The Inner Kālacakratantra

The Inner Kālacakratantra

A Buddhist Tantric View of the Individual

Vesna A. Wallace

OXFORD
UNIVERSITY PRESS

2001

OXFORD
UNIVERSITY PRESS

Oxford New York
Athens Auckland Bangkok Bogotá Buenos Aires Cape Town
Chennai Dar es Salaam Delhi Florence Hong Kong Istanbul Karachi
Kolkata Kuala Lumpur Madrid Melbourne Mexico City Mumbai Nairobi
Paris Shanghai Singapore Taipei Tokyo Toronto Warsaw

and associated companies in

Berlin Ibadan

Published by Oxford University Press, Inc.,
198 Madison Avenue, New York, New York 10016

Library of Congress Cataloging-in-Publication Data
Wallace, Vesna A.
The inner kalacakratantra : a Buddhist tantric view of the individual / Vesna A. Wallace.
p. cm.
Includes bibliographical references and index.
ISBN 0-19-512211-9
1. Tripiòaka. Såtrapiòaka. Tantra. Kålacakratantra—Criticism, interpretation, etc.
2. Man (Buddhism) 3. Body, Human—Religious aspects—Buddhism.
4. Tantric Buddhism—Doctrines. I. Title.
BQ2177.W35 2000
294.3'85—dc21
00-022893

1 3 5 7 9 8 6 4 2

Printed in the United States of America
on acid-free paper

Preface

The *Kālacakratantra* and its commentarial literature are a rich textual source for the study of diverse but mutually related fields of South Asian studies in general and of South Asian Buddhism in particular. The works that belong to the Kālacakra literary corpus warrant careful research for several reasons. They express the doctrinal and social theories and the relevant tantric practices that were characteristic of north Indian Buddhism in its final stages. A study of those theories and practices reveals the ways in which the Indian tantric Buddhists from the early eleventh century on interpreted and further developed earlier Buddhist ideas and their practical applications. The *Kālacakratantra* literature also sheds light on the religious and social conditions of eleventh-century India in general and on the social standing and role of Indian tantric Buddhism of that era in particular.

For these reasons, a main focus of this book is on the Kālacakra tradition as an Indian Buddhist tradition. Although the Kālacakra tradition has been a significant component of Tibetan Buddhism to this day and has produced a large body of tantric literature in Tibet, for a number of reasons the intended task of this book is not to provide a detailed analysis of the Indo-Tibetan Kālacakra tradition as a whole. The Kālacakra tradition as a whole includes a plurality of texts and interpretative perspectives, some of which are not in agreement with each other; and it deals with an extensive variety of topics, which deserve separate scholarly analyses. Likewise, the diverse and complex historiographical, textual, and philosophical problems surrounding the Kālacakra literature of both India and Tibet, which should be addressed in great detail, require a collaborative effort of scholars who are willing to undertake such a task.

The central topic of this book is the *Kālacakratantra*'s view of the nature of the individual and one's place in the universe and society. Accordingly, a primary theme of the book is a textual, historical, and philosophical analysis of the second chapter of the *Kālacakratantra*, called the "Chapter on the Individual" (*adhyātma-paṭala*), and its principal commentary, the *Vimalaprabhā*. However, since the Kālacakra tradition's theory of the human being permeates all the chapters of the *Kālacakratantra*, the second chapter of the *Kālacakratantra* is intimately related to the other chapters of this *tantra*. For example, the Kālacakratantra's view of the individual is inseparable from its view of the universe as discussed in the first chapter of the *tantra*. Likewise, the purpose of the *Kālacakratantra*'s presentation of the individual's psycho-physiology in the "Chapter on the Individual" becomes clear only when examined in light of the tantric yogic practices described in the third, fourth, and fifth chapters. Therefore, in this book the topics of the inner *Kālacakratantra* are dealt with in their relationship to the larger context of the *Kālacakratantra*'s theory and practice.

In accordance with the *Kālacakratantra*'s theory of nonduality, this book analyzes the Kālacakra tradition's view of the individual in terms of the individual as cosmos, society, gnosis, and the path of spiritual transformation. For this reason, the main chapters of this book are entitled the "Gnostic Body," the "Cosmic Body," the "Social Body," and the "Transformative Body."

Santa Barbara, California V. A. W.
August 1999

Acknowledgments

I owe a great debt of gratitude to the Fetzer Institute, and especially to the former director of the research program there, Professor Arthur Zajonc, for its generous financial support, which enabled me to continue the research and writing that I initially started during my graduate studies at the University of California in Berkeley. My former professors and distinguished scholars in the Department of South and Southeast Asian Studies and in the Department of East Asian Languages and Literature at the University of California, Berkeley, prepared me for this work and facilitated my initial research and writing of this book. I am very grateful to Ms. Cynthia Reed, editor at Oxford University Press, who believed in me and in this project long before it was finished. I also wish to express my appreciation to the editors at Oxford University Press, especially to Mr. Robert Milks and Mr. Theodore Calderara, for their meticulous work and graciousness.

I am also greatly indebted to Mr. Calvin Smith for his patience and endurance in the painstaking task of proofreading the manuscript and correcting the awkward expressions to which I as a nonnative English speaker am prone. I thank him for all the hours that he spent in making and adjusting the graphics in the book. My sincere gratitude also goes to Mr. Brian Bailey for his professional help in creating the graphics for chapter 7 on the "Cosmic Body" and to Mr. David Reigle for his generosity in providing me with copies of the Sanskrit manuscripts.

I would like to express my heartfelt gratitude to my husband, Alan Wallace, for reading the manuscript and offering his useful comments, for supporting me in my work, and bringing light to the darkness of my ruminations. Finally, I wish to thank my daughter, Sarah, for her enduring love that inspires all my worthy endeavors.

Contents

The Inner Kālacakratantra

Introduction

The *Kālacakratantra* is an early eleventh-century esoteric treatise belonging to the class of unexcelled *yoga-tantras* (*anuttara-yoga-tantra*). To the best of our knowledge, it was the last *anuttara-yoga-tantra* to appear in India.

According to the Kālacakra tradition, the extant version of the *Kālacakratantra* is an abridged version of the larger original *tantra*, called the *Paramādibuddha*, that was taught by the Buddha Śākyamuni to Sucandra, the king of Sambhala and an emanation of Vajrapāṇi, in the Dhānyakaṭaka *stūpa*, a notable center of Mahāyāna in the vicinity of the present-day village of Amarāvatī in Andhra Pradesh. Upon receiving instruction on the *Paramādibuddhatantra* and returning to Sambhala, King Sucandra wrote it down and propagated it throughout his kingdom. His six successors continued to maintain the inherited tradition, and the eighth king of Sambhala, Mañjuśrī Yaśas, composed the abridged version of the *Paramādibuddhatantra*, which is handed down to us as the *Sovereign Abridged Kālacakratantra* (*Laghukālacakratantrarāja*). It is traditionally taught that it is composed of 1,030 verses written in the *sradgharā* meter.[1] However, various Sanskrit manuscripts and editions of the *Laghukālacakratantra* contain a somewhat larger number of verses, ranging from 1,037 to 1,047 verses. The term an "abridged *tantra*" (*laghu-tantra*) has a specific meaning in Indian Buddhist tantric tradition. Its traditional interpretation is given in Naḍapāda's (Nāropā) *Sekoddeśaṭīkā*, which states that in every *yoga*, *yoginī*, and other types of *tantras*, the concise, general explanations (*uddeśa*) and specific explanations (*nirdeśa*) make up a tantric discourse (*tantra-saṃgīti*), and that discourse, which is an exposition (*uddeśana*) there, is an entire abridged *tantra*.[2]

The tradition tells us that Mañjuśrī Yaśas's successor Puṇḍarīka, who was an emanation of Avalokiteśvara, composed a large commentary on the *Kālacakratantra*, called the *Stainless Light* (*Vimalaprabhā*), which became the most authoritative commentary on the *Kālacakratantra* and served as the basis for all subsequent commentarial literature of that literary corpus. The place of the *Vimalaprabhā* in the Kālacakra literary corpus is of great importance, for in many instances, without the *Vimalaprabhā*, it would be practically impossible to understand not only the broader implications of the *Kālacakratantra*'s cryptic verses and often grammatically corrupt sentences but their basic meanings. It has been said that the *Kālacakratantra* is explicit with regard to the tantric teachings that are often only implied in the other *anuttara-yoga-tantras*, but this explicitness is actually far more characteristic of the *Vimalaprabhā* than of the *Kālacakratantra* itself.

According to Tibetan sources, the *ācārya* Cilupā from Orissa, who lived in the second half of the tenth century, after reading the *Kālacakratantra* in the monastery in Ratnagiri, undertook a journey to Sambhala in order to receive oral teachings that would illuminate the text. After his return to southern India, he initially had three students, one of whom was the great *paṇḍita* Piṇḍo, who was originally from Bengal. The *ācārya* Piṇḍo became a teacher of Kālacakrapāda the Senior, who was from northern Bengal (Varendra). After returning to eastern India, Kālacakrapāda the Senior taught the *Kālacakratantra* to his disciples, the most famous of whom was Kālacakrapāda the Junior, who built the Kālacakra temple in Nālanda, believing that the propagation of the *Kālacakratantra* in Magadha would facilitate its propagation in all directions. I shall not discuss here all the variants in the accounts given by the Tibetan Rwa and 'Bro traditions of the history of the *Kālacakratantra* in India, for these accounts have already been narrated in other readily available works by other Western scholars and in English translations of the Tibetan sources.[3]

One of the references that seems significant for establishing the period of the propagation of the *Kālacakratantra* in India is the reference in the *Kālacakratantra* (Ch. 2, v. 27) and the *Vimalaprabhā* to the end of the sexagenary cycle that comes 403 years after the Hijrī, or Islamic era (*mlecchendra-varṣa*), of 622 CE. Likewise, the same texts assert that the hundred and eighty-second year after the Hijrī era is the period of the eleventh Kalkī, the king Aja, which is corroborated by the *Kālacakrānusāriganita*,[4] which states further that after the time of Kalkī Aja, 221 years passed till the end of the sexagenary cycle. Thus, adding 221 years to 182, one arrives at the number of 403 years after the Hijrī era. In light of this, I agree with G. Orofino in determining the year to be 1026 CE, relying on the Indian system of reckoning years, in which 623 CE is included in the span of 403 years.[5] This is in contrast to G. Grönbold and D. Schuh, who assumed without substantial evidence that the Kālacakra tradition incorrectly calculated the Hijrī era as beginning at 642 CE and thus determined the year to be 1027 CE by adding the span of 403 years to the year of 624 CE.[6]

According to the *Vimalaprabhā* commentary, the *Paramādibuddhatantra* was composed of twelve thousand verses, written in the *anuṣṭubh* meter.[7] However, we cannot determine now with certainty whether the *Paramādibuddhatantra* ever existed as a single text or as a corpus of mutually related writings, since we know from the *Vimalaprabhā*[8] that the *Sekoddeśa*, which circulated as an independent text in early eleventh-century India, has traditionally been considered to be a part of the *Paramādibuddhatantra*. Nearly two hundred and ten verses from the *Ādibuddhatantra* are cited throughout the five chapters of the *Vimalaprabhā*; and some verses attributed to the *Paramādibuddhatantra* are also scattered in other writings related to the Kālacakra literary corpus, such as the *Sekoddeśaṭippanī*[9] and the *Paramārthasaṃgraha*,[10] which cites the verse from the *Paramādibuddhatantra* that coincides with the opening verse of the *Ḍākinīvajrapañjaratantra*.[11] Likewise, some citations from the *Paramādibuddhatantra* are found in the commentarial literature on the *Hevajratantra*, specifically—in the *Hevajrapiṇḍārthaṭīkā*[12] and in the *Vajrapādasārasaṃgrahapañjikā*.[13]

In addition to these, there are other pieces of textual evidence found in the *Abridged Kālacakratantra* and in the *Vimalaprabhā*, such as the repeated references to the *Hevajratantra*, the *Guhyasamājatantra*, the *Cakrasaṃvaratantra*, and to the *Mañjuśrīnāmasaṃgīti*, which the *Vimalaprabhā* identifies as the sixteenth chapter of the *Māyājālatantra*. These suggest that the *Paramādibuddhatantra* must have been composed after these tantric traditions of the seventh and eighth centuries were already well established.

The works of the eminent Indian *Kālacakratantra* adepts, such as those of Dārika, Anupamarakṣita, and Sādhuputra, which are preserved in the different versions of the Tibetan Bstan 'gyur, can be dated to the beginning of the eleventh century. The writings of the Bengali author Abhayākāragupta, who was a contemporary of the Bengali king Rāmapāla, and the works of Raviśrījñāna from Kaśmīr, can be traced to the late eleventh and early twelfth centuries. Likewise, the writings of the Bengali author Vibhūticandra who studied in Magadha, and the works of the Kaśmīr author Śākyaśrībhadra can be dated to the second half of the twelfth and the beginning of the thirteenth centuries. Some Tibetan authors indicate that although writing on the *Kālacakratantra* might have ceased in India with the Turkish invasions of Bihar and Bengal at the beginning of the thirteenth century, the Kālacakra tradition did not completely die in India until the fifteenth century.[14] In his *History of Indian Buddhism*,[15] Tāranātha mentions one of the last of the Indian Buddhist *paṇḍitas*, Vanaratna, from eastern Bengal, who in 1426 was the last Indian *paṇḍita* to reach Tibet through Nepal. Having reached Tibet, he taught and cotranslated several works of the Kālacakra corpus from Sanskrit into Tibetan. According to the *Blue Annals*, the best of the initiations and precepts of the *Kālacakratantra* came at that time from Vanaratna.[16] Thus, it seems that the doctrine and practice of the *Kālacakratantra* were promulgated in India for almost five centuries.

It is difficult to determine with certainty the parts of India in which the first authors of the Kālacakra tradition resided. The Tibetan accounts, however, indicate that even though the Kālacakra tradition initially may have started in south India, the *Kālacakratantra*'s sphere of influence in India was confined to Bengal, Magadha (Bihar), and Kaśmīr, wherefrom it was transmitted to Nepal, Tibet, and eventually to Mongolia, where Kālacakra was instituted as the protective deity of the Mongol nation.

The Broader Theoretical Framework of the *Kālacakratantra*

The *Kālacakratantra* belongs to the class of the unexcelled *yoga-tantras* (*anuttara-yoga-tantra*); and together with its most authoritative Indian commentary, the *Vimalaprabhā*, it stands as the most comprehensive and informative *tantra* of its class. According to the Kālacakra tradition itself, the *Kālacakratantra* is the most explicit *tantra*, which imparts its teaching by revealing the actual meanings; whereas the other *anuttara-yoga-tantras*, which are regarded as secret, or concealed, *tantras*, convey their meanings in an implicit manner.

Accordingly, the *Vimalaprabhā* asserts that in every king of *tantras* (*rāja-tantra*)—specifically, in the method *tantras* such as the *Guhyasamājatantra*, and in the wisdom *tantras* such as the *Cakrasaṃvaratantra*—the Buddha taught the blissful state that arises from sexual union, but concealed it out of his great compassion for the sake of the spiritual maturation of simple-minded people. For those who seek understanding of other *anuttara-yoga-tantras*, the *Kālacakratantra* is of inestimable value for it explains the meanings in detail.[1] In the instances in which other systems of the *anuttara-yoga-tantras* offer only scant information, the *Kālacakratantra* system explicates in detail. For example, the *Vimalaprabhā* points out that unlike the other *tantras* of its class, which only suggest that the fourth initiation is like the third, the Kālacakra tradition reveals in full its content and implications.[2] The Kālacakra tradition also gives the most elaborate presentation of the human psycho-physiology and the individual's natural and social environments and their relevance to tantric practices.

With regard to the *Kālacakratantra*'s explicit and elaborate manner of presenting its topics, the *Vimalaprabhā*, just like the *Sekoddeśa*, asserts that in the *Ādibuddhatantra*, the Buddha illuminated the *vajra*-word by means of general expositions (*uddeśa*), detailed descriptions (*nirdeśa*), and repeated references (*pratinirdeśa*).[3]

In light of its explicitness, the *Kālacakratantra* claims superiority over all other *tantras* in the following manner:

> In every king of *tantras*, the Vajrī concealed the *vajra*-word, and in the *Ādibuddha*, he taught it explicitly and in full for the sake of the liberation of living beings. Therefore, Sucandra, the splendid *Ādibuddhatantra*, a discourse of the supreme lord of Ji-

nas, is the higher, more comprehensive and complete *tantra* than the mundane and supramundane [*tantras*].[4]

According to the *Vimalaprabhā* commentary on this verse, the Buddha Śākyamuni, who abides in the *vajra* of indivisible gnosis, the inconceivable mind-*vajra*, concealed the supreme, imperishable bliss (*paramākṣara-sukha*) in those *yoginī* and *yoga tantras*, because otherwise the conceited Buddhist *paṇḍitas* in the land of the Āryas, who did not wish to listen to the spiritual mentor (*guru*), would read the book and claim that they understood the *vajra*-word. Thus, they would not receive the initiation and would go to hell, due to their self-grasping (*ahaṃ-kāra*). In contrast, he taught it explicitly in the *Ādibuddhatantra* in order to mature those who were born in the land of Sambhala and whose minds were free of self-grasping. On these grounds, the *Vimalaprabhā* affirms that the *Ādibuddhatantra*, which is the discourse of the innate Sahajakāya, is more comprehensive and higher than the *kriyā* and *yoga tantras*.

This is one way in which the *Kālacakratantra* system substantiates its self-designation as unexcelled (*anuttara*). Likewise, interpreting *yoga* as the union, or absorption, of bliss and emptiness, or of method and wisdom, this tantric tradition presents itself as a nondual (*advaya*) *yoga-tantra*, which is ultimately neither a wisdom *tantra* nor a method *tantra*. It views its nonduality of wisdom and method as an expression of nondual gnosis, without which Buddhahood could never occur.[5]

The Kālacakra tradition also affirms its unexcelled status by claiming that the *Ādibuddhatantra* does not come from a succession of transmissions of spiritual mentors, nor is it established by means of the spiritual mentor's authority (*ājñā*).[6] The *Vimalaprabhā* states that one cannot achieve omniscient Buddhahood and lordship over the three worlds by the mere blessing and authority of a spiritual mentor.[7] The *Ādibuddhatantra* asserts the same in this manner:

> The perishable mind, which is stained by attachment and other mental afflictions, is the cause of transmigratory existence. It is pure due to its separation from these [impurities]. It is pure and stainless by nature.
>
> None [of the impurities] can be taken out nor thrown into [the mind] by the authority of a spiritual mentor. The sublime, imperishable, pure reality (*tattva*) cannot be given or taken away.
>
> A spiritual mentor is neither a giver nor a remover of the pure reality. In the case of those who are devoid of the accumulation of merit, the omniscient lord himself [cannot give or remove the pure reality].[8]

In light of this, the *Vimalaprabhā* disparages the Śaiva tantric tradition, which claims that its teaching regarding the supreme Īśvara who brings forth pleasure (*bhukti*) and liberation (*mukti*) is handed down by a succession of teachers and through the blessing of the spiritual mentor. It warns against the dangers of following teachings that come in this way by deprecating the Śaiva tantric teachers on the basis that they have trifling knowledge but have become the spiritual mentors of the childish due to showing a few limited *siddhis*. They require trust from their deluded followers, who, thinking that their spiritual mentor is liberated, do everything that he commands. They kill, speak falsehood, steal, drink liquor, and so on. In this way, they perform the deeds of Māras and do not obtain the bodily *siddhis* by the blessing and authority of the supreme Īśvara. At death, their bodies are either incinerated by fire or eaten by dogs and birds, and their consciousness does not become Śiva.[9]

According to the *Vimalaprabhā*, one cannot teach the *tantra* without knowing first the list of the principles of the Buddha Dharma (*dharma-saṃgraha*) for one who does not know it teaches the evil path. One becomes a knower of the *dharma-saṃgraha* and a teacher of the three Vehicles—the Vehicles of the Śrāvakas, Pratyekabuddhas, and Samyaksambuddhas—only by accomplishing these two: (1) gnosis (*jñāna*), which is the apprehending mind (*grāhaka-citta*) and wisdom (*prajñā*), and (2) space (*ākāśa*), or the empty form (*śūnya-bimba*), which is the apprehended object (*grāhya*) and method (*upāya*).[10]

The *Vimalaprabhā* entreats those who desire to enter the Vajrayāna to completely investigate a potential tantric teacher, and it points to the danger of practicing a distorted Dharma and going to hell due to honoring a spiritual mentor who lacks the necessary qualifications.[11] The *Kālacakratantra* provides a list of the qualifications of a *vajrācārya*, who must have tantric pledges (*samaya*). These qualifications, according to the *Vimalaprabhā*, are of two kinds—external and internal—and must be understood in terms of their definitive and provisional meanings. Likewise, the tantric teacher is expected to practice meditation on reality, and that meditation is also of two kinds—one which accomplishes mundane *siddhis* and the other which accomplishes full and perfect awakening (*samyaksaṃbodhi*). He must be free of greed, not grasping onto his sons, wife, his own body, or anything else. He must be devoid of all mental afflictions (*kleśa*). He is to be patient, not having any expectations, and he must follow the path of full and perfect awakening. The *Kālacakratantra* asserts that a spiritual mentor who has these qualifications is able to provide his disciples with the path and to remove their fear of death, because as a "celibate" (*brahmacārin*), meaning, as one who has attained supreme, imperishable bliss (*paramākṣara-sukha*), he is like a *vajra*-rod to the four classes of Māras.[12] In contrast to the qualified tantric teacher, a corrupt spiritual mentor is said to be full of conceit, which is of many kinds: conceit in one's own learning, in one's own wealth, seeing others as beneath oneself, and so on. His absence of humility is seen as an indication of his lack of compassion. Likewise, one is advised to shun a tantric teacher who is overcome by anger, who is devoid of tantric pledges, and who publicly practices the secret pledges that disgust the world.[13] Similarly, a *vajrācārya* who is greedy and attached to mundane pleasures, or who is an uneducated fool, ignorant of the true path and not initiated into the *tantra*, or who is fond of liquor or sex, is to be avoided, for he leads his disciples to hell.[14] In light of this, the *Vimalaprabhā* points out that the well-known saying that one should look for the *ācārya*'s good qualities and never for his faults has been misunderstood in the past and will be in the future by foolish people who have lost the true path. It suggests that sayings like this should be understood in terms of both ultimate and conventional truths, that is to say, in terms of their definitive and provisional meanings. In terms of the ultimate truth, an *ācārya* refers to the Buddha Śākyamuni, to "the omnipresent and omniscient *vajrācārya*, who practices (*ācarati*) the *vajra*-word in order to benefit sentient beings within the three realms." Thus, the aforementioned saying is to be understood literally only when examined from this point of view. Supporting the *Kālacakratantra*'s position that before honoring a spiritual mentor one should investigate his faults and his good qualities, the *Vimalaprabhā* cites the following verses from the *Gurupañcāśikā*, which support the Kālacakra tradition's stand on this issue.

> An intelligent disciple should not make him who is devoid of compassion, who is angry, cruel, stubborn, unrestrained, and self-aggrandizing his spiritual mentor.
>
> [A qualified spiritual mentor] is steadfast, disciplined, intelligent, patient, sincere, honest, versed in the tantric practices of *mantras*, compassionate, a knower of the *śāstras*,
>
> Fully acquainted with the ten principles,[15] a knower of the art of drawing *maṇḍalas*, an *ācārya* who explains *mantras*, who is propitious and has subdued his senses.[16]

With regard to the hierarchy of the *vajrācāryas*, the Kālacakra tradition distinguishes the *vajrācārya* who is an ordained monk as the highest type of a *vajrācārya*.[17] It states that ordained monks should only mentally revere the *vajrācārya* who is a householder in order that they may be free of sloth and pride; but when there is a *vajra*-holder who is an ordained monk, then neither the monks nor the king should honor a spiritual mentor who is a householder. The reason for this injunction is based on the association of the white garment, which is generally worn by householders, with the Barbarian Dharma. The *Vimalaprabhā* explicitly states that the Buddhist system (*bauddha-darśana*) is never associated with the white robe. It asserts that in the land of Mañjuśrī, when a monk or a wandering ascetic is expelled from a Buddhist monastery due to committing a sin of immediate retribution, he is allowed to leave the monastery only after he gives back his red robe and puts on a white robe. In light of this, the author of the *Vimalaprabhā* abhors the possibility of a householder who wears a white robe being a spiritual mentor to those who wear the red robe or of a householder dwelling in a Buddhist monastery. He sees it as an insult to the Buddhist monastic community and as a great defect in Buddhists' judgment.[18]

Likewise, it asserts that among men who are worthy of veneration, the *vajrācārya* who is endowed with extrasensory perceptions (*abhijñā*) and has attained at least the first *bodhisattva-bhūmi* is to be venerated for his knowledge. Such a man, be he an ordained monk or a householder, is said to be equal to ten respectable monks. In the absence of this kind of *vajrācārya*, a monk who is an elder should be venerated for his asceticism by the monks whose ordination was later than his; and he should be venerated by tantric householders, since his initiation was prior to theirs. The third kind of venerable man is said to be a learned *paṇḍita* who can illuminate the doctrine and tame the Māras who propound contrary doctrines.[19] In contrast, a householder who is devoid of extrasensory perception is not considered worthy of veneration.[20] Statements such as these reveal the strong monastic orientation of the Kālacakra tradition.

With regard to tantric disciples, the Kālacakra tradition distinguishes three kinds of tantric trainees—the superior, the middling, and the inferior. The superior disciple is one who has his mind set on the deep and profound Dharma that consists of wisdom and compassion, who delights in the ten virtues and has not violated the tantric precepts, who is free of attachment, who does not care about the mundane *siddhis* but desires a *sādhana* on the *mahāmudrā-siddhi*, and who does not associate with evil people such as *ācāryas* who are greedy householders and ascetics who live off the temples and monasteries. Such a disciple is considered to be qualified to receive the first seven and the other four higher initiations in order to meditate on the path of emptiness. The middling disciple is one who is endowed with mediocre qualities and who seeks a *sādhana* on the mundane *siddhis*, and he is qualified to receive only the first seven initiations in order to meditate on the *maṇḍala*, *mantras*, *mudrās*, and the like. Lastly, the disciple of inferior qualities who respects the spiritual mentor is said to be qualified to be a lay practitioner, and he may receive the five Buddhist precepts but not the initiations.[21]

In light of this, the *Kālacakratantra* classifies the Buddhist community at large into two groups—Śrāvakas and Anuttaras—each consisting of four types of Buddhist practitioners. The four categories of Śrāvakas are the Buddhist nuns (*bhikṣunī*) and monks (*bhikṣu*) and the great female (*mahopāsikā*) and male (*mahopāsaka*) lay disciples. The group of Anuttaras includes the *yoginīs* and *yogīs* who delight in innate bliss—that is to say, those who have received the higher initiations and who practice the stage of completion—and the female (*upāsikā*) and male (*upāsaka*) lay tantric practitioners, who have received the first seven initiations and who practice the stage of generation.[22] The *Kālacakratantra* asserts the superior quality of the Anuttaras on the ground that there is no monk or celibate who can equal one who has taken the tantric vows and precepts and who is self-empowered by means of *mantras*.[23]

The theoretical principles of the *Kālacakratantra* are imbedded in the conceptual context of Vajrayāna as a whole. Therefore, in order to understand the conceptual framework of the Kālacakra tradition in India, one needs to examine its own interpretation of Vajrayāna. According to the Kālacakra tradition's explanation of the term Vajrayāna, the word *vajra* signifies liberation (*mokṣa*), or the indivisible omniscience that cannot be destroyed by conceptualization;[24] and the word *yāna* is understood as a vehicle that is of a dual nature. It is the means by which the tantric adept advances toward liberation and the aim toward which the tantric adept progresses.[25] The *Vimalaprabhā* also identifies Vajrayāna as Samyaksaṃbuddhayāna (the "Vehicle of a Fully Awakened One"), since it cannot be damaged by the vehicles of heterodox groups (*tīrthika*), Śrāvakas, or Pratyekabuddhas.[26]

The Kālacakra tradition also interprets Vajrayāna as the system of *mantras* (*mantra-naya*) and the system of perfections (*pāramitā-naya*).[27] As the system of *mantras*, it characterizes itself as the system that includes ideas pertaining to both mundane (*laukika*) and supramundane (*lokottara*) truths. Teachings pertaining to the mundane truth are said to be discussed from the conventional point of view, and teachings pertaining to the supramundane truth are said to be discussed from the ultimate point of view. Moreover, the ideas that are taught from the mundane, or conventional, point of view are said to have a provisional meaning (*neyārtha*); and the ideas that are taught from the ultimate point of view are said to have the definitive meaning (*nītārtha*). Likewise, the ideas that are discussed from the conventional point of view are regarded as ideations (*kalpanā*) of one's own mind, which lead to the attainment of mundane *siddhis*. They are said to be taught for mediocre Vajrayāna students who seek nothing more than the accomplishment of mundane *siddhis*.[28] The ideas that are imparted from the ultimate point of view are considered as clear manifestations, or reflections (*pratibhāsa*), of one's own mind, which are not of the nature of ideations. As such they are believed to lead to the achievement of the supramundane *siddhi*, called the *mahāmudrā-siddhi*, or the attainment of supreme and imperishable gnosis (*paramākṣara-jñāna-siddhi*); and they are said to be taught for superior Vajrayāna students, who aspire to spiritual awakening.

Likewise, the *Vimalaprabhā* views Vajrayāna as a unified system that consists of both the cause and the result. Thus, the system of *mantras* is said to refer to compassion (*karuṇā*) and is characterized as the result.[29] In this tantric system, as in the related systems of the *anuttara-yoga-tantras*, in addition to the standard Mahāyāna practices of developing compassion, the cultivation of compassion also entails seminal nonemission. In this regard, compassion is here also referred to as the gnosis of sublime bliss (*mahā-sukha-jñāna*). The system of perfections, on the other hand, refers to the wisdom (*prajñā*) that cognizes the emptiness (*śūnyatā*) of inherent existence. This wisdom is viewed as the cause of the aforementioned result.

Although the Kālacakra tradition acknowledges the Mādhyamika view of emptiness as its primary theoretical foundation, it has its own unique interpretation of emptiness, not only as a mere negation of inherent existence (*svabhāva*), but also as the absence of material constituents of the individual's body and mind. Hence, this emptiness, which is also called the "aspect of emptiness" (*śūnyatākāra*), or the "form of emptiness" (*śūnyatā-bimba*), is a form that is empty of both inherent existence and physical particles. It is a form that is endowed with all the signs and symbols of the Buddha. That form of emptiness, also known as the "empty form," is also regarded as the "animate emptiness" (*ajaḍā-śūnyatā*). Due to being animate, this emptiness is the cause of supreme and immutable bliss (*paramācala-sukha*). The nonduality of the cause and effect is the essential teaching of this *tantra*.

From that unique view of emptiness stem the *Kālacakratantra*'s unique goal and path to that goal. The *Kālacakratantra*'s most significant goal is the transformation of one's own gross physical body into a luminous form devoid of both gross matter and the subtle body of *prāṇas*. The transformation of one's own mind into the enlightened mind of immutable bliss occurs in direct dependence upon that material transformation. The actualization of that transformation is believed to be perfect and full Buddhahood in the form of Kālacakra, the Supreme Primordial Buddha (*paramādibuddha*), who is the omniscient, innate Lord of the Jinas,[30] the true nature of one's own mind and body. Thus, according to this tantric system, the supreme Ādibuddha refers not only to the Buddha Śākyamuni, who is said to be the first to attain perfect awakening by means of the supreme, imperishable bliss,[31] but also to the innate nature of the mind of every sentient being.

This points to another unique feature of the *Kālacakratantra*'s theory, namely, the assertion that all sentient beings are Buddhas, which will be discussed in greater detail in chapter 7 on the "Gnostic Body". The *Kālacakratantra*'s view of the ultimate nature of sentient beings and their environment as blissful is reflected in the *Kālacakratantra*'s explicit usage of sexual tantric practices on the spiritual path. The generation of sexual bliss without emission of regenerative fluids is regarded in this *tantra* as the most direct method of generating the mental bliss that refines the mind by diminishing conceptualizations and thus makes it fit for the realization of the empty nature of phenomena. One who practices the generation of sexual bliss without emission, which is referred to as sublime, imperishable bliss, is considered to be like a young virgin. Such bliss is believed to empower one's mind, just as the mind of a young virgin, who has not experienced sexual bliss with emission, can be empowered by deities and *mantras* that enable her to see appearances in a prognostic mirror. Thus, it is thought that the empowerment of the tantric adept's mind, which enables him to perceive the three worlds as mere appearances in space, does not come from some external source such as the blessing or permission of a spiritual mentor, just as a young virgin's ability to see appearances in a prognostic mirror does not come from the blessing or permission of a spiritual mentor.

To those adherents of the Brāhmaṇic tradition who claim that many noncelibates who do not practice sexual bliss with nonemission demonstrate isolatory knowledge (*kaivalya-jñāna*) and predict the future, the Kālacakra tradition responds that their isolatory knowledge is nothing but a branch of astrology, which is common to all people and which enables one to predict the future events by means of calculations.[32]

Likewise, it is believed in this tantric tradition that the five extrasensory perceptions (*abhijñā*) cannot arise without the practice of seminal nonemission. It is said that those Bodhisattvas who have the five extrasensory perceptions despite the fact that they occasionally practiced sexual bliss with seminal emission, should be considered celibate, because their seminal emission is an intentional emission, characterized by the motivation to reenter transmigratory existence for the sake of helping others. According to the *Vimalaprabhā*, there are two types of seminal emission—one that is due to the power of wholesome and unwholesome *karma*, and one that is due to the power of controlling the mind. Of these two types of emission, the first one, which is characteristic of ordinary human beings, is for the sake of wandering in transmigratory existence, and the other one, which is characteristic of Bodhisattvas, is for the sake of showing the path to those who are driven by *karma* in the cycle of transmigration.[33]

The Classification of the Families in the Kālacakra Tradition

The Kālacakra tradition, like the other tantric traditions of the *anuttara-yoga* class, categorizes the family of its principal deity into three, four, five, and six families (*kula*). The Kālacakra tradition's classification and interpretation of the Kālacakra family can be summarized in the following manner.

In terms of the individual, the classification into three families corresponds to the classification of the body, speech, and mind, or the left, right, and central *nāḍīs*; and in terms of the universe, the three families are the three realms—the realms of desire, form, and formlessness. With regard to ultimate reality, however, the three families are the three bodies of the Buddha—the Nirmāṇakāya, Saṃbhogakāya, and Dharmakāya.[34]

In terms of the individual, the classification into four families corresponds to the classification of uterine blood, semen, mind, and gnosis, or to the classification of the body, speech, mind, and gnosis, which accords with the classification of the four drops (*bindu*) and with the four states of the mind—namely, waking, dreaming, deep sleep, and the fourth state. In terms of the universe, the four families are the families of the sun, moon, Rāhu, and Agni (Ketu), and in terms of society, they are the four castes. With regard to ultimate reality, the four families are the four bodies of the Buddha—the aforementioned three bodies and the Jñānakāya.

With regard to the individual, the five families are the five psycho-physical aggregates (*skandha*), and in terms of society, they are the four castes and the outcastes. With regard to ultimate reality, they are the five types of the Buddha's gnosis manifesting as the five Buddhas—Akṣobhya, Vairocana, Ratnasambhava, Amitābha, and Amoghasiddhi.[35]

In terms of the individual, the six families are the five psycho-physical aggregates and their emptiness; and in terms of society, they are the four castes and the classes of Ḍombas and Caṇḍālas. With regard to ultimate reality, the six families are the five aforementioned Buddhas and the Svābhāvikakāya.[36]

The Mādhyamika Critique of Other Philosophical Systems in the *Kālacakratantra*

Although it has many unique features, as will be demonstrated in the subsequent chapters of this book, the Kālacakra tradition shares some of its fundamental ideas with other Buddhist systems. The *Kālacakratantra* summarizes its fundamental philosophical views in this single verse:

> Identitylessness, the maturation of *karma*, the three realms, the six states of existence, the origination due to the twelve-limbed dependence, the Four Truths, the eighteen unique qualities of the Buddha, the five psycho-physical aggregates, the three bodies and the Sahajakāya, and animate emptiness. The [system] in which these [tenets] are taught is the clear and definite instruction of the Vajrī.[37]

Positioning itself in the above-mentioned philosophical views, it criticizes all other philosophical systems, including the Buddhist schools other than Madhayamaka. Although the Kālacakra tradition's refutation of the non-Buddhist philosophical systems is based on the standard Mādhyamika arguments, at times it uses some new and interesting examples in its logical analysis of other systems. It regards its critique of certain tenets of other philosophical systems as a means of leading individuals of different mental dispositions to some understanding of emptiness, which would be the foundation of their attainment of mundane *siddhis*. The following brief summary of the Kālacakra tradition's rebuttal of the dogmas that in one way or another contradict the view of the absence of inherent existence best demonstrates the degree to which the Kālacakra tradition follows the Mādhyamika mode of investigation.

The *Kālacakratantra* critiques Viṣṇuism for its view of the Veda as being self-existent, eternal, and similar to space. It refutes the notion of the Veda as self-existent and eternal on the basis that the word "Veda" signifies a referent that is produced by the activity of the throat, palate, and the like. It further argues that the Veda is also not identical with the referent, since a word and its referent cannot be identical. If there were such an identity, then when one utters the word "fire," it would burn one's mouth. Likewise, it repudiates the notion that the Veda is similar to space on the grounds that it is local in usage and recited by the mouth. It also objects to the notion that the Veda is a standard for learned and knowledgeable men, since low castes such as Śūdras read and write.[38]

Furthermore, the *Kālacakratantra* critiques the Śaiva notion of Īśvara as the creator. The *Kālacakratantra* argues that if one asserts Īśvara as the creator, one implies that Īśvara is one who experiences *karma*, since it is never the case that one person eats a salty cake and another person experiences the result and dies from thirst. An agent is never established without *karma*. And if he is not an agent of *karma*, as Śaivas claim, then it implies that he is dependent on another agent, who is his instigator. This, it says, contradicts the very term "Īśvara," which implies independence. Thus, according to the *Kālacakratantra*, Īśvara has never been the creator who bestows the results of virtue and sin, disregarding the *karma* of living beings. Likewise, if the creator is devoid of the atoms of the elements, then in the absence of matter, he does not create anything; and if he is devoid of the sense-objects, as Śaivas say, then that creator has neither perceptual nor inferential means of valid knowledge.[39]

In light of its view of dependent origination, the *Kālacakratantra* asserts that the efficacy of phenomena is not caused by anyone in the triple world but that the origination of all phenomena takes place due to the conjunction of things. Thus, due to the conjunction of a moon-stone with moon-rays, water appears from the moon-stone, and due to the conjunction of an iron-stick with a lode-stone, the iron stick is set in motion, and so on. By means of these and other examples, it tries to demonstrate that things never occur by the will of the creator.[40]

From the vantage point of identitylessness, the *Kālacakratantra* critiques the notion of the Self (*ātman*) as being omnipresent and permanent. It argues that the Self cannot be omnipresent, since it experiences suffering due to separation from relatives. If it were omnipresent, it would exist as one and would not suffer due to being separated from loved ones. Likewise, if the Self were omnipresent, then one sentient being would experience the suffering of all sentient beings. Moreover, it argues that one cannot say that there are many Selves, because that would imply that there is no omnipresence of many Selves. It refutes the notion of the permanent Self, pointing to its susceptibility to change, as in the case of falling in love.[41]

In light of its refutation of the Self, the *Kālacakratantra* asserts that there is no one who departs to liberation—there is only a collection of phenomena in cessation—and yet there is a departure to liberation. Likewise, there is bondage for originated phenomena, but there is no one who is bound. The state of the Buddha is identical with existence and nonexistence, and it is without inherent existence, devoid of conceptualizations and matter, and free of momentariness. Therefore, the teachings of the Buddha, which are free of the demons of conceptualizations, cannot be destroyed by the words of gods and *nāgas*, which are accompanied by demons, just like a wrestler who is free of demons cannot be killed by a wrestler who is possessed by demons.[42]

The *Kālacakratantra* refutes the teachings of Rahman, or the Dharma of Tājikas, on the basis of their assertion that in this life the individual experiences the result of actions that he performed earlier in this lifetime, and that a person who dies experiences pleasure or suffering in heaven or hell through another human form. It argues that if it is as the Tājikas teach, then one could not annihilate one's own *karma* from one birth to another, and consequently, one could not escape transmigratory existence or enter liberation even in the course of an immeasurable number of lives.[43]

It critiques the doctrine of the Materialists (Cārvāka), which denies the existence of god and the maturation of *karma* and claims that one experiences only the amassment of atoms, arguing that this Materialist doctrine destroys the path of liberation for people. The *Kālacakratantra* argues that if, just like the power of intoxicating drink, the witnessing mind arises due to configurations of the elements, then trees would also have consciousness due to the agglomeration of the elements. But if inanimate things lack the efficacy of living beings, then the agglomeration of the elements is inadequate for producing consciousness.[44]

The Kālacakra tradition also repudiates the Jaina doctrine, specifically, the Jaina assertion of a permanent soul (*jīva*) that has the size of the body, and the Jaina view of the permanence of atoms. The *Kālacakratantra* argues that if the soul would have the size of the body, it would perish after the removal of the arms and legs. Likewise, it argues that atoms are not permanent, since they are liable to change, as are gross and subtle bodies.

The *Vimalaprabhā* critiques the Jaina argument that the substance of the soul is permanent, as gold is permanent, whereas its modes are impermanent, just as the modes of gold such as earrings are impermanent. The *Vimalaprabhā* rejects this argument as invalid, on the basis that if the substance and its mode were identical, then there would be no difference between the two; and if they were different, there could be no mode without the substance; nor can one say that they are both identical and different, because of their mutual exclusion. Likewise, it refutes the Jaina notion that the three worlds are permanent on the basis that whatever is made of atoms never remains permanent. It also critiques the Jaina view that one soul acquires one body, such that plants and grains are also living beings. It argues against this view, stating that if a single soul is in a single body, then when one breaks the stem of a sugar cane into pieces, there would not be many pieces. But since there are many pieces, then the soul must have entered one of those pieces due to its *karma*. That does not stand up to logical analysis, because a sprout arises from each of the pieces of sugar cane that are replanted in the earth.[45]

The Kālacakra tradition also critiques the Vaibhāṣikas, Sautrāntikas, and Yogācārins as simple-minded Buddhist *tīrthikas* who, grasping onto their own dogmatic positions (*pakṣa*), grasp onto the dogmatic positions of others and see the similarity or the contrariety with this or that dogmatic position of others. The *Kālacakratantra* refutes the Vaibhāṣikas' assertion of the reality of the person (*pudgala*) endowed with a body at birth as the implication of the inherent existence of the *pudgala*. It argues that the *pudgala* cannot be one's inherent nature, because if the *pudgala* were of the nature of cognition, then it would be impermanent, for the nature of cognition is impermanent; and if the *pudgala* were of the nature of noncognition, then it would be unaware of its happiness and suffering.

It critiques the Sautrāntikas for asserting objects by means of conventional truth and claims that for this reason they consider the unknown ultimate truth that has the Jñānakāya ("Gnosis-body") as nonexistent, like the son of a barren woman. Explaining the basis for the *Kālacakratantra*'s critique of Sautrāntikas, the *Vimalaprabhā* cites the following verse from Āryadeva's *Jñānasārasamuccaya*:

Sautrāntikas know this: mental factors (*saṃskāras*) are not inanimate (*jaḍa*), there is nothing that proceeds through the three times, and an unimpeded (*apratigha*) form does not exist.[46]

The *Vimalaprabhā* argues on the part of the *Kālacakratantra* that if the unimpeded form, that is, the Dharmakāya, does not exist, then the omniscient one would not exist either. It asserts that *nirvāṇa* is not the same as the extinction of a lamp, that is to say, it is not the same as the cessation of all awareness. In the absence of the four bodies, there would not be Buddhahood with a localized body. Without the unimpeded body, there would be no displays of the extraordinary powers of all the forms of the Buddha.

The *Kālacakratantra* refutes the Yogācāra's assertion of the inherent reality of consciousness and its classification of consciousness. In light of this rejection, the *Vimalaprabhā* asks the following: If there is no form of an external object other than consciousness, then why does the external form of visual consciousness as the apprehender manifest itself as being of the nature of the apprehended? It cannot be due to the power of the habitual propensities of spiritual ignorance, as the Yogācārins say, because spiritual ignorance has the characteristic of the three realms, and the three realms are mere consciousness. Thus, mere consciousness is of the nature of spiritual ignorance, therefore, spiritual ignorance is not the disappearance of consciousness; but if the three realms are not mere consciousness, then the Yogācārins' position has failed. The *Vimalaprabhā* also refutes the Yogācāra's assertion that self-knowing awareness arises and ceases in an instant, resorting to the standard Mādhyamika argument that the origination, cessation, and duration of phenomena do not occur simultaneously, for if they were to exist in a single moment, then due to the fact that time is a moment, birth, old age, and death would be identical. Moreover, if consciousness were to arise from a consciousness that has ceased, then it would be like the origination of a flame from a flame that has ceased, and this makes no sense. But if another consciousness were to arise from a consciousness that has not ceased, then it would be like the origination of a flame from a flame that has not ceased, which means that from origination to origination there would be a series of consciousness, like a series of flames. In this case, one cannot say that after the cessation of an earlier consciousness there is an origination of another consciousness, nor can one say that there is an origination of another consciousness from the earlier unceased consciousness, nor from the combination of the aforementioned two manners of origination, because of their mutual contradiction.[47]

However, the *Kālacakratantra* indicates that the Mādhyamika's negation of the inherent existence of consciousness, which inspired some to say that the Buddha's wisdom is not located anywhere, is a danger for those who, devoid of the self-aware gnosis of imperishable bliss, will grasp onto that emptiness and will thus fall into the trap of a doctrinal view and attain nothing.[48]

After refuting the preceding tenets of the Indian systems of thought in the above-demonstrated ways, in order to assure one of the pure motivation behind its criticisms, the *Kālacakratantra* states that its assertion of the absence of inherent existence is free from mundane concerns and intended to be of service to others.[49] Likewise, in order to establish one's confidence in the supremacy of the source of its teaching and to bring one to final conversion, the *Kālacakratantra* ends its critique of other philosophical systems with these words of the Buddha to the king Sucandra:

> I am Indra, the spiritual mentor of thirty-three men in heaven, the universal monarch (*cakravartin*) on the earth, the king of *nāgas* in the underworld, revered by serpents. I am the highest, gnosis, the Buddha, the lord of sages, the imperishable, supreme sovereign, the *yogī*'s *vajra-yoga*, the Veda, self-awareness, and the purifier (*pavitra*). O king, take refuge in me with all your being.[50]

With regard to the criticism of one's own or other Buddhist tantric systems, the Kālacakra tradition views this as the major cause of committing the sixth of the fourteen root downfalls (*mūlāpatti*), which is specified in the *Kālacakratantra* (Ch. 3, v. 102) and the *Vimalaprabhā* as reviling the *siddhāntas* of the system of perfections within the *mantra*-system. The *Vimalaprabhā* indicates that criticism of one's own or other Buddhist tantric systems is often an expression of one's own ignorance with regard to the relation between the subject and predicate in Buddhist *tantras*, and as such, it leads the faultfinder to hell.[51]

The Concept of the Ādibuddha in the Kālacakra Tantric System

One of the most important concepts in the Kālacakra system is that of the Ādibuddha. Even though the concept of the Ādibuddha is not unique to the *Kālacakratantra*, it is most emphasized and discussed in the Kālacakra literature. To the best of our knowledge, the earliest reference to the Ādibuddha is found in the *Mahāyānasūtrālaṃkāra* (Ch. 9, v. 77), which refutes the notion of the Primordial Buddha on the grounds that there is no Buddhahood without the accumulations of merit (*puṇya*) and knowledge (*jñāna*). Later references to the Ādibuddha are found in the *Mañjuśrīnāmasaṃgīti* (v. 100), in the commentarial literature of the *Guhyasamāja* corpus, and in the *yoginī-tantras*. The Kālacakra tradition's interpretation of the Ādibuddha is primarily based on the *Nāmasaṃgīti*'s exposition of Vajrasattva, who is Vajradhara.

According to the Kālacakra tradition, the Ādibuddha is called the Primordial Buddha because he was the first to obtain Buddhahood by means of the imperishable bliss characterized by perfect awakening in a single moment.[52] In connection with this interpretation, the *Vimalaprabhā* asserts that according to the words of the Buddha in the *Nāmasaṃgīti* (v. 85), which praises Vajradhara as one who is free of mental obscurations, a person who is devoid of merit and knowledge does not in any way become a Buddha.[53] Such an interpretation does not seem to contradict the *Mahāyānābhisamayālaṃkāra*'s assertion that there is no Buddha who has been enlightened since beginningless time. On the other hand, the *Vimalaprabhā* interprets the word *ādi* ("primordial") as meaning "without beginning or end," meaning, without the origination and cessation.[54] This interpretation of the word *ādi* with regard to the Buddha is reiterated by Naḍapāda in his *Sekoddeśaṭīkā*, which further interprets the Ādibuddha's freedom from origination and cessation as omniscience.[55] The Kālacakra tradition's interpretation of the word is based on the *Nāmasaṃgīti*, v. 100, which begins with: "Without beginning or end, he is the Buddha, Ādibuddha. . . ."[56] This interpretation of the word *ādi* appears to contradict the aforementioned interpretation of the Primordial Buddha. However, analysis of the Kālacakra literature reveals that when the Kālacakra tradition speaks of the Ādibuddha in the sense of a beginningless and endless Buddha, it is referring to the innate gnosis that pervades the minds of all sentient beings and stands as the basis of both *saṃsāra* and *nirvāṇa*. Whereas, when it speaks of the Ādibuddha as the one who first attained perfect enlightenment by means of imperishable bliss, and when it asserts the necessity of acquiring merit and knowledge in order to attain perfect Buddhahood, it is referring to the actual realization of one's own innate gnosis. Thus, one could say that in the Kālacakra tradition, Ādibuddha refers to the ultimate nature of one's own mind and to the one who has realized the innate nature of one's own mind by means of purificatory practices.

The *Kālacakratantra* and the Mañjuśrīnāmasaṃgīti

The Kālacakra tradition views its essential topic, which is the Jñānakāya, or Vajrasattva, as indivisible from that of the *Nāmasaṃgīti*, which, according to the *Vimalaprabhā*, makes the Jñānakāya of Vajradhara evident. The *Vimalaprabhā* remarks that in every king of *tantras*, the Buddha described the *vajra*-word as the imperishable bliss of *yogīs*; and in them he designated that *vajra*-word as the Jñānakāya, which is described by the *Nāmasaṃgīti*.[57] Accordingly, the *Kālacakratantra* teaches that one should meditate every day on Kālacakra, the progenitor of all the Buddhas, only after one "has taken apart," or investigated, this *vajra*-word.[58]

The *Vimalaprabhā* comments that the path of purification that brings forth the *mahāmudrā-siddhi* was written explicitly in the *Paramādibuddhatantra* only after the Buddha made the *Nāmasaṃgīti* an authoritative scripture. Knowing that in the future sentient beings will be free of doubts, the Buddha taught Vajrapāṇi the definitive meaning of all the tantric systems, in accordance with the *Nāmasaṃgīti*. In light of this, it affirms that in order to know the *Nāmasaṃgīti*, one must know the *Ādibuddhatantra*. If one does not know the *Nāmasaṃgīti*, one will be ignorant of the Jñānakāya of Vajradhara, and not knowing the Jñānakāya of Vajradhara, one will not know the Mantrayāna. Being ignorant of the Mantrayāna, one will be devoid of the path of Vajradhara and remain in transmigratory existence.[59]

In verses 12–13, the *Nāmasaṃgīti* asserts its durability, claiming that the Buddhas of the past, present, and future have taught and recited the *Nāmasaṃgīti* and that innumerable Buddhas have praised it. On the basis of these verses, the *Vimalaprabhā* affirms that it is due to Vajrapāṇi requesting the Buddha to teach the *Nāmasaṃgīti* that all the Tathāgatas taught the Mantra Vehicle.[60] This statement may clarify just why it is that most Buddhist tantric traditions mention Vajrapāṇi as one who both requests the teachings and compiles the *tantras* such as the *Guhyasamāja* and the *Ādibuddha tantras*.

Similarly, according to the *Vimalaprabhā*, the *yoga* that is the imperishable bliss, the sublime goal (*mahārtha*) of the *Kālacakratantra*, has already been declared in the *Nāmasaṃgīti* by fourteen verses (28–36) in praise of the *maṇḍala* of the *vajra-dhātu*. The *Vimalaprabhā* remarks that the fully awakened one, who is described by those fourteen verses, is taught in all the *tantras*, in accordance with the superior, middling, and inferior dispositions of sentient beings.[61]

In light of its view of the inseparability of the *Kālacakratantra* and the *Nāmasaṃgīti*, throughout its five chapters, the *Vimalaprabhā* altogether cites sixty-five verses from the *Nāmasaṃgīti* in order to explain or substantiate the *Kālacakratantra*'s views of Buddhahood and the path of actualizing it. Thus, the Kālacakra tradition's view of the omniscient Buddha, who stands at the extreme limit of transmigratory existence and is superior to the Hindu gods such as Hari and Hara, who are born in the realm of gods within cyclic existence, is based on the *Nāmasaṃgīti*'s statement in verse 54, which reads:

> Standing at the far limit of transmigratory existence, having his task accomplished, he rests on the shore. Having rejected isolatory knowledge, he is a cleaving sword of wisdom.[62]

Likewise, the *Kālacakratantra*'s interpretation of the Jñānakāya as the fully awakened one who is imbued with *nirvāṇa* without remainder (*nirupadhi*) and transcends the reality of consciousness (*vijñāna-dharmatā*) is in full accord with that of the *Nāmasaṃgīti* (vs. 87, 99), according to which, the fully awakened one, being free of all remainders, dwells in the path of space, and transcending the reality of consciousness, is a spontaneous nondual gnosis that is free of conceptualization.

Furthermore, the *Kālacakratantra*'s interpretation of enlightened awareness as the mind that, though free of the habitual propensities of *karma* (*karma-vāsanā*), supports transmigratory happiness and suffering and terminates them, is based on the *Nāmasaṃgīti's* (v. 96) description of the discriminating gnosis (*pratyavekṣaṇa-jñāna*) of the Buddha as the mind that ends happiness and suffering. Likewise, the *Vimalaprabhā* suggests that the *Kālacakratantra*'s interpretation of the self-awareness that knows the nature of all things has its basis in the *Nāmasaṃgīti*'s (v. 98) characterization of the Buddha's gnosis as omniscient, fully awake, and wide awake to itself.[63]

The Kālacakra tradition also substantiates its exposition of Jñānakāya as devoid of form (*rūpa*) on the basis of the *Nāmasaṃgīti*'s (v. 73) description of Vajrasattva as one whose hundred eyes and hair are blazing like a *vajra*; and it asserts that it is not the Rūpakāya of the Buddha that is the subject of investigation in the *Nāmasaṃgīti* but the Vajradharakāya of Vajrapāṇi.[64] Likewise, it bases its argument that the Buddha's body is not a localized (*prādeśika*) body on verses 61–63 of the *Nāmasaṃgīti*, which speak of the Buddha as a torch of gnosis that arises instantly in space, and so on.[65]

At times, the Kālacakra tradition offers an interpretation of certain passages from the *Nāmasaṃgīti* that radically differs from those found in the commentarial literature on the *Nāmasaṃgīti*. For example, it interprets the *Nāmasaṃgīti*'s (v. 45) depiction of the Buddha as having ten aspects (*daśākāra*) in terms of the Vajrakāya that is the existence of ten kinds of phenomena—namely, the body, gnosis, space, wind, fire, water, earth, the inanimate, the animate, and the invisible deities of the formless realm.[66] Whereas, Mañjuśrīmitra's *Nāmasaṃgītivṛtti* (176. 1. 7) specifies the ten aspects as ten truths—provisional truth, conventional truth, and so on—whose words and meanings the Buddha intends to teach;[67] and Vilāsavajra's *Nāmasaṃgītiṭīkā* (196. 5. 5) interprets the ten aspects as the ten types of grasping onto the Self,[68] on the grounds that the Buddha himself should be understood as undesirable mental factors and as their antidotes. This cryptic interpretation makes sense when examined in the light of the Kālacakra tradition's view of enlightened awareness as the support of both *saṃsāra* and *nirvāṇa*.

Similarly, the Kālacakra tradition gives its own interpretation of the *Nāmasaṃgīti*'s (v. 133) description of the Buddha as the referent of the truth that has twelve aspects, and as one who knows the sixteen aspects of reality and is fully awakened with twenty aspects. According to the *Vimalaprabhā*, he is the referent of the truth with twelve aspects, because he has attained the twelve *bodhisattva-bhūmis* due to the cessation of the twelve zodiacs;[69] and according to the *Nāmasaṃgītivṛtti* (182. 5. 1), he is the referent of the truth with twelve aspects, because he has the twelve sense-bases (*āyatana*), which are his aspects in terms of conventional truth. Although the Kālacakra tradition and the *Nāmasaṃgītivṛitti* agree that the sixteen aspects of reality refer to the sixteen types of emptiness—to be discussed in chapter 7 on the "Gnostic Body"—the Kālacakra tradition offers its own reason for the manifestation of the sixteen aspects: the cessation of the sixteen digits of the moon. With regard to the full awakening with twenty aspects, the Kālacakra tradition also departs from the interpretation given in the *Nāmasaṃgītivṛtti* (182. 5. 2). According to the *Vimalaprabhā*, the Buddha has spiritual awakening with twenty aspects because he fully knows the five purified psycho-physical aggregates, the five sense-faculties, the five sense-objects, and the five types of consciousness, since they were purified in the central *nāḍī* by means of the six-phased *yoga*. According to the *Nāmasaṃgītivṛtti* (182. 5. 3), on the other hand, the twenty aspects are the earlier mentioned sixteen aspects and the four types of the Buddha's gnosis.

The Kālacakra tradition also considers its exposition of Kālacakra as consisting of the four families—specifically, the four bodies of the Buddha—to accord completely with the *Nāmasaṃgīti*'s (v. 108) description of the Buddha as the sublime mind (*mahā-citta*) of all the Buddhas, as the desire of the mind (*mano-gati*), as the sublime body (*mahā-kāya*) of all the Buddhas, and as the speech (*sarasvatī*) of the Buddhas.[70] Thus, it interprets the sublime mind of all the Buddhas as the Viśuddhakāya, the desire of the mind as the Dharmakāya, the sublime body of all the Buddhas as the Nirmāṇakāya, and the speech of all the Buddhas as the Dharmakāya. Likewise, the *Vimalaprabhā* suggests that the *Nāmasaṃgīti*'s (v. 93) characterization of the Buddha as one who has five faces and five hair-knots is most relevant to the Kālacakra tradition's presentation of the Buddha as one who, due to the classification of the five psycho-physical aggregates and elements, consists of the five families.[71] Finally, it asserts that the *Nāmasaṃgīti*'s (v. 35) description of the Buddha Vajradhara as one who bears the sublime illusions is taught there in terms of the Kālacakra tradition's classifications of the six families and the hundred families.[72]

The *Nāmasaṃgīti*'s presentation of Vajrasattva has also influenced certain forms of *Kālacakratantra* practice, whose goal is the actualization of Vajrasattva as he is described in the *Nāmasaṃgīti*. For example, verse 111 from the *Nāmasaṃgīti*, which states that the sublime Vajradhara of the Buddha bears all illusions, is considered to be a theoretical basis for the *Kālacakratantra* practice of the stage of generation, more specifically, for the practice of meditation on the universal form (*viśva-rūpa*) of the empty and blissful Buddha that has many arms, legs, colors, and shapes.[73] Similarly, the *Nāmasaṃgīti*'s (vs. 61–62) description of the self-arisen Vajrasattva as the sublime fire of wisdom and gnosis that has arisen from space and its (v. 56) characterization of the Buddha as one who has abandoned all thoughts and is free of ideation are pointed out as reasons why the *Kālacakratantra* practice of the stage of completion is to be practiced in the form of meditation that is free of ideation.[74] Moreover, the *Vimalaprabhā* indicates that the *Nāmasaṃgīti*'s (v. 53) assertion that the Buddha is free of the sense of "I" and "mine" is the reason why at the stage of completion practice one should not practice self-identification with Vajrasattva but should resort to ultimate truth.[75]

The recitation of certain verses from the *Nāmasaṃgīti* also forms an integral part of *Kālacakratantra* practice. Thus, at the end of the stage of generation practice, after the tantric adept has meditated on the *kālacakra-maṇḍala* and on the enlightened activities of the deities in the *maṇḍala*, and after he has practiced *sādhanas* on the *yoga* of drops (*bindu-yoga*) and the subtle *yoga* (*sūkṣma-yoga*), he recites verse 158 from the *Nāmasaṃgīti*, with which he expresses his reverence for the enlightenment of the Buddha, whose essence is emptiness. By reciting this verse, he establishes the appropriate attitude with which he is able to purify his four drops within the four *cakras* by emanating the principal deities within those *cakras*.

With regard to the *Kālacakratantra* initiation, the Kālacakra tradition's interpretation of the *Kālacakratantra*'s four higher initiations as a symbolical passage from being a lay Buddhist practitioner to being a wandering ascetic, a monk, and a Buddha is justified in the light of the *Nāmasaṃgīti* (vs. 81, 51–52, 94–95), which describes the Buddha as being a youth, an elder (*sthavira*), and an old man, as a leader of the Pratyekabuddhas, an Arhat, a monk, and the progenitor (*prajāpati*), and as one who has the great vow, great austerity, and so on. Likewise, the receiving of diadem (*paṭṭa*) and crown (*mauli*) during the four higher initiations is explained in terms of the *Nāmasaṃgīti*'s (v. 93) description of the Buddha as an ascetic with a crest of hair and diadem.[76]

A Brief Analysis of the Inner *Kālacakratantra*

The entire *Kālacakratantra* is divided into five main chapters—the chapters on the world system (*loka-dhātu*), the individual (*adhyātma*), initiation (*abhiṣeka*), *sādhana*, and gnosis (*jñāna*). The subjects of these five chapters delineate the Kālacakra tradition's vision of the gradual transformation from the macrocosmic and microcosmic aspects of provisional reality to ultimate reality, culminating in gnosis. They also represent a unitary reality that manifests as the universe, the individual, the path of purification, and its result.

The first chapter of the *Kālacakratantra* begins with the words of King Sucandra requesting the teaching on the *yoga* of the *Kālacakratantra* from the Buddha Śākyamuni for the sake of the liberation of human beings who live in the *kali-yuga*; and the last chapter concludes with Sucandra's homage to Kālacakra, who is the *tantra*, the presiding deity Vajrasattva, the union of wisdom and method (*prajñopaya-yoga*), and the reality (*tattva*) with sixteen aspects. Each of the other four chapters also begins with Sucandra's request for teachings on the main topic of the chapter, and the remaining verses of each chapter contain the Buddha's response to Sucandra's request.

The inner *Kālacakratantra*, or the "Chapter on the Individual," begins with Sucandra's question to the Buddha: "How can the entire three worlds be within the body?" It continues with the Buddha's summary of how all phenomena in the world are the three modes of the Buddha's existence that are present in the human body, all of which should be known by means of the classifications of emptiness. This is followed by a further exposition on the origination of the individual's body, speech, and mind by means of the agglomeration of atoms and the power of time. The detailed description of the conception and development of the fetus in the womb indicates the author's familiarity with embryology, as taught in the earlier Buddhist writings such as the *Abhidammatasaṃgaha*, *Āhārasutta*, and the *Āyuṣmannandagarbhāvakrāntinirdeśasūtra*, in tantric works such as the *Vajragarbhaṭīkā* and the *Amṛtahṛdayāṣṭāṅgaguhyopadeśatantra*, and in the Buddhist medical treatises. For example, the *Kālacakratantra*'s description of the conditions necessary for conception, the characteristics of the fetus, and its growth correspond to that in the *Āyuṣmannandagarbhāvakrāntinirdeśasūtra*.[77] The view of the six tastes as arising from the six elements is common to the *Kālacakratantra* and the *Vajragarbhaṭīkā*.[78] Likewise, the *Kālacakratantra's* statement that the marrow, bones, and ligaments of the fetus arise from the father's semen, and the skin, blood, and flesh arise from the mother's uterine blood corresponds to a great degree with the *Amṛtahṛdayāṣṭāṅgaguhyopadeśatantra*'s assertion that the bones, brain, and spinal cord of the fetus arise from the father's sperm, and the muscles, blood, and viscera arise from the mother's uterine blood.[79] Similarly, the *Kālacakratantra*'s classification of the human life into ten stages corresponds to that given in earlier works such as the *Āyuṣparyantasūtra*[80] and the *Nandagarbhāvasthā*.[81]

Explaining the functions of each of the elements in the formation of the human being and of the conditions in the mother's womb, the author tries to demonstrate the manner in which the principles of dependent origination (*pratītya-samutpāda*) apply to the origination of the human psycho-physiology.

This first section of the inner *Kālacakratantra* continues with an exposition of the preciousness of human birth and continues with an explanation of the ways in which the four bodies of the Buddha are present in the body of the individual. It represents the individual in the specific stages of life within and outside the womb, as the provisional manifestations of each of the four bodies of the Buddha. It identifies the individual with the four bodies of the Buddha in accordance with the degree of development of the individual's bodily, verbal, mental, and sexual capacities. It shows further the manner in which the elements, the psycho-physical aggregates, the *prāṇas*, and the mind support each other in the body of the individual; and it explains the relation among the sense-faculties and their corresponding sense-objects in terms of one type of element apprehending a different type of element. For example, the olfactory sense-faculty, which arises from the water-element, apprehends taste as its sense-object, which arises from the fire-element. Explaining their relation in this way, the author tries to demonstrate that all the constituents of the individual and all his experiences arise due to the union of opposites, often referred to in this tantric system as the "different families." He specifies the elements from which each of the psycho-physical aggregates, the *prāṇas*, and the *cakras* arise in order to demonstrate the material nature of the transmigratory body.

The second section of the inner *Kālacakratantra* (vs. 27–47) specifies the locations of the four bodies of the Buddha and of the six families within the individual's four *cakras*. It describes the manner in which mental states enter the body and the body enters mental states, and thus they become of the same taste. Likewise, it discusses the elements of the bodily constituents in terms of wisdom and method, and it suggests that everything pertaining to the body and the mind of the individual comes into existence due to the union of these two. In this way, it provides the reader with a description of the *kālacakra-maṇḍala* in terms of the human being. It further depicts the ways in which the presence of time and the universe is to be recognized in one's own body and shows the correspondences between the passage of time in the world and the passage of *prāṇas* within the body. In this regard, this section also discusses the different functions and locations of the diverse types of the *prāṇas* in the body.

The third section of the inner *Kālacakratantra* (vs. 48–60) begins with a description of the current battle between the universal monarch (*cakravartin*) and the lord of the Barbarians (*mleccha*) within the body of the individual, which will take place in the land of Mecca and be between the external manifestations of good and evil. It also discusses the ways in which the *yoga* and *yoginī tantras*, such as the *Māyājāla* and the *Guhyasamāja*, and the tantric families of their deities are present within the individual and included in the *kālacakra-maṇḍala*. In this regard, it further describes the location of the male and female deities of the *kālacakra-maṇḍala* within the body of the individual and identifies them with the *nāḍīs* and the passage of time in the body.

The fourth section of the "Chapter on the Individual" (vs. 61–81) gives a detailed description of the characteristics of the unfavorable signs of death, beginning with descriptions of the ways in which one can determine the number of the remaining days of life by examining the flow of the *prāṇas* in the *nāḍīs*. For example, if the *prāṇa* uninterruptedly flows in the left *nāḍī* for a day and a night, then one has one more year to live, and so on. It associates the unfavorable signs of untimely death with the gradual ceasing of the *prāṇas*' flow in the individual *nāḍīs* of the navel-*cakra*. It also describes the characteristics of timely death, which begins with the disintegration of the *nāḍīs* in the navel-*cakra* and progresses throughout the body through the severance of the *nāḍīs* within all the other *cakras* and bodily joints. It compares the process of death to the moon and the sun leaving their lunar and solar mansions. The gradual severance of the *nāḍīs* is said to manifest for six days in the acidity of urine and in the *prāṇas*' departure from the sense-faculties. During the other six days, it is said to manifest in the following symptoms: one perceives the tip of one's own nose as dangling down, one perceives the sun as being black and the full moon as being yellow, and the planets as the sparks of fire, and a black line appears below one's tongue, and so on.

The fifth section of the inner *Kālacakratantra* (vs. 82–106) discusses the *kālacakrī*, or the moment of seminal emission, in terms of conventional reality, as an agent of the creation and annihilation of the individual. It also points to the individual's conceptualizations and *karma* that is contained in the *guṇas* of *prakṛti* as causes of transmigratory suffering and happiness. It classifies the *karma* of human beings into three kinds: gross, subtle, and subtlest, in accordance with the classification of the body, speech, and mind. It also distinguishes a *karma* with regard to the individual's grasping onto the agent of action. When one thinks, "I am the agent," this is a distinct *karma*; when one thinks, "The supreme Īśvara is the agent," this is a *karma*; but when one thinks, "Neither I nor someone else devoid of *prakṛti* is the agent," this is not a *karma*. It further asserts that it is the mind of the deluded person that creates his own suffering and happiness and not the Bhagavān Kālacakra, who is devoid of the *guṇas* and conceptualizations. In light of this, it affirms that the mental state that characterizes the individual's mind at the time of death determines the state of his next rebirth.

The sixth section of the "Chapter on the Individual" (vs. 107–160) is dedicated to the discussion of the ways of guarding the body from illness and untimely death. It first depicts various tantric yogic practices and practices of *prāṇāyāma* as methods of eliminating malignant illnesses and preventing untimely death. In addition to these practices, it also prescribes herbal medication, elixirs, and dietary regulations. It also gives guidance on storing medicinal herbs and spices and preparing their combinations, and on preparing and storing rolls of incenses, unguents, and fragrances. Additionally, it discusses ritual tantric methods of protecting pregnant women and infants from diseases caused by malevolent spirits, and it describes the symptoms of such diseases.

The last section of the inner *Kālacakratantra* (vs. 161–180) discusses the *Kālacakratantra*'s philosophical views and those of other Indian Buddhist and non-Buddhist systems of thought. After briefly expounding the fundamentals of its own philosophical tenets, the author presents the tenets of other systems, without offering any comment on them. Upon giving an overview of the other systems, he engages in a critique of those tenets that he finds contrary to the *Kālacakratantra*'s philosophical orientation.

A History of the *ṣaḍ-aṅga-yoga* of the *Kālacakratantra* and Its Relation to Other Religious Traditions of India

A close look at the *Kālacakratantra*'s six-phased *yoga* reveals its correlation and historical connection to earlier forms of the six-phased *yoga*, found in both Hinduism and Buddhism. Moreover, it also reveals the unique character of the practical applications and implications of the *Kālacakratantra*'s six-phased *yoga*. To the best of my knowledge, the earliest reference to a six-phased *yoga* is found in the *Maitrāyaṇīya*, or *Maitrī Upaniṣad*, which belongs to the branch of the black Yajur Veda and is considered to be the last of the classical Upaniṣads. The *ṣaḍ-aṅga-yoga* of the *Maitrāyaṇīya Upaniṣad*, Ch. 6, v. 18, contains the following six phases: breath-control (*prāṇāyāma*), retraction (*pratyāhāra*), meditative stabilization (*dhyāna*), concentration (*dhāraṇā*), contemplative inquiry (*tarka*), and *samādhi*.[1] It is taught in this Upaniṣad as a method for achieving union with the supreme Self (*paramātman*). If we accept that the *Maitrāyaṇīya Upaniṣad* predates Patañjali, we can assume that this six-phased *yoga* also predates the eight-phased *yoga* (*aṣṭāṅga-yoga*) of the classical Yoga system. The fact that Patañjali never makes any reference to a six-phased *yoga* and that his *Yogasūtra* never mentions contemplative inquiry (*tarka*) is not sufficient evidence to regard the six-phased *yoga* as a later revision of the eight-phased *yoga*, as Günter Grönbold suggests.[2] Even if the sixth chapter of the *Maitrāyaṇīya Upaniṣad*, which incorporates a six-phased *yoga*, is a later interpolation, as Mircea Eliade speculates,[3] the antecedence of the sixth-phased *yoga* to the *yoga* of Patañjali is still quite plausible. The phrase "for it is said elsewhere," which often occurs at the beginning of the verses of the sixth chapter, indicates that the *Maitrāyaṇīya Upaniṣad* draws its yogic elements from the earlier yogic sources. Even though we are unable to determine the exact sources of the yogic elements in the *Maitrāyaṇīya Upaniṣad*, it is obvious that different forms of its six-phased *yoga* have very early origins in India. The six-phased *yoga* was later modified into diverse forms of *yoga* with varying numbers of phases.

For example, in one of the earliest Purāṇas, the *Vāyu Purāṇa*, Ch. 10, v. 76,[4] one encounters a five-phased *yoga*, whose fifth phase is recollection (*smaraṇa*), corresponding in name to the fifth phase of the *Kālacakratantra*'s six-phased *yoga*. In this Purāṇa as in the *Kālacakratantra*, contemplative inquiry (*tarka*) is replaced by recollection. Considering that the Purāṇas underwent many revisions after the majority of their material was composed during the Gupta reign (c. 320–c. 500 CE), it is extremely difficult to establish whether the recollection phase of *yoga* was established first in the Purāṇic tradition or in the Buddhist tradition, specifically, in the *Guhyasamājatantra*, which some scholars date as early as the fourth century CE and some as late as the eighth century CE.

Within later Hindu sources, a six-phased *yoga* is also mentioned in a number of texts belonging to the Upaniṣads of the Yoga class—specifically, in the *Amṛtabindu Upaniṣad*—and in the Śaiva Āgamas, Śaiva *tantras*, and some Dharma Sūtras, where there is a slightly different order of phases than that found in the six-phased *yoga* in the *Maitrāyaṇīya Upaniṣad*. For example, in the *Amṛtabindu Upaniṣad*, v. 6, the six phases of *yoga* are retraction (*pratyāhāra*), meditative stabilization (*dhyāna*), breath-control (*prāṇāyāma*), concentration (*dhāraṇā*), contemplative inquiry (*tarka*), and *samādhi*. This particular sequence of the phases of *yoga* is almost identical to that of the *Kālacakratantra*. The difference between the two lies in the designation of the fifth phase of *yoga* as contemplative inquiry (*tarka*) instead of recollection (*anusmṛti*).[5] Even though contemplative inquiry is not explicitly mentioned among the six phases of the *Kālacakratantra*'s six-phased *yoga* as a separate member, it is not absent from there. Rather, it is included within the phase of meditative stabilization (*dhyāna*), along with wisdom (*prajñā*), analysis (*vicāra*), joy (*rati*), and immutable bliss (*acala-sukha*).[6] Contemplative inquiry as a constituent of the phase of meditative stabilization is explained in the *Vimalaprabhā* as the apprehension of the phenomenon of empty form that is being observed or meditated upon during this phase.[7] As such, it is an indispensable element in the practice of the *Kālacakratantra*'s six-phased *yoga*. Nevertheless, it is not given superiority over all other phases of the six-phased *yoga* and their elements as it is in Kaśmīr Śaivism—specifically, in the Śaivāgamas and in the works of Abhinavagupta and Jayaratha. Abhinavagupta (975–1025) in his *Paratrīśikavivaraṇa* asserts that "among all the lights of the component parts of *yoga*," contemplative inquiry (*tarka*) has already been determined in the earlier *Mālinīvijaya* "to be the brilliant sun by which one gets liberated and liberates others."[8] When commenting on Abhinavagupta's *Tantrāloka*, Jayaratha (thirteenth century) in his *Tantrālokaviveka* mentions the six-phased *yoga* that has breath control (*prāṇayāma*) as its first member and contemplative inquiry (*tarka*) as its fifth member and exalts it as the highest (*uttama*) phase.[9] Moreover, just as contemplative inquiry is included in the six-phased *yoga* of the *Kālacakratantra*, even though it is not regarded as a separate phase, so too are meditative posture (*āsana*) and restraint (*niyama*) implicitly included in this *yoga*. The *vajra*-posture (*vajrāsana*) is often referred to as the posture in which an adept of the *Kālacakratantra* does his meditative practice, whereas *niyama* is included in the observance of the *Kālacakratantra*'s ethical discipline, in the form of restraint from indulging in the five objects of desire and keeping the twenty-five tantric precepts (*vrata*), which are deemed prerequisites for the successful outcome of the practice of the six-phased *yoga*.[10] The *Vimalaprabhā* defines *niyama* as a Buddha's command (*buddhānujñā*) with regard to the twenty-five precepts.[11] Since these two prerequisites to the *Kālacakratantra*'s six-phased *yoga* are present in each phase of the *yoga* as qualifying conditions, they are not considered to be separate phases.

Within later Hindu sources there are also those who speak of a six-phased *yoga* that does not include the phase of contemplative inquiry but includes meditative posture (*āsana*) as the first phase. For example, some Yoga Upaniṣads—specifically, the *Dhyānabindu Upaniṣad*, v. 41 and the *Yogacūḍāmaṇi Upaniṣad*, v. 2—several texts of the *Gorakṣa* corpus (c. twelfth century), and the *Netratantra*, cited in Kṣemarāja's *Vimarśinī* (eleventh century) commentary on the *Śiva Sūtra* 6, contain the following list of the six phases: posture (*āsana*), breath-control (*prāṇāyāma*), retraction (*pratyāhāra*), meditative stabilization (*dhyāna*), concentration (*dhāraṇā*), and *samādhi*. This form of the six-phased *yoga* seems to be later than that found in the *Guhyasamājatantra* and later incorporated into the *Kālacakratantra*. Thus, it is most likely that the Buddhist six-phased *yoga* chronologically succeeds the six-phased *yogas* containing contemplative inquiry (*tarka*) as the fifth phase, which continued to be in practice in later times as well. However, it is more difficult to determine with certainty whether the Buddhist six-phased *yoga* precedes the six-phased *yoga* of Kaśmīr Śaivism that contains meditative posture (*āsana*) as its first phase or whether it was contemporaneous with it. If one were to rely only on the extant Śaiva texts that refer to the sixth-phased *yoga* having meditative posture as its first member, it would seem that the Buddhist sixth-phased *yoga* preceded that particular *yoga* of Kaśmīr Śaivism. Considering the incompleteness of textual and historical information, it is impossible to reconstruct an accurate and precise history of the six-phased *yoga* in India. Therefore, I offer here only a limited comparative table of the different types of six-phased *yogas* that were cited in specific Śaiva, Vaiṣṇava, and Buddhist texts. As table 2.1. indicates, not only teachers of different religious traditions but also various teachers of different schools within the same tradition taught diverse forms of the six-phased *yoga*, according to their intended goals. Even though these diverse types of the six-phased *yoga* were couched within the different theoretical and practical frameworks of disparate traditions, they all share some commonalities. The most salient point of commonality is that each form of the six-phased *yoga* is viewed within its own tradition as inducive to the accomplishment of both limited, or mundane, and supreme *siddhis*. There are also certain commonalities in the more general interpretations of some phases of the diverse types of six-phased *yoga*, despite the clear divergence in the manner in which particular phases are structured and practiced within the different traditions. For example, in both Kaśmīr Śaivism and Buddhism, the phase of breath-control (*prāṇāyāma*) involves bringing the *prāṇas* into the central *nāḍī*; the phase of retraction (*pratyāhāra*) involves the withdrawal of the senses from external objects; and meditative stabilization (*dhyāna*) implies meditation on a divine form, and so on. Their interpretations also coincide to a certain degree with Patañjali's definitions in the *Yoga Sūtras*. For the variant listings of the six members of the *ṣaḍ-aṅga-yoga* within the different schools of the Hindu and Buddhist traditions see table 2.1.

Within the Indian Buddhist tradition, teachings on the six-phased *yoga* are found within two Buddhist *tantric* systems—the *Guhyasamājatantra* and the *Kālacakratantra*. The *Hevajratantra* (Ch. 8, vs. 21–22) also mentions a six-phased *yoga*, but it does not list its members nor does it elaborate on it. Even though the six-phased

TABLE 2.1 The Variants of the Ṣaḍaṅga-yoga

The Tarka class of the Ṣaḍaṅga-yoga			
Maitrāyaṇīya Upaniṣad, 16:18	Yoga Upaniṣads *Amṛtanāda, 6, etc.*	*Viṣṇu Saṃhitā*, 30:57–58	*Tantrālokaviveka*, 3
prāṇāyāma	*pratyāhāra*	*prāṇāyāma*	*prāṇāyāma*
pratyāhāra	*dhyāna*	*pratyāhāra*	*dhyāna*
dhyāna	*prāṇāyāma*	*dhāraṇā*	*pratyāhāra*
dhāraṇā	*dhāraṇā*	*tarka*	*dhāraṇā*
tarka	*tarka*	*samādhi*	*tarka*
samādhi	*samādhi*	*dhyāna*	*samādhi*
The Anusmṛti class of the Ṣaḍaṅga-yoga			
Guhyasamājatantra, 18:140		*Kālacakratantra*, 4:116	
pratyāhāra		*pratyāhāra*	
dhyāna		*dhyāna*	
prāṇāyāma		*prāṇāyāma*	
dhāraṇā		*dhāraṇā*	
anusmṛti		*anusmṛti*	
samādhi		*samādhi*	
The Āsana class of the Ṣaḍaṅga-yoga			
Netratantra (*Mṛtyujit*)		Gorakṣa Texts, *Gorakṣaśataka*, 7, etc.	
āsana		*āsana*	
prāṇāyāma		*prāṇayāma*	
pratyāhāra		*pratyāhāra*	
dhyāna		*dhāraṇā*	
dhāraṇā		*dhyāna*	
samādhi		*samādhi*	

yogas of the Kālacakra and Guhyasamāja systems accord in the names and in the sequences of their phases, they differ in their content and practical implications. Among the Indian sources of these two traditions, the majority of treatises and commentaries on the six-phased *yoga* belong to the Kālacakra corpus. According to the *Blue Annals*, the six-phased *yoga* of the *Kālacakratantra* was initially taught by Vajradhara in the form of Avadhūtipa to Anupamarakṣita (c. eleventh-twelfth centuries), who passed it on to his friend Śrīdhara.[12] Two works on the six-phased *yoga* are traditionally attributed to Anupamarakṣita: the *Ṣaḍaṅgayoga* and the *Ṣaḍaṅgayoganāma*. The later Indian author Raviśrījñāna (eleventh–twelfth centuries)—in the introductions to his *Guṇabharaṇī*, a commentary on the *Ṣaḍaṅgayoga* and to his *Ṣaḍaṅgayogaṭīkā*, a commentary on the *Ṣaḍaṅgayoganāma*—gives a brief account of Anupamarakṣita's revelatory experience.[13] According to the accounts recorded in the *Guṇabharaṇī* and the *Ṣaḍaṅgayogaṭīkā*, Anupamarakṣita studied Buddhism and other Indian systems of thought. Under the guidance of Śrīkhasarpana, he practiced for twelve years a meditation on reality without an object and free of conceptualizations, but was unable to gain a special insight. Depressed, he fell asleep, during which Vajrayoginī appeared to him, instructing him to go to Vikramapura, where he would attain that special insight. After arriving at midnight in Vikramapura—accompanied by his disciple, the great *paṇḍita* Śrīdhara—Anupamarakṣita received instruction on the six-phased *yoga* directly from the Buddha in the form of Avadhūta. By merely receiving the instruction that confirmed, "This is reality," he entered *samādhi*; and upon emerging from his *samādhi* in the early morning, Anupamarakṣita taught this knowledge to Śrīdhara.

With some variations, this story is repeated several times in later Tibetan chronicles of Buddhism and the lineage of the *Kālacakratantra*'s six-phased *yoga*.[14] Apart from Padma dkar po, who mistook Vikramapura for Vikramaśīla monastery in Bihar, none of the sources specify the location of Vikramapura nor the place from which Anupamarakṣita went to Vikramapura. It is likely that the Vikramapura to which Raviśrījñāna refers is Vajrayoginī village in contemporary Dacca, located in east-central Bengal, which is also thought to be the birthplace of Atīśa.[15] This is perhaps the same Vikramapura mentioned in the inscriptions found in north India. In the inscriptions related to the rulers of the Varman and Vikramāditya dynasties of northern India, Vikramapura is mentioned as their capital during the eleventh and twelfth centuries. The Varman dynasty ruled eastern Bengal in the second quarter of the eleventh century, and their Vikramapura was eventually overtaken by Vijayasena, the greatest king of the Sena dynasty, in the middle of the twelfth century. Thus, Raviśrījñāna, who, according to Tāranātha's *History of Buddhism in India*, lived during the reign of the Sena dynasty, could have been referring to that Vikramapura.[16] Some inscriptions mention Vikramapura as a capital founded by Vikramāditya VI (*c.* 1076–1126). His father, Someśvara I, reigned in Magadha and eastern Bengal, and he himself conquered central Bengal shortly before 1068 CE, after defeating Vigrahapāla III. According to Tāranātha's *History of Buddhism in India*, Anupamarakṣita lived during the period of the Bhayapāla and Nayapāla kings of the Pāla dynasty.[17] Nayapāla, the father of the mentioned Vigrahapāla III, ascended the throne in the early eleventh century and ruled the kingdom that extended on the west up to Bihar and to the east to central Bengal. Tāranātha's information coincides with 'Gos lo tsa ba gzhon nu dpal's assertion in the *Blue Annals* that Anupamarakṣita could not have been later than Nāro (956–1040 CE), since Nāro cites Anupamarakṣita's teaching in his *Sekkodeśaṭīkā*.[18] Thus, whether Raviśrījñāna was referring to the Vikramapura of the Pālas, Varmans, or Vikaramādityas, according to Buddhist tradition the *Kālacakratantra*'s six-phased *yoga* was first disseminated in Bengal.

Anupamarakṣita's name could have been easily related to the well-known Anupama monastery (*vihāra*) in Kaśmīr, which produced Buddhaśrījñāna, Sarvajñaśrīrakṣita, and Śākyaśrībhadra, the great early eleventh-century Kaśmīr scholars of the *Kālacakratantra*. His name also could have been related to Anupamapura, the seat of the two greatest Buddhist centers of learning in Kaśmīr during the eleventh and twelfth centuries—the monasteries of Ratnagupta and Ratnarāśmi. In either case, Anupamarakṣita could have come to Bengal from Kaśmīr.

It is clear from the extant Indian and Tibetan sources that there were several lineages of the *Kālacakratantra*'s six-phased *yoga* in India. As these sources indicate, the most important among those lineages was that of Anupamarakṣita. In the *Guṇabharaṇī*, Raviśrījñāna gives the following lineage: Anupamarakṣita[19]—Śrīdhara—Bhāskara—Raviśrījñāna. The same lineage, but in an extended form, is also given in the *Blue Annals*, the fifteenth-century Tibetan chronicle of Buddhism in Tibet, which also mentions the famous lineages of Indian Buddhist masters. According to the *Blue Annals*, the most famous lineage of the *Kālacakratantra*'s six-phased *yoga* in

India begins with Anupamarakṣita and ends with the Bengali *mahā-paṇḍita*, Vanaratna (1384–1468). Vanaratna received the transmission of the six-phased *yoga* from the *mahā-siddha* Śavaripa, one of the eighty-four legendary *mahā-siddhas* of India, and he taught it extensively in Tibet during the first half of the fifteenth century.[20] The extended lineage is given as follows: Anupamarakṣita—Śrīdharanandana (Sādhuputra)[21]—Bhāskaradeva—Raviśrījñāna (Sūryaśrī)—Dharmākāraśānti—Ratnarakṣita—Narendrabodhi—Muktipakṣa—Śākyarakṣita—Sujata—Buddhaghoṣa—Vanaratna. The exact same lineage of Indian masters is also mentioned in Padma dkar po's (sixteenth century) *Dpe med 'tsho'i lugs kyi rnal 'byor yan lag drug pa'i khrid rdo rje'i tshig 'byed*.[22]

Earlier Tibetan historians of Buddhism in India and Tibet recorded a shorter branch of Anupamarakṣita's lineage in India. In his *Dpe med 'tsho'i sbyor drug gi br gyud pa*, included in the *Gsang sngags rgyud sde bzhi'i gzungs'bum*,[23] Bu ston offers the following list for the Indian masters following the lineage of Anupamarakṣita: Anupamarakṣita—Śrīdhara—Bhāskaradeva—Dharmākaraśānti—Raviśrījñāna—Ratnarakṣita—Vibhūticandra. This line of Indian Buddhist masters ends with Vibhūticandra (twelfth–thirteenth centuries). According to Padma gar dbang,[24] Vibhūticandra received his *Kālacakratantra* initiation and teachings from three Indian scholars: Śākyaśrībhadra, the *mahā-paṇḍita* of Kaśmīr,[25] who was his principal spiritual mentor, Vikhyātadeva, and Dharmadāsa. In Nepal, he mastered the *Kālacakratantra* under the guidance of Ratnarakṣita, the Newari *mahā-paṇḍita*, from whom he received the teachings of the six-phased *yoga* of the *Kālacakratantra* in the tradition of Anupamarakṣita. During his stay in Nepal, Vibhūticandra became an expert in the *Kālacakratantra* and in the practice of the six-phased *yoga*. According to Padma gar dbang,[26] he wrote annotations to the *Kālacakratantra* and the *Vimalaprabhā*, which influenced later Tibetan translators and commentators on the *Kālacakratantra*. As one of the Indian *mahā-paṇḍitas*, Vibhūticandra visited Tibet three times and became fluent in the Tibetan language. He himself translated his *Ṣaḍaṅgayoganāma* (*Rnal 'byor yan lag drug pa*)[27] into Tibetan. According to the Tibetan six-phased *yoga* tradition, the *Ṣaḍaṅgayoganāma* is the direct transmission of the six-phased *yoga* practice that Vibhūticandra received from Śavaripa during his stay at Stham Bihar monastery in Kathmandu, upon which he attained *dhāraṇā*, the fourth phase of this *yoga*. In subsequent centuries, this text became one of the most important and authoritative texts for the direct transmission of the *Kālacakratantra*'s six-phased *yoga* in Tibet, especially in the Jonangpa tradition. According to Tāranātha,[28] the teachings on the six-phased *yoga* that Śavaripa revealed to Vibhūticandra were based on the *dohas* of Saraha, and Saraha's yogic practice itself was based on the six-phased *yoga*.

In the *Sbyor ba yan lag drug gi rdzogs rim gyi gnad bsdus pa*, Tshong kha pa[29] (fourteenth–fifteenth centuries), following his teacher Bu ston, cites the Indian lineage of Anupamarakṣita in this way: Anupamarakṣita—Śrīdhara—Bhāskaradeva—Dharmākaraśānti—Raviśrījñāna—Ratnarakṣita—Vibhūticandra.

3

The Nature of Syncretism in the *Kālacakratantra*

Reading the *Kālacakratantra*, one immediately notices its prominent, syncretistic character, but close examination of this *tantra* and its commentarial literature reveals that the Kālacakra tradition has preserved a distinctively Buddhist orientation, and that its affiliation with non-Buddhist Indian systems is in form rather than content. The syncretism of this tantric system is a self-conscious absorption, or appropriation, of the modes of expression that are characteristic of the rival religious systems of India. This self-conscious syncretism variously permeates several areas of the *Kālacakratantra*, such as its theoretical system, language, medicine, and cosmology; and it is often inextricably related to Buddhist tantric conversionary efforts. For this reason, the term syncretism does not quite fit this tradition, whose rhetorical strategies and linguistic divergences, though cleverly disguised, are firmly rooted in Buddhist doctrine. The Kālacakra tradition expressly justifies its adaptive character as a skillful means for leading individuals of diverse mental dispositions to spiritual maturation. The *Paramādibuddhatantra* asserts that "one should teach the Dharma in whatever manner matures sentient beings."[1]

The conversionary mission of the *Kālacakratantra* is not the sole basis of its syncretistic character. The growing pluralism within the inner life of Indian Mahāyāna communities could have been another contributing factor in the proliferation of syncretism, for the flourishing of religious pluralism often makes syncretism a necessity rather than just a possibility. The pluralism that is characteristic of Indian tantric Buddhism can be described as a self-conscious recognition that although the Buddhist tradition is shared by all the members of a specific Buddhist community, the way it is interpreted, analyzed, and experienced differs within that community. It seems that the Kālacakra tradition tried to find grounds for dialogue with other Buddhist and non-Buddhist systems without ignoring their differences; while at the same time, it was apprehensive about losing its own distinct identity. Its ambivalence with regard to its own syncretism is evident throughout the *Kālacakratantra* and the *Vimalaprabhā*. For example, while refuting the particular views of the Indian non-Buddhist and the so-called Buddhist heterodox schools, the *Kālacakratantra* states:

> Kālacakra imparts instruction on the earth for the sake of this and other knowledge of people who have dull, sharp, and other mental dispositions due to the power of their karmic habitual propensities.[2]

At the same time, it warns against the dangers of grasping onto one's own dogmatic position or falling under the influence of other teachings by familiarizing oneself with those teachings in order to refute them:

> Since the mind, like a crystal, is colored by the colors of the objects in its proximity, the *yogī* should not criticize any teaching that belongs to his own or to another family.[3]

The *Vimalaprabhā* justifies the Kālacakra tradition's syncretism, asserting that the principle (*niyama)* of the Bhagavān Kālacakra is that "whatever is identical to the words of the Buddha either in terms of conventional or ultimate truth must not be criticized."[4] In accordance with this principle, it cites passages from the writings of heterodox Buddhist schools at times—the Vaibhāṣikas, for example—in order to substantiate its theory; and at other times, it vehemently criticizes other passages from the same writings that express views contrary to those of the Kālacakra tradition.

Likewise, on the one hand, the *Kālacakratantra* asserts that even when one's own mind is pure, one should not create discord among intelligent and unintelligent people, since they are all Buddhas;[5] and on the other hand, it states that one should not use ferocious *mantras* to kill living beings but to terrify the host of Māras who are "the authors of the Smṛtis and other murderous heterodox groups (*tīrthika*) who are fond of fighting."[6] The *Vimalaprabhā* interprets here "Māras" as proponents of the Vedic Dharma, and it affirms that a Bodhisattva should use ferocious *mantras* to generate fear in heterodox groups that their Dharma will be destroyed.[7]

The Theoretical Syncretism of the *Kālacakratantra*

As mentioned earlier, the philosophical position advocated in the *Kālacakratantra* and its related literature is that of the Mādhyamikas, following the line of Nāgārjuna. According to the *Kālacakratantra*, only Mādhyamikas who assert the nonduality of compassion and emptiness avoid philosophical failure. Thus, adhering to the ontological view of the Mādhyamikas as the only valid one, the *Kālacakratantra* refutes the tenets of all other Buddhist and non-Buddhist systems. Although the *Vimalaprabhā* acknowledges diverse Buddhist systems such as Vaibhāṣika, Saütrāntika, Yogācāra, and Madhyamaka as equally authentic teachings of the Buddha, it presents the Madhyamaka system as the pinnacle of the Buddha's teaching, and it claims that the Mādhyamikas are the only ones who are qualified to attain "the non-abiding (*apratiṣṭhita*) *nirvāṇa* that is without remainder (*upadhi-rahita*), due to the cessation of causes and results, and that is devoid of the waking and deep sleep states and is similar to the dream and the fourth state."[8] It affirms the superiority of the Madhayamaka school over other Buddhist schools on the grounds that the Mādhyamika treatises, unlike the scriptures of the aforementioned Buddhist schools, elucidate ultimate reality.[9]

The *Vimalaprabhā* interprets the differences among the four schools of Buddhism as the Buddha's response to different mental dispositions of sentient beings, some of whom have the fortune of being closer to enlightenment, while some are further from enlightenment. It also views the differing teachings of the four Buddhist schools as the Buddha's response to the teachings of four different non-Buddhist groups, that is, as his conversionary means. It asserts:

> Since beginningless time, all sentient beings have been heterodox (*tīrthika*), devoted to the Dharmas of gods, spirits (*bhūta*), and *asuras*, deprived of the path of omniscience, placing themselves into one of the four castes, desiring the pleasures that are the reward of heaven, and asserting [the existence of] a creator and the Self (*ātman*). Among them, those who rely on the Dharmas of gods and *pretas* are proponents of "correct words" (*śabda-vādin*), Īśvara, the Self, and social discrimination (*jāti-vādin*). Those who rely on the Dharmas of the Barbarians (*mleccha*) and *asuras* are proponents of a creator and a soul (*jīva*) and are devoid of the propagation of social discrimination.[10]

Thus, according to the Kālacakra tradition, all followers of the four schools of Buddhism at some time or another belonged to the heterodox groups, and as they further pursued the issues related to the religious teachings they followed and finally settled with Buddhist answers to those issues, they converted to Buddhism. Thus, the Vaibhāṣikas are said to be Buddhist converts who previosly followed the Barbarian Dharma. The Sautrāntikas are Buddhist converts who previously propagated the theories of a creator, correct words, Īśvara, and class discrimination; and the Yogācārins are Buddhist converts who previously held the view of the permanent Self and the creator; whereas, the Mādhyamikas are the converts who abandoned not only the aforementioned heterodox views but also the dogmatic positions and related meditative practices that are characteristic of the other three Buddhist schools. The *Vimalaprabhā* describes the manner of their conversion to Buddhism in the following way:

> Among those Barbarians (*mleccha*) there are two types of grasping—grasping onto the agglomeration of atoms and grasping onto the [truly existent] person (*pudgala*) who has origination. Their belief is: "If a person who has the origination and dwells in the body that consists of the agglomeration of atoms does not exist, then who will take on another body after the body that consists of the agglomeration of atoms has perished? Therefore, a spontaneously arisen person (*upapāduka-pudgala*) does exist. By meditating on this, the reward of heaven, or the reward of *nirvāṇa*, comes about. Apart from the reward of heaven, there is no other *nirvāṇa*." At the time when they sought the truth, knowing the thoughts of their minds, the Bhagavān who knows reality said: "There is a person who carries the burden, but I do not say that he [exists] permanently or impermanently." This is true, since according to the Bhagavān's words, it is not possible to say that a person who is [a manifestation of] mental habitual propensities in the dreaming state is permanent or impermanent. Abandoning the Dharma of Barbarians due to this statement of the Tathāgata, they have become the Buddhist Vaibhāṣikas. Moreover, some, hearing the highest Dharma as it was being taught to the Bodhisattvas and abandoning the grasping onto the [truly existent] person, resorted to the path of the Samyaksaṃbuddha.
>
> Furthermore, among the Sautrāntikas, there is grasping onto the agglomeration of atoms. The belief of these substantialists (*artha-vādin*) is: "If the animate and inanimate things that inhabit space do not exist, then the triple world would not exist

either. In the absence of *saṃsāra*, there would be nonfavorable or unfavorable states of existence. Likewise, neither Buddhas nor Bodhisattvas would exist, nor would the supreme *nirvāṇa* exist. One could not see the Bhagavān's relics because of the absence of the substance present in the matter." At the time when they sought the truth in this way, the Bhagavān, knowing the thoughts of their minds, said: "There is the final body [of the Bhagavān] that consists of the agglomeration of atoms and is endowed with thirty-two characteristics of the Great Man, by means of which the state of the Samyaksaṃbuddha and the sublime *parinirvāṇa* come into existence." This is true because of the appearance of the Bhagavān's relics. Thus having heard of the power of the body that consists of the agglomeration of atoms and abandoning the propagation of social discrimination, correct words, Īśvara, and a creator, they became the Buddhist Sautrāntikas. Moreover, some, hearing the instruction on the supramundane Dharma to Bodhisattvas and abandoning the grasping onto that substance (*artha*), resorted to the path of the Samyaksaṃbuddha.

Among the Yogācārins, there is grasping onto consciousness. The belief of these proponents of consciousness is: "The entire three worlds are consciousness only. The so-called atom does not exist because it is a division that consists of the six constitutent parts. Just as in the dreaming state the things that are mere appearances of the mind engage in activities even though there is an absence of atomic matter, so too in the waking state a thing appears by means of an unreal thing, like a hair-net or a golden conch appearing to the eye soiled with dark dirt." At the time when they sought the truth in this way, the Bhagavān, knowing the thoughts of their minds, said: "The triple world is consciousness only. Apart from consciousness, there is no other *saṃsāra*. The cessation of the seed of cyclic existence is due to the cessation of mundane consciousness (*laukika-vijñāna*). Due to that, there is *nirvāṇa*." This is true. The manifestation of suffering and happiness arises from the animate and not from the inanimate. So-called suffering and happiness are *saṃsāra*, and their absence is *nirvāṇa*. Thus, hearing the Bhagavān's words and abandoning the theory of the creator and the Self, they became the Buddhist Yogācārins. Moreover, some, hearing the instruction on the supramundane Dharma to Bodhisattvas and abandoning the propagation of consciousness, resorted to the path of the Samyaksaṃbuddha.[11]

It further argues that just as the Buddha taught different theories to the four types of Buddhists, so he taught them different meditative practices that were in accordance with their differing views. For example, he taught meditation on the impermanence of a person to the Pudgalavādins, meditation on the *kṛtsnās* to the Arthavādins, meditation on cognition only (*vijñapti-mātra*) to the Vijñānavādins, and to the Mādhyamikas, he taught meditation on the dreamlike and imperishable gnosis.[12] Thus, in light of its view of the superiority of the advanced Mādhyamika teachings and practices, the Kālacakra tradition associates the Mādhyamikas with spiritually mature Buddhists who, abandoning all dogmatic positions and related meditative practices of the other three Buddhist schools, succeed in reaching the highest spiritual goal.

Nevertheless, the Kālacakra tradition argues that there is no distinction between the Mādhyamikas and the heterodox groups with regard to the manner in which conventional reality appears. It regards the investigation of conventionally existent phenomena and the notions of the conventional creator, means of action, and action as common to all, Buddhists and non-Buddhists alike. It affirms that the only major difference between its philosophical views and those of the heterodox groups is in its understanding of the nature of emptiness, which is identitylessness of two kinds—personal identitylessness (*pudgala-nairātmya*) and phenomenal identitylessness (*dharma-nairātmya*).[13]

That view of the commonality of the Mādhyamika's and the heterodox groups' speculative approaches to conventional reality facilitated the *Kālacakratantra*'s import of certain ideas and theoretical models from other philosophical systems and induced its theoretical syncretism. By incorporating the ideas characteristic of other philosophical systems into its own theoretical framework and by attributing conventional validity to them, the *Kālacakratantra* attempts to accomplish two objectives: namely, to provide rational explanations pertaining to human psycho-physiology, and to convert heterodox groups. Textual study of this tantric tradition reveals the following two goals of the Kālacakra tradition's theoretical syncretism: the conversion of heterodox groups, and the modeling of conventional reality for meditational purposes.

For example, the Sāṃkhya's qualitative dualism of consciousness (*puruṣa*) and matter (*prakṛti*) is adopted by the *Kālacakratantra* as a heuristic device for explaining the nature of the human being from the conventional point of view. However, the Sāṃkhya's concepts of *puruṣa* and *prakṛti*, which permeate the theoretical framework of this *tantra*, are not taken literally from the Sāṃkhya philosophical system. Rather, they are reinterpreted and adapted to the *Kālacakratantra*'s own unique system.

Thus, in the context of the *Kālacakratantra*, the twenty-five principles of *prakṛti* are the five aggregates (*skandha*), the five elements (*dhātu*), the twelve sense-bases (*āyatana*), intellect (*buddhi*), self-grasping (*ahaṃkāra*), and the mind (*manas*). The *prakṛti* of the human being is devoid of inherent nature (*svabhāva*), and from the ultimate point of view, it is luminous. In contrast, in the Sāṃkhya philosophical system, the twenty-four principles of *prakṛti* forming the human being include the primordial *prakṛti* (*mūla-prakṛti*), which is an independently existent and inherently generative phenomenon, and its twenty-three temporal subdivisions. Likewise, in the *Kālacakratantra*, the aggregates, elements, and sense-bases form the *prakṛti* of the transmigratory body,[14] and the five elements, intellect, self-grasping, and the mind form the *prakṛti* of the transmigratory mind.[15] In Sāṃkhya, on the other hand, only the intellect, self-grasping, and the mind form the "inner organ" (*antaḥ-karaṇa*); and when combined with the sense-faculties (*buddhīndriya*), faculties of action (*karmendriya*), and subtle elements (*tanmātra*), they form the subtle body (*liṅga-śarīra*), which is separable from the gross body and thus capable of transmigrating through a series of gross bodies which are aggregations of the five gross elements.

There is also a difference in terms of the origination of the gross and subtle elements. According to Sāṃkhya, the five gross elements are derivatives of the subtle elements beginning with sound, and so forth;[16] whereas in the *Kālacakratantra*, the five gross elements are said to give rise to sound and other subtle elements.[17]

It is not quite clear what is meant in the *Kālacakratantra* by the terms *buddhi*, *manas*, and *ahaṃkāra*. The Indian commentarial literature does not elucidate these points, and Tibetan commentaries understand them in different ways. For mKhas grub rje, the eight constituents of the *prakṛti* of the transmigratory mind are eight of the twenty-five principles of *prakṛti* and *puruṣa*, as categorized by the Sāṃkhya philosophical system. mKhas grub rje does not mention whether or not we should understand *buddhi*, *manas*, and *ahaṃkāra* in the way in which Sāṃkhya interprets them. He thus leaves us with a puzzle and room for speculation. Bu ston's annotations [438], on the other hand, suggest that *buddhi* here refers to the five sensory faculties (*buddhīndriya*), that *manas* designates conceptualization (*vikalpa*), and that *ahaṃkāra* refers to the defiled, or afflicted mind (*kliṣṭa-manas*), referring to a subtle feeling of "I." This concept of an afflicted mind is characteristic of the Yogācāra's classification of the mind and not of the Mādhyamika. Bu ston's interpretation of the term *buddhi* definitely differs from that in Sāṃkhya, which considers *buddhi* a part of the "inner organ" that makes decisions, cognitively and ethically.[18] However, Bu ston's explanations of the terms *manas* and *ahaṃkāra* correspond in some ways to the implications of those terms in Sāṃkhya, which regards conceptualization as one of the functions of the *manas*,[19] and interprets *ahaṃkāra* as a part of the "inner organ" that appropriates all experiences to itself. The fact that the *Kālacakratantra* uses these philosophical terms without clearly explaining their meaning is one more indication of the author's conscious attempt to incorporate the Sāṃkhya system into its universal model of conventional reality.[20]

Likewise, despite some striking similarities between the Sāṃkhya's and the *Kālacakratantra*'s interpretations of *puruṣa*, there are some basic differences with regard to the nature of the *puruṣa* and its relation to *prakṛti*. In both systems, the *puruṣa* refers to consciousness which pervades *prakṛti* but itself is neither *prakṛti* nor its derivative, and which is free of the three properties—namely, *sattva*, *rajas*, and *tamas*—and is neither bound nor liberated by anything. However, whereas in the Sāṃkhya philosophical system, the *puruṣa* is an independently existent reality, a contentless presence, or an *inactive* witness devoid of bliss, in the *Kālacakratantra*, the *puruṣa* is of the nature of innate gnosis (*sahaja-jñāna*), which is blissful omniscience; and it transcends both *saṃsāra* and *nirvāṇa*, and yet is *active* in supporting both.

For the schematization of the above mentioned differences between the Sāṃkhya's and *Kālacakratantra*'s interpretations of *puruṣa* and *prakṛti*, see table 3.1.

Similarly, the *Kālacakratantra*'s way of understanding the *guṇas* of *prakṛti* does not correspond in every way to the Sāṃkhya's interpretation. In some instances, instead of *sattva*, *rajas*, and *tamas*, the *Kālacakratantra* specifies the five sense-objects—smell, sound, form, taste, and touch—as the *guṇas* of *prakṛti*.[21] Being subject to origination and cessation, they are said to have the characteristics of conceptualizations and bind the individual to the cycle of existence. In other instances, the three *guṇas*—*sattva*, *rajas*, and *tamas*—correspond to the moral distinctions among sentient beings' mental dispositions that are induced by their own *karma*.[22] In yet other instances, the Kālacakra tradition refers to the three *guṇas* in ways that are open to multiple interpretations. For example, when it speaks of the gross, subtle, and supreme natures (*prakṛti*) of the mind as being contained in the three *guṇas*, it does not fully explain the manner in which it understands the three *guṇas* in this particular context. The *Vimalaprabhā* suggests only that in the *Kālacakratantra's* classification of the nature of awareness as gross, subtle, and supreme, the gross nature of the transmigratory mind, which apprehends phenomena with the gross sense-faculties, is characterized by the waking state. This state is said to correspond to *sattva*, that is to say, to the daytime. The subtle nature of the mind, which apprehends mental phenomena that are like an illusion, is characterized by the dreaming state, which is said to correspond to *ra-*

TABLE 3.1 Puruṣa and Prakṛti in Sāṃkhya and in the *Kālacakratantra*

Sāṃkhya	*Kālacakratantra*
Puruṣa	
contentless presence	omniscience
passive witness	active support
devoid of bliss	blissful
Prakṛti	
primordial materiality (*mūlaprakṛti*)	
intellect (*buddhi*)	intellect (*buddhi*)
self-grasping (*ahaṃkāra*)	self-grasping (*ahaṃkāra*)
mind (*manas*)	
the five sense-faculties (*buddhīndriya*)	**the six sense-faculties (*indriya*)**
auditory faculty (*śrotra*)	auditory faculty
tactile faculty (*tvac*)	tactile faculty
visual faculty (*cakṣu*)	visual faculty
gustatory faculty (*rasana*)	gustatory faculty
olfactory faculty (*ghrāṇa*)	olfactory faculty
	mental faculty
the five faculties of action (*karmendriya*)	**the five psycho-physical aggregates (*skandha*)**
speaking (*vāc*)	the form-aggregate (*rūpa-skandha*)
grasping (*pāṇi*)	the feeling-aggregate
walking (*pāda*)	the discernment-aggregate
excreting (*pāyu*)	the aggregate of mental formations
procreating (*upastha*)	the aggregate of consciousness
the five subtle elements (*tanmātra*)	**the six sense-objects (*viṣaya*)**
sound (*śabda*)	form (*rūpa*)
contact (*sparśa*)	sound (*śabda*)
form (*rūpa*)	smell (*gandha*)
taste (*rasa*)	taste (*rasa*)
smell (*gandha*)	touch (*sparśa*)
	mental object (*citta*)
the five gross elements (*mahā-bhūta*)	**the five elements (*dhātu*)**
space (*ākāśa*)	earth (*pṛthivī*)
wind (*vāyu*)	water (*ap*)
fire (*tejas*)	fire (*tejas*)
water (*ap*)	wind (*vāyu*)
earth (*pṛthivī*)	space (*ākāśa*)

jas, or to twilight. The supreme nature of the mind, which discards all phenomena, is characterized by the state of deep sleep, which is thought to correspond to *tamas*, or to midnight. If not examined within its own context and in light of the Madhyamaka view of *sattva*, *rajas*, and *tamas*, this threefold classification of the nature (*prakṛti*) of the mind, related to *sattva*, *rajas*, and *tamas*, may appear identical to that of non-Buddhist tantric systems, particularly of the nondual Kaśmīr Śaivism.[23] It is quite plausible that the *Kālacakratantra* introduced that type of categorization of the nature of awareness from Kaśmīr Śaivism as a useful model to describe the conventional aspects of the transmigratory mind.[24]

In light of the fact that the Kālacakra tradition explicitly reaches out to a non-Buddhist audience, *sattva*, *rajas*, and *tamas* may be interpreted in accordance with the Sāṃkhya philosophy. On the other hand, there are some internal indications that for Buddhists not committed to that interpretation, the names of these three *guṇas* can simply be taken as ciphers to relate the three humors in the body—phlegm (*kapha*), bile (*pitta*), and wind (*vāyu*)—to the three *nāḍīs* in the body—*iḍā* on the left, *piṅgalā* on the right, and *suṣumnā* in the center—and to specific physiological or mental processes of three kinds, and so on.[25]

Likewise, it is plausible that the *Kālacakratantra*'s description of the fourth nature of the mind comes originally from the Śaiva *tantras*, for the classification of the four types of awareness was known in non-Buddhist Indian traditions since the time of the Upaniṣads. Within the context of the *Kālacakratantra*, the fourth state of the mind is a state that supports the three aforementioned states. It is characterized by the emission of regenerative fluids. Comparative analysis of the expositions of the fourth state of the mind in the *Kālacakratantra* and in Śaiva *tantras* reveals striking similarities, and yet it shows some fundamental differences with regard to the nature of that state. They agree that the fourth state of the mind marks the blissful state of consciousness in which all conceptualizations disappear and any sense of duality vanishes. However, in Śaiva *tantras*,[26] the fourth state of the mind is also a state of self-realization, a state in which one becomes aware of one's undivided, essential Self, and consequently becomes free of spiritual ignorance (*avidyā*). It is a condition by which one rises to the fifth state, or the state of liberation, within one's lifetime (*jīvan-mukti*). In the *Kālacakratantra*, on the other hand, the fourth type of awareness, though nondual at the time of the emission of regenerative fluids, is still tainted with the habitual propensities of spiritual ignorance (*avidyā-vāsanā*) and is thus embedded in the cycle of existence.

The aforementioned examples demonstrate some of the ways in which the *Kālacakratantra* endeavors to simultaneously achieve both its goals—to offer rational explanations concerning the individual, and to convert Śaivites and other heterodox groups adhering to the Sāṃkhya's world view—without compromising its fundamental tenets.

Similarly, in order to attract the Vaiṣṇavas and to illustrate its view of the physical and mental development of the human being, the *Kālacakratantra* uses the model of the ten *avatāras* of Viṣṇu as an analogy for the ten phases of human life. By so doing, it introduces its own unique interpretation of Viṣṇu's *avatāras*. Thus, in the *Kālacakratantra*,[27] Viṣṇu is also referred to as Viṣṇu Vajradhara, the individual's mind-*vajra*. He is identified here with the *gandharva* being, or the being of the intermediate state (*antar-bhāva*), being conveived in the womb and undergoing different stages in the different phases of life inside and outside the womb. For example, as a fetus, one assumes the forms of a fish, tortoise, and boar; at birth, one becomes a man-lion; in early childhood, one is in the dwarf-stage; at the time when the first teeth grow until they fall out, one is in the stage of Rāma; in adolescence, one experiences the stage of Paraśurāma; from adolescence until the appearance of gray hair, one experiences the stage of Kṛṣṇa; in old age, one is in the stage of a Buddha, and on the day of death, one attains the stage of Kalkī. Interpreting Viṣṇu's *avatāras* in this manner, the *Vimalaprabhā* cautions against adopting the standard interpretation of the

Purāṇic teachings on the grounds that they are meaningless, lead to hell, and are devised by corrupt Brāhmaṇas in order to deceive simple-minded people.[28]

This is one of many instances in which the *Kālacakratantra* tradition contemptuously disparages the Vaiṣṇava tradition and its teachings. It frequently refers to the Brāhmaṇic teachings, especially those of the Purāṇas, as false teachings, devoid of reasoning, creating confusion among foolish people, and composed by corrupt Brāhmaṇic sages for the sake of promoting their own social class.[29] One reason for such assertions was the overt animosity between the Buddhists and the adherents of the Brāhmaṇic tradition in the northern India of the late tenth and eleventh centuries. This was an era in which the influence of the Purāṇas and strength of Brāhmaṇism steadily increased, and in which orthodox Brāhmaṇic schools jointly stood in opposition to Buddhist ideology, posing a threat to the entire Buddhist tradition. One of many examples of internal evidence of the antagonism between the Brāhmaṇic and Buddhist traditions of that time is their contention over the issue of which Dharma is the best one. The *Vimalaprabhā* refutes the Brāhmaṇic claim that the Vedic Dharma is superior to the Buddha Dharma because it is earlier and innate (*sahaja*), whereas the Buddhist Dharma is later and fabricated (*kṛtaka*). It argues that just as the earlier and innate ignorance is not better than later knowledge, so too the fact that the Vedic Dharma is earlier and innate does not mean that it is best. Even though it is earlier and innate, it does not illuminate the path to omniscience, for it is characterized by the darkness of ignorance. Therefore, the *Vimalaprabhā* states, the later Buddha Dharma was created in order to destroy the great darkness of the Vedic Dharma. Speaking from the Buddhist tantric point of view, the *Vimalaprabhā* argues that the Buddhist Dharma is superior to the Vedic Dharma because *nirvāṇa* comes about only by means of a *sādhana* on the supreme, imperishable gnosis (*paramākṣa-rajñāna*) and not by means of the Vedic Dharma, which consists of nothing but the habitual propensity of seminal emission.[30]

In addition to the aforementioned instances in which the *Kālacakratantra* adopts and redefines concepts characteristic of non-Buddhist systems, it also incorporates non-Buddhist cosmological views without reinterpreting them. For example, in its classification of the infernal realms and its description of the size of Meru, the Kālacakra tradition closely parallels the Jaina cosmological view; and its description of the four cosmic *maṇḍalas* also parallels those in the Purāṇas.[31]

The fact that the conversion of heterodox groups was one of the motivations behind the *Kālacakratantra*'s adoption of specific non-Buddhist ideas implies that its teachings pertaining to the Kālacakra worldview were not kept secret from the public; that is, they were not guarded as secret teachings intended for an initiated elite. Moreover, the Kālacakra tradition's preference for explicitly presenting its specific tantric views is a result of its openly professed conversionary endeavors.

The Syncretism of *Kālacakratantra* Practice

There is clear evidence in the Kālacakra literature that even the teachings and practices pertaining to the Kālacakra initiation were accessible to heterodox groups, whether they were seeking only mundane *siddhis* or the realization of the supramundane gnosis. With regard to its initiation, the *Kālacakratantra*[32] asserts that whether one is a Buddhist, a Śaiva, a Brāhmaṇa, a naked mendicant (*nagna*), a *snātaka* (a Brāhmaṇa beggar), a *kāpālī* (a follower of a Śaiva sect, who wears a garland of human skulls and eats and drinks from them), a Jaina mendicant (*lupta-keśa*), a hermit (*maunī*), or a follower of the left-hand Śāktism (*kaulī*), one will obtain purity and all virtues by receiving the Kālacakra initiation. It substantiates that assertion on the grounds that through initiation into the *kālacakra-maṇḍala* one becomes initiated into all *maṇḍalas*, including those of the deities belonging to those heterodox groups.[33]

In its attempt to attract heterodox groups, the *Kālacakratantra* includes in its *maṇḍala* the deities that were equally accepted by Hindus, Jainas, and Buddhists as objects of worship and meditation. In this way it introduced its practical syncretism into the practice of the stage of generation. However, just as the *Kālacakratantra*'s theoretical syncretism often lends itself to both Buddhist and non-Buddhist interpretations, so too can these deities of the heterodox groups be viewed either as non-Buddhist deities or—as the *Vimalaprabhā*[34] suggests—as symbolic representations of the diverse factors of Buddhahood.[35] The Kālacakra tradition is the only Buddhist tantric tradition that fully discloses the symbolic representations of its adopted non-Buddhist deities.

While the *Kālacakratantra* incorporates into its *maṇḍala* the diverse deities that were worshipped by both Buddhists and non-Buddhists, the *Vimalaprabhā* admonishes the Buddhist tantric *yogīs* who seek liberation and wish to advance in *Kālacakratantra* practice by meditating on the supramundane *siddhis* not to perform *sādhanas* on the deities and *mantras* of the outsiders. Its rationale for this is that the deities of the outsiders cause minor misfortunes, and even when they are meditated upon, they look for the faults of the meditator and become his enemies. It points to the futility of meditation on non-Buddhist deities in this manner:

> Meditated upon, what will they, who are like poor men, give? When meditated upon, they say: "Hey *sādhaka*, we will obey your every command." If the *sādhaka* says, "Tie the king and bring him here," then they refuse, [saying]: "We are incompetent in this matter." Likewise, the insignificant deities who are meditated upon refuse [to help] with regard to omniscience.[36]

Moreover, textual study of the *Kālacakratantra* shows that receiving the *Kālacakratantra* initiation did not entail taking refuge in the Buddha, Dharma, and Saṅgha. It is clear that non-Buddhist recipients of the Kālacakra initiation did not have to become Buddhists. However, the fact that the subsequent tantric practice of the stage of generation begins with taking refuge[37] implies that those wishing to engage in more advanced Kālacakra practices had to commit themselves to the Buddhist path. Study of the fourth chapter of the *Kālacakratantra*, which describes the practice of the stages of generation, suggests that that mode of practice was introduced partly with the intention of accommodating new converts to this tantric path. Moreover, the *Vimalaprabhā*[38] asserts that the Kālacakra *sādhana* is to be taught first as a dualistic practice, based on the differentiation between the visualized deity as permanent (*nitya*) and the meditator as impermanent (*anitya*), for the sake of the mental purification and conversion of the foolish who have not yet realized that their visualized object is ultimately their own mind. The term "foolish" (*bāla*) is recurrently used in the Kālacakra literature to describe the members of heterodox groups.

The examples given above demonstrate two important facts. The first is that the Kālacakra tradition's reconciliation of non-Buddhist views with its own is primarily achieved through its reinterpretation of non-Buddhist ideas; and the second fact is that its conversionary effort was the most important factor in inducing its theoretical and practical syncretism.

The Syncretism of the *Kālacakratantra's* Language

The *Kālacakratantra*'s aforementioned expressions of syncretism are also reflected in its language. They induce the specific types of lexical and semantical syncretism found in this *tantra*, which is characterized by a diverse mixture of Buddhist and non-Buddhist terms. As we saw earlier, at times the terms borrowed from non-Buddhist systems convey the ideas characteristic of those systems; at other times, they convey traditional Buddhist ideas; and at yet other times, they designate new Buddhist ideas specific to this tantric system.

The *Vimalaprabhā* interprets the *Kālacakratantra*'s linguistic divergences as its way of transcending the class discrimination of the rivaling Hindu groups, which prohibit the Vaiṣyas, Śūdras, and other low classes from studying their scriptures, saying, "Here in the land of mortals, the Vaiṣyas, Śūdras, and others born in degraded wombs, must not study the Vedas and must not take up the mendicant's life and staff."[39] It also views the *Kālacakratantra*'s linguistic syncretism as a way of overcoming the alienation created by conservative Buddhist ways of institutionalizing the language of the north Indian Buddhist tradition, upheld by Buddhists who, "seeing the arrogance of the heterodox *paṇḍitas* who propound the proper words, think: 'Just as the chosen deities of the Brāḥmaṇas, Vaiṣṇavas, Śaivas, and others—Brahmā, Hari, Hara, and others—speak Sanskrit, so too our chosen deities, the Buddhas and Bodhisattvas, speak Sanskrit." '[40]

Another facet of the *Kālacakratantra*'s lexical syncretism manifests in the usage and reinterpretation of Buddhist terms of different Buddhist schools. For example, the *Kālacakratantra* frequently employs the Yogācāra's term *ālaya-vijñāna* (repository consciousness) simply to designate *vijñāna* (consciousness). Taking into account the interpretation of the *Vimalaprabhā* commentary, which glosses *ālaya-vijñāna* as *vijñāna* and *jīva*, the *Kālacakratantra*'s general view of the nature of the mind, and its refutation of the Yogācāra's classification of the mind, one may infer that the term *ālaya-vijñāna* in this tantric tradition designates not the Yogācāra's concept of an ethically neutral repository of the habitual propensities of *karma*, but a continuum of mental consciousness. This particular type of lexical syncretism results from the *Kālacakratantra*'s effort to convert the adherents of Buddhist schools other than Madhyamaka. The *Vimalaprabhā* explicitly refers to Yogācārins, Sautrāntikas, and Vaibhāṣikas as simple-minded Buddhist heretics (*bauddha-tīrthika*).[41]

The Kālacakra tradition's conversionary endeavors may also be traced to yet another facet of its lexical syncretism, namely, the usage of terms originating from Indian vernaculars. For example, the terms *chandoha*, *upachandoha*, *melāpaka*, *upamelāpaka*, and others, which designate the names of the specific bodily joints, do not have clear Sankrit etymologies. Since the author of the *tantra* demonstrates his familiarity with the Āyurvedic medical treatises such as the *Caraka* and *Suśruta*

Saṃhitās, which employ standard Sanskrit terms to designate those bodily parts, it is certain that the usage of these terms was not accidental.

In light of the preceding discussions, one may draw several conclusions. First, the above-mentioned characteristics of the *Kālacakratantra*'s pervasive syncretism demonstrate the diversity of that syncretism. Second, it is the prevailing reinterpretative aspect of the *Kālacakratantra*'s syncretism that ensures this *tantra*'s coherence and gives it a distinctively Buddhist character. Third, the different features of the *Kālacakratantra*'s syncretism are incidental to the various immediate goals that this *tantra* attempts to accomplish by resorting to syncretism. As mentioned earlier, there are several reasons for the *Kālacakratantra*'s syncretism. The first is to enhance and enrich its presentation of conventional reality. The second is its expressed aim of proselytism. In support of this claim, it is well to remember that during the late tenth and early eleventh centuries, northern India was subjected to frequent raids by the Muslim chief Amīr of Ghaznī and his son Sultan Mahmūd, whose forces took tens of thousands of slaves and plundered the country's treasures. In the midst of this brutal invasion, the author of the *Kālacakratantra* may well have sought to form a united front of heterodox groups and Buddhists, a new ecumenical movement that would stand up against this common foe, who exemplified the "Barbarians" (*mleccha*). Likewise, dangerous times like these often create a world of religious uncertainty that can sometimes be warded off by precarious theoretical and practical forms of religious affirmations, which may be seen as heretical.

The fact that a conversionary mission is the most compelling factor in inducing the *Kālacakratantra*'s syncretism brings us to a simple but pertinent question: Why does the *Kālacakratantra* resort to syncretism in order to fulfill its conversionary goals? The answer may be threefold. First, by incorporating heterodox theories and practices, it makes its own system more accessible to those whom it is trying to attract. That is, by presenting its own views in terms that the heterodox groups are steeped in and with which they are comfortable, it makes its own theory more readily understandable to them. Second, it acknowledges aspirations already cherished by its potential Buddhist and non-Buddhist followers—such as physical health, mundane *siddhis*, immortality, and liberation—and shows them how to accomplish these aims by means of *Kālacakratantra* practice. Third, by means of syncretism, it tries to demonstrate that in terms of conventional reality there is no fundamental difference between the views of the heterodox systems and the *Kālacakratantra*, and that no theory describes any purported inherent nature of the world. However, this assertion of the essential compatibility between the heterodox and *Kālacakratantra* views appears to be contradictory, for the Kālacakra tradition undeniably refutes and reinterprets others' views concerning the conventional nature of phenomena. This dilemma may be a philosophical one which the Kālacakra tradition, due to its adoptive strategies, cannot avoid; but there may perhaps be a deeper justification that can be discovered through further research into this subject.

4

The Concept of Science in the Kālacakra Tradition

When the issue of science is raised within the context of Indian Buddhist thought, there are no more advanced or comprehensive matrices of theory and practice than those presented in the literature of the Kālacakra tradition. A textual study of the Indian literary sources of this tantric tradition reveals that when Brāhmaṇic formal education in eleventh-century India was exclusively theological and disdainful of technical knowledge,[1] north Indian Buddhist monastic education incorporated training in nontheological skills that required knowledge of medicine, alchemy, mathematics, artisanship, and even weaponry.[2] The sharp split between theological and scientific education, which impaired the Brāhmaṇic educational system of that time, was absent in Buddhist monastic education due to the prevailing Buddhist view that theological knowledge and technical and scientific learning are not only compatible but complementary as well.[3] The literature of the Kālacakra tradition with its diverse and well-integrated topics and applications of the diverse fields of knowledge best attests to that fact. The integration of diverse fields of knowledge by this tantric tradition has its roots in the Buddhist monastic, educational system.

The study of the five fields of knowledge (*pañca-vidyā*)—linguistics, logic, inner science (metaphysics and philosophy), medicine, and creative arts—was incorporated in Buddhist education at the time of the emergence of the Mahāyāna Buddhist monastic universities. Mahāyāna monasteries were the first to offer educational opportunities to both the monastic and lay Buddhist communities; and they were the first to provide them with religious and secular education as well. This is very significant in light of the fact that in the Indian Buddhist world, educational opportunities did not exist apart from monasteries. In early Buddhism, Buddhist education was entirely monastic in its content and available only to those who entered or intended to enter the Buddhist monastic order. The origin of the Buddhist educational system was closely tied to the inception of the Buddhist monastic order. The Buddhist educational system actually arose from the need for instructing monastic novices. Each novice (*śrāmaṇera*) at his ordination (*pravrajyā*) was placed under two senior monks, one called a preceptor (*upadhyāya*) and the other a personal teacher (*ācārya*). From the description given in the early Buddhist Pāli texts (*Mahāvagga*, Ch. 1.), it seems that the *upadhyāya* was responsible for instructing the novice in Buddhist texts and doctrine, whereas the *ācārya* was responsible for training the novice in the proper conduct of a fully ordained monk. After the novitiate period was over, a novice aged twenty or older underwent a second ordination (*upasaṃpadā*). As a fully ordained monk (*bhikṣu*), one received further training to become well versed in Buddhist scriptures and meditation. That period was called *niśraya*, or "dependence," and it could be reduced to five years or extended for a lifetime. Once that period was over, a trained monk was allowed to teach younger monks as an independent *ācārya*. Thus, in early Buddhism the unit of the Buddhist educational system was a young monk or a group of young monks living under the supervision of two elders who were responsible for their entire well-being. Many such groups of students and teachers resided together within a single monastic institution. This pattern of collective life and organization of education carried over to the educational system of Mahāyāna Buddhism where it was further developed. However, unlike the Mahāyāna texts, the early Buddhist writings[4] refer to the creative arts, craftsmanship, scribing, and similar fields of knowledge as vulgar fields of knowledge (*tiracchāna-vijjā*), which are studied only by lay people. Likewise, in the early Buddhist period, the Buddhist laity had to seek other educational centers when they needed nonreligious education. With the advent of Mahāyāna, there was greater emphasis on promoting general education for the entire Buddhist community. There were two main reasons for that shift in the priorities. One reason was Mahāyāna's recognition of the Buddhist lay life as a viable way of life in the pursuit of spiritual awakening, and the other reason lay in the Bodhisattva ideal and the ideal of perfect enlightenment characterized by omniscience. Therefore, whereas in early Buddhism attention was given almost exclusively to the elimination of spiritual ignorance, Mahāyāna Buddhism was concerned with the eradication of every kind of ignorance. As some Mahāyāna texts attest, a Bodhisattva was encouraged to gain proficiency in all kinds of knowledge in order to attain the six perfections and assist others in every way needed. The *Bodhicaryāvatāra*, for instance, declares, "there is nothing that the Children of the Jina should not learn."[5] In this regard, in the Mahāyāna Buddhist tradition, the study of the five fields of knowledge was considered necessary in both pursuits—the pursuit of one's pragmatic, mundane ends and the pursuit of spiritual awakening. It is said in the *Mahāyānasūtrālaṃkāra*:

> An Ārya who does not undergo training in the five fields of knowledge in no way attains omniscience. He trains in them in order to defeat and assist others, and in order to gain knowledge for himself.[6]

The text further explains that by studying linguistics and logic one is able to defeat opponents in debate; by studying medicine, the creative arts, and similar disciplines, one assists those who desire so; and by studying the inner science, or Buddhism proper, one gains knowledge for oneself.

Likewise, mastery of the five fields of knowledge was considered as one of the characteristics of Buddhahood itself. In the *Vyākhyāyukti*,[7] or the *Sūtravyākyāyuktyupadeśa*, Vasubandhu states that Buddha's teaching is called comprehensive because it demonstrates his proficiency in every field of knowledge. In tantric literature, specifically in the *Vajrapañjaratantra*, a good *vajrācārya* is said to be completely versed in all fields of knowledge. As I will try to demonstrate throughout this book, the Kālacakra tradition supports this view of the Buddha's omniscience as inclusive of all forms of learning, and it accordingly integrates the diverse branches of exoteric learning into its esoteric theories and practices. The fact that the entire *Kālacakratantra* can be divided into two main parts—one dealing with diverse disciplines pertaining to the theoretical knowledge of the world and the other pertaining to meditation—indicates that the Kālacakra tradition also agrees with the Mahāyāna view that one is unable to get the firm footing in Buddhist teachings and practice by study and analysis alone, without the practice of meditation, or with meditation alone, without study. In this way, it concords with the earlier Mahāyāna view expressed by the following verse from the *Mahāyānasūtrālaṃkāra*:

> Meditation would be useless if reality could be perceived through mere study; and the teaching would be useless if one could practice meditation without having studied.[8]

The topics of the *Kālacakratantra*'s first two chapters—called respectively "The Universe" and "The Individual"—deal with the investigation of the universe as macrocosm and of the individual as its microcosm. The *Kālacakratantra*'s inquiry into the nature of the external world and the individual as two facets of the phenomenal world—the external (*bāhya*) and internal (*adhyātma*)—utilizes knowledge of the various branches of Buddhist science. Disciplines analogous to cosmology, astronomy, astrometry, chronometry, embryology, physiology, psycho-physiology, anatomy, medical therapeutics, pharmacology, alchemy, botany, psychology, and philosophy are either directly or indirectly incorporated into the *Kālacakratantra*, especially into its first two chapters. For this tantric tradition, those diverse scientific disciplines provide a systematic analysis of the natural world, provisionally viewed as an object of purification, and humans' place and interactions in that world. Thorough understanding of the structures and functions of conventional reality (*saṃvṛti-satya*) is considered here indispensable for the realization of ultimate reality (*paramārtha-satya*), or Buddhahood.

Since the earliest period of Buddhism, Buddhists' investigation of the world has been based on their understanding of nature as an orderly system governed by discernible causal laws. This same theoretical basis of investigation also permeates the discussions of the universe and the individual in the *Kālacakratantra*. An analysis of this *tantra* and its related literature indicates that the primary goal of the tantric Buddhist investigation of the natural world is to discover the causal factors operating within the universe as macrocosm and within the individual as microcosm. The secondary goal is to demonstrate the correspondence between the universe and the individual by identifying the properties of the external physical universe in the body of the individual.[9] This goal reflects the Kālacakra tradition's intent that its very presentation of Buddhist scientific truths be nondual, that is, without drawing an absolute distinction between subject and object. The tertiary objective of the Buddhist tantric scientific investigation is to ascertain the properties of the cosmos and the individual as mere appearances invoked by the power of the individual's habitual propensities. Finally, the ultimate aim is to see things as they are (*yathā-bhūta*) by means of acquiring direct knowledge of the nature of reality. Seeing things as they are means perceiving the illusory nature of conventional reality and realizing the nonduality of conventional and ultimate realities. The nature of this nonduality is that conventional reality, although manifesting as the universe, has the form of emptiness (*śūnyatā-rūpiṇī*), and emptiness has the form of conventional reality (*saṃvṛti-rūpiṇī*).[10]

The realization of the fundamental nonduality of the conventional and ultimate realities and the contemplative path to that realization are the chief topics of the other three chapters of the *Kālacakratantra*, called respectively the "Initiation," "Sādhana," and "Gnosis." An analysis of those three chapters indicates that this Buddhist tantric path of actualizing Buddhahood is structured on two theoretical grounds. One is a theory that the universe is contained within the body of the individual as demonstrated by the diverse disciplines of Buddhist natural sciences; and the second is that the natural world as we experience it and explain it through scientific analysis is already *nirvāṇa* but needs to be recognized as such.

Thus, in the context of Buddhist tantric soteriology, the proper understanding of the conventional world that is the object of purification, the genuine practice of the Buddhist tantric path that is the means of purification, and the authentic actualization of Buddhahood, which is the result of that purification, are directly contingent upon adequate knowledge of the Buddhist natural and social sciences.

The concept of science in the *Kālacakratantra* is indicated by the Sanskrit word *vidyā*, meaning "knowledge." Already in some of the early Buddhist expositions on *vidyā*, the term signifies more than knowledge regarding the Four Noble Truths. In the *Nettipakaraṇa*,[11] the definition of *vidyā* includes such concepts as investigation (*vicaya*), scrutiny or observation (*upaparikkhā*), and correct views or theories (*sammā-diṭṭhi*). Thus, from early times, Indian Buddhists have recognized the relevance of rational and empirical methods in their studies of the natural world and human thought and relations. However, just as the Western concepts of religion and philosophy do not clearly apply to Buddhism as a whole, so too the Western concept of science *does not directly correspond* to the phenomenon of Buddhist science. There are several critical reasons for that—namely, Buddhist science is characterized by widely known and used contemplative and introspective methods of scientific investigation,[12] its application of extrasensory perception as one of the means of scientific verification, the difficulty of demonstrating the knowledge acquired by contemplative means, and its goal of progress toward, not unprecedented knowledge, but knowledge previously acquired by Buddha Śākyamuni and other Buddhist contemplatives. Nevertheless, I think the term "science" is justified here for several reasons. First, in Buddhist science there are working hypotheses that are tested by means of experience and that are capable, in principle, of being refuted experientially. Moreover, the conclusions drawn from experience are formulated as rational theories that are internally consistent and make intelligible a wide range of phenomena.

In light of the *Kālacakratantra*'s classification of reality into the provisional and ultimate, this tantric system speaks of two types of science (*vidyā*).[13] The first type of scientific knowledge is knowledge of conventional reality, which is acquired by means of investigation. As such, it is described as perishable scientific knowledge (*kṣara-vidyā*), since it is provisional and highly subjective.[14] It is subjective in the sense that it is affected by the habitual propensities of *saṃsāra*, which are nothing other than the measure of the habitual propensities of one's own mind. Scientific knowledge of conventional reality is provisional also due to its being perceptual and conceptual. The verification of provisional scientific truths is based on the sensory perceptions and on inference based on perceptual experiences; but one's perceptions and conceptions of the world are said to depend on the power of one's own merit, or virtue (*puṇya*).[15] Scientific knowledge of conventional reality is also provisional due to its being characterized by a series of momentary cognitions that arise and cease with the arising and ceasing of cognized impermanent phenomena. A transmigratory mind, which observes conventional reality, is momentary because to that mind phenomena appear to arise, remain, and cease in separate, consecutive moments. Such a mind does not perceive the unity, or simultaneity, of the moment of the phenomena's arising, remaining, and ceasing.[16] Thus, as the mind perceives conventional reality, it discriminates the moments as one and many, and consequently, it discriminates all other phenomena as separate from one another, since they appear to arise and cease in their own separate times. This discriminatory, dualistic manner of perceiving the conventional world as a multiplicity of temporal phenomena is seen as the most prominent characteristic of provisional scientific knowledge. The *Vimalaprabhā* asserts that this provisional scientific knowledge is inconsequential scientific knowledge to which the human mind is strongly attached.[17]

The Kālacakra tradition affirms that that which is scientific knowledge (*vidyā*) in terms of conventional reality is ignorance (*avidyā*) with regard to the ultimate nature of phenomena.[18] Ignorance is a habitual propensity of *saṃsāra*, and it is knowledge accompanied by attachment that often manifests in scientific inquiry as an expectation. Since attachment gives rise to aversion and aversion is of the nature of delusion, provisional scientific knowledge of conventional reality is fundamentally a mental affliction, which subjectively creates all the worlds in every single moment and perceives the world in a biased manner. In contrast, knowledge of ultimate reality, or as-it-is-ness, is viewed as ultimate and imperishable scientific knowledge, because it is not affected by the habitual propensities of *saṃsāra*. It is a nonconceptual, unmediated knowledge, in which the distinction between the perceiver and the perceived no longer appears. Therefore, this type of scientific knowledge (*vidyā*) is said to be devoid of an object (*analambinī*).[19] It is nonperceptual knowledge, because it is not acquired through the sense-faculties or any conventional means of scientific investigation, nor is it acquired even by means of meditation. It is free of momentariness, for it does not discriminate moments as one or many. In this way, it dwells in the absence of origination and cessation. Just as *saṃsāra* is the measure of one's own mind, so too is ultimate reality the measure of one's own mind. Thus, ultimate scientific knowledge is nothing other than self-knowledge, knowledge of the extent of one's own mind. However, even though provisional scientific knowledge of the world is regarded as ultimately incorrect, it is seen as indispensable for gaining eventual knowledge of ultimate reality, which is omniscience, for it facilitates one's understanding of impermanence and emptiness and thereby indirectly brings about the eradication of one's afflictive and cognitive obscurations. Thus, provisional scientific knowledge is seen as an integral part of ultimate scientific knowledge.

A careful study of the Kālacakra literature reveals that the scope of science in tantric Buddhism includes not only a wide range of natural sciences but cognitive sciences as well. Those diverse branches of Buddhist science present systematized knowledge of the nature and composition of the natural world and humans' place and interactions in that world. Adequate knowledge of the Buddhist scientific disciplines and its practical application in an integrated form on the tantric Buddhist path are viewed as highly relevant for one's spiritual maturation and liberation. For that reason, it is thought that the *Kālacakratantra* practitioner should acquire and cultivate such knowledge and its practical applications for the sake of liberation and for the sake of temporary well-being as well. Thus, within the Kālacakra system, all the aspects of the natural world become legitimate fields of Buddhists' scientific investigation, and knowledge of the various scientific fields becomes a significant component of the Buddhist Dharma as the body of verifiable truths.[20]

The Kālacakra literature also demonstrates the ways in which the natural sciences become integrated with cognitive and social sciences on that Buddhist tantric path. Disciplines classified in the modern world as history, philosophy, fine arts, and psychology are presented in the Kālacakra literature alongside astronomy, cosmology, physics, medicine, biology, pharmaceutics, and alchemy and are jointly utilized in the varied modes of *Kālacakratantra* practice. The integration of different sciences on this Buddhist tantric path is facilitated by the earlier mentioned tantric view of the nonduality of the individual and the individual's environment. That particular view implies that all psycho-physiological processes of the individual correspond to the physical and socio-historical processes occurring in the individual's environment. For example, the passage of days, seasons, and years corresponds to the passage of *prāṇas* in the human body; and the individual's spiritual battle with one's own mental afflictions has its external aspect in the religious war of Kalkī with the king of Barbarians in the land of Mecca, and so forth.[21] Thus, one may say that in this tantric system, the themes addressed in the Buddhist natural sciences are analogous to the themes of modern science.

In all of the above-mentioned disciplines of Buddhist tantric science, the verification of the Buddhist scientific truths appears to be based on the following four means: sensory perceptions, mental perceptions, extrasensory perceptions, and inference. Since earliest times, extrasensory perceptions have been regarded in the Buddhist tradition as a valid means of scientific verification. In its last two chapters, the *Kālacakratantra* presents rational psychological and physiological conditions for bringing about extrasensory perceptions. The verification of Buddhist scientific truths concerning the relative nature of the world, as expressed in natural causal laws, is based on all the aforementioned means of verification. Correspondingly, knowledge of relative scientific truths is viewed in this tantric system as perceptual and conceptual and as provisional knowledge of the world as it appears to the dualistic, biased mind. The verification of absolute scientific truth regarding the ultimate nature of the world, as expressed in emptiness, is presented as a form of nondualistic contemplative perception. Knowledge of absolute truth, however, is described as the nonconceptual (*avikalpita*), unmediated knowledge of all things, in which the distinction between the perceiver and the perceived no longer appears.[22]

An important, common feature of the aforementioned disciplines of Buddhist tantric science is their individual syncretism that permeates the theories and modes of their practical application. The syncretistic nature of Buddhist tantric science, as evidenced in the *Kālacakratantra*, stems from the Buddhist tantric view of the commonality of the Buddhists' and heterodox groups' (*tīrthika*) teachings concerning conventionally existent phenomena. The *Kālacakratantra* contends that there is no distinction between the Buddhists and heterodox groups with regard to the manner in which conventional reality appears. That view of the commonality of the Buddhists' and heterodox groups' approaches to conventional reality justifies the Buddhist tantric incorporation of specific ideas from other Indian religious and scientific systems and resulted in the syncretism of Buddhist tantric science. By amalgamating the ideas characteristic of non-Buddhist systems into its own theoretical framework, the Kālacakra tradition attempts to accomplish two objectives: to facilitate its modeling of conventional reality and to convert heterodox groups. In this way, the Buddhist tantric proselytizing efforts significantly contributed to the complex nature of most of the Buddhist tantric scientific disciplines. However, the syncretism of Buddhist tantric medicine appears less related to those efforts, for it stems chiefly from the distinctive Buddhist tantric emphasis on the favorable effects of physical health on one's spiritual development.

The Kālacakra tradition gives great importance to the preservation of one's health on the grounds that the achievements of supernormal abilities and liberation are contingent upon proper bodily functioning. Since its earliest stages, the Buddhist tradition has been concerned with medical knowledge and its practical application as supplementary systems of Buddhist learning and religious practice. The favorable effects of physical health on one's spiritual development are already indicated in the earliest Buddhist Pāli literature. As recorded in the *Majjhimanikāya*,[23] Buddha Śākyamuni himself saw health as the individual's finest possession and pointed out the difficulty of reaching enlightenment with an impaired body. For that reason, understanding of the human body and knowledge of maintaining and restoring health have been given soteriological significance in all of Indian Buddhism. However, it is within the context of tantric Buddhism that the preservation of one's health becomes of paramount importance. The *Kālacakratantra* gives the following reason for that:

> Firstly, a *mantrī* should preserve the entire body of the Jina for the sake of *siddhis*. In the absence of the body, neither any *siddhi* nor supreme bliss is attained in this life.[24]

Consequently, in the Kālacakra tradition as in other related tantric traditions, Buddhist medicine has been regarded as a major facet of Buddhist Dharma.

The earliest records of Buddhist theoretical and practical approaches to medicine are already found in the Pāli *Tipiṭaka*. Those records reveal that the early Buddhists' understanding of human anatomy and physiology was generally in accord with that of classical Āyurveda, whose basic contents were already formed and well known throughout the Indian subcontinent. The early Buddhist *materia medica* was also similar to that of the Āyurveda. Nevertheless, early Buddhist records frequently present the knowledge of illnesses and medicinal substances in a less systematic manner and on a more popular level than in the later Āyurvedic texts and later Buddhist medical treatises. Also, the Āyurvedic concept of the *prāṇa* as a support of life is only mentioned in the Buddhist Pāli Canon and not yet developed and medically utilized as it is in the *Kālacakratantra*.

By the time of Mahāyāna Buddhism in India, a rational system of classical

Āyurvedic medicine was in general use among Buddhists, and it strongly influenced the scientific framework of later Buddhist medicine.[25] Several medical treatises—such as *Yogaśataka*,[26] *Jīvasūtra*, *Avabheṣajakalpa*, *Āryarājanāmavaṭikā*, and *Āryamūlakoṣamahauṣadhāvalī*[27]—which the Buddhist tradition ascribes to an author by the name of Nāgārjuna, contain systematized knowledge of selected collections of medicinal formulas, discussions of physiological aspects of diseases, and medical treatments that accord with Āyurveda.

The disciplines of alchemy and magic developed alongside the traditional and empirico-rational system of Buddhist medicine. According to a tradition no later than the seventh century CE, those disciplines were already in practice by the time of Nāgārjuna, the alchemist, whose name is mentioned by the Chinese pilgrim Hsüan-tsang. The *Rasaratnākara* and the *Kakṣapuṭa*[28] have been traditionally attributed to Nāgārjuna, as his writings on alchemy and magic respectively. The Mahāyāna Buddhist tradition considered Āyurvedic medicine, alchemy, and magic as separate but complementary branches of knowledge. It resorted to alchemical preparations, recitation of *mantras*, and drawing of *maṇḍalas* as supplementary methods of healing.

However, Buddhist tantric medical treatises and the *Kālacakratantra* literature integrate classical Āyurvedic medicine, alchemy, and magic even more strongly into a unique and comprehensive system of Buddhist tantric medicine. The broad scope of the tantric medical system, evidenced in the *Kālacakra* literary corpus, also encompasses knowledge of preparing incenses and perfumes used for worshipping Buddhas and Bodhisattvas during healing rites. The *Vimalaprabhā* indicates that the *Kālacakratantra*'s instructions on preparing incenses and perfumes are based on information contained in specialized treatises on the preparation of perfumes and incenses (*gandha-śāstra*).[29] Thus, the manuals on preparing perfumes and incenses form a significant supplementary branch of Buddhist tantric medical literature.

As in the earlier Buddhist medical systems, so too in Buddhist tantric medicine, one may find distinctions between magico-religious treatments and rational therapeutics based on induction from observation. In Buddhist tantric medicine, the determination of a medical treatment is contingent upon determining the nature of a disease. Illnesses induced by malevolent spirits (*bhūta*), also known as nonhuman diseases, and snakebites are commonly treated by means of religious healing rites and *mantras*.[30] *Mantras* are also implemented as the protective, or preventive, methods of counteracting the evil intentions of nonhuman entities.[31] Likewise, carrying a precious stone of the color red, which belongs to the class of the substances that predominantly arise from the fire-element, is believed to prevent evil spirits from entering one's body, whereas gems that belong to the class of substances that are related to the space-element are said to ward off the cast of an evil eye.[32]

The *Kālacakratantra* mentions diverse types of evils spirits and malicious Siddhas who are to be appeased by building specific *maṇḍalas* outside a village, or under a tree, in a cemetery, in a temple, or at the confluence of rivers, with offerings of delicacies, incenses, perfumes, flowers, candles, praises, and *mantras*.[33] The *yakṣas*, *grahas*, *rākṣasas*, *piśācas*, *śākinīs*, evil *nāgas*, who delight in human blood, *ḍākinīs*, *rūpikās*, vampire-ghouls feeding in cemeteries (*kumbhāṇḍa*), protectors of fields (*kṣetrapāla*), *gaṇapatis*, *pretas*, goblins, the lords of *ḍākinīs* who are accompanied by epilepsy, and malicious Siddhas are all considered to be powerful entities that may cause both illnesses and great well-being. Therefore, worshiping them is seen as beneficial for the patient's safe recovery. However, the *Kālacakratantra* warns against the pacification of malevolent spirits when the symptoms of irrevocable death appear, which cannot be warded off by gods, men, or *nāgas*.[34] It gives two reasons for this caution.[35] The first is that religious healing rites are ineffective in such a case, and the second reason is that this situation may create temptation for the tantric *yogī* to perform the rites simply for the sake of his own material gain, while knowing that they will be of no benefit to the patient.

Tantric healing rites also entail the drawing of *yantras*, the initiation of a patient in a *maṇḍala*, and ablutions. For example, a *yantra* consisting of thirty-four numbers placed within its respective sections should be shown to a pregnant woman when her womb stiffens at the time of childbirth.[36] Children afflicted by *grahas* are bathed with the five ambrosias (*amṛta*): water, milk, sour milk, ghee, honey, molasses, and fragrant water, that are contained within seven unbaked vessels.[37]

At times, certain herbal medications, empowered by *mantras*, are administered to those possessed by malevolent spirits in order to alleviate the symptoms of afflictions. For instance, in the case of a pregnant woman's sharp uterine pains caused by malevolent entities, the pregnant woman is to be given pounded *kuṣṭha*, *uśīra*,[38] *kaseru* grass, *tagara*,[39] blue water-lilly (*keśara*), and a filament of a lotus with cold water, all of which are consecrated by *mantras* and *vajras*.[40]

Thus, the boundaries between magico-religious and empirico-rational treatments become far less noticeable in Buddhist tantric medicine than in its precedents. In the tantric rites of healing the afflictions caused by nonhuman entities, the magico-religious and empiricio-rational approaches clearly concur. The empirico-rational approach involves diagnosing a disease based upon the observation of its symptoms and the occasions for their occurrence; it establishes the causes of affliction and determines the treatment according to those causes. For example, unpleasant symptoms such as bodily convulsions, sharp pains in the eyes, a yellowish color of the face, arms, and legs, a distinctively yellow color of the urine, fever, vomiting, emaciation, and fainting are described as the symptoms characteristic of a children's disease that are caused by the possession by cruel spirits; and this can be treated by a ritual oblation of the child in the *maṇḍala*.[41] In this way, the empirico-rational approach essentially underlies the magico-religious healing rites.

Furthermore, the treatments of other ailments provoked by the disequilibrium of the three humors—wind (*vāta*), bile (*pitta*), and phlegm (*kapha*)—external actions, poor hygiene, inadequate diet, and other similar factors predominantly follow an empirico-rational approach. Thus, the application of slightly warmed *akṣobhya* in the mouth is administered in the case of an infection of the mouth; anointing of the neck with *karkoṭī*,[42] *lāṅgalī*,[43] and *indrī*[44] is applied in the case of the inflammation of the glands of the neck, and so on.[45] Nevertheless, meditation, visualization of tantric deities, and the recitation of *mantras*, which are the common healing factors in magico-religious healing rituals, often accompany the administering of medicaments in empirico-rational therapeutics. For example, in the case of the malignant boils in the throat, one abiding in *samādhi* annihilates strong pains in the following way: while practicing *prāṇāyāma*, one visualizes in the heart-*cakra* Viśvamātā appearing as the stainless moon, with her hands in the wish-granting posture and holding a lotus, sitting on a lotus-seat in the *vajra* posture, and having one face and two arms.[46]

Tantric medicinal *mantras* mentioned in the *Kālacakratantra* can be classified into three main categories: protective *mantras*, supplicatory *mantras* such as "*oṃ phre* Viśvamātā, eliminate, eliminate *vajra*-like sharp and stingent pains, bring on my forbearance, bring on *svāhā*,"[47] and consecratory *mantras* such as "*oṃ āḥ huṃ* take away, take away pains in the womb of such and such person *svāhā*."[48] In many instances, one *mantra* can perform more than one function. Thus, in treatments of malignant diseases that are accompanied by fever and pain in the joints, the *mantra* "*oṃ phre vajra*" is said to simultaneously empower medicinal herbal ingredients and to protect the patient's bodily *cakras*.[49]

The recitation of protective and supplicatory *mantras* that induce a physiological change by directly influencing the patient's *prāṇas* may be regarded as an empirico-rational treatment. The Kālacakra tradition's definition of *prāṇa* as the principal deity of a *mantra*[50] and its view of the individual's *vajras*, or capacities, of body, speech, mind, and gnosis as the source (*yoni*) of *mantras*[51] indicate a close and reciprocal influence between the *mantras* and the individual's mind and body. In light of this view, one may infer that in the context of Buddhist tantric medicine, the recitation of *mantras* is utilized as a medical treatment of both the mind[52] and the body. Although the *Vimalaprabhā* acknowledges that the power of *mantras*, medicinal herbs, gems, and other potent substances arises due to the transformation of the mind of the individual who empowers them, it emphasizes that neither *mantras* nor the empowered substances have limitless powers, since they are not empowered by the mind of the supreme, imperishable gnosis of the Buddha, but by the limited mind of the tantric *yogī*.[53]

As its rational methods of cure, Buddhist tantric medicine utilizes the techniques of *haṭha-yoga*, particularly, the practices of *prāṇāyāma* and different *yogic* postures (*āsana*). For instance, in the *Kālacakratantra*, the *vajra* posture (*vajrāsana*)[54] is recommended for the elimination of backache, the head-stand posture (*śīrṣāsana*) for the cure of a disease induced by a disorder of phlegm, the vase technique (*kumbhaka*) of *prāṇāyāma* is recommended for the alleviation of abdominal ailments, leprosy, and similar diseases. In the case of leprosy,[55] the patient is advised to practice the *kumbhaka* for a period of six months, during which he should not emit semen during sexual intercourse. The *Kālacakratantra*[56] also cautions that one should practice *prāṇāyāma* only until heat in the heart or pain in the head occurs. If one continues to practice the *prāṇāyāma* after those symptoms occur, the *prāṇa* congeals in the navel-*cakra*, or if unrestrained, it causes death by violently splitting the *uṣṇīṣa* and leaving the body.

Sometimes, especially in the cases of the malignant diseases, *prāṇāyāma* is recommended as an alternative therapy to the application of medicaments. It is chiefly recommended to experienced Buddhist tantric *yogīs* who are capable of developing profound meditative concentration (*samādhi*) and who do not always have access to appropriate medication. Thus, to *yogīs* suffering from a malignant disease of the throat which is accompanied by fever, pains in the joints of the arms and legs, and headache, the following practice of *prāṇāyāma* is recommended: having entered a windowless house, the *yogī* should let his arms hang down toward the feet, as far as the thighs, and he should practice the *kumbhaka* for as long as he does not fall on the ground and for as long as his fever does not diminish.[57]

The most prevalent empirico-rational therapeutics of Buddhist tantric medicine encountered in the Kālacakra literature are dietary therapy, hydrotherapy, massage, and treatments carried out by means of nasal inhalation and oral consumption of drugs, fumigation, and anointing. For example, everything bitter, combined with three myrobalans (*kaṭuka*),[58] is said to obliterate disorders of phlegm, so goat's milk, combined with the three myrobalans, is recommended to those suffering from phlegm-disorders. Since sweet and astringent substances are believed to eliminate bile-disorders, buffalo-cow's milk is administered to those suffering from such an ailment. Camel's milk is administered to those suffering from a disorder of wind, because camel's milk, combined with rock salt (*saindhava*), becomes an alkaline fluid (*kṣārāmbu*) that removes wind-disorders. Nasal inhalation of the *akṣobhya* plant or nasal inhalation of water in the morning is prescribed as a cure for a headache.[59] In the case of boils, pustules, and similar skin disorders, fumigation with ghee and sea-salt wrapped in a cloth and anointing with the sap of *arka*[60] are suggested as an effective therapy.[61] In the case of infections of the ear and eye, the application of warm urine in the ear and of cold urine in the eye is recommended. In the case of sunstroke, the oral ingestion of a decoction containing an equal portion of *dhātrī*, coriander, and powder of tamarind leaves for three nights is suggested as an effective cure.

The curative efficacy of the specific tastes that characterize diverse nutritional, herbal, and mineral ingredients of medicinal preparations is thought to stem from the elements that give rise to the diverse tastes.[62] Therefore, consuming the appropriate preparations, one supplements the lack of the particular elements in the body that directly caused a disorder of one of three humors.

The aforementioned types of empirico-rational treatments best illustrate the classical Āyurvedic and early Buddhist medical heritage in Buddhist tantric medicine. The *Kālacakratantra*'s *materia medica* is also similar to that of Āyurveda and early Buddhist medicine. In addition to herbal and other remedial substances that are well-known from Āyurveda and earlier Buddhist medical treatises, the *Kālacakratantra* mentions medicinal substances that are not specified in Āyurvedic texts or in earlier Buddhist medical works. It is possible, however, that those medicinal substances are known in Āyurvedic and earlier Buddhist writings by different names, since the *Kālacakratantra* occasionally designates the medicinal herbs by terms that seem to be regional folk names—such as "lion's urine" (*siṃhamūtra*), "son's hair" (*putrakeśa*)[63]—instead of by their generally accepted names.

Indian tantric Buddhists, concerned with the preservation of the body, expanded the already existent science of rejuvenation and longevity and structured it as an additional branch of Buddhist tantric medicine. Since Buddhist monastic schools of the eleventh-century India attracted scholars from other countries such as China, Persia, and so forth, one may suspect that tantric Buddhist methods of rejuvenation were influenced to some degree by Taoist and other methods for the prolongation of life. Tantric Buddhists composed various tantric works that deal exclusively with diverse methods of rejuvenation and prolongation of life, which involve the arts of extracting rejuvenating essences and knowledge of performing rituals for longevity.[64]

In its exposition of Buddhist tantric medicine, the *Kālacakratantra* indicates the following individual methods of rejuvenation: meditation (*dhyāna*) that involves bringing the *prāṇas* into the central *nāḍī* (*madhyamā*), practices of *prāṇāyāma*, ingestion of the five combined ambrosias (*amṛta*),[65] ingestion of life-giving essences extracted from herbs and foods, and ingestion of elixirs produced by means of complex alchemical processes. For example, the *kumbhaka*, accompanied by the retention of regenerative fluids in sexual union, mentioned earlier with regard to the elimination of leprosy, is also seen as having a rejuvenating power. It is said that if practiced for two years, it eradicates old age and its symptoms. Also, the nasal inhalation of uterine blood and the honey of black bees (*keśarājikā*), accompanied with meditation, is suggested as a six-month therapy for rejuvenation. The *Kālacakratantra* also discusses intricate procedures for preparing tonics, elixirs, and gold, which are also called external elixirs (*bāhya-rasāyana*) and are regarded by Buddhist tantric tradition as nutrients that induce the attainment of a divine body (*divya-deha*) that is free of wrinkles and gray hair.

Thus, with respect to Buddhist tantric therapeutics, one may draw the following conclusions. Buddhist tantric therapeutics establishes four aims, namely, to prevent and cure disease, to secure longevity, and to bring forth liberation. The first three goals are of a temporal nature. They are not mere ends in themselves but ancillary to the actualization of the ultimate goal, which is enlightenment. In order to actualize its goals, Buddhist tantric therapeutics utilize the syncretized knowledge and practices of tantric *yoga*, *haṭha-yoga*, Āyurveda, folk medicine, religious esoteric rites of healing and exorcism, the science of distillation, and alchemy into its distinctive Buddhist tantric medical theory and practice. Thus, the immediate objective of the syncretism of the Buddhist tantric medicine is to utilize all available medical knowledge and to provide all possible means of cure and disease-prevention in order to facilitate one's liberation. However, the syncretism of the Buddhist tantric medicine should not be understood as a *reconciliation* of disparate views and practices but rather as their *synthesis*. The *Kālacakratantra* does not attempt to reinterpret diverse medical theories and practices; it pragmatically juxtaposes them.

The *Kālacakratantra*'s medical therapeutics rest on several theoretical grounds that are characteristic of Buddhist tantric medicine as a whole. The primary theoretical basis of *Kālacakratantra* medicine is tantric Buddhist soteriology that focuses on the intimate relationship among the mind, body, and liberation. On that foundation rests the *Kālacakratantra*'s principal medical theory of the predominant effects of *prāṇas* on one's mental, physical, and spiritual condition. To that theory the *Kālacakratantra* adds the theoretical framework of the secular system of Āyurvedic medicine, operating on the presumption that good health is maintained by the equilibrium of the three humors—wind, phlegm, and bile. The fourth element of this theoretical context is the principles of *haṭha-yoga*, which are based on the view of a causal relationship among bodily postures, breathing exercises, and mental and physical health. Finally, the last theoretical basis of Buddhist tantric medical therapeutics is the premises of folk medicine and occult beliefs concerning bewitchment and spirit possession, according to which, spirits can possess and thereby influence an individual's mental and physical states.

Likewise, the theoretical syncretism of *Kālacakratantra* medicine yields a wide variety of medical treatments. Among the aforementioned medical treatments, the tantric yogic practices of manipulating the *prāṇas* and retaining regenerative fluids are believed to most directly affect the accomplishment of medical and soteriological ends. Thus, according to the *Kālacakratantra*, the yogic methods of actualizing supernormal powers (*siddhi*) are a part of the Buddhist tantric medical theory and practice. The tantric yogic practices of manipulating the flows of the *prāṇas* and retaining regenerative fluids during sexual intercourse have a dual purpose: spiritual and medical. When practiced by *yogīs* endowed with good health, the tantric yogic practices induce spiritual powers and liberation. To those facing premature death, that is, death prior to the age of one hundred, and to those suffering from various diseases—such as abdominal ailments,[66] asthma, cough, eye-diseases, poisoning, dysuria, and leprosy—they serve as preventive and curative therapeutics. For example, when the signs of untimely death occur, the following *yogic* practices are sequentially performed. The first is the obstruction of the *prāṇas* in the left and right *nāḍīs*; the next phase entails bringing the *prāṇas* into the central channel *nāḍī* and making them circulate there for a day; the third phase involves filling one's arms, legs, and fingers with *prāṇas*; and the final phase involves visualizing the Buddhas' six female consorts with their hands in the protection-*mudrā* and standing within one's own six *cakras*. In the case of the abdominal and other diseases mentioned previously, one is advised to contract the wind of *apāna* from below the navel and the wind of *prāṇa* from above. In this way, those two winds colide and cause a strong digestive fire to arise and spread throughout the entire body. It is said that after a month of practicing this *yoga*, one averts maladies of the liver, spleen, hemorrhoids, asthma, headache, cough, and so on.[67]

Lastly, the syncretism of the *Kālacakratantra*'s medical theory reduced the boundaries between magico-religious and empirico-rational therapeutics. The concurrence of magico-religious and empirico-rational treatments in individual cases was invariably used for two purposes: simultaneously to alleviate the symptoms of the disease and to eliminate the cause of the disease.

These multiple aims and means of cure in *Kālacakratantra* medicine required the incorporation of different sciences as additional branches of medicine. For example, the earlier mentioned science of preparing perfumes and incenses, the science of extracting elixirs from foods and herbs, the science of alchemy, etc. became supplementary fields of medical study. In this way, the syncretism of the Buddhist tantric medical theory and practice broadened the scope of Indian Buddhist medicine as a whole, and it extended the Buddhist tantric framework of theory and practice.

The Cosmic Body

The Cosmos, the Individual, and the Cosmos as the Individual

The *Kālacakratantra*'s cosmology is structured on several theoretical models. In its interpretation of the conventional nature of the cosmos, the *Kālacakratantra* combines to some degree the Vaibhāṣika atomic theory, the Sāṃkhya model of the twenty-five principles of the *puruṣa* and *prakṛti*, and Jaina and Purāṇic cosmographies with its own measurements of the cosmos (*loka-dhātu*)[1] and its own theories of the cosmos's nature and relation to the individual. The Kālacakra tradition intentionally uses this form of syncretism in order to provide a useful theoretical model of the Buddhist tantric view of the cosmos that will accord with its interpretation of the individual and with its model of practice. As already indicated in chapter 3 on syncretism, the Kālacakra tradition itself justifies this syncretism in terms of its proselytizing efforts[2] and in terms of the multiplicity and relativity of conventional realities.

According to this tantric tradition, knowledge of the constitution of the cosmos and of the manner in which the cosmos originates and dissolves is pertinent to one's spiritual maturation. The *Vimalaprabhā* explicitly states that in order to fully comprehend the three Vehicles, one must first know the origination and dissolution of the cosmos as taught by the Vaibhāṣikas, who assert the true existence of the individual (*pudgala*) and of the cosmos, which consists of an agglomeration of atoms.[3] While supporting the Madhyamaka view of phenomenal and personal identitylessness, the Kālacakra tradition affirms the conventional existence of the cosmos and the individual and acknowledges the validity and usefulness of the Vaibhāṣikas' atomic theory of the evolution and disintegration of the cosmos. Consequently, it holds that within the context of the Kālacakra system, one investigates the conventional nature of the cosmos by way of the Vaibhāṣika doctrine and gains a thorough knowledge of the three Vehicles, thereby enhancing one's understanding of the entire Buddhist Dharma. Resorting to the Vaibhāṣika atomic theory, the *Kālacakratantra* asserts that all inanimate phenomena that constitute the cosmos originate from atomic particles that evade sensory perception—namely, the atoms of the earth, water, fire, wind, and space elements, which are pervaded by the sphere of reality (*dharma-dhātu*).[4] Likewise in the case of the individual, the atomic particles of earth, water, fire, wind, and space that form the father's seminal fluid and the mother's uterine blood eventually become the body of the individual.[5] Thus, the inanimate phenomena in the individual's body and environment share the same atomic structure and originate in a similar fashion by means of the agglomeration of atomic particles, which takes place due to the efficacy of time. This is one way in which the Kālacakra tradition attempts to demonstrate that the individual and the individual's natural environment are identical not only with regard to their ultimate nature, but also with regard to their conventionally established atomic structure and their manner of origination and destruction.

The Origination and Dissolution of the Cosmos and the Individual

According to the *Kālacakratantra*,[6] cyclic existence consists of the immeasurable Buddha-fields (*buddha-kṣetra*), which have limitless qualities, and of the five elements. It is characterized by their origination, duration, and destruction. This entire cosmos is said to arise and dissolve because sentient beings are experiencing the results of their wholesome and unwholesome actions. The collective *karma* of sentient beings produces karmic winds, which mold and dissolve the cosmos by amassing and disintegrating the atomic particles that constitute the cosmos. Thus, the external karmic winds (*karma-vāta*) accord with the characteristic qualities of sentient beings' consciousness (*vijñāna-dharma*).

The karmic wind that produces the cosmos of a Buddha-field is considered to be of a dual nature, because it produces two types of cosmos: inanimate and animate. Like the heavenly constellations (*nakṣatra*), the inanimate cosmos of a Buddha-field is stationary; whereas the animate cosmos is in motion, just as the circle of astrological houses (*rāśi-cakra*) moves in space. At the time of the dissolution of the inanimate cosmos, the bodies of all humans and other living beings composed of atoms also disintegrate. In this way, the destiny of the inanimate cosmos, which is due to the actions of sentient beings, is also the destiny of the sentient beings who inhabit that cosmos.

The limitless karmic winds generate the numerous world-systems of the Buddha-fields just as the karmic winds of the *prāṇas*, which invariably accompany a transmigratory consciousness, generate the body of a sentient being. Just as the internal karmic winds of living beings induce bodily growth, the external karmic winds cause the growth of inanimate things.[7]

There are three types of external karmic winds: the holding (*saṃdhāraṇa*), churning (*manthāna*), and shaping (*saṃsthāna*) wind. The supporting wind holds together the atoms of the earth and the other elements in the same way that a rain-wind holds together the atoms of rain-water. Following that, the churning wind churns the atoms to their very core until the elements become solidified. Just as salt crystallizes due to its exposure to the sun, the elements solidify due to such churning. The churning wind makes the elements absorb each other into the agglomorate in which the atomic particles of one element become a predominant substance, while the atomic particles of other elements become secondary substances. As in a human body so too in the cosmos, with regard to solidity, the atoms of the earth become primary and the other atoms secondary. Likewise, the water, fire, and wind elements become primary in terms of fluidity, heat, and motility, respectively. In the case of space, however, all other atomic particles that are devoid of their own properties become primary.[8] Once the agglomeration of the atomic particles of the elements takes place, the great shaping wind moves through the entire Buddha-field in the form of the ten winds.[9] These ten karmic winds that fashion the inanimate cosmos also shape the body of the individual, in which they circulate and carry the habitual propensities of the individual's *karma*. Therefore, one can say that for this tantric tradition, all *karma* of sentient beings is stored in the atomic particles of the karmic winds. The *Kālacakratantra* itself asserts that "one's own *karma* is contained in the *guṇas* of *prakṛti*,"[10] which is conventionally established as physical. It also indicates that the ten karmic winds, which fashion the inanimate environment and the body of the individual, themselves arise from the five elements.

> The three winds of *āpāna* arise from the gnosis-element, and the three winds of *prāṇa* arise from the space-element. *Samāna* arises from the wind, *udāna* arises from the fire, *vyāna* arises from the water, and *nāga* arises from the earth. These four—*kūrma*, *kṛkara*, *devadatta*, and *dhanaṃja*—arise respectively from the wind, fire, water, and earth.[11]

In the final analysis, this suggests that the *karma* of sentient beings, which manifests in the form of atomic substances, is of a physical nature. In this regard, the *Kālacakratantra*'s view of *karma* conforms to the Jaina theory of *karma* as subtle clusters of matter that constitute a karmic body. In the Kālacakra tradition, however, this view of *karma* does not preclude the traditional Buddhist view of all actions as being ultimately mental. Even when the Kālacakra tradition acknowledges that one's own transmigratory mind (*saṃsāra-citta*) is a conventionally established agent of all actions and a fundamental cause of the origination and destruction of the entire cosmos, it specifies that the five elements are the material components of the transmigratory mind. It does so pointing to the fact that the agent who is devoid of material substances neither acts nor creates anything.[12] Thus, one may infer that *karma* is material, because the transmigratory mind that generates it is itself material. Likewise, all cyclic existence, which manifests due to sentient beings' *karma*, is material because the *karma* that creates it is itself material. I surmise that this causal relationship among the material nature of the transmigratory mind, *karma*, and the environment that one perceives is implied in the *Kālacakratantra*'s assertion that the cosmos that one perceives is a mere manifestation of one's own mind.

According to this tantric tradition, a Buddha-field always comes into existence accompanied by a world-system, just as the origination of the individual's body is always accompanied by the seventy-two thousand *nāḍīs*.[13] At the time of the origination of the cosmos, very subtle particles (*aṇu*), which are imperceptible to the sense-faculties, are said to be present in the form of atomic particles (*paramāṇu*). These atomic particles are of the five types: wind, fire, water, earth, and space.

Under the influence of time, the wind-element originates first among these atomic particles. This origination begins with the atomic particles of wind adhering to each other. Then, owing to their adherence, a subtle fluttering motion takes place, and this we call "wind." After that, the atoms of fire begin to adhere to one another, and lightning, accompanied by wind, comes forth as fire. Following this, the atoms of water adhere to one other, and rain, accompanied by the wind and fire, comes into existence as water. Lastly, the atomic particles of the earth-element appear, and a rainbow called "earth" arises in space. The atoms of space pervade all of the above-mentioned elements.

Upon the formation of the five elements, the seven continents, mountains, and oceans start to arise from the five elements due to the conjunction of the supporting, churning, and shaping winds.[14] The seven mountains and the seven continents arise from the earth-element, which is solidity. The seven oceans arise from the water-element, which is fluidity. The fire of the sun, lightning, and domestic fire originate from the fire-element, which is heat. The wind-element is motility, and the space-element is the domain that allows for movement and growth. This is the manner in which the entire cosmos arises from the atomic particles of the five elements in order for sentient beings to experience the results of their actions.

At the time of the dissolution of the cosmos, the fire that burns the cosmos to ashes (*kālāgni*), kindled by the winds of *karma*, melts the atomic agglomerates of the entire cosmos. Its function is comparable to the fire of gnosis (*jñānāgni*), or the fire of sexual desire (*kāmāgni*), which incinerates the material nature of the transmigratory body and consciousness during the completion-stage of *Kālacakratantra* practice. It is also worth noting that both fires—*kālāgni* and *kāmāgni*—are identified in this tantric tradition as two types of deities, namely, Kālāgni and Caṇḍālī.[15] Their respective locations in the cosmos and the body of the individual are also comparable, since both dwell in the lower regions of the cosmic and individual bodies, where they can become aroused or ignited. Kālāgni dwells in the underworld, and Caṇḍālī abides in the navel of the human body. Caṇḍālī flames due to the constriction of the winds of *prāṇa*, and it is therefore called "the fire of *prāṇāyāma*."[16] Similarly, *kālāgni* inflames when the karmic winds of the *prāṇas* of the cosmic body are extinguished.

The time of the incineration of the cosmos is characterized not only by the destruction of the cosmos but also by its origination. At the time of the disintegration of the cosmos, the atomic particles of the earth-element do not perish; they remain due to their cohesion with the atomic particles of the water and other elements. When the cosmos dissolves, a karmic wind draws out the atoms of the earth from their agglomerates, separating the individual atoms from the mass of earth atoms and hurling them into the mass of the water atoms. Following this, it draws them out of the water-element and hurls them into the fire-element. Then it draws them out of the fire-element and hurls them into the wind-element. Lastly, it draws them out of the atomic particles of the wind-element and spreads them one by one into space. Upon the destruction of the inanimate cosmos, living beings go to another Buddha-field and to another cosmos, which are produced by their karmic winds, in order to experience the further results of their actions.

The manner in which the inanimate cosmos originates and dissolves corresponds to the manner in which a human being comes into existence and dies. As in the inanimate world, the human body, due to the power of the ten karmic winds, arises from the agglomerations of atomic particles of the earth, water, fire, wind, and space elements. At the time of conception, the father's semen and mother's uterine blood, which are made of the five elements, are "devoured" by the consciousness which, accompanied by subtle *prāṇas*, enters the mother's womb. When conception takes place due to the power of time, the semen and uterine blood within the womb slowly develop into the body of the individual. This occurs due to the spreading of *prāṇas*. The growing fetus consumes food comprised of six flavors—bitter, sour, salty, pungent, sweet, and astringent—and these six flavors originate from the six elements, sixth being gnosis. Consequently, the body of a fetus becomes a gross physical body, composed of the agglomerates of the atomic particles. The elements of the father's semen give rise to the marrow, bones, *nāḍīs*, and sinews of the fetus; and the elements of the mother's uterine blood give rise to the skin, blood, and flesh of the fetus. Thus, all the elements and psycho-physical aggregates that constitute the human being come into existence due to the union of the atomic agglomerates of the father's semen and mother's uterine blood. The five elements of the father's semen and mother's uterine blood facilitate the growth of the fetus, just as they facilitate the growth of a plant's seed in the natural environment. The earth-element supports the semen that has entered the womb, just as it holds a seed in the ground; and the water-element makes it sprout from there. The fire-element makes it blossom and digest the six flavors that arise from the six elements. The wind-element stimulates its growth, and the space-element provides the room for growth. The earth-element causes the body to become dense, and it gives rise to the bones and nails. The water-element causes moisture in the body, giving rise to the seven kinds of bodily fluids. The fire-element induces the maturation of the fetus and gives rise to blood. The ten principal winds of *prāṇas* expand its skin, and the space-element becomes the bodily apertures.

On the basis of these similarities in atomic nature of the inanimate world and the body of the individual, the Kālacakra tradition identifies the seven mountains, continents, and oceans with the elements of solidity, softness, and fluidity in the body of the individual. Tables 5. 1.a–c illustrate the correspondences among the seven mountains, continents, and oceans and the specific constituents of the human body.

After the moment of conception, the semen and uterine blood grow in the womb for a month. Following this, the ten subtle *nāḍīs* arise within the heart of the fetus. Likewise, within the navel, there arise the sixty-four *nāḍīs* that carry the *daṇḍas* in the body and the twelve subtle *nāḍīs* that carry the twelve internal solar mansions. Due to the *prāṇas*' power of spreading, all the *nāḍīs* in the navel gradually expand into

TABLE 5.1.A The Hard Earth-element in the Environment and in the Body

Seven mountains	The hard elements of the body
Vajra mountains	the nails of the hands and feet
Sīta	the bones of the hands
Droṇa	the bones of the forearms
Maṇikara	the bones of the upper arms
Niṣadha	the bones of the legs
Mandara	the bones of the shanks
Nilābha	the upper bones

TABLE 5.1.B The Soft Earth-element in the Environment and in the Body

Seven continents	The soft elements of the body
Jambudvīpa with its twelve sections	twelve joints of the arms and legs
Raudra	flesh
Krauñca	liver
Kiṃnara	heart
Kuśa	fat
Sitābha	urine
Candra	*nāḍīs*

the regions of the arms, legs, and face. After the second month, there are some indications of arms, legs, and a face. At the end of the third month, the arms, legs, neck, and the whole head are clearly developed. The five fingers of each hand and the five toes of each foot arise respectively from the five elements.[17] During the fourth month, subtle *nāḍīs* spread into the hands, feet, face, and neck, and during the fifth month, three hundred and sixty bones and joints begin to develop within the flesh. At the completion of the sixth month, the fetus is endowed with flesh and blood, and it begins to experience pleasure and pain. At the completion of the seventh month, the bodily hair, eyebrows, bodily apertures, and remaining *nāḍīs* come into existence. At the end of the eighth month, the joints, bones, marrow, tongue, urine, and feces are fully developed. The complete body is said to consist of 20.5 million constituents, for there are that many modifications of the five elements of the father's semen and the mother's uterine blood. During the ninth month, the fetus experiences pain as if it were being baked in a potter's oven. At the completion of the ninth month, one is born, being squeezed by the womb and experiencing pain as if one were being crushed by an anvil and a hammer. Thus, propelled by the habitual propensities of one's own *karma*, which are carried by the ten *internal* winds of *prāṇas*, a human being enters the world that is likewise brought into existence by his own *karma*, which, again, is carried by the ten *external* winds of *prāṇas*.

Thus, the cosmos and the individual share a common material nature and common causes of origination and destruction. They also originate in similar ways, with their respective components arising in the same sequence. Table 5.2 illustrates the correspondences between the origination of the specific bodily parts and the various parts of the cosmos.[18] A classification of the different components of the human and cosmic bodies into the sequentially arising sets of the four, five, six, four, five, and

TABLE 5.1.C The Water-element in the Environment and in the Body

Seven oceans	The fluid elements of the body
Salty ocean	urine
the ocean of wine	sweat
the ocean of fresh water	saliva
the ocean of milk	women's milk and men's phlegm
the ocean of curd	brain
the ocean butter	fats
the ocean of honey	semen

TABLE 5.2 A Classification of the Human and Cosmic Bodies

The body of the individual	The cosmos
The fourfold first set at conception	**Four heavenly bodies**
a transmigrating consciousness	Rāhu
the father's and mother's bliss	Kālāgni
uterine blood	the sun
semen	the moon
The fivefold second set	**The five maṇḍalas**
the bones	the earth-*maṇḍala*
bile	the water-*maṇḍala*
blood	the fire-*maṇḍala*
flesh and skin	the wind-*maṇḍala*
marrow	the space-*maṇḍala*
The sixfold third set	**Six planets**
the visual sense-faculty	Mars
the auditory sense-faculty	Mercury
the gustatory sense-faculty	Jupiter
the olfactory sense-faculty	Venus
the faculty of action	Saturn
the mental sense-faculty	Ketu
The fourfold fourth set	**The four islands of the Great Jambudvīpa**
the left hand	Pūrvavideha (eastern island)
the right hand	Small Jambudvīpa (southern island)
the right foot	Godanīya (western island)
the left foot	Uttarakuru (northern island)
The set of the five fingers and toes	**The five external sense-objects**
a thumb/a big toe	smell
a forefinger/a second toe	taste
a middle finger/a middle toe	form
a ring-finger/ the fourth toe	touch
a small finger/a small toe	sound
The three knuckles of every finger/toe	**The three *guṇas***
the first knuckle at the tip of a finger	*sattva*
the middle knuckle	*rajas*
the last knuckle	*tamas*

three, as presented in table 5.2, is used in this tantric tradition as a model for practicing a *sādhana* on the sequence (*krama*) of the arising of the five tantric families (*kula*) within a larger bodily or cosmic family.

Just as a sequence of the origination of the diverse parts of the cosmos corresponds to that of the individual, so too does the sequence of the dissolution of the cosmos accord with that of the individual. In the process of the dissolution of the cosmos, the karmic winds that support the elements sequentially withdraw from the agglomerates of the five elements in the five cosmic discs that make up the cosmos. Similarly, in the process of dying, the winds of *prāṇas* sequentially cease carrying the elements of earth, water, fire, wind, and space within the respective *cakras* of the navel, heart, throat, *lalāṭa*, and *uṣṇīṣa*.[19]

According to the Kālacakra tradition, one's own body, which was produced by one's own *karma* from the material particles of the father's semen, also dissolves due to the emission of one's own semen. At a human's death, semen, which consists of the five elements, flowing out of the dead body initiates the disintegration of the body. Several passages on this topic in the Kālacakra literature suggest that semen leaves the body at the time of death due to the power of the individual's habitual propensities of seminal emission in sexual bliss. The habitual propensities (*citta-vāsanā*) of the mind of the human being, who consumes the food of the six flavors that originate from the five elements, themselves consist of the five elements. Therefore, semen, which leaves the body during the experience of sexual bliss and at death, is composed of the five elements. At the time of death, the habitual propensities of the mind, together with semen, upon leaving the dead body, make up the body of the habitual propensities (*vāsanā-śarīra*) of the mind. Even though this body of the habitual propensities of the mind is made of fine atomic particles, it is similar to a dream body (*svapna-śarīra*), in the sense that it is devoid of perceptible agglomerations of atoms. The body of the habitual propensities of *karma* does not cease at death. Due to this remaining body of habitual propensities, a transmigratory consciousness acquires a new gross body consisting of atoms. As a transmigratory consciousness forsakes the habitual propensities of the former gross body, the habitual propensities of the new gross body arise in the mind. Consequently, the adventitious psycho-physical aggregates (*āgantuka-skandha*) arise from the empty (*śūnya*) psycho-physical aggregates of the habitual propensities of the mind (*citta-vāsanā-skandha*). Likewise, the empty psycho-physical aggregates of the habitual propensities of the mind arise from the adventitious psycho-physical aggregates. The atomic particles of the former, dead body do not go to another world, for after leaving the earlier psycho-physical aggregates, a transmigratory consciousness acquires different atomic particles.[20]

This process of rebirth is said to be the same for other sentient beings of the three realms of cyclic existence. The only difference is in the number of the elements that constitute the bodies of the diverse classes of gods. Instead of having five elements, the bodies and semen of the gods in the desire-realm, form-realm, and formless realm consist of four, three, and one element, respectively. This is because gods consume food that consists of five, four, or one flavor. For example, the bodies and semen of the gods inhabiting the six types of desire-realm consist of the agglomerations of the elements of water, fire, wind, and space. The bodies of these gods are devoid of the earth-element and are therefore characterized by lightness. Likewise, their mental habitual propensities are devoid of smell as the sense-object that arises from the earth-element. The bodies and semen of the sixteen types of gods dwelling in the form-realm consist of the agglomerations of the atoms of fire, wind, and space; and their mental habitual propensities are endowed with taste, touch, and sound as their sense-objects. The bodies and semen of the gods inhabiting the formless realm consist of the space-element alone, and their mental habitual propensities have only sound as their sense-object.[21] Thus, the bodies, mental habitual propensities, and experiences of different sentient beings are closely related to the nature of the elements contained in the semen with which they undergo birth and death.

According to this tantric system, a habitual propensity of transmigratory existence cannot arise from a single attribute of the elements but only from an assembly of attributes. In the case of all sentient beings dwelling in the three realms, during sexual bliss and at death, semen—the elements of which may be the five, four, three, or one in number—leaves the body under the influence of the habitual propensities. In this way, seminal emission is instrumental in both the birth and death of sentient beings. For the Kālacakra tradition, the cycle of birth and death does not take place in any other way. Thus, one may say that for this tantric tradition, the entire cosmos, with all of its inhabitants, manifests and dissolves due to the power of the moment of seminal emission.

The Configuration and Measurements of the Cosmos and the Individual

Since the entire cosmos comes into existence due to the efficacy of the habitual propensities of sentient beings' minds, one may regard it as a cosmic replica of sentient beings' bodies. Thus, the configuration and measurements of the cosmos are seen in this tantric system as analogous and correlative to the structure and measurements of the individual's body. Likewise, since the cosmos arises and dissolves as a manifestation of the individual's mind, the *Kālacakratantra* considers the cosmos as being fundamentally nondual from the individual. Due to their common material nature, the cosmos and the individual are viewed as mutually pervasive, even in terms of their conventional existence; and due to their fundamental nonduality, the cosmos and the individual inevitably influence each other.

In terms of conventional reality, the cosmos and the body of the individual are nondual in the sense that they share a common nature (*prakṛti*) consisting of the twenty-four principles (*tattva*), which are the objects of the individual's (*puruṣa*) experience. The eight constituents of the primary nature (*prakṛti*) of the individual—namely, the five elements, the mind (*manas*), intellect (*buddhi*), and self-grasping (*ahaṃkāra*)—are the microcosmic correlates of the primary nature of the individual's environment. Likewise, the sixteen modifications (*vikṛti*) of the primary nature of the individual—specifically, the five sense-faculties, the five sense-objects in the body, the five faculties of action, and the sexual organ—evolve from the primary nature of the individual in the same way that the five planets, five external sense objects, and six flavors evolve from the primary nature of the cosmos.

Table 5.3 illustrates the exact correspondences between the individual and the cosmos in terms of their primary nature and its modifications.

In terms of ultimate reality, the cosmos and the individual are also of the same nature, the nature of gnosis (*jñāna*), which manifests in the form of emptiness (*śūnyatā-bimba*). Those who are free of the afflictive and cognitive obscurations nondually perceive the world as the form of emptiness in a nondual manner; that is, they perceive the world as an inseparable unity of form and emptiness. On the other hand, ordinary sentient beings, whose perception is influenced by the afflictive and cognitive obscurations, see the world in a dual fashion, as something other than themselves. They see the world as an ordinary place inhabited by ordinary sentient beings. But in reality, the entire cosmos, with Meru in its center, is a cosmic body of the Jina, a cosmic image or reflection (*pratimā*) of the Buddha, having the nature of form. As such, it is similar to the Nirmāṇakāya of the Buddha.[22] Therefore, according to this

TABLE 5.3 The Corresponding Elements of the Human and Cosmic Bodies

The individual	The cosmos
Eight *Prakṛtis*	**Eight *Prakṛtis***
the earth-element	the earth-element
the water-element	the water-element
the wind-element	the wind-element
the fire-element	the fire-element
the space-element	the space-element
the mind (*manas*)	Rāhu
the intellect (*buddhi*)	the sun
the self-grasping (*ahaṃkāra*)	the moon
Sixteen *Vikṛtis*	**Sixteen *Vikṛtis***
the visual faculty	Mars
gustatory faculty	Venus
olfactory faculty	Jupiter
auditory faculty	Ketu
mental faculty	Saturn
the five sense-objects	**the five sense-objects**
the anus	salty taste
the hands	hot taste
the feet	sweet
the larynx	bitter
the female sexual organ	astringent
the male sexual organ	sour

tantric system, one should attend to this cosmic image of the Buddha, as one attends to the statue of the Buddha, created for the sake of worship.

The immediate aim of the *Kālacakratantra*'s exposition of the interrelatedness of the individual and the cosmos is not to directly induce the unmediated experience of their nonduality by eradicating the afflictive and cognitive obscurations, but to facilitate a thorough understanding of conventional reality. In this tantric system, a proper understanding of the structure and functions of conventional reality provides a theoretical basis for the realization of ultimate reality. I see two main reasons for this. First, conventional reality is the starting point from which a tantric practitioner ventures into tantric practices; and second, a thorough knowledge of the ways in which conventional reality operates facilitates insight into the nature of conventional reality, which is fundamentally not different from ultimate reality. Before one can understand the nonduality of conventional and ultimate realities, one must first understand that a seemingly multiform conventional reality is itself unitary. This, I surmise, is one of the reasons why the *Kālacakratantra*'s initial two chapters are dedicated to discussions of the ways in which the cosmos and the individual correlate to and pervade each other.

"As it is outside so it is within the body" (*yathā bāhye tathā dehe*) is one of the most frequently used phrases in the *Kālacakratantra* and its commentarial literature. This maxim underlies the pervading themes of the *Kālacakratantra*'s chapters on the cosmos and the individual. To the phrase "as it is outside so it is in the body," the

Ādibuddhatantra adds "as it is in the body so it is elsewhere" (*yathā dehe tathā anyatra*), meaning, in the *kālacakra-maṇḍala*.[23] The cosmos, the human body, and the *kālacakra-maṇḍala* are taught here in terms of conventional truth as three *maṇḍalas* representing the outer (*bāhya*), inner (*adhyātma*), and alternative (*anya*), or sublimated, aspects of a single reality. Therefore, these three *maṇḍalas* are said to be the three abodes of the Buddha Kālacakra. Knowledge of how these three conventional aspects of ultimate reality are interrelated is seen as soteriologically significant, for such knowledge provides an indispensable theoretical framework for *Kālacakratantra* practice, which aims at the unmediated experience of their fundamental unity. It is for this reason that the Kālacakra literature frequently points out the correlations among the arrangements and measurements of the cosmos, the human body, and the *kālacakra-maṇḍala*.

There is sufficient textual evidence in the Kālacakra literature to indicate that the *Kālacakratantra* refers to these three aspects of reality as circular *maṇḍalas*, not because it considers a circular form to be their true form, but merely as a heuristic model for meditative purposes. In showing the parallels among the cosmos, the human body, and the *kālacakra-maṇḍala*, the Kālacakra tradition uses various paradigms, which reflect the diverse ways in which this tantric tradition interprets the cosmos as a cosmic body of the individual and of enlightened awareness. All the diverse models of the relations between the cosmos and the individual that the Kālacakra tradition provides have a practical purpose: they serve as devices for furthering one's understanding of the interconnectedness of all phenomena and for training the mind to perceive the world in a nondual fashion. Moreover, they are the contemplative models with which one can diminish the habitual propensities of an ordinary, dualistic mind.

The configuration and measurements of the cosmos as described in the *Kālacakratantra* frequently differ from those given in the *Abhidharmakośa*. The Kālacakra tradition departs from the *Abhidharmakośa* not only with regard to the arrangement and size of the cosmos but also in terms of the units of measurements.[24] Nevertheless, the Kālacakra tradition does not attempt to authenticate its own presentation of the arrangement and measurement of the cosmos over that given in the *Abhidharmakośa*. The *Vimalaprabhā*[25] asserts that in terms of the ultimate truth, the cosmos has no spatial dimensions. The conventionally established size of the cosmos appears differently to different sentient beings due to the power of their virtue (*puṇya*) and sin (*pāpa*). The cosmos is merely an insubstantial apparition of the mind, like a five-cubits wide cave inhabited by a Śrāvaka or a Bodhisattva due to whose powers a universal monarch (*cakravartin*) and his army can enter the cave without the cave being extended and without the universal monarch's army being contracted. Similarly, the *Kālacakratantra*[26] itself asserts that for the Buddhas and for knowledgeable people, the dimensions of the cosmos that were taught by the Buddhas are not its true dimensions, since for the Buddha, one cubit can be many cubits due to the power of the Sahajakāya. It also affirms that the Buddha reveals only the dimensions that corresponds to the perceptions of sentient beings, because if he were to say that the dimensions of the cosmos which he taught were in accordance with the inclinations of living beings dwelling in the land of *karma* (*karma-bhūmi*), then the gods would call him a nihilist (*nāstika*). Thus, the Kālacakra tradition implicitly suggests that both Buddhist accounts of the configuration and size of the cosmos—those of the *Abhi-dharmakośa* and the *Kālacakratantra*—are ultimately invalid. Nevertheless, it considers both accounts to be provisionally valid expressions of the Buddha's skillful means. Justifying the *Kālacakratantra*'s account of the dimensions of the cosmos in terms of skillful means, the *Vimalaprabhā* cites the following verses from the *Paramādibuddhatantra*:

> A falsehood that benefits sentient beings causes an accumulation of merit. A truth that harms others brings Avīci and other hells.
>
> Miserly *pretas* perceive a homely dwelling as a mountain. Evil-doers perceive a home in the form of a needle-pointed mountain.
>
> *Siddhas* who have attained the *siddhi* of the underworld perceive the solid earth as full of holes everywhere and visit the city of celestial nymphs (*apsaras*).[27]

In a similar manner, the following verse from the abridged *Kālacakratantra*[28] expresses its view that one's perception of one's own natural environment is relative, for it is conditioned by the degree of one's own virtue and sin.

> Wish-fulfilling trees, quicksilver, supreme potions, other medicinal herbs, and philosopher's stones, which eliminate all diseases, appeared on the earth along with atoms. However, sentient beings do not see them. They see ordinary grass, trees, water, dust, stones, and copper. *Pretas* perceive rivers as blazing fires, and men in hell perceive spears and other weapons.

In this way the Kālacakra tradition interprets the disparities in the measurements and arrangement of the cosmos within the two Buddhist traditions as evidence of the diversity of sentient beings' perceptions and experiences of the cosmos, which results from their diverse mental dispositions and actions. However, this same interpretative principle is not applied to the divergent measurements of the cosmos given in Hindu Siddhāntas. The *Vimalaprabhā* denies even the conventional validity of the Hindu view of the cosmos as Brahmā's egg (*brahmāṇḍa*), ten million leagues (*yojana*) in size. In light of its criticism of the Hindu Siddhāntas, the *Vimalaprabhā* claims that the *Kālacakratantra* establishes the size of the cosmos using the zodiacal circle (*rāśi-golā*) for the calculation of planets in order to abolish the Hindu measurements of the cosmos for the sake of the spiritual maturation of Buddhist sages.[29]

According to the *Kālacakratantra*, within every single world-system (*loka-dhātu*) there is one great world system (*cakravāla*), just as on every single body of a human being there are bodily hairs and skin. The world-system that is of the nature of *karma* is in the center of a Buddha-field, just as the *avadhūti* is in the center of the body among all the *nāḍīs*. The remaining world-systems that are of the nature of enjoyment (*bhoga*) stand in the same relation to the land of *karma* (*karma-bhūmi*) as do the other *nāḍīs* to the *avadhūti*. These lands of enjoyment (*bhoga-bhūmi*) bring pleasure to the senses, as do the *nāḍīs* in the body. They are filled with jewels, as the *nāḍīs* are filled with blood.

Vajrasattva, the progenitor of the three worlds, dwells in space until the time of expansion of the cosmos. But sentient beings do not witness the arising of the Buddha as long as they lack the accumulations of merit and knowledge. During the time when sentient beings lack merit and knowledge, Vajrasattva resides in space, abiding in the Dharmakāya; and by means of the Jñānakāya, he perceives the entire Buddha-field as it truly is, free of *karma* and karmic winds.[30] It is said that Vajrasattva, together with all other Buddhas, abides in a single pure atom (*śuddhāṇu*), which is not of the nature of an atomic particle (*paramāṇu*) but of the twelve *bodhisattva-bhūmis*.[31] Thus, while ordinary sentient beings, endowed with afflictive and cognitive obscurations, have atomic particles as their material support, the Buddhas, free of all obscurations, have the twelve *bodhisattva-bhūmis* as their pure, immaterial support. In other words, that which is perceived as an agglomeration of atomic particles by those with mental obscurations is perceived as pure gnosis by those without obscurations.

Even though the *Kālacakratantra* agrees to some extent with the *Abhidharmakośa* about the manner in which the cosmos evolves, its description of the configuration and measurements of the cosmos differs significantly from that of the *Abhidharmakośa*. According to the Kālacakra tradition, the cosmos measures twelve hundred thousand leagues in circumference and four hundred thousand leagues in diameter.[32] It is composed of the five *maṇḍalas*, or the five discs (*valaya*)—namely, the earth, water, fire, wind, and space *maṇḍalas*—just as the human body is composed of the five elements. These *maṇḍalas* support one another in the same sequence in which the five elements support one another in the body.[33] Although each of the first four *maṇḍalas* measures fifty thousand leagues in height, they vary in diameter and circumference. The earth-*maṇḍala*, measuring one thousand leagues in diameter, or three hundred thousand leagues in circumference, rests on the water-*maṇḍala*. The water-*maṇḍala*, measuring two hundred thousand leagues in diameter, or six hundred thousand leagues in circumference, rests on the fire-*maṇḍala*. The fire-*maṇḍala*, measuring three hundred thousand leagues in diameter, or nine hundred thousand leagues in circumference, rests on the wind-*maṇḍala*. The wind-*maṇḍala*, measuring four hundred thousand leagues in diameter, or twelve hundred thousand leagues in circumference, rests on the sphere of space (*ākāśa-dhātu*). Thus, space is the support of all the *maṇḍalas*, just as it is the support of all the elements in the body.

The four *maṇḍalas* that rest in space not only correspond to the *maṇḍalas* of the four elements in the human body, but they are also the cosmic representations of particular bodily components. Within different contexts, the Kālacakra tradition draws different correspondences among the four *maṇḍalas* of the cosmic body and the components of the human body. Here are several illustrations of the ways in which the Kālacakra tradition correlates the four cosmic *maṇḍalas* with the bodily parts.

Table 5.4.a illustrates the identification of the four *maṇḍalas* with all the bodily

TABLE 5.4.A The Common Features of the Four Cosmic Maṇḍalas and Bodily Parts

The cosmos	The individual
the earth-*maṇḍala*	the soft and hard bodily parts
the water-*maṇḍala*	the fluid bodily parts
the fire-*maṇḍala*	blood
the wind-*maṇḍala*	skin

TABLE 5.4.B The Four Cosmic Maṇḍalas and the Upper Bodily Parts

The cosmos	The individual
the earth-disc	a half of the chest
(50,000 leagues in radius from the center of Meru to the outer limit of the earth-disc)	(12 finger breadths)
the water-disc	an upper arm
(50,000 leagues in radius from the outer limit of the earth-disc to the outer limit of the water-disc)	(12 finger breadths)
the fire-disc	a forearm
(50,000 leagues in radius from the outer limit of the water disc to the outer limit of the fire-disc)	(12 finger breadths)
the wind-disc	from the wrist to the end of the hand
(50,000 leagues in radius from the outer limit of the fire-disc to the outer limit of the wind-disc)	(12 finger breadths)

parts in terms of their qualitative characteristics. Table 5.4.b demonstrates the correspondences among the four *maṇḍalas* with the upper parts of the body in terms of their measurements; and table 5.4.c illustrates the identification of the four *maṇḍalas* with the four bodily *cakras*, which bear the characteristics of the four elements.

From the uppermost *maṇḍala* downward, each *maṇḍala* is one hundred thousand leagues smaller in diameter than the one that supports it, and each *maṇḍala* rests in the center of the one beneath it. In each of the first four *maṇḍalas* there are two types of underworlds (*pātāla*), each measuring twenty-five thousand leagues in height. Thus, there are altogether eight underworlds: seven hells and the city of *nāgas*. The two underworlds contained in the earth-*maṇḍala* are the City of *nāgas* and the Gravel Water hell (*śarkārāmbhas*), one half of the city of *nāgas* being inhabited by *asuras*, and the other by *nāgas*.[34] The two hells located in the water-*maṇḍala* are the Sandy Water hell (*vālukāmbhas*) and the Muddy Water hell (*paṅkāmbhas*). The two hot hells in the fire-*maṇḍala* are the Intense Smoke hell (*tīvradhūmra*) and the Fire hell (*agni*). Lastly, the two cold hells located in the wind-*maṇḍala* are the Great Severe hell (*mahākharavāta*) and the Great Darkness hell (*mahāndhakāra*).

TABLE 5.4.C The Four Cosmic Maṇḍalas and the Four Bodily Cakras

The cosmos	The individual
the earth-*maṇḍala*	the navel-*cakra*
the water-*maṇḍala*	the heart-*cakra*
the fire-*maṇḍala*	the throat-*cakra*
the wind-*maṇḍala*	the forehead-*cakra*

As indicated in chapter 3 on syncretism, the *Vimalaprabhā*'s account of the eight underworlds is remarkably similar to that given in the Jaina classic, the *Tattvārthādhigamasūtra*, which is traditionally ascribed to Umāsvati, a prolific Jaina author of the second century CE who was equally accepted by both Digambaras and Śvetāmbaras. For example, the corresponding hells enumerated in the *Tattvārthādhigamasūtra* have the following sequence and names: the Jewel-hued (*ratna*), Pebble-hued (*śarkara*), Sand-hued (*vāluka*), Mud-hued (*paṅka*), Smoke-hued (*dhūma*), Darkness-hued (*tamas*), and the Great darkness-hued (*mahā-tamas*) hells.[35] There are also certain similarities among the hells mentioned in the *Vimalaprabhā* and those in the *Tattvārthādhigamasūtra* with regard to the temperature and sequential increase in the size of hells, but not with regard to their shape and specific measurements.[36] Thus, the *Vimalaprabhā*'s classification of the eight types of underworld and its description of their location clearly differ from those in the *Abhidharmakośa*.[37]

It is interesting that in the *Vimalaprabhā*'s account of the configuration of the underworld there is no mention of the Avīci hell, even though the *Ādibuddhatantra* and the *Vimalaprabhā* make references to Avīci in other contexts.[38] So far, I have not encountered an explanation for this omission in any of the commentarial literature on the *Kālacakratantra*. The only thing the *Vimalaprabhā* says about hell in general is that it is "a state of an infernal being (*nārakatva*), which originates from the habitual propensities of the six elements (*ṣaḍ-dhātu-vāsanā*), and is like a dream."[39] But this intepretative principle can also be applied to the other hells and the rest of the universe. It is possible that the author of the *Vimalaprabhā*, being aware of other Buddhist classifications of hells, writes of Avīci in terms of the broader Buddhist context. It is also possible that Avīci and some of the other hells described in the *Abhidharmakośa* and other earlier Buddhist texts are implicitly included here as subcategories of the various hells. Since neither the *Vimalaprabhā* nor the *Kālacakratantra* offers a more detailed description of the contents of the hells and the nature of suffering in them, it is difficult to determine with certainty the extent to which the mentioned hells correspond to and differ from the hells described in the *Abhidharmakośa* and the *Tattvārthādhigamasūtra*. It is clear, however, that the Kālacakra tradition finds the Jaina classification of hells to be more applicable to its own schematization of the underworld, consisting of the four elemental *maṇḍalas* than that of the earlier Buddhist traditions.[40] The names of the hells reveal that each pair of hells is physically characterized by the element of the *maṇḍala* to which it belongs. This fundamental fourfold classification of the underworld is obviously designed to conform closely to the *Kālacakratantra*'s fourfold classifications of the elemental *maṇḍalas* in the body of the individual, the four *vajras* of the individual, the four states of the mind, the four castes, four *vajra*-families, and the four bodies of the Buddha. The configuration of the underworld, beginning with the city of the *nāgas* in the earth-*maṇḍala* and ending with the Great Darkness (*mahāndhakāra*) hell in the wind-*maṇḍala*, is structurally similar to the individual's body at death. In the dying process, the earth-element of the individual's body disintegrates first, followed by the respective elements of water, fire, and wind.[41] See figure 5.1.

Thus, the Kālacakra tradition departs from the *Abhidharmakośa* in terms of both the configuration and the measurement of the cosmos. According to the *Abhidharmakośa*, the cosmos measures 3,610,350 leagues in circumference and 1,203,450

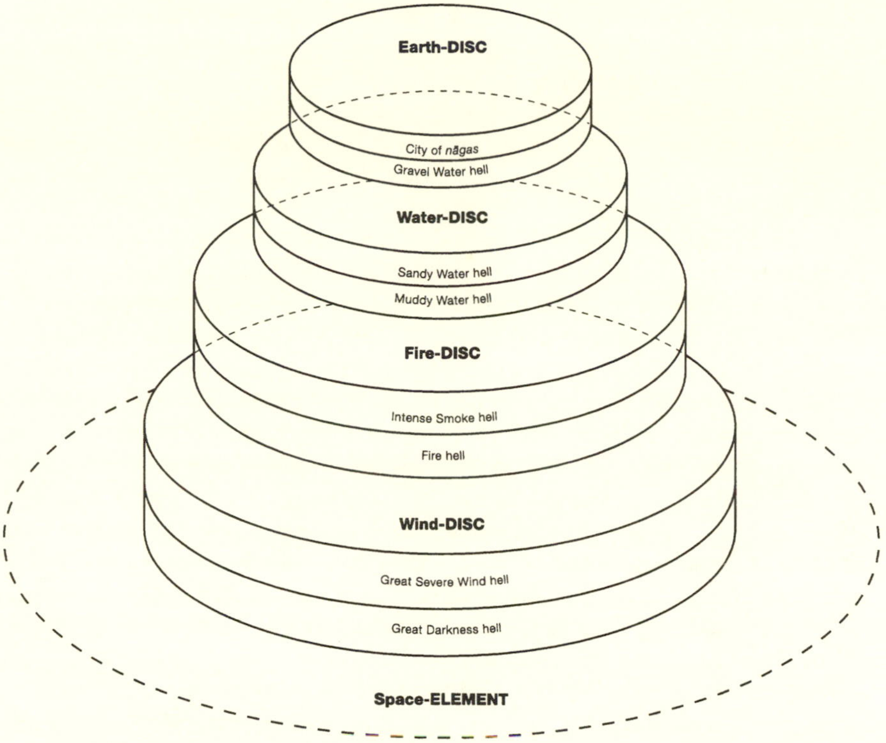

FIGURE 5.1 The universe and its divisions

leagues in diameter.[42] The human world is supported by three instead of four *maṇḍalas*—the golden earth-*maṇḍala*, the water-*maṇḍala*, and the wind-*maṇḍala* that rests in space. The golden earth-*maṇḍala*, which measures 1,203,450 leagues in diameter and 320,000 leagues in height, rests on the water-*maṇḍala*, which is, in turn, 1,203,450 leagues in diameter and 800,000 leagues in height. The water-*maṇḍala* rests on the wind-*maṇḍala*, which is immeasurable in circumference and 1,600,000 leagues in height.[43]

The account of the configuration of the surface of the earth-*maṇḍala* in the Kālacakra tradition also differs from that of the *Abhidharmakośa*. According to the Kālacakra tradition, on the surface of the earth-*maṇḍala* there are seven continents (*dvīpa*), including Great Jambudvīpa (*mahā-jambudvīpa*) as the seventh. Furthermore, there are seven mountains in addition to Mt. Meru, which is in the center of the earth-*maṇḍala*; and there are seven oceans, with the water-*maṇḍala* as the seventh.[44] The six continents—Candra, Sītābha, Varaparamakuśa, Kiṃnara, Krauñca, and Raudra—are the lands of enjoyment (*bhoga-bhūmi*),[45] while the seventh continent, which is the earth-*maṇḍala*, or the Great Jambudvīpa, is the land of *karma* (*karma-bhūmi*), inhabited by humans and animals. On the surface of Great Jambudvīpa, the six oceans—the oceans of wine, fresh water, milk, curd, butter, and honey—surround the six continents. The seventh, the salt ocean, surrounds Great

Jambudvīpa,[46] and from the center of Mt. Meru, the salt ocean measures one hundred thousand leagues in all directions. Seventy-two thousand rivers flow into the oceans,[47] and they correspond to the seventy-two thousand *nāḍīs* in the body. The seven mountains that surround the seven continents in concentric circles are Nīlābha, Mandara,[48] Niṣadha,[49] Maṇikara, Droṇa, Sīta, and the *vajra*-mountain, Vādavāgni, which is situated at the edge of the salt ocean and the earth-*maṇḍala* and beneath the salt ocean.

Mt. Meru is at the very center of Great Jambudvīpa, just as the spine is at the center of the body. It is said to have the shape of a *bindu* and is dark green in the center, due to the nature of the space-*maṇḍala*. Meru's four sides have four different colors. It is blue in the east, red in the south, yellow in the west, and white in the north due to the nature of the elements of wind, fire, earth, and water. In total, it measures one hundred thousand leagues in height.[50] The height of its head is fifty thousand leagues, and its neck and immovable peak are each twenty-five thousand leagues in height. Its upper width is fifty thousand leagues, and its width on the surface of the earth-*maṇḍala* is sixteen thousand leagues. Meru is the spine and head of the cosmic body; and as such, it is an external representation of the individual's head and spine, expanding from the buttocks up to the shoulders. Accordingly, its measurements correspond to those of the spine and the head of the human body.

Table 5.5 illustrates the metrical correspondences bewteen Mt. Meru and the individual's spine and head, as presented in this tantric system.

This measurement of Mt. Meru differs from that described in the *Abhidharmakośa*, in which the height of Mt. Meru is said to be 1,600,000 leagues. Here again, the *Kālacakratantra*'s measurement of Mt. Meru accords with that given in the Jaina commentarial literature on the *Tattvārthādhigamasūtra*, in which Mt. Meru is said to be one hundred thousand leagues in height, with one thousand leagues being below the surface of the earth.[51] See figure 5.2.

The circle of astrological houses, together with innumerable stellar constellations, revolves day and night around Mt. Meru's summit. In the eight directions of Mt. Meru there are eight planets, just as around the spine there are the sense-faculties and faculties of action. The sun and Mars are on the right; Ketu and Saturn are in the front; the moon and Mercury are on the left; and Venus and Jupiter are on the back. On the top of Mt. Meru there are five peaks that penetrate the earth. In all di-

TABLE 5.5 Mt. Meru and the Human Body

Mt. Meru	The bodily spine and the head
100,000 leagues in height from the earth-*maṇḍala* to the top of the peak	1 cubit in height from the waist to the bottom of the neck
Mt. Meru's neck is 25,000 leagues in height	the neck is 6 finger breadths in height
Mt. Meru's head is 50,000 leagues in height	the head from the neck to the end of the *lalāṭa* is 12 finger breadths in height
Mt. Meru's immovable peak is 25,000 leagues in height	the top of the head from the *lalāṭa* to the *uṣṇīṣa* is 6 finger breadths

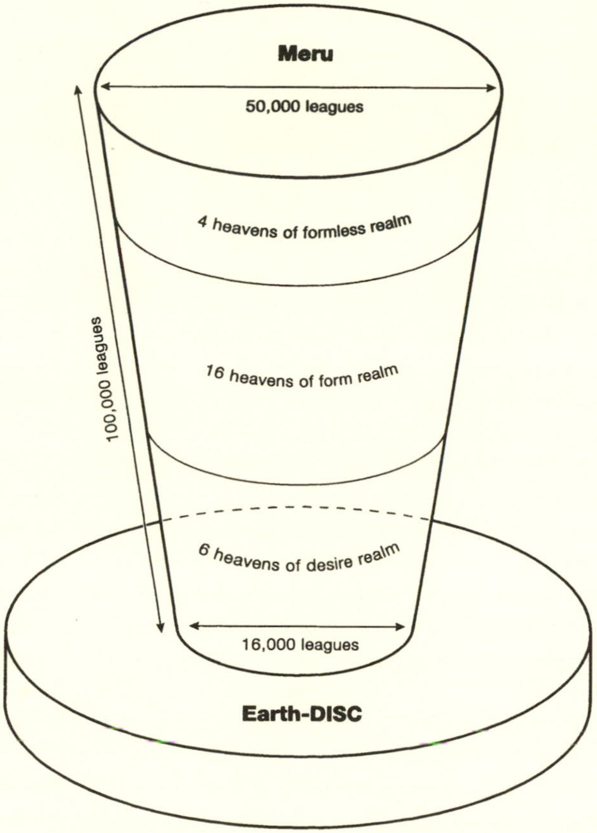

FIGURE 5.2 Dimensions of Mt. Meru

rections from Brahmā's abode in the lower region of the center of Mt. Meru, there are eight thousand leagues in width. All around Mt. Meru is a mountain range (*cakravāḍa*), which measures one thousand leagues in breadth. Outside that mountain range, in the cavities in between the four peaks of Mt. Meru that penetrate the earth, there are the alternating discs of the six continents with their oceans and mountains. Each of the six continents, oceans, and mountains measures roughly 889 leagues in diameter,[52] thus measuring sixteen thousand leagues altogether. Outside all of this, in the eight directions of Mt. Meru, Great Jambudvīpa measures twenty-five thousand leagues.

Outside Great Jambudvīpa is a disc of salty water, which measures fifty thousand leagues in all directions from the outer limit of Great Jambudvīpa to the end of the water-*maṇḍala*. In every direction from Brahmā's place in Meru to the outer limit of the wind-*maṇḍala*, there are two hundred thousand leagues.[53] In this way, the entire breadth of the cosmos extends up to four hundred thousand leagues in diameter, its size corresponding to the size of the human body measuring four cubits (*hasta*). However, when one includes the space-*maṇḍala* in the breadth of the cosmos, then the body of the cosmos measure five hundred thousand leagues from the top of Mt. Meru up to the end of space. With the reasoning that the cosmos pervades the body of the individual, the human body is said to measure five cubits up to the tips of the hair on the head.

This type of arrangement of Great Jambudvīpa is not found in the *Abhidharmakośa*. The numbers and the concentric layout of the seven continents and seven oceans correspond to those mentioned in the Purāṇas,[54] as do the shape and measurement of Great Jambudvīpa.[55] Although the Kālacakra tradition accepts to a large extent the Purāṇic representation of the configuration of the cosmos, it criticizes the Purāṇic account of the origination of the cosmos. With regard to the shapes and sizes of Great Jambudvīpa and the salt ocean, the Kālacakra tradition's account corresponds to that of the Jaina cosmology. According to the *Tattvārthādhigamasūtra*, Ch. 3, v. 9, and its earlier mentioned commentarial literature, Great Jambudvīpa has the shape of a ring with a diameter of one hundred thousand leagues, and it is surrounded by the salt ocean, which is twice as wide as Jambudvīpa.[56]

Although the *Kālacakratantra*'s account of the configuration of Great Jambudvīpa seems to be based on that of the Purāṇas, it includes to some degree the model of the four continents found in the *Abhidharmakośa* and other Buddhist texts.[57] The four continents that are mentioned in the *Abhidharmakośa* and other earlier Buddhist literature are incorporated into this larger picture of the cosmos as the four islands that are located in the four directions of Great Jambudvīpa. Their arrangement in relation to Mt. Meru as depicted in the Kālacakra literature corresponds to that in the *Abhidharmakośa*, but the measurements and shapes of the islands in most cases differ.

According to the Kālacakra tradition, there are four islands on Great Jambudvīpa. Each of the four islands is of the nature of one of the four elements—wind, fire, water, and earth. The nature of each of the mentioned elements influences the shapes and colors of the islands.[58] Thus, in the eastern side of Great Jambudvīpa, in front of Mt. Meru, there is the dark blue Pūrvavideha, which is semicircular in form, due to the nature of the wind-*maṇḍala*. It measures seven thousand leagues. On the south of Great Jambudvīpa, to the right of Mt. Meru, there is Small Jambudvīpa, which is red and triangular in shape, due to the nature of the fire-element. It measures eight thousand leagues.[59] On the north of Great Jambudvīpa, to the left of Mt. Meru, there is the white Uttarakuru, which is circular in shape, due to the nature of the water-*maṇḍala*. It measures nine thousand leagues. On the west of Great Jambudvīpa, facing the back of Mt. Meru, there is the golden island Godanīya, which is yellow and quadrangular in shape, due to the nature of the earth-element. It measures ten thousand leagues.[60] See figure 5.3.

The formation of the four islands in relation to Mt. Meru and the characteristics of their colors and shapes correspond to the four sides of the individual's body, each of which is characterized by the elemental nature of one of the four bodily *maṇḍalas*. Table 5.6 demonstrates the way in which the Kālacakra tradition correlates the four islands of Great Jambudvīpa with the four sides of the individual's body.

The colors of the four islands correspond to the colors of the four sides of Mt. Meru. Likewise, their colors and formations on Great Jambudvīpa correspond to the four faces of the Buddha Kālacakra in the *kālacakra-maṇḍala*. The four faces of Kāla-

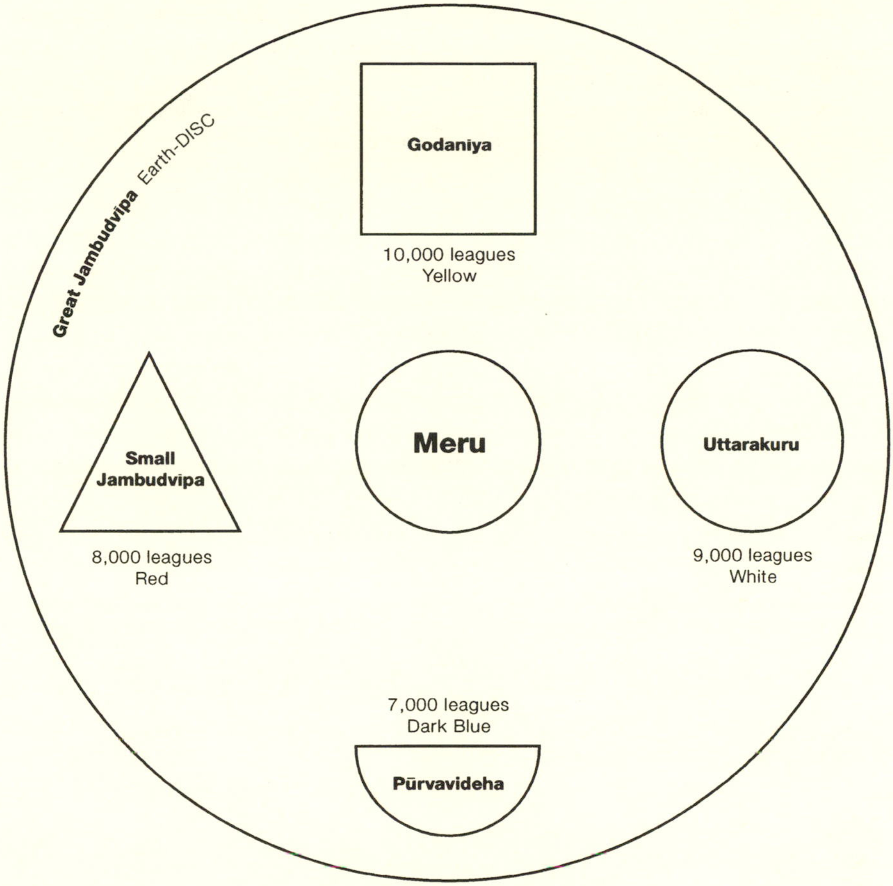

FIGURE 5.3 Great Jambudvīpa

TABLE 5.6 Great Jambudvīpa and the Human Body

Great Jambudvīpa	The individual
Pūrvavideha: the eastern, semicircular island having the nature of the wind-*maṇḍala*	The front part of the body having the nature of the wind-*maṇḍala*
Godanīya: the western, quadrangular island having the nature of the earth-*maṇḍala*	The back of the body having the nature of the earth-*maṇḍala*
Uttarakuru: the northern, circular island having the nature of the water-*maṇḍala*	The left side of the body having the nature of the water-*maṇḍala*
Small Jambudvīpa: the southern, triangular island having the nature of the fire-*maṇḍala*	The right side of the body having the nature of the fire-*maṇḍala*

cakra symbolize the four aspects in which enlightened awareness manifests itself. Thus, the four islands of Great Jambudvīpa and the corresponding sides of the human body are the geographical and anatomical representations of the four aspects of the Buddha's mind. When these phenomenal aspects of the Buddha's mind become purified, they manifest as the four bodies of the Buddha.

Great Jambudvīpa looks like a twelve-spoked wheel, for it is divided into twelve sections (*khaṇḍa*). Each of the sections measures twenty-five thousand leagues. In the center of the section belonging to the Small Jambudvīpa there is the mountain Kāilāśa, surrounded by snow mountains. Together with the surrounding snow mountains, Kāilāśa occupies one-third of that section. Outside that range there are twelve countries and districts in the twelve subsections of Small Jambudvīpa.[61]

In each section of Great Jambudvīpa there is one universal monarch (*cakravartin*), who turns the Wheel of Dharma in his section. Thus, the twelve sections of Great Jambudvīpa have twelve universal monarchs, who are likened to twelve suns that dispel the darkness of ignorance by introducing the Buddhist Dharma. They are twelve in number in the same sense that one can speak of "twelve suns" due to the classification of the twelve solar mansions. Thus, Great Jambudvīpa, together with its twelve sections, is an earthly reflection of the circle of solar mansions and of the twelve-spoked wheel of cyclic existence.

Every eighteen hundred human years, the universal monarch enters one section of the earth-*maṇḍala*,[62] moving progressively from one section to another, from the front to the back of Meru. He establishes his Dharma in each section that has entered the *kali-yuga* and thereby introduces the *kṛta-yuga*. Thus, the *kali-yuga* is always in front of him, and the *tretā-yuga* is behind him.[63]

This belief that at different times, the universal monarch, visiting and teaching Dharma in the twelve sections of Great Jambudvīpa, sanctifies each of the sections with his presence, is one of reasons that the Kālacakra tradition identifies the twelve sections of the Great Jambudvīpa as the twelve groups of cosmic pilgrimage sites—namely, *pīṭhas*, *upapīṭhas*, *kṣetras*, *upakṣetras*, *chandohas*, *upachandohas*, *melāpakas*, *upamelāpakas*, *veśmas* (*pīlavas*), *upaveśmas* (*upapīlavas*), *śmaśānas*, *upaśmaśānas*. Each of the twelve groups of sacred pilgrimage sites comprises a specific number of sites. The Kālacakra tradition classifies and subdivides the twelve classes of pilgrimage sites in various ways in order to demonstrate the multiple models of interpreting the correspondences between the cosmic body and the human body. One of the *Kālacakratantra*'s goals in outlining the correspondences and identities among the pilgrimage sites and the bodily components of the individual is to demonstrate the pointlessness of visiting the pilgrimage sites, for they are already present within one's own body. Visits to the external pilgrimage sites lead neither to spiritual awakening nor to mundane *siddhis*. The *Vimalaprabhā* asserts that the pilgrimage sites such as Jalāndhara and others are mentioned only for the benefit of foolish people (*bāla*) who wander about the country.[64] This same statement also appears in Nāropā's *Vajrapādasārasaṃgraha*, XVII, 3*b* 2.[65] In both cases, it suggests that foolish people, who lack understanding of nonduality, do not see that the places of pilgrimage are omnipresent. The entire cosmos is a pilgrimage site, as is the individual.

The *Vimalaprabhā* states that according to the *Paramādibuddhatantra*, due to the pervasiveness of the earth-element, the external pilgrimage sites are present also in

Tibet, China, and other countries. According to the abridged *Kālacakratantra*, they are also present in every city.[66] In this way, the Kālacakra tradition rejects the inherent sacredness of one place or one human being over another. It suggests that all regions of the world and all human bodies are equally sacred. This view of the human body as containing within itself all the pilgrimage sites is not unique to the Kālacakra tradition. It is also found in other *anuttara-yoga-tantras* and in the literature of the Sahajayāna. For example, the well-known Sahajīya poet, Sarahapāda, affirms in his *Dohākoṣa* that he has not seen another place of pilgrimage as blissful as his own body.[67]

With regard to the individual, the Kālacakra literature identifies the twelve categories of pilgrimage sites with the twelve characteristics of transmigratory existence and enlightened existence. In terms of conventional reality, the Kālacakra tradition identifies the twelve categories of pilgrimage sites with the twelve links of dependent origination and the twelve signs of the zodiac—starting with spiritual ignorance (*avidyā*) arising in Capricorn and ending with old age and death (*jarā-maraṇa*) arising in Sagittarius. In terms of ultimate reality, the *Kālacakratantra* sees the twelve categories of pilgrimage sites as the symbolic representations of both the twelve *bodhisattva-bhūmis*—which impede the arising of the twelve links of dependent origination and the twelve zodiacs—which are the temporal basis of the twelve links of dependent origination.

This identification of the twelve categories of pilgrimage sites with the twelve *bodhisattva-bhūmis* is equally characteristic of other *anuttara-yoga-tantras*—specifically, the *Cakrasaṃvara* and the *Hevajra tantras*. However, the Kālacakra literature gives a more explicit explanation of this type of identification. The Kālacakra tradition identifies the twelve types of pilgrimage sites with the twelve *bodhisattva-bhūmis* on the ground that throughout the three times, the elements of the Buddha's purified psycho-physical aggregates and sense-bases assume the form of deities. These deities then arrive at and leave from these pilgrimage sites, and due to the *prāṇas*' flow in the bodily *cakras*, they arrive at and leave from those *cakras*.

Furthermore, a group of *yoginīs* who roam the earth for the benefit of sentient beings dwells in each of the eight directions of Mt. Meru, expanding as far as the end of the wind-*maṇḍala*. These *yoginīs* also journey in the cosmic *maṇḍalas* of water, fire, wind, and space, which are the seats of the cosmic *cakras*, just as the *prāṇas* move through the *cakras* of the invidivual's body. Just as the human body has six *cakras*, so too does the body of the cosmos. The six *cakras* of the cosmos are the locations of the cosmic pilgrimage sites. In the center of the summit of Mt. Meru, there is the inner lotus (*garbha-padma*) of the Bhagavān Kālacakra, which has sixteen petals and constitutes the bliss-*cakra* (*ānanda-cakra*) of the cosmic body.[68] The gnosis-*cakra*, which has eight spokes, occupies two-thirds of the earth-*maṇḍala*. The earth-*cakra* is in one half of the salty ocean, and the water-*cakra* is in the other half. Likewise, the fire-*cakra* is in one half of the fire-*maṇḍala*, and the wind-*cakra* is in the other half. The space-*cakra* is in one half of the wind-*maṇḍala*. In the space-*maṇḍala* there are sixteen pilgrimage sites of the *śmaśāna* type.

Tables 5.7.a–h illustrate the specific locations of the pilgrimage sites within the six cosmic and six bodily *cakras*. They also demonstrate the manner in which the Kālacakra tradition asserts that the cessation of the twelve zodiacs and twelve links

TABLE 5.7.A Locations of the Cosmic and Bodily Pilgrimage Sites

Pilgrimage sites	The cosmos	The individual
four *pīṭhas* [1] Kāmarūpa Jālandhara Pūrṇagiri Oḍḍiyāṇa	in the four cardinal directions of the earth-*maṇḍala*	in the four cardinal directions of the *cakra* of the gnosis-element due to the cessations of Sagittarius and the twelfth link of dependent origination (*jarā-maraṇa*)

[1] The names of the four *pīṭhas* correspond to those given in the *Hevajratantra*, Part 1, Ch. 7, v. 13. According to P. Gupta, 1973, p. 27, the region of Kāmarūpa is marked by the river Karatoyā and is placed around the Gauhati region of Assam. It was also known under the name Prāgjyotiṣa. H. H. Wilson in his translation of *The Viṣṇu Purāṇa: A System of Hindu Mythology and Tradition*, 2 vols., Delhi: Nag, 1989, vol. 1. p. 263, fn. 6, identifies Kāmarūpa as the northeastern part of Bengal and western portion of Assam. This seems to accord to some degree with Tāranātha's account, 1990, p. 330, which also places Kāmarūpa in northeastern India.

According to Bu ston [188], Kāmarūpa is in eastern India and has the river Lohitā in its center, which flows north to south.

P. Gupta identifies Jālandhara as Jullundur, the headquarters of the same district in Punjab. In the *Padma Purāṇa*, Jālandhara is mentioned as the capital of the great *daitya* king Jālandhara. Bu ston [188] identifies Jālandhara as being northwest of the Guge region in Tibet; and he places Pūrṇa to the north of Oḍḍiyāna. Tāranātha, 1990, pp. 91, 121, 274, associates Jālandhara with the celebrated king Kaniṣka of the first century CE and places it in northern India.

Oḍḍiyāna was situated on the Śubhavāstu river (the modern Swāt river). It includes the four modern districts of Pangkora, Bijāwar, Swāt, and Bunir, and its capital was Maṅgala. According to Fa-hien, who visited India in the fifth century CE, it was a part of northern India and was situated north of the Punjab along the Subhāvastu river. It was an important center of Mahāyāna Buddhism.

TABLE 5.7.B Locations of the Cosmic and Bodily Pilgrimage Sites

Pilgrimage sites	The cosmos	The individual
four *upapīṭhas* [1] Godāvarī Rāmeśa Devikoṭṭa Mālava	in the four intermediate directions of the earth *maṇḍala*	in the four intermediate directions of the *cakra* of the gnosis-element due to the cessations of Scorpio and the eleventh link of dependent origination (*jāti*)

[1] Godāvarī is the name of the largest and longest river in south India, which rises from the Western Ghats. According to the *Viṣṇu Purāṇa*, Book 2, Ch. 2, vs. 11–12, Godāvarī flows from the Sahya mountains. According to P. Gupta, 1973, p. 73, there was a famous pilgrimage site at Govardhan-Gaṅgapura on the right bank of the river, about six miles west of Nasik. The *Mārkaṇḍeya Purāṇa*, Ch. 57, v. 34, mentions the river Godāvarī in connection with a region where Govardhanapura stood.

It is possible that Rāmeśa refers to Rāmeśvara, a sacred island in the Bay of Bengal. However, according to Bu ston [188], Rāmeśa is a synonym for Rāmeśvara, or Nandeśvara, located on the shore of Śrī Laṅkā. Tāranātha, 1990, p. 336, places Rāmeśvara at the extremity of the apex of the triangular region of the south.

Devikoṭṭa may be another name for Devīkoṭa, or Devakoṭa, the ancient capital of Koṭivarṣa in northern Bengal, which is often mentioned in the epigraphic records of the Pālas and Senas of Bengal. However, there were several places in India under this name. H. H. Wilson, 1989, vol. 2, p. 823, fn. 1, identifies Devikoṭa as a synonym for Śoṇiputra, corresponding to the modern Devicotta in the Karnatic. The name Devikoṭa also designates the capital of Munja in Dekhin on the banks of the Godāvarī and the place in Assam near Goalpara.

Mālava was the country of the Mālava tribes who settled in Punjab. The location of the exact territory that they occupied is difficult to determine. Different authors locate them in different areas. According to B. C. Law, 1984, p. 110, it seems that the Mālavas eventually migrated southward and settled in Rajaputana at the time of Samudragupta. Tāranātha, 1990, pp. 47, 49, 68, places the Mālava country in western India and associates it with the cities of Kośāmbi and Ujjayinī.

Cf. the *Hevajratantra*, Part 1, Ch. 7, v. 13, which mentions the following three *upapīṭhas*: Mālava, Sindhu, and Nagara.

TABLE 5.7.C Locations of the Cosmic and Bodily Pilgrimage Sites

Pilgrimage sites	The cosmos	The individual
four *kṣetras* [1] Arbuda Munmunī Oḍra Kāruṇyapāṭaka	in the four cardinal directions of the inner half of the water-*maṇḍala*	in the four cardinal directions of the earth-*cakra* due to the cessations of Libra and the tenth link of dependent origination (*bhava*)
four *upakṣetras* [2] Triśakuni Karmārapāṭaka Kośala Lāḍadeśa	in the four intermediate directions of the inner half of the water-*maṇḍala*	in the four intermediate directions of the earth-*cakra* due to the cessations of Virgo and the ninth link of dependent origination (*upādāna*)

[1] B. C. Law, 1984, p. 304, and P. Gupta, 1973, p. 251, agree that Arbuda is the mountain Abu in the southern end of the Aravalli range in the Sirohi state of Rajputana. Bu ston [188] places Arbuda and Munmunī in eastern India.

According to B. C. Law, 1984, p. 178, Odra is the modern Orissa. According to Bu ston [189], Oḍra and Kāruṇyapāṭaka are northwest of Rājagṛha, on the southern bank of Gaṅgā in the country of Aśoka.

Cf. the *Hevajratantra*, Part 1, Ch. 7, v. 13: Kāruṇyapātaka, Devīkoṭa, and Karmārapāṭaka.

[2] Bu ston [188] identifies Karmārapāṭaka as a district of many blacksmiths, a part of Bhagala in eastern India. Bhagala is most likely a synonym for Bhaṅgala (Bengal), since Tāranātha, 1990, p. 121, mentions Gauḍa as its capital.

Lāḍadeśa is, according to Bu ston [188], a region of Ruka in western India.

Kośala was an important kingdom in eastern Deccan at the time of early Buddhism. In the *Aṅguttara Nikāya*, 1958, vol. 1, it is listed among the sixteen Mahājanapadas of Jambudvīpa. The capital cities of Kośala were Śrāvastī, where the Buddha reportedly spent much time, and Sāketa.

Cf. the *Hevajratantra*, Part 1, Ch. 7, v. 14: Kulatā, Arbuda, Godāvarī, and Himādri.

TABLE 5.7.D Locations of the Cosmic and Bodily Pilgrimage Sites

Pilgrimage sites	The cosmos	The individual
four *chandohas* [1] Kaliṅga Harikela Candradvīpa Lampāka	in the four cardinal directions of the outer half of the water-*maṇḍala*	in the four cardinal directions of the water-*cakra* due to the cessations of Leo and the eighth link of dependent origination (*tṛṣṇā*)

[1] Kaliṅga is the seacoast, west of the mouths of the Ganges, together with the upper part of the Coromandel coast. According to Bu ston [188], Kaliṅga is in the southwest, sixty leagues from Vajrāsana.

Harikela was also an eastern country. According to B. C. Law, 1984, p. 222, it was located west of the river Meghnā, some forty leagues north of Tāmralipti. Some think that it was a coastal country between Samatata and Orissa, and some identify it with parts of Backerganj and Noakhali. For different opinions on its exact location see B. C. Law, pp. 221–222. According to Bu ston [189], Harikela is a district of Bhagala in the east.

Candradvīpa was also located in eastern India. According to B. C. Law, p. 215, it is mentioned in the Rāmpāl grant of Śrīcandra as being ruled by the king Trailokyacandra in the tenth or eleventh century CE. According to Bu ston [189], it is the island of Bhagala.

According to S. M. Ali, 1966, p. 143, Lampāka was a territorial unit in the northern mountain zone of the Indus Basin, associated with the upper Kabul valley. The region is the same as the Lambagae of the Greeks and modern Lamghan.

Cf. the *Hevajratantra*, Part 1, Ch. 7, v. 15: Harikela, arising from the salt-ocean, Lampāka, Kāñcika, and Saurāṣṭra.

TABLE 5.7.E Locations of the Cosmic and Bodily Pilgrimage Sites

Pilgrimage sites	The cosmos	The individual
four *upachandohas*[1] Kāñcī Koṅkaṇaka Himālaya Nepāla	in the four intermediate directions of the outer half of the water-*maṇḍala*	in the four intermediate directions of the water-*cakra* due to the cessations of Cancer and the seventh link of dependent origination (*vedanā*)
four *melāpakas*[2] Mātṛgṛha Prayāga Kollagiri Gṛhadevatā	in the four cardinal directions of the inner half of the fire-*maṇḍala*	in the four cardinal directions of the fire-*cakra* due to the cessations of Gemini and the sixth link of dependent origination (*sparṣa*)

[1] The city of Kāñcī was an important place of pilgrimage in southern India since early times. It has been identified as Conjeevaram, the capital of Drāviḍa or Coḷa on the Palār river, forty-three miles southwest of Madras. It contains many Śaiva, Vaiṣṇava, and Jaina temples. It was one of the well-known centers of Buddhist learning. Bu ston [189] mentions Kāñci as Dharmakīrti's place.

According to Bu ston [188], Koṇkaṇaka was a city in the southwest. Its borders were surrounded by rivers, and it had seven divisions. Koṅkaṇaka is most likely Koṅkana, also mentioned by Tāranātha, 1990, p. 325, as a region in the south of India, in which there was a famous Buddhist shrine Mahābimba.

Cf. the *Hevajratantra*, Part 1, Ch. 7, v. 16: Kāliṅga, the Isle of Gold, and Kokaṇa.

[2] I have been unable to identify Mātṛgṛha and Kollagiri. According to the *Chos kyi rnam grangs*, 1986, pp. 457–458, Gṛhadevatā is in northwestern China. Prayāga is modern Allahabad. The *Mahābhārata*, 85. 79–83, mentions it as the holiest place in the world. The early Pāli texts mention Prayāga as a pilgrimage site (*tīrtha*) or *ghāṭ* on the river Ganges.

According to Huien-stang, there were only a few Buddhist establishments in Prayāga at the time of his visit. The *Hevajratantra* does not list any site belonging to the group of *melāpakas* or *upamelāpakas*.

of dependent origination is causally related to the transformation of the six cosmic and six bodily *cakras* into the twelve *bodhisattva-bhūmis*, or the twelve groups of pilgrimage sites. These tables further suggest that in the context of the *Kālacakratantra* practice, the sequential attainment of the twelve *bodhisattva-bhūmis* is an internal pilgrimage to spiritual awakening. A tantric adept undertakes an internal pilgrimage by purifying the bodily *cakras* by means of the six-phased *yoga* (*ṣaḍ-aṅga-yoga*), which, in turn, purifies the external *cakras* of his environment. Thus, one may say that in this tantric system, the path of spiritual awakening is metaphorically seen as the ultimate pilgrimage. See tables 5.7.a–h for the correlations among the locations of pilgrimage sites in the cosmos and within the body of the individual.

According to the schema given above, each of the twelve categories of pilgrimage sites includes the four pilgrimage sites. Thus, for this tantric tradition, there are altogether forty-eight pilgrimage sites.[69] The number of the subdivisions of the twelve pilgrimage sites and their names as given in the Kālacakra tradition differ from those given in other Buddhist tantric systems.[70] This should not come as a surprise, though, since one encounters various numberings even within each of the mentioned Buddhist tantric systems. The *Vimalaprabhā* justifies these contradictions as the skillful means of liberating those with sharp mental faculties from grasping onto any physical place.[71] A closer look at the illustrated paradigms of the ways in which the Kālacakra tradition draws the correlations among the external pilgrimage sites and the

TABLE 5.7.F Locations of the Cosmic and Bodily Pilgrimage Sites

Pilgrimage sites	The cosmos	The individual
four *upamelāpakas*[1] Saurāṣṭra Kāśmīra Suvarṇadvīpa Siṃhala	in the four intermediate directions of the inner half of the fire-*maṇḍala*	in the four intermediate directions of the fire-*cakra* due to the cessations of Taurus and the fifth link of dependent origination (six *āyatanas*)
four *śmaśānas*[2] Nagara Mahendraśaila Sindhudeśa Kirātaka	in the four cardinal directions of the outer half of the fire-*maṇḍala*	in the four cardinal directions of the wind-*cakra* due to the cessations of Aries and the fourth link of dependent origination (*nāma-rūpa*)

[1] According to S. M. Ali, 1966, p. 146, the *Matsya Purāṇa* identifies Saurāṣṭra as the region occupying the southern half of the Kathiawar peninsula. The *Viṣṇu Purāṇa* also mentions Saurāṣṭra as one of the western regions of India. The Buddhist tradition considers it as the birthplace of Śāntideva.

Suvarṇadvīpa could be a synonym for Suvarṇabhūmi (Lower Burma and Malay islands), mentioned in the early Pāli texts, specifically, in the *Majjhima* and *Saṃyutta Nikāyas*. According to the *Chos kyi rnam grangs*, 1986, pp. 457–458, Suvarṇadvīpa designates Indonesia. Siṃhala is another name for Ceylon.

[2] Mahendraśaila is perhaps Mahendragiri, or Mahendrācala, the portion of the eastern Ghats between the Godāvarī and Mahānādī rivers. A portion of the eastern Ghat near Ganjam is still called the Mahendra hill. H. H. Wilson, vol. 1, p. 259, fn. 2, specifies Mahendra as the chain of hills that extends from Orissa and the northern Circas to Gondwana near Ganjam. According to Bu ston [189], Mahendraśaila is in the district of Dhāṇyakaṭaka, the famous site of Mahāyāna Buddhism.

According to P. Gupta, 1973, p. 17, the ancient Sindhudeśa was to the west of the lower Indus. According to Bu ston [189], Sindhudeśa designates the region in eastern India through which flows the great river Sindhu.

Kirātaka probably refers to the country of Kirātas, which was in the Himālayas. Kirātas were nomadic people according to Megasthenes. According to Ptolemy, they lived in the northern region of Uttarāpatha. In the *Bhāgavata Purāṇa*, II. 4, 18, they are mentioned as people living outside the Āryan fold. Bu ston [189] only glosses Kirātaka as the Kirātadeśa.

Cf. the *Hevajratantra*, Part 1, Ch. 7, v. 17: Caritra, Kośala, Vindhyā, and Kaumārapaurikā.

bodily parts reveals that the diverse numberings of pilgrimage sites are not contradictory or randomly arranged but complementary and carefully designed. They exemplify the multiple ways in which this tantric system delineates the correspondences it sees. As the given correspondences themselves vary, there are different ways of structuring and numbering. The diverse ways of identifying the pilgrimage sites with the components of the individual's body have their specific roles in the different phases of the *Kālacakratantra* practice.

For example, identifying the twelve groups of pilgrimage sites with the twelve sections of Great Jambudvīpa and with the twelve joints of the individual's body, the Kālacakra tradition attempts to demonstrate a close link among the purifications of the twelve bodily joints and the attainment of the twelve *bodhisattva-bhūmis* and the purification of the twelve sections of Great Jambudvīpa. A purification of bodily joints implies here a cessation of the ordinary body that is accompanied by afflictive and cognitive obscurations. Therefore, as the tantric adept gradually purifies his bodily joints by means of the *Kālacakratantra* practice, he also eradicates the obscurations and attains the twelve *bodhisattva-bhūmis*. The identification of the twelve bodily joints with the twelve sections of Great Jambudvīpa is based on the *Kālacakratantra*'s

TABLE 5.7.G Locations of the Cosmic and Bodily Pilgrimage Sites

Pilgrimage sites	The cosmos	The individual
four *upaśmaśānas* [1] Marudeśa Gahvara Kulatā Samala	in the four intermediate directions of the outer half of the fire-*maṇḍala*	in the four intermediate directions of the wind-*cakra* due to the cessations of Pisces and the third link of dependent origination (*vijñāna*)
four *pīlavas/veśmas* [2] Caritra Harikela Vindhya Kaumārikapurī	in the four cardinal directions of the inner half of the wind-*maṇḍala*	in the four cardinal directions in the space-*cakra* due to the cessations of Aquarius and the second link of dependent origination (*saṃskāra*)

[1] Marudeśa most likely refers to the district of Maru, mentioned in the Junagarh rock inscription. According to P. Gupta, 1973, p. 19, Maru perhaps denoted the territory of Marwar in Rajasthan. Tāranātha, 1990, p. 253, places Maru in western India.

There is a slight possibility that Gahvara refers to the mountains extending from Kabul to Bamian, which provide numerous cave habitats.

[2] B. C. Law, 1984, p. 221, identifies Harikela as an eastern country, on the basis that the *Kārpuramaṇjarī* mentions it as such. Some have identified it with Bengal, and some suggest that it occupied the parts of Backerganj and Noakhali districts. Tibetan translation reads Raṇa instead of Harikela.

According to Bu ston [189], Vindhya mountains is a place where Dignāga practiced a *sādhana*, and Kaumārikapurī is a place inhabited only by women.

view of their common relation to the elements of wind, fire, water, and earth.[72] Thus, as one purifies the atomic nature of one's own body, one simultaneously purifies one's own perception of the twelve sections of Great Jambudvīpa as ordinary, physical places.[73]

Table 5.8 illustrates the aforementioned correspondences among the twelve pilgrimage sites in the cosmic and individual bodies, which are the phenomenal aspects of the twelve *bodhisattva-bhūmis*.

TABLE 5.7.H Locations of the Cosmic and Bodily Pilgrimage Sites

Pilgrimage sites	The cosmos	The individual
four *upapīlavas/ upaveśmas* [1] Virajā Koṅka Tripurī Śrīhaṭṭaka	in the four intermediate directions of the inner half of the wind-*maṇḍala*	in the four cardinal directions in the space-*cakra* due to the cessations of Capricorn and the first link of dependent origination (*avidyā*)

[1] Koṅka may be another name for Koṅkān, which, according to the *Mārkaṇḍeya Purāṇa*, 25, lies on the river Veṇvā. P. Gupta, 1973, p. 16, refers to Tripurī (Tewar) as a city in central India. B. C. Law, 1984, p. 196, mentions that the ninth-century Ratnapur stone inscription of Jājalladeva of the Cedi speaks of Tripurī as being ruled by one of the Cedi rulers, named Kokalla. According to Bu ston [189], Tripurī is on the Labda island in the south.

Śrīhaṭṭaka could be Śrīhaṭṭa in eastern India, or Sylhet, which is identified by B. C. Law, p. 261, as the region that occupies the lower valley of the Surma river and which is surrounded by high hills. According to Bu ston [189], Śrīhaṭṭaka is in the south of India, the birthplace of Aruṇagapo.

TABLE 5.8 Twelve Cosmic and Bodily Pilgrimage Sites

Twelve pilgrimage sites	The cosmos	The individual
pīṭhas	the four islands in the four cardinal directions of the Great Jambudvīpa	the twelve joints of the arms and legs
upapīṭhas	the four intermediate directions of the Great Jambudvīpa	
kṣetras and *upakṣetras*	the inner half of the salt ocean	
chandohas and *upachandohas*	the outer half of the salt ocean	
melāpakas and *upamelāpakas*	the inner half of the fire-*maṇḍala*	
veśmas and *upaveśmas*	the outer half of the fire-*maṇḍala*	
śmaśānas and *upaśmaśānas*	the inner half of the wind-*maṇḍala*	

In some other contexts, the Kālacakra tradition classifies the twelve groups of pilgrimage sites into thirty-six subcategories. It presents thirty-six pilgrimage sites as the dwelling places of thirty-six families of *yoginīs*, who are the sublimated aspects of thirty-six social classes (*jāti*), thirty-six bodily constituents of the individual, and thirty-six factors of spiritual awakening (*bodhi-pākṣika-dharma*). As table 5.9 illustrates, the Kālacakra tradition identifies these thirty-six pilgrimage sites with thirty-six components of the cosmos and the individual. This identification is taught in the "Chapter on Initiation," in the context of tantric yogic practices performed during a tantric feast (*gaṇa-cakra*), in which the thirty-six social classes of the Indian society of that time had to be represented.[74] It exemplifies one of the ways in which this tantric tradition identifies the individual with his social environment. This particular manner of identifying the external and internal pilgrimage sites as the abodes of *yoginīs* is seen as relevant for the purification of tantric pledges (*samaya*). It is relevant because the purification of tantric pledges takes place only when the initiate is cognizant of the correspondences given below and applies them in viewing his body and his natural and social environments as nondual and equally sacred. Bringing to mind the sublimated aspects of the participants in a tantric feast and viewing the parts of one's own body and the cosmos as their pure abodes, one purifies one's own vision of the individual, social, and cosmic bodies. By so doing, one transforms one's own body and the cosmos into the sacred pilgrimage sites and brings forth a certain degree of purification.

For the specific correlations among the pilgrimage sites and the constituting elements of the cosmos, individual, and *kālacakra-maṇḍala*, which a tantric practitioner must know in order to purify his vision and attitude toward his natural environment and toward his own body, see table 5.9.

TABLE 5.9 Pilgrimage Sites as the Cosmos, Individual, and Kālacakra-maṇḍala

Pilgrimage sites	The cosmos	The individual	The Kālacakra-maṇḍala
four *pīṭhas*	Kālāgni moon sun Rāhu	feces urine blood flesh	the mansions of Tārā, etc.
six *kṣetras*	Mars Mercury Jupiter Venus Saturn Ketu	ear nose eye tongue anus vulva	the mansions of Rūpavajrā, etc.
eight *chandohas*	earth water fire wind the earth-born the water-born the fire-born the wind-born	pus phlegm louse worm saliva fat bodily hair hair of the head	the mansions of Carcikā, etc., born from *bhūtas*
ten *melāpakas*	six tastes smell color sound touch	intestines bile bones marrow liver lungs *nāḍīs* skin heart lymph	the mansions of Jambhikāsyā, etc., born from *krodhas*
eight *śmaśānas*	a decay of the four elements, colors, etc.	the ear-secretion nasal secretion the eye-secretion gustatory secretion uterine secretion intestinal secretion penile secretion armpit secretion	the mansions of Śvānāsyā, etc., born from *asuras*

There are several other ways in which the Kālacakra tradition identifies the pilgrimage sites with the individual's body, and these are equally relevant to the aforementioned phase of the *Kālacakratantra* practice. The following two models are specifically related to the practice of the unification of the tantric pledges (*samaya-melāpaka*), or of the female and male consorts, during tantric sexual *yoga* performed after a tantric feast. Identifying the sacred pilgrimage sites with the various parts of the male and female body during sexual tantric *yoga*, a tantric practitioner sanctifies a sexual act, which becomes a kind of bliss-generating pilgrimage. This type of identification also suggests that the bliss and spiritual benefits resulting from a single yogic sexual act equal those resulting from visiting ten kinds of pilgrimage sites.

TABLE 5.10 Ten Pilgrimage Sites in the Female and Male Bodies

Ten pilgrimage sites	The individual
pīṭha	the female sexual organ
upapīṭha	the male sexual organ
kṣetras	the six sense-bases (*āyatanas*) of a woman
upakṣetras	the six sense-bases of a man
chandohas	the eight *samāna*-winds of a woman
upachanodhas	the eight *samāna*-winds of a man
melāpakas	the ten faculties of action (*karmendriya*) of a woman
upamelāpakas	the ten faculties of action of a man
śmaśānas	a discharge of secretions from the nostrils, ears, eyes, mouth, and anus of a woman
upaśmaśānas	a discharge of secretions from the nostrils, ears, eyes, mouth, and anus of a man

Table 5.10 illustrates the manner in which the Kālacakra tradition classifies ten pilgrimage sites into two main categories—those corresponding to ten parts of the female body and those corresponding to ten parts of the male body. Whereas table 5.11 demonstrates the way in which each of ten groups of pilgrimage sites is identified with the same male and female bodily parts.

All of the aforementioned classifications of the pilgrimage sites illustrate the Kālacakra tradition's premise that on this tantric path to spiritual awakening, one transforms one's own environment, or more precisely, one's own experience of the environment, by transforming one's own physical constituents.

The Three Realms of Cyclic Existence as the Individual

The *Kālacakratantra*'s earlier mentioned principle, which states that "as it is outside so it is within the body, and as it is within the body so it is elsewhere," also applies to its view of the interconnectedness of human beings with all other sentient beings. The *Kālacakratantra* suggests that one should look at the triple world as similar to space and as unitary.[75] The Kālacakra tradition provides a variety of methods for training the mind to perceive all sentient beings as nondual from oneself. These methods are considered to be applicable at any stage of the *Kālacakratantra* practice, for they reinforce the underlying premise and objective of all *Kālacakratantra* practices, which are the nonduality of all phenomena and its realization.

The Kālacakra tradition points out that all six states of transmigratory existence are already present within every individual. In the *Kālacakratantra*'s view, the origi-

TABLE 5.11 Ten Pilgrimage Sites as Ten Bodily Parts of Men and Women

Ten pilgrimage sites	The individual
pīṭhas	the left sides of a woman's and a man's body
upapīṭhas	the right sides of a woman's and a man's body
kṣetras	the left sense-faculties (*indriya*) of a woman and a man
upakṣetras	the right sense-faculties of a woman and a man
chandohas	the *kūrma*, *kṛkara*, *devadatta*, and *dhanaṃjaya prāṇas* of a woman and a man
upachandohas	the *samāna*, *udāna*, *vyāna*, and *nāga prāṇas* of a woman and a man
melāpakas	the left faculties of action (*karmendriya*) of a woman and a man
upamelāpakas	the right faculties of action (*karmendriya*) of a woman and a man
śmaśānas	a discharge of secretions from the left nostril, etc., of a woman and a man
upaśmaśānas	a discharge of secretions from the right nostril, etc., of a woman and a man

nation of a sentient being within a particular state of existence is directly influenced by one or the combination of the three *guṇas*—*sattva*, *rajas*, or *tamas*. The three *guṇas* of one's mind are, in turn, the direct result of sentient beings' *karma*. Thus, the existence as a god is caused by the *sattva-guṇa*, which, due to wholesome *karma*, gives rise to the peaceful state of mind. Existence as a denizen of hell is caused by *tamas*, which due to unwholesome *karma*, gives rise to the violent state of mind. Existence as an animal is caused by *rajas*, which, due to the medially unwholesome *karma*, gives rise to the passionate state of mind. Finally, existence as a human is characterized by the combination of the three *guṇas*. Similarly, the existences of *asuras* and *pretas* are characterized by a combination of two of the three *guṇas*. Since human existence is caused by a combination of the three *guṇas*, the individual's mental states and experiences are often determined by the prevalence of one of the three *guṇas*. Thus, due to the prevalence of *sattva*, a person experiences happiness; due to the prevalence of *rajas*, one experiences suffering; and due the prevalence of *tamas*, one experiences constant suffering. Because the prevalence of the three *guṇas* tends to alternate throughout one's lifetime, an ordinary person may experience the mental states that characterize all six states of existence.[76] In this way, the individual who mentally experiences different states of existence in a single lifetime already embodies all six states of existence.

TABLE 5.12 Commonalities among Living Beings and the Human Body

Living beings inhabiting the cosmos and their origins	The bodily constituents and sentient beings inhabiting the body
the earth-origin	
stationary beings	the bodily hairs
the wind-origin	
the egg-born beings	lice on the head
the water-origin	
worms and others born from sweat	worms and the like in the body
the womb-origin	
those born from womb and semen	bodily semen
the space-element	
apparitional beings	subtle living beings, living in the body and having the form of an egg

One of the *Kālacakratantra*'s methods of training a tantric practitioner to view all sentient beings as a part of himself is patterned on the fivefold classification of sentient beings, who have five different origins (*yoni*) of birth. The four different classes of beings who originate from the four respective sources—namely, the earth, wind, water, and womb, and the self-arisen, or apparitional beings (*upapāduka*), who arise from the element of space—inhabit both the cosmos and the individual. On this tantric path of developing a nondual vision of the world, one should recognize that one's own body, like the body of the cosmos, is the birthplace for diverse sentient beings and is thereby most intimately connected with diverse forms of life. It is a microcosmic representation of the cosmos and its inhabitants. Table 5.12 exemplifies the way in which the Kālacakra tradition correlates the five types of sentient beings in the natural environment with the constituents of the human body and living organisms that inhabit the body.[77]

Similarly, to realize the nonduality of oneself and the triple world, one must train oneself to view the three realms of the cosmos—the realms of desire, form, and formlessness—as one's own three *vajras*—namely, the body, speech, and mind *vajras*. Only then can one understand that the diverse sentient beings within the three realms of cyclic existence are nondual from one's own mental, verbal, and bodily capacities. Different states of existence are simply the cosmic manifestations of one's own body, speech, and mind, whose sublimated aspects are the body, speech, and mind *maṇḍalas* of the *kālacakra-maṇḍala*.

Tables 5.13.a–b illustrate the specific correspondences among the three realms of cyclic existence and the three *vajras* of the individual and their locations in the bodily *cakras*, as they are explained in this tantric system.

As tables 5.13.a–b demonstrate, the Kālacakra tradition, like other Buddhist systems, classifies the three realms of cyclic existence into thirty-one categories. According to this tantric system, from among these thirty-one categories of cyclic existence, four belong to the formless realm, sixteen to the realm of form, and eleven to the desire-realm. Here again, one encounters some departure from the *Abhidhar-*

TABLE 5.13.A The Realms of Formlessness and Form within the Human Body

The cosmos	The individual
The formless realm (*arūpa-dhātu*)	**The mind-*vajra***
The fourfold Saudharmakalpa	*uṣṇīṣa-cakra*
4. The sphere of neither perception nor nonperception	
3. The sphere of nothing at all	
2. The sphere of limitless consciousness	
1. The sphere of limitless space	
The form-realm (*rūpa-dhātu*)	**The speech-*vajra***
The fourfold Brahmakalpa	the *lalāṭa-cakra*
16. Akaniṣṭha	
15. Sudarśana	
14. Atapa	
13. Avṛha	
The fourfold Brahmalokottarakalpa	the nose
12. Bṛhatphala	
11. Puṇyapravasa	
10. Ānabhra	
9. Śubhakṛtsna	
The fourfold Śrīkalpa	the area beneath the nose up to the chin
8. Apramāṇaśubha	
7. Parīttaśubha	
6. Ābhāsvara	
5. Apramāṇabha	
The fourfold Śvetakalpa	the throat-*cakra*
4. Parītābha	
3. Mahābrahmāṇa	
2. Brahmapurohita	
1. Brahmakāyika	

makośa, according to which, the realm of form contains seventeen types of existence, and the desire-realm is comprised of ten. The Kālacakra tradition omits the class of Sudṛśa gods of the realm-form and adds *asuras* as the eleventh class of beings belonging to the desire-realm. Likewise, the names of the heavens of the realms of form and formlessness differ from those in the *Abhidharmakośa* and accord with some of the names of heavens listed in the Jaina *Tattvārthādhigamasūtra*, Ch. 4, v. 20.

According to the Kālacakra tradition, at the top of the cosmos, above the thirty-one types of cyclic existence, in the crest of Mt. Meru's peak, abides Kālacakra, the indestructible Vajrakāya. He is accompanied by all the Buddhas and surrounded by the guardians of the ten directions.[78] The location of the three realms in the body of the cosmos corresponds to their location in the body of the individual. Below Meru's *uṣṇīṣa*, in the area of its head, there are the four divisions of Saudharmakalpa, a heavenly abode of the formless realm.[79] Those who have developed a meditative concentration (*samādhi*) on the four types of the space-*kṛtsna* are born in the formless

TABLE 5.13.B The Realm of Desire within the Human Body

The cosmos	The individual
The desire-realm (*kāma-dhātu*)	**The body-*vajra***
Six types of gods	the body beneath the throat
6. Paranirmitavaśavartin	
5. Nirmāṇarati	
4. Tuṣita	
3. Yāma	
2. Trāyastriṃśa	
1. Cāturmahārājakāyika	
Asuras	
Humans	
Animals	
Pretas	
Denizens of eight hells	

realm. The four heavens of the form-realm are sequentially located in the regions of Meru's *lalāṭa* and nose, in the area beneath the nose that extends up to the chin, and in the region of Meru's throat. One is born within one of the four divisions of the form-realm by developing a meditative concentration on the respective wind, fire, water, and earth *kṛtsnas* and by the power of ethical discipline (*śīla*). The desire-realm extends from the bottom of Meru's throat to the bottom of the wind-*maṇḍala*. Sentient beings are born as gods of the desire-realm due to the power of generosity (*dāna*) and due to the recitation of *mantras*. The remaining types of existence in the realm of desire are those of *asuras*, humans, animals, *pretas*, and denizens of hells. The existence of *asuras* comes about by the power of generosity. Human existence is due to the power of one's wholesome and unwholesome actions. Animal existence results from lesser sins. The existence of *pretas* is due to the power of middling sins, and the existence of the denizens of hell comes about through the power of the greatest sins.

Tables 5.14.a–b give a schematic presentation of the life spans of the sentient beings in the cyclic existence, as taught in the Kālacakra tradition.[80]

According to this tantric tradition, the life spans of all sentient beings are related to and measured by the number of their breaths. Within the six states of existence, breaths of the different types of sentient beings have different durations. For example, the duration of one breath in the human realm is one solar day for an insect, a duration of thirty human breaths is one breath for a *preta*, one human year is one breath of the gods in the Akaniṣṭha heaven, and a hundred years in the human realm is one breath of the gods in the formless realm. Thus, just as the cosmos is perceived and experienced differently by different sentient beings—relative to their *karma* and state of existence—so too is time a relative phenomenon, experienced differently by different sentient beings.

The Kālacakra tradition considers the age of one hundred years as the full life span of the individual, which can decrease or increase in accordance with the indi-

TABLE 5.14.A The Life Spans of Sentient Beings

The realms of formlessness and form	The duration of life
The formless realm	
The fourfold Saudharmakalpa	
4. The sphere of neither perception nor nonperception	four great eons (*mahā-kalpa*)
3. The sphere of nothing at all	three great eons
2. The sphere of limitless consciousness	two great eons
1. The sphere of limitless space	one great eon
The form-realm	
The fourfold Brahmakalpa	
16. Akaniṣṭha	sixteen eons
15. Sudarśana	fifteen eons
14. Atapa	fourteen eons
13. Avṛha	thirteen eons
The fourfold Brahmalokottarakalpa	
12. Bṛhatphala	twelve eons
11. Puṇyapravasa	eleven eons
10. Ānabhra	ten eons
9. Śubhakṛtsna	nine eons
The fourfold Śrīkalpa	
8. Apramāṇaśubha	eight eons
7. Parīttaśubha	seven eons
6. Ābhāsvara	six eons
5. Apramāṇabha	five eons
The fourfold Śvetakalpa	
4. Parītābha	four eons
3. Mahābrahmāṇa	three eons
2. Brahmapurohita	two eons
1. Brahmakāyika	one eon

vidual's own *karma*. It increases for *yogīs* and ascetics who, by the power of their *yoga* and meditative concentration, extend the duration of a single breath for up to one *ghaṭikā*; and it decreases for evil people due to the power of their sins. Thus, the duration of one's life is directly related to the duration and number of one's breaths, which, in turn, is directly related to one's mental states. As the mind becomes more afflicted and agitated, one's breathing becomes faster, breaths become shorter, and thereby one's life becomes shorter. It is in the form of the breaths, minutes (*pāṇipalas*), *ghaṭikās*, and solar days that death takes its course in the body. As these measures of time gradually increase within the right and left *nāḍīs*, death advances in the body, until the *prāṇa* finally leaves the *nāḍīs*, which dissolve and cause a bodily disintegration.

The notion of the full human life span being one hundred years goes back to the early Brāhmaṇic period. In support of this notion, the *Vimalaprabhā* cites a line from the *Aitareya Brāhmaṇa*, II. 17. 4. 19, which states that a person (*puruṣa*) has a life span of a hundred years.[81] The *Vimalaprabhā* interprets this statement in terms of both its

TABLE 5.14.B The Life Spans of Sentient Beings

The realm of desire	The duration of life
The desire-realm	
Six types of gods	
6. Paranirmitavaśavartin	six short eons
5. Nirmāṇarati	five short eons
4. Tuṣita	four short eons
3. Yāma	three short eons
2. Trāyastriṃśa	two short eons
1. Cāturmahārājakāyika	one short eon
Asuras	
Humans	one hundred years
Animals	
Pretas	
Denizens of the eight hells	
nāgas	one short eon
those in the second and third hells	one medium eon (*madhyama-kalpa*)
those in the fourth and fifth hells	one extended eon (*utkṛṣṭa-kalpa*)
those in the sixth and seventh hells	one great eon
those in the eighth hell	till the dissolution of the cosmos

provisional and definitive meanings. In terms of a provisional meaning, a person has a life span of a hundred years, due to the increase of the human life span during the *kṛta-yuga*. In terms of the definitive meaning, the word "person" (*puruṣa*) designates here every solar day and every year. This implies that with regard to the individual, there are one hundred solar days, and with regard to the cosmos, there are one hundred years. Thus, one year in the individual's environment corresponds to one solar day in the body of the individual, in accordance with the number of the individual's breaths. On the grounds that the individual takes twenty-one thousand and six hundred breaths each solar day, two hundred such solar days in a human body are said to equal 4,320,000 years in the environment, which make up four cosmic *yugas*.[82] Thus, with each round of 4,320,000 breaths, which the individual takes in the course of two hundred solar days, a cycle of four cosmic *yugas* takes place in the body. In this way, all temporal and physical changes that occur in the body of the cosmos have already taken place in the body of the individual.

A goal of the *Kālacakratantra* practice is to transmute these phenomenal bodies of the cosmos and the individual into the transcendent body of the Buddha Kālacakra, into the Vajrasattva, who is the indivisible unity of the three realms of cyclic existence. The process of their transmutation entails their generation in the form of the *kālacakra-maṇḍala* by means of the stage of generation practice and their dissolution by means of the stage of completion practice. At the time of the transformation of the individual's body into the transcendent body of Kālacakra, the constituents of the phenomenal body manifest as the constituents of spiritual awakening. Thus, certain bodily components—bodily hair, skin, flesh, blood, water, bones, marrows, and the like—manifest as the *bodhisattva-bhūmis*. The four great elements of the ordinary body—earth, water, fire, and wind—manifest as the four *brahma-vihāras*—loving kindness (*maitrī*), compassion (*karuṇā*), sympathetic joy (*muditā*), and equanimity (*upekṣā*). The five ordinary pshycho-physical aggregates, accompanied by afflictive and cognitive obscurations, manifest as the five types of unobscured psycho-physical aggregates, or the five types of gnosis—the mirror-like gnosis (*ādarśa-jñāna*), the gnosis of equality (*samatā-jñāna*), the discriminating gnosis (*pratyavekṣana-jñāna*), the accomplishing gnosis (*kṛtyānuṣṭhāna-jñāna*), and the gnosis of the sphere of reality (*dharma-dhātu-jñāna*). When the bodily constituents become free of obscurations and atomic matter, they manifest as the empty form. Although the empty form is endowed with aspects of fire, earth, water, and the like, due to its immateriality, it is neither a fire, nor is it solid or liquid. Likewise, although appearing with various colors, it has no color. It is said to appear like an illusory city.[83] The *Kālacakratantra* states that although the empty form is endowed with all aspects (*sarvākāra*), "foolish people are unable to see it anywhere, due to the power of their mental obscurations, which are sustained by the flow of the *prāṇas* in the right and left *nāḍīs*."[84] Thus, even though the entire universe is ultimately the omnipresent, empty form, it is not perceived as such by those whose perception is obscured by their materiality.

The Wheel of Time, the Individual, and the Wheel of Time as the Individual

In this tantric system, the term "wheel of time" (*kāla-cakra*) designates the dynamic and nondual nature of a single reality that manifests primarily in two ways—the conventional (*saṃvṛti*) and the ultimate (*paramārtha*). The conventional reality itself appears in two ways—the individual (*adhyātma*) and the individual's environment (*bāhya*), the macrocosmic and microcosmic aspects of that single reality. With regard to the external aspect of conventional reality, the term "wheel of time" refers to the passage of days, month, and years in the cycle of time. The *Vimalaprabhā* defines time (*kāla*) as a circle of twelve solar mansions or zodiacs (*rāśi-cakra*).[85] The unit day-and-night (*aho-rātra*) is also called "time."[86]

With regard to the individual, the "wheel of time" denotes a circulation of *prāṇas* within the wheel of the *nāḍīs* in the body. In view of the close interrelatedness of these two aspects of conventional reality, the "wheel of time" also designates a circulation (*cakra*) of twenty-one thousand and six hundred pairs of inhalations and exhalations, which takes place in the course of a day-and-night called "time."

Even though the cosmos ultimately neither arises nor ceases, conventionally, the entire cosmos, with its three worlds, is said to arise and cease due to the power of time. More specifically, this is said to occur due to the union of the time of origination and the time of destruction. It is stated in the *Ādibuddhatantra*:

> Time brings forth phenomena, and time always destroys phenomena, for time is the Bhagavān, *vajrī*, who has the nature of a day and a night.[87]

> In accordance with the classification of the mind, a day is the sun, uterine blood, and vulva; a night is the moon, semen, and male sexual organ. Their union is Kālacakra, the supreme bliss (*mahā-sukha*).[88]

Likewise, the unit day-and-night is interpreted as "time," and a circle of solar mansions (*rāśi-cakra*) is seen as its "wheel." In terms of the individual, the unit day-and-night is also understood as "time"; whereas its "wheel," the circle of solar mansions, is understood as the circle of twelve *nāḍīs* in the navel-*cakra*, which is the seat of the transmigratory mind. This internal circle of twelve zodiacs consists of twenty-one thousand and six hundred pairs of breaths and is characterized by the twelve links of dependent origination. Due to the flow of the wind of *prāṇa* through the twelve internal zodiacs, a human being comes into existence, dies, and is born again. It is in this sense that the Kālacakra tradition views time as the sole cause of the origination and cessation of all living beings.[89]

In all of cyclic existence, the union of "time" and its "wheel" (*kāla-cakra-yoga*) has *nirvāṇa*, or the gnosis-element (*jñāna-dhātu*), as its beginning and the earth-element as its end. In between are the elements of space, wind, fire, and water, which are pervaded by the gnosis-element, or *nirvāṇa*, which itself is without attributes. Thus, the "wheel of time" is the nonduality of the ultimate and conventional realities.

With regard to the ultimate reality, the "wheel of time" indicates the nonduality of two facets of a single reality—namely, wisdom (*prajñā*), or emptiness (*śūnyatā*), and method (*upāya*), or compassion (*karuṇā*). The word "time" refers to the gnosis of imperishable bliss (*akṣara-sukha-jñāna*), which is a method consisting of compassion; and the word "wheel" designates wisdom consisting of emptiness.[90] Their unity is the Buddha Kālacakra.

As the purified aspects of time, emptiness and compassion are the ultimate aspects of the sun and the moon, of a day and a night, and of the dark and bright lunar fortnights (*pakṣa*). Sixteen types of emptiness are the purified aspects of the sixteen lunar days (*tithi*) of a dark lunar fortnight, and sixteen types of compassion are the purified aspects of the sixteen lunar days of a bright lunar fortnight.[91] Their union is Kālacakra.

Tables 5.15 and 5.16 illustrate the manner in which the Kālacakra tradition identifies the sixteen types of emptiness and compassion with sixteen lunar days.

TABLE 5.15 Temporal Aspects of the Sixteen Types of Emptiness

Sixteen types of emptiness	Sixteen lunar days
1. **The five types of emptiness (*śūnyatā*)** the emptiness of the five aggregates (*skandha*)	five lunar days of the dark fortnight, beginning with the first lunar day (*pratipad*)
2. **The five types of great emptiness (*mahā-śūnyatā*)** the emptiness of the five elements (*dhātu*)	five lunar days of the dark fortnight, beginning with the sixth lunar day
3. **The five types of the emptiness of the *Ultimate Reality* (*paramārtha-śūnyatā*)** the emptiness of the five sense-faculties (*indriya*)	five lunar days of the dark fortnight, beginning with the eleventh lunar day (*umā*)
The sixteenth emptiness having all Aspects (*ṣoḍaśī sarvākārā śūnyatā*)	in between the end of the fifteenth lunar day of the dark fortnight and the first lunar day of the bright fortnight

TABLE 5.16 Temporal Aspects of the Sixteen Types of Compassion

Sixteen types of compassion	Sixteen lunar days
Compassion having sentient beings as its object (*sattvāvalambanī karuṇā*)	five lunar days of the bright fortnight, beginning with the first lunar fortnight
Compassion having phenomena as its object (*dharmāvalambanī karuṇā*)	five lunar days of the bright fortnight, beginning with the sixth lunar day
Compassion without an object (*anavalambanī karuṇā*)	five lunar days of the bright fortnight, beginning with the eleventh lunar day
Sixteenth Compassion (*ṣoḍaśī karuṇā*)	in between the last day of the bright lunar fortnight and the first day of the dark lunar fortnight

Resorting to the Madhyamaka's four-point analysis (*catuṣ-koṭi*), the Kālacakra tradition tries to demonstrate that from the ultimate point of view, the Sahajakāya of the Buddhas is neither compassion—a bright lunar fortnight (*śukla-pakṣa*)—nor wisdom—a dark lunar fortnight (*kṛṣṇa-pakṣa*)—nor is it both because of their mutual contradiction, nor is it without the both. Thus, the Sahajakāya is neither female nor male but neuter (*napuṃsaka*). It is the sixteenth digit (*kalā*), which is characterized by emptiness and purified through the four-point analysis.[92]

In terms of the Buddha's mind and body, "time" refers to the Buddha's mind, which is the moment of supreme, indestructible bliss (*paramākṣara-sukha*), in which the moment of perishable bliss, or seminal emission, perishes forever. This moment is the vajra-*gnosis* (*vajra-jñāna*). The "wheel" indicates the Buddha's body, which is brought forth by that supreme bliss and is comprised of the aggregates and elements that are free of the afflictive and cognitive obscurations. This body, which has all aspects and the form of a *bindu*, is the unity of the three worlds, the object of knowledge (*jñeya*).[93] The *Sekoddeśaṭīkā* interptets it in a similar way, stating that the word "time" designates "the supreme, imperishable, moment of nonemission" (*acyuta-kṣaṇa*), which is gnosis; and its "wheel" is the wheel whose psycho-physical aggregates, elements, and sense-bases are free of obscurations. That very wheel is a "sublime *maṇḍala* of the *vajra*-sphere" (*vajra-dhātu-mahā-maṇḍala*), the Bhagavān's body that consists of wisdom and method, that has all aspects and all sense-faculties and holds all illusions.[94]

The Kālacakra tradition also interprets the "wheel of time" as the unity of the Buddha's mind and body, in terms of the nonduality of knowledge (*jñāna*) and the object of knowledge (*jñeya*). "Time" is the supreme indestructible gnosis (*paramākṣara-jñāna*), the supreme bliss, and the cause of the eradication of all afflictive and cognitive obscurations. Its "wheel" is the triple world, which is characterized by innumerable phenomena and is the object of that knowledge.[95]

Similarly, "time" is a supreme, indestructible moment (*paramākṣara-kṣaṇa*) of seminal nonemission, known as the *vajra*-gnosis. This moment of seminal nonemission is sometimes referred to as the indestructible time (*akṣara-kāla*), a termination of attachment (*rāga*), of the time of origination (*utpāda-kāla*), and of the time of cessation (*nirodha-kāla*). Its "wheel"—the unobscured aggregates and elements—is the unity of the three worlds, which is the object of knowledge that is free of obscurations. That very "wheel" is also called "the supreme *maṇḍala* of the *vajra*-sphere" (*vajra-dhātu-mahā-maṇḍala*), which has all aspects, holds all illusions, and is the Buddha's body, which consists of wisdom and compassion.[96]

"Time" is also understood as an image (*mūrti*) of wisdom and compassion, which has the form of conventional reality (*saṃvṛti-rūpin*); and its "wheel" is the emptiness (*śūnyatā*) of that image.[97] As an image, "time" is revered as an incomparable person (*puruṣa*)—omnipresent, free of elaborations (*niṣprapañca*), standing at the far limit (*kūṭa-stha*), and having the ears, nose, mouth, eyes, body, arms, and legs as its "wheel." Yet this Wheel of Time is neither a *puruṣa* nor a *prakṛti*, neither the mind nor the sound, smell, taste, touch, or form. That Kālacakra is the end of sentient beings and their lord. It is the holder of the three worlds, the cause of causes (*kāraṇaṃ kārāṇām*), yet it is not a creator. It is spiritual knowledge (*vidyā*), the highest state of bliss, which is attainable through *yoga*.[98]

In terms of the *Kālacakratantra* practice, the "wheel of time" refers to the integration of the cause, result, and method of actualizing the unified mind, known as Kālacakra. The syllable *kā* designates the cause (*kāraṇa*), which is peace (*śānta*). The syllable *la* signifies the absorption (*laya*) of the unsteady mind (*cala-citta*), indicated by the syllable *ca*, into that peace, which takes place due to the joining of the flows (*krama-bandha*) of drops. The joining of the flows, which is denoted by the syllable *kra*, implies the joining of the flows of the drops of the body, speech, mind, and gnosis by means of innate bliss.[99]

Thus, one can say in conclusion that the "wheel of time" signifies not only the manifestations of the cyclic existence and *nirvāṇa* but their causes as well. In this tantric system, the "wheel of time" represents a single, unified reality that is called by different names: Kālacakra, Vajra-yoga, Ādibuddha ("Primordial Buddha"), Sahajakāya ("Innate Body"), Jñānakāya ("Gnosis-body"), Viśuddhakāya ("Pure Body"), Sahajānanda ("Innate Bliss"), and the like. When this single reality manifests itself in numerous phenomenal forms, it is called cyclic existence. According to the *Vimalaprabhā*'s hermeneutical explanation of the term *kāla-cakra*, conventional reality is a provisional meaning (*neyārtha*) of the term "wheel of time," whereas the ultimate reality is the definitive meaning (*nītārtha*) of the term.

The identification of time with the phenomenal and ultimate realities is neither invented by nor is unique to the Kālacakra tradition. Its precursors can be found already in the Vedas. In the early Vedic texts, the word "time" designated both phenomenal time and supreme being, the source of living beings. For example, the *Atharva Veda* reads: "The mind is in time, the *prāṇa* is in time, and the name is placed in time. . . . Time created living beings. In the beginning, time created Prajāpati."[100] Likewise, some of the aforementioned definitions of the term *kāla-cakra* reveal striking similarities between the *Kālacakratantra*'s interpretation of Kālacakra and the early Brāhmaṇic notion of Prajāpati. Like the *Kālacakratantra*, the Brāhmaṇas speak of Prajāpati as "time," which, by means of days and nights, brings forth and destroys living beings. Like the body of Kālacakra, the body of Prajāpati is a year, consisting of days and nights, the cosmos, and sentient beings.[101] Furthermore, some of the ways in which the *Kālacakratantra* correlates specific bodily parts with the digits of the moon and other temporal phenomena strikingly resemble the correlations given in the Brāhmaṇas.[102] In the *Sekoddeśa* one even encounters a reference to Kālacakra as Prajāpati, the progenitor of all the Buddhas.[103]

Similarly, the *Kālacakratantra*'s notion of the "wheel of time" as manifesting in the form of the temporary, phenomenal world, in which it is characterized by the movement of the sun, and as the timeless, unitary reality, whose form is emptiness, shows some similarity to the Upaniṣadic notion of time. The *Maitrī Upaniṣad* identifies time with the two aspects of Brahma—the embodied and formless, temporary and timeless. The formless, or timeless, aspect of Brahma precedes the sun and is indivisible; but time that is related to the movement of the sun is a temporal aspect of Brahman, which manifests as a year, or Prajāpati, by whose efficacy living beings originate, grow, and perish.[104] Likewise, the earlier cited line from the *Ādibuddhatantra*, which states that time brings forth phenomena and time always destroys phenomena, also resonates with the following line appearing in the *Mahābhārata* and in the *Kūrma Purāṇa*, which reads: "Time creates beings, and time destroys people."[105] Different passages in the *Mahābhārata* and in the *Kūrma* and *Viṣṇu* Purāṇas also speak of time as a conventional phenomenon and as the omnipresent, self-existent, supreme Īśvara, who is without beginning and end, who is the Self (*ātman*) of all.[106] In the *Bhagavadgīta*, Kṛṣṇa speaks of himself as the imperishable time that brings forth the destruction of the worlds.[107] These similarities between the *Kālacakratantra*'s intepretation of the wheel of time and those of the aforementioned works of the Hindu tradition suggest that it is likely that these non-Buddhist interpretations of time inspired to some degree the *Kālacakratantra*'s formulation of the "wheel of time."

Time in the Cosmos and in the Individual

According to this tantric tradition, time in the human realm is externally measured according to the movement of planets and internally according to the number of the individual's breaths.[108] The arrangement and movement of the planets in the sky influence the body of the individual and correlate to the arrangement and flow of the *nāḍīs* in the body. Thus, in accordance with the sun's passages (*saṃkrānti*) through the twelve solar mansions, twelve very subtle *nāḍīs* originate in the navel, which is the seat of the transmigratory mind.[109] Likewise, the sun's passing through the twelve signs of the zodiac in the course of a year correlates with the *prāṇa*'s daily passing through the twelve petals, the internal signs of the zodiac, in the navel-*cakra*.[110]

The manner in which the sun passes through the twelve zodiacs also corresponds to the manner in which the *prāṇa* flows within the twelve *nāḍīs* of the navel. For example, one solar passage occurs in the course of eighteen hundred *daṇḍas*, just as a passage of *prāṇa* within a single petal occurs in the course of eighteen hundred breaths. Likewise, within a single solar passage, the passing of the five *maṇḍalas* takes place, just as within the petal of a single passage of *prāṇa*, there are five localities—the west, north, south, east, and center—where the respective *maṇḍalas* of earth, water, fire, wind, and space flow. Similarly, every single *maṇḍala* within a solar passage passes in the course of three hundred and sixty *daṇḍas*, just as a single passage of *prāṇa* from one *nāḍī* to another takes place in three hundred and sixty exhalations. The cosmic *maṇḍalas* of space and the other elements pass through the uneven solar mansions,[111] just as in the body, the *maṇḍalas* of space and the other elements flow in the left nostril. The cosmic *maṇḍalas* of earth and the other elements pass through the even solar mansions,[112] in the same manner in which the bodily *maṇḍalas* of the earth and the other elements flow in the right nostril. Furthermore, just as in the north, the moon governs Aries, Gemini, Leo, Libra, Sagittarius, and Aquarius, so the element of semen (*bodhicitta-dhātu*) governs the left *nāḍī* in the body of the individual. Likewise, in the south, the sun governs Taurus, Cancer, Virgo, Scorpio, and Capricorn, just as the element of uterine blood (*rajo-dhātu*) governs the right *nāḍī* in the body.[113]

The sun and the moon in the sky and their manifestations in the body of the individual—semen and uterine blood—are equally set in motion by the power of *prāṇas*. Just as the karmic winds of *prāṇas* bring these constituents of the cosmos and the individual into manifestation, so they keep them in motion until the karmic winds of *prāṇas* become exhausted and desert them at the time of dissolution and death.

According to this tantric tradition, the twelve links of dependent origination arise due to the efficacy of the solar passages through the twelve zodiacs and due to the passing of the lunar fortnights (*pakṣa*) and lunar days (*tithi*). In this way, the daily coursing of the sun and the moon in the cosmic body and the daily passing of the *prāṇa* in the right and left *nāḍīs* within the individual's body perpetuate cyclic existence in the world and in the body. Therefore, both the external and internal circles of zodiacs are the temporal causes of transmigratory existence and the temporal manifestations of the twelve links of dependent origination. For this reason, the twelve phases of the stage of completion (*saṃpanna-krama*) practice of the *Kālacakratantra* directly relate to the eradication of the twelve internal and external zodiacs.

In terms of ultimate reality, however, the internal and external circles of zodiacs are the temporal manifestations of the *vajras* of the individual's mind, speech, body, and gnosis, and of the four bodies of the Buddha, which are characterized by the cessation of the twelve links of dependent origination. Therefore, in the course of the *Kālacakratantra* practice, one starts to sublimate the twelve signs of the zodiac by visualizing them as the twelve gates of the *kālacakra-maṇḍala*, as the body of the Buddha Kālacakra, and as his twelve faces.[114]

The internal circle of zodiacs within the navel-*cakra*, which corresponds to the external circle of zodiacs and gives rise to the twelve links of dependent origination in the body, is of the nature of causes and effects. Therefore, time, or transmigratory existence, ceases when these causes and effects cease. There are several ways in which the Kālacakra tradition interprets the twelve zodiacs and twelve links of dependent origination in terms of causes and effects. Table 5.17 illustrates the manner in which this tantric system explains the interdependence of the twelve links of dependent origination and of the twelve zodiacs, starting from Capricorn, the month of conception in the womb. Capricorn is always considered as the month of conception, because after conception, the *prāṇa* begins to move from the *nāḍī* of Capricorn into the navel-*cakra* of the fetus.

Table 5.17 also illustrates the cycle of existence (*saṃsāra-cakra*), in which mental affliction gives rise to *karma*, *karma* gives rise to suffering, and suffering gives rise to mental affliction. Thus, each link of dependent origination is a cause and a result of another link. For this tantric tradition, the very cycle of existence can be seen as

TABLE 5.17 Twelve Zodiacs and Links of Dependent Origination

Twelve zodiacs	Twelve links of dependent origination	Causes and effects
Capricorn	spiritual ignorance (*avidyā*)	mental affliction (*kleśa*)
Aquarius	karmic formations (*saṃskāra*)	*karma*
Pisces	consciousness (*vijñāna*)	suffering (*duḥkha*)
Aries	the mind-and-body (*nāma-rūpa*)	mental affliction
Taurus	six sense bases (*ṣaḍ-āyatana*)	*karma*
Gemini	sensory contact (*sparśa*)	suffering
Cancer	feeling (*vedanā*)	mental affliction
Leo	craving (*tṛṣṇā*)	*karma*
Virgo	grasping onto existence (*upādāna*)	suffering
Libra	becoming (*bhava*)	mental affliction
Scorpio	birth (*jāti*)	*karma*
Sagittarius	old age and death (*jarā-maraṇa*)	suffering

a cause and the entire world as its result. There are no other sentient beings apart from this cycle of transmigratory existence, which consists of causes and effects. Due to the relation between the cause and effect and the cycle of existence, this phenomenal wheel of time ceases when these causes and effects cease.

The Kālacakra tradition's classification of the twelve links of dependent origination into three categories—mental affliction, *karma*, and suffering—goes back to the earlier works of Abhidharma and Mahāyāna.[115] However, the specific links of dependent origination that it includes in those three categories differ from the classifications of the earlier Buddhist systems. For example, in Nāgārjuna's *Pratītysamutpādahṛdayakārikā*,[116] spiritual ignorance (*avidyā*), craving (*tṛṣṇā*), and grasping onto existence (*upādāna*) belong to the category of mental afflictions; karmic formations (*saṃskāra*) and becoming (*bhava*) belong to the category of *karma*; and the remaining seven belong to the category of suffering.

Table 5.18 illustrates yet another manner in which the Kālacakra tradition relates the twelve links of dependent origination to the twelve zodiacs and twelve lunar months. In this particular scheme, the three aforementioned aspects of the twelve links of dependent origination are reduced to two—cause and effect. Thus, the first five links of dependent origination, which correspond to the first five zodiacs and lunar months, are interpreted as the causal phenomena; and the remaining seven are viewed as the resultant phenomena, characterized by suffering.[117] This particular manner of classifying the twelve links of dependent origination into the two categories seems to be specific to the Kālacakra tradition.

Due to the power of this cycle of time within the body and outside the body, the twelve links of dependent origination constantly revolve in the sequence of creation and destruction. The respective links of dependent origination arise and cease not only when the sun enters a zodiac and when the day of a new lunar month begins,

TABLE 5.18 Twelve Zodiacs, Lunar Months, and Links of Dependent Origination

Twelve zodiacs	Twelve lunar months	Twelve links of dependent origination
Capricorn	beginning of Māgha	spiritual ignorance *cause*
Aquarius	beginning of Phālguna	karmic formations *cause*
Pisces	beginning of Caitra	consciousness *cause*
Aries	beginning of Vaiśākha	mind-and-body *cause*
Taurus	beginning of Jyeṣṭha	six sense bases *cause*
Gemini	beginning of Āṣāḍha	sensory contact *effect*
Cancer	beginning of Śrāvaṇa	feelings *effect*
Leo	beginning of Bhādrapada	craving *effect*
Virgo	beginning of Āśvinī	grasping onto existence *effect*
Libra	beginning of Kārttikā	becoming *effect*
Scorpio	beginning of Mārgaśīrṣa	birth *effect*
Sagittarius	beginning of Puṣya	old age and death *effect*

but also with the coming and passing of every lunar day. For example, spiritual ignorance arises on the first lunar day of the month of Puṣya (in the sign of Sagittarius) during the bright lunar fortnight (*śukla-pakṣa*). Karmic formations arise on the second day, and so on. During the bright lunar fortnight, the twelve links of dependent origination arise in the sequence of creation. However, when spiritual ignorance arises on the first lunar day of the dark lunar fortnight (*kṛṣṇa-pakṣa*), then the twelfth link arises on the second day, and so on. Thus, during the dark lunar fortnight, the twelve links of dependent origination arise in the sequence of destruction. As during the month of Puṣya, the twelve links of dependent origination arise first in the sequence of creation and then in the sequence of destruction; and this is due to the classification on the bright and dark lunar fortnights. Therefore, within the following month of Māgha, they arise first in the sequence of destruction, starting with the second link, the karmic formations, and ending with spiritual ignorance as the twelfth. The sequences of their arising alternate with each lunar month. In this way, due to the efficacy of the bright and dark lunar fortnights, a full cycle of origination and destruction takes place in a single lunar month. Thus, a cycle of the twelve links of dependent origination of a solar year contains the twenty-four shorter cycles of dependent origination of the twelve lunar months. When the twelve links of a solar cycle of dependent origination are added to the twenty-four links of a lunar cycle of dependent origination, they make up thirty-six links of dependent origination, which correspond to the thirty-six *padas* ("stations") of the sun and the moon in the sky and of the semen and uterine blood in the body of the individual. Likewise, if one multiplies the twenty-four lunar cycles of dependent origination by the twelve links of a single solar cycle of dependent origination, one gets the number that corresponds to the two hundred and eighty-eight *padas* of the sun and the moon, which are obtained by the multiplication of their thirty-six *padas* by the eight watches of the day (*prahara*).

Similarly, every single day, the eight watches of the day and the four junctures (*sandhyā*) of the day make up together the twelve links of dependent origination, the twelve microcosmic zodiacs. In the body of the individual, each of these twelve links has eighteen hundred flows of *prāṇa*, just as outside the body, each link of dependent origination has eighteen hundred *daṇḍas* in the course of a lunar month. In this way, just as one solar year consists of three hundred and sixty days, so one lunar cycle of dependent origination consists of three hundred and sixty daily cycles of dependent origination. Likewise, every two links of dependent origination make up a season (*ṛtu*), consisting of two months, which has thirty-six hundred flows of *prāṇas* in the body and thirty-six hundred *daṇḍas* outside the body. In this way, the six seasons of a year also make up the twelve links of dependent origination.[118]

Thus, in the cosmic body and in the body of the individual, the multiple shorter cycles of dependent origination make up the successively larger cycles of dependent origination, in accordance with the division of a solar year into the smaller units of time. This implies that each cycle of dependent origination, which comprises progressively smaller cycles of dependent origination, arises in dependence upon other cycles of dependent origination and is therefore itself empty of inherent existence. This implies further that even within one lifetime, the individual is nothing other than the embodiment of the multiple cycles of dependent origination. Likewise, this analysis of time in terms of the successively smaller cycles of dependent origination suggests that time itself is not an inherently existent phenomenon, since there is nothing within the cycle of time that can be established as its ontological basis. In this manner, the *Kālacakratantra* supports the Nāgārjuna's position on time, presented in the nineteenth chapter of the *Mūlamadhyamakakārikā*, which argues that time is not an independent, inherently existent phenomenon but a dependent set of temporal relations.

This analysis also suggests that the individual is merely a cycle of transmigration (*saṃsāra-cakra*), a wheel of time manifesting in human form. The Kālacakra tradition affirms that apart from this phenomenal wheel of time, there is no other sentient being.[119] This assertion reminds one of Nāgārjuna's *Bodhicittavivaraṇa*, v. 60, which states that there is no other sentient being apart from the twelve-spoked wheel, which rolls along the path of cyclic existence.[120] This is a way in which the Kālacakra tradition analyzes the emptiness of the inherent existence of the phenomena existing in time. By means of such analysis, it tries to demonstrate that since it is a wheel of time, the body of the individual and personal identitylessness (*pudgala-nairātmya*) are mutually pervasive and nondual. This is one of the *Kālacakratantra*'s unique ways of interpreting the early Madhyamaka's reconciliation of the traditional Buddhist theory of the twelve-limbed dependent origination with the doctrine of emptiness, as found in

TABLE 5.19 Units of Time and the Individual

Time	The individual
360 solar days (21,600 *ghaṭikās*)	360 *nāḍīs* of the 360 joints
30 lunar days (*tithi*)	30 *nāḍīs* of the 30 joints of the fingers
15 lunar days of a bright fortnight (*śukla-pakṣa*)	15 *nāḍīs* of the 15 joints of the fingers of the left hand, starting with the small finger and ending with the thumb, due to the classification of space and other elements
15 lunar days of a dark fortnight (*kṛṣṇa-pakṣa*)	15 *nāḍīs* of the 15 joints of the fingers of the right hand, starting with the thumb and ending with the little finger, due to the classification of the earth and other elements
16 digits (*kalā*) of the moon	**16 bodily constituents**
the first	fine hair
the second	long hair
the third	skin
the fourth	skin
the fifth	blood
the sixth	blood
the seventh	flesh
the eighth	flesh
the ninth	*nāḍīs*
the tenth	*nāḍīs*
the eleventh	bones
the twelfth	bones
the thirteenth	marrow
the fourteenth	marrow
the fifteenth	semen
the sixteenth	semen

Nāgārjuna's *Mūlamadhyamakakārikā*[121] and *Pratītyasamutpādahṛdayakārikā*. Identifying phenomenal existence with emptiness, the Kālacakra tradition also affirms the old Mahāyāna assertion stated in the *Prajñāpāramitāhṛdayasūtra* that form is emptiness and emptiness is form.

The Kālacakra tradition presents the human body as a wheel of time in a variety of ways. Table 5.19 demonstrates the manner in which this tantric tradition identifies the solar and lunar days and the digits (*kalā*) of the moon with the specific *nāḍīs* of the individual's body.

Tables 5.20.a–b illustrate the manner in which this tantric system sees the *nāḍīs* of the six bodily *cakras* as the inner supports, or seats, of the wheel of time.

The wheel of time that is embodied in the individual is stirred by the ten winds of *prāṇas* in sixteen hundred and twenty bodily *nāḍīs*, called "the *nāḍīs* of the wheel of time." As table 5.21 indicates, the *nāḍīs* of the wheel of time are one hundred and sixty-two *nāḍīs*, which are of ten kinds due to the circulation of the ten kinds of *prāṇas* in each *nāḍī*.[122]

These *nāḍīs* of the wheel of time bring death to ordinary people, for in the course

TABLE 5.20.A Locations of the Inner Padas of the Moon and Constellations

Fourteen padas of the moon	The *lalāṭa*
the *pada* consisting of 5 *ghaṭikās*	in the first, second, and third *nāḍīs*
the *pada* consisting of 4 *ghaṭikās*	in the fourth *nāḍī*
the *pada* consisting of 3 *ghaṭikās*	in the fifth *nāḍī*
the *pada* consisting of 2 *ghaṭikās*	in the sixth *nāḍī*
the *pada* consisting of 1 *ghaṭikās*	in the seventh and eighth *nāḍīs*
the *pada* consisting of 2 *ghaṭikās*	in the ninth *nāḍī*
the *pada* consisting of 3 *ghaṭikās*	in the tenth *nāḍī*
the *pada* consisting of 4 *ghaṭikās*	in the eleventh *nāḍī*
the *pada* consisting of 5 *ghaṭikās*	in the twelfth, thirteenth, and fourteenth *nāḍīs*
nothing	in the fifteenth and sixteenth *nāḍīs*
Constellations	**The throat-*cakra***
twenty-eight constellations	in twenty-eight *nāḍīs*
nothing	in the remaining 4 *nāḍīs*

of time they become disturbed by the elements of phlegm (*kapha*), bile (*pitta*), and wind (*vāta*).[123] However, they are said to give bliss to those *yogīs* who meditate upon them as the *nāḍīs* of the Buddha Kālacakra—the deities of the *kālacakra-maṇḍala*—and who protect them in the body by means of the six-phased *yoga* (*ṣaḍ-aṅga-yoga*).

Since the transmigratory wheel of time is nondual from the body of the cosmos and the body of the individual, it is of the nature of the elements and their modifications. For example, Capricorn is of the nature of the space-element and the aggregate of consciousness (*vijñāna-skandha*): Aquarius is of the nature of the wind-element and the aggregate of mental factors (*saṃskāra-skandha*); Pisces is of the nature of the fire-element and the aggregate of feelings (*vedanā-skandha*); Aries is of the na-

TABLE 5.20.B Locations of the Inner Days, Ghaṭikās, and Digits of the Moon

Days of the week	The Heart-*cakra*
Sunday	in the eastern *nāḍī*
Monday	in the southeastern *nāḍī*
Tuesday	in the southern *nāḍī*
Wednesday	in the southwestern *nāḍī*
Thursday	in the western *nāḍī*
Friday	in the northwestern *nāḍī*
Saturday	in the northern *nāḍī*
the day of Ketu's and Rāhu's passing through *kulikā*	in the northeastern *nāḍī*
Ghaṭikās	**The navel-*cakra***
60 *ghaṭikās*	in 60 *nāḍīs*
nothing	in the remaining 4 *nāḍīs*
Digits of the Moon	**The secret-*cakra***
16 digits of the bright lunar fortnight	in 32 *nāḍīs*
16 digits of the dark lunar fortnight	

TABLE 5.21 Inner Conveyers of the Wheel of Time

Nāḍīs of the Wheel of Time (*kāla-cakra*)
162 *nāḍīs* of the six *cakras*
1. 4 *nāḍīs* in the *uṣṇīṣa*, which carry the 4 junctures of the day
2. 16 *nāḍīs* in the *lalāṭa*, which carry 16 lunar days
3. 32 *nāḍīs* in the throat-*cakra*, which carry 28 constellations and 4 *daṇḍas*
4. 8 *nāḍīs* of the heart-*cakra*, which carry the 8 watches of the day
5. 64 *nāḍīs* of the navel-*cakra*, which carry 54 *daṇḍas*
6. 32 *nāḍīs* of the secret *cakra*, which carry 32 elements
7. **6 other *nāḍīs***
lalanā, *rasanā*, *avadhūti*, and the three *nāḍīs* carrying feces, urine, and semen

ture of the water-element and the aggregate of discernment (*saṃjñā-skandha*); Taurus is of the nature of the earth-element and the aggregate of form (*rūpa-skandha*); Gemini is of the nature of the gnosis-element and the aggregate of gnosis (*jñāna-skandha*); and the remaining six zodiacs, beginning with Cancer, are of the same nature as the aforementioned six but in reverse order.[124]

Likewise, the classification of the units of time is due to the efficacy of the six elements. For example, as in the case of the aforementioned six solar mansions, the classification of six months is due to the classification of the six elements, the six seasons alternating in accordance with the nature of the six elements. Among three seasons of six months, the first season is characterized by *sattva*, the second by *rajas*, and the third by *tamas*.[125] Similarly, the following threefold classification in which a lunar fortnight is of the nature of *sattva*, a lunar month is of the nature of *rajas*, and a season is of the nature of *tamas*, is due to the classification of the three *guṇas*.[126]

Thus, in terms of conventional reality, wherever there is corporeality there is time, for everything material, which is characterized by the origination and cessation, is temporary. Therefore, a goal of *Kālacakratantra* practice is to transform this corporeal wheel of time into the transcendent wheel of time, which is devoid of matter and free of origination and cessation. When the locally embodied and temporary wheel of time becomes the omnipresent and everlasting wheel of time, it is called the Buddha Kālacakra, the unity of emptiness and bliss.

The actualization of the transcendent wheel of time is charaterized by the transformation of the twelve zodiacs into the twelve *bodhisattva-bhūmis*. Likewise, at the time of this transformation, the thirty-two digits of the moon manifest as the thirty-two marks of a Great Man (*mahā-puruṣa*). Similarly, the moon becomes the supreme mind (*mahā-citta*) of the Buddha, and the last of its sixteen digits becomes the supreme emptiness (*mahā-śūnyatā*), the supreme body (*mahā-kāya*) of the Buddha. This sixteenth digit of the moon, or the supreme emptiness, comes at the end of the bright lunar fortnight, which is passion, or attachment (*rāga*); and it comes at the beginning of the dark lunar fortnight, which is dispassion, or detachment (*arāga*). Thus, the supreme emptiness of enlightened awareness is the cessation of the phenomenal aspects of the bright and dark lunar fortnights. It is the heart of all the Tathāgatas in the same way that personal identitylessness is the heart of dependent origination. This is the manner in which the Kālacakra tradition explains, in terms of the cessation of phenomenal time and its causes, its definition of Buddhahood as the mind that has emptiness as its form (*śūnyatā-bimba-citta*) and transcends both attachment and detachment. Likewise, by transforming the atomic nature of the five elements that constitute the internal moon, sun, and Rāhu into the nature of gnosis, one transforms these heavenly bodies within oneself and outside oneself into the different types of gnosis, or into the aggregates that are free of obscurations (*nirāvaraṇa-skandha*). The moon in the sky, or semen in the body, becomes the Buddha's mirror-like gnosis (*ādarśa-jñāna*), the unobscured form-aggregate (*rūpa-skandha*), or Vairocana. The sun in the sky, or uterine blood in the body, becomes the gnosis of equality (*samatā-jñāna*), the unobscured aggregate of feeling, or Ratnasaṃbhava. Rāhu in the sky, or consciousness in the body, becomes the discriminating gnosis (*pratyavekṣaṇa-jñāna*), the unobscured aggregate of discernment, or Amitābha. The unification of these three in the wind of *prāṇa* becomes the accomplishing gnosis (*kṛtyānuṣṭhāna-jñāna*), the unobscured aggregate of mental formations, or Amoghasiddhi. When consciousness becomes endowed with all the components of these four members, it transforms into the gnosis of the sphere of reality (*dharma-dhātu-jñāna*), the unobscured aggregate of consciousness, or Akṣobhya. Thus, due to the purification of afflictive and cognitive obscurations, which are stored in subtle atomic particles, the phenomenal wheel of time, which is characterized by the twelve limbs of dependent origination, manifests as the transcendent wheel of time, which is characterized by the twelve *bodhisattva-bhūmis*.

This transcendent wheel of time knows itself to be devoid of the past and future, and yet it sees the past and future.[127] Perceiving that time is empty of inherent existence, it knows itself to be of empty nature (*śūnya-svabhāva*).

Appendix

Table A.1 outlines yet another way of seeing the correspondences among the ten pilgrimage sites and the human limbs, joints, and nails.[1]

TABLE A.1 Pilgrimage Sites in the Human Body

Pilgrimage sites	The individual
pīṭha	the left arm
upapīṭha	the right arm
kṣetras	the joint of the left upper arm and the joint of the left thigh
upakṣetras	the joint of the right upper arm and the joint of the right thigh
chandohas	the joint of the left forearm and the joint of the left knee
upachandohas	the joint of the right forearm and the joint of the right knee
melāpakas	the joints of the left hand and the left foot
upamelāpakas	the joints of the right hand and the right foot
śmaśānas	the nails of the left fingers and toes
upaśmaśānas	the nails of the right fingers and toes

In the schema presented in table A.2, the twenty-four pilgrimage sites, grouped into ten main categories and subdivided into the groups of two and four, correspond to the joints in the body of the individual.[2]

TABLE A.2 Pilgrimage Sites and the Bodily Joints

Pilgrimage sites	The individual
two *kṣetras*	two joints of the upper arms
two *upakṣetras*	two joints of the thighs
two *chandohas*	two joints of the lower arms
two *upachandohas*	two joints of the knees
two *melāpakas*	two joints of the wrist
two *upamelāpakas*	two joints of the feet
two *śmaśānas*	two joints of the palms of the hands
two *upaśmaśānas*	two joints of the soles of the feet
four *mahāśmaśānas*	the joints of the two thumbs
four *upamahāśmaśānas*	the joints of the two big toes

Table A.3 illustrates the Kālacakra tradition's interpretation of different heavenly lights in terms of the *nāḍīs* in the body of the individual and in terms of the different types of gnosis (*jñāna*).

TABLE A.3 Heavenly Lights and the Nāḍīs in the Body

The universe	The individual
The white light in the north	the left *nāḍī* (*lalanā*)
Rāhu	
the moon	
Mercury	
Venus	
Ketu	
rain	
water	
The red light in the south	the red *nāḍī* (*rasanā*)
Kālāgni	
the sun	
Mars	
Jupiter	
Saturn	
lightening	
fire	
The yellow light in the west	the yellow *nāḍī* of the flow of feces
dim stars	*udāna-prāṇa*
bright stars	*nāga-prāṇa*
rainbow	*kṛkara-prāṇa*
earth of two types: soil and stone	
The green light above	*prāṇa* in the *nāḍī* of consciousness (*vijñāna-nāḍī*)
The blue light below	*apāna* in the *nāḍī* of gnosis (*jñāna-nāḍī*)
The black light in the east	*samāna-prāṇa*
	vyāna-prāṇa
	kūrma-prāṇa
	devadatta-prāṇa
	dhanaṃjaya-prāṇa

Table A.4 shows the manner in which the Kālacakra tradition sees the correspondences among the ten planets and the individual's bodily apertures.

TABLE A.4 Planets and the Bodily Apertures

Ten planets	Ten bodily apertures
Moon	the aperture of the anus
Sun	the urinary aperture
Kālāgni	the aperture for semen
Rāhu	the aperture of the mouth
Mars	the aperture of the right eye
Mercury	the aperture of the left eye
Jupiter	the aperture of the right nostril
Venus	the aperture of the left nostril
Saturn	the aperture of the right ear
Ketu	the aperture of the left ear

Table A.5 demonstrates the Kālacakra tradition's interpretation of stellar constellations as macrocosmic correlates of the individual's teeth.

TABLE A.5 Constellations and the Individual's Teeth

Constellations	The individual
28 constellations (*nakṣatra*), Abhijit constellation, and 4 *daṇḍa* constellations located at the four corners of the *śālāka* constellations	32 teeth

Table A.5a illustrates the Kālacakra tradition's identification of the meteorological phenomena with the body of the individual.

TABLE A.5A Meteorological Phenomena within the Human Body

Meteorological phenomena	The individual
rain	saliva
clouds	intestines
thunder	heartbeat and intestinal rumbling
rainbow	excrement

In table A.6 the three realms of transmigratory existence are seen as corresponding to the three types of bodily extremities.

TABLE A.6 The Three Realms and the Bodily Extremities

The universe	The individual
heavenly world	the head and the throat
the world of mortals	the arms
the underworld	the legs

The correspondences between time in the individual's body and time outside the body are the following:
1 fortnight = 900 breaths
24 fortnights of a year = 21,600 breaths, making up a solar day
1 period (*yuga-samaya*)[3] = 5,400 breaths
four periods of a year = 21,600 breaths/a solar day
1 time (*kāla*) = 7,200 breaths
three times of a year = 21,600 breaths/a solar day
1 half a year = 10,800 breaths
2 halves of a year = 21,600 breaths/a solar day
1 day and a night (*ahorātra*) = 60 breaths
360 days and nights of a year = 21,600 breaths/a solar day
1 *lagna* = 5 breaths
4,320 *lagnas* of a year = 21,600 breaths/a solar day

6

The Social Body

The Individual and Society

The *Kālacakratantra*'s views of the individual's place in society and of the individual as society are closely interrelated. These provide a sociological framework for the traditional interpretation of the *Kālacakratantra*'s history, and for its eschatology and soteriology. The Kālacakra tradition's interpretation of social relations and its sharp criticism of caste divisions and social bias have multiple goals and practical applications. Some of them are unique to the Kālacakra tradition, and some are characteristic of all Indian Buddhist systems. From its very inception, Indian Buddhism prided itself on its inclusiveness of all social classes and ethnic groups. Throughout its history, it criticized the Brāhmaṇical views of the divine origin of the four castes (*varṇa*) and the hereditary nature of their moral and spiritual qualities. It censured the Brāhmaṇical insistence on the preservation of the hierarchy of the caste system and the Brāhmaṇic position on the soteriological implications of one's social status and relations.[1] Even though Indian Buddhist communities at times fell short of Buddhist social ideals, Buddhist scriptures continually emphasized the provisional nature of social differences, the lack of any inherent, moral qualities of any social class or ethnic group, and the equal qualifications of all social classes for venturing onto the Buddhist path of spiritual maturation and awakening.

Buddhist scriptures often refer to the populace as the intended audience of Buddhist teachings. The early Pāli literature depicts Buddha Śākyamuni as turning the Wheel of Dharma for the benefit and happiness of the multitudes of people (*bahu-jana-hita, bahu-jana-sukha*); and later Mahāyāna works portray the Buddhas and Bodhisattvas as those who teach the Dharma for the well-being of all sentient beings (*sarva-sattvārtha*). Among the renowned male and female Arhats, Bodhisattvas, and Siddhas, many are said to have been born into families of barbers, fishermen, cowherds, hunters, courtesans, and outcasts. In one of the earliest Buddhist texts, the *Suttanipāta*, the Buddha teaches that human beings cannot be divided into different species as are animals and plants. Rather, their differences are determined only by convention. Diverse social classes (*jāti*) exist by mere designation. Since there is no real difference among social classes, one cannot speak of the four castes.[2] Consequently, the moral superiority of the individual does not lie in the caste, clan, or family into which one is born but in the individual's spiritual achievements—specifically, in freedom from mental afflictions (*kleśa*) and in ethical conduct (*śīla*). According to the *Vāseṭṭha Sutta*, the Buddha Śākyamuni stated the following:

> I do not call a man a Brahmin because of his mother or because of his breeding. Just because a man is entitled to be called "Sir," it does not mean that he is free from habit and attachment. He who is free from attachment and he who is free from grasping is the person I call a Brahmin.
>
> When all the chains are shattered, when there is no more agitation, and a man has freed himself and thrown off his shackles—that is the person I call a Brahmin.[3]

According to the *Theragāthā*, the Buddha said similar words to Sunīta, an outcast, who was said to be revered by Indra and Brahmā after attaining Arhatship.

> By austerity, by living the religious life, by self-restraint and self-taming, by this one becomes a Brāhmaṇa; this is the supreme state of being a Brāhmaṇa.[4]

The *Majjhimanikāyāṭṭhakathā* distinguishes two types of sons of a noble family—one who is a son of a noble family by birth (*jāti-kula-putta*), referring to one who is born into the family of an upper social class, and the other who is a son of a noble family by conduct (*ācāra-kula-putta*), referring to a Buddhist monk. Thus, the early Buddhists attempted to transcend class discrimination in their communities by creating a socially integrated, monastic community.

In the early Buddhist canonical texts, the terms *gotra* and *kula*, meaning "family, clan, or lineage," have often been used as synonyms for a Buddhist spiritual family or lineage. In the context of Mahāyāna, the term *kula* remained a general term designating a community of Mahāyāna practitioners, and the term *gotra* assumed an additional, technical meaning, specifying one's spiritual disposition or inclination. Indian Buddhist *tantras*, on the other hand, conflated and expanded the meanings of these two terms beyond their meanings in the Mahāyāna scriptures. The difference in the interpretations of these two terms is explained by the fact that different theoretical and practical implications were attributed to the notion of a spiritual family or lineage by different Buddhist traditions and schools. Even though the interpretative differences are obvious, they are historically related in the sense that the later interpretations are formulated on the basis of the earlier ones.

In early Buddhism, the Pali terms *gotta* and *kula* primarily signified a Buddhist monastic community of the spiritual heirs of the Buddha and secondarily a Buddhist lay community. A monastic community unified through social integration and shared beliefs, spiritual goals, and practices was seen as an ideal type of family. According to the *Mahāvagga* of the *Aṅguttara Nikāya* (XIX. 14), the Buddha taught that those who left home for homelessness in the Buddhist Dharma and monastic discipline (*vinaya*) renounced their former lineages (*nāma-gotta*) and became members of the integrated, Buddhist monastic family. The text expresses this point as follows:

Monks, just as great rivers—namely, Gaṅgā, Yamunā, Aciravatī, Sarabhū, and Mahī—descending into the great ocean, lose their former names and are called the great ocean, so, monks, these four castes—Kṣatriyas, Brāhmaṇas, Vaiśyas, and Śūdras—having gone from home to homelessness in the Dharma and monastic discipline, which are taught by the Tathāgata, renounce their former lineages and are called the wandering ascetics (*samaṇa*) belonging to the son of Śakyas.[5]

Likewise, in the *Aggañña Sutta* of the *Dīgha Nikāya* (III. 84. 9), the Buddha asserts that a monk who has firmly rooted and unshakable faith in the Tathāgata can truly call himself "a Son of the Bhagavān, who is born of his mouth, born of Dharma, generated by Dharma, and who is an heir of Dharma, since the Tathāgata is the Body of Dharma." This formula is undoubtedly modeled on the example of the Brāhmaṇic claim to the moral and spiritual superiority of the Brahmin caste, cited by the Buddha in the *Madhurā Sutta* of the *Majjhima Nikāya*, which reads: "Master Kaccanā, the Brāhmaṇas say thus: '. . .Brāhmaṇas alone are the sons of Brahmā, the offspring of Brahmā, born of his mouth, born of Brahmā, created by Brahmā, heirs of Brahmā.'"[6]

Early Pāli texts indicate that even a person who has not yet become a Stream-enterer but is endowed with the conditions conducive to stream-entry becomes of the lineage (*gotta-bhū*) of Āryas, thereby surpassing the inferior lineage of ordinary people (*puthuj-jana*).[7] Even though he is lacking experiential insight (*dassana*) and full confidence (*saddhā*) in the Buddha's teachings, by becoming disillusioned with the world of desires and by aspiring for *nibbāna*, a person becomes of the lineage of Āryas and thereby becomes capable of clearly discerning the first Noble Truth.[8] Thus, according to the early Buddhist scriptures, a Buddhist spiritual family includes two main categories of individuals: (1) those endowed with spiritual accomplishments such as experiential insight into the Four Noble Truths and freedom from mental afflictions, and (2) those showing *potential* for attaining those accomplishments.

These early Buddhist notions of a spiritual family are the precursors to later Mahāyāna theories of the Buddha-family. Some Indian Mahāyāna authors continued to advocate a social integration of the Buddhist spiritual family, and to some degree, they extended this social ideal to Buddhist lay communities as well. Following the example of the earlier *Suttanipāta*, they denied any significant differences among social classes and explained social class as mere designation (*saṃjñā-mātram*), or convention (*vyavahāra*). Reinterpreting the Vedic *Puruṣasūkta* in their rejection of the traditional Brāhmaṇic interpretations of the origin of the four castes, they claimed that in this world there is only one, universal social group (*sāmānya-jāti*), since human beings do not differ among themselves as do different species of animals and plants.[9] The *Śārdulakarṇāvadāna* asserts the unity of all social classes, declaring: "this all is one, and one is this all."[10] It tries to demonstrate that the Brāhmaṇic account of the origination of the four social classes from the four different parts of Brahmā's body does not justify social discrimination but proves instead that all the members of Indian society are of the same class and value by birth, since they all originate from the same source. The text argues this point, stating: "Since Brahmā is one, therefore his progeny belongs only to one social class (*jāti*)."[11] It supports this argument by affirming that if all the members of one social class originated from the same part of the Brahmā's body, then:

Your sister would be your wife, and that is not appropriate for a Brāhmaṇa.

> If this world was first generated by Brahmā himself, then a Brāhmaṇī is a Brāhmaṇa's sister, a Kṣatriyā is a Kṣatriya's sister, a Vaiśyā is a Vaiśya's [sister], and a Śūdrā is a Śūdra's [sister].

> A sister is not suitable to be a wife, if she is generated by Brahmā. Sentient beings are not generated by Brahmā but are generated by their mental afflictions and *karma*.[12]

Aśvaghoṣa, a renowned Mahāyāna scholar and poet belonging to approximately the same period as the *Śārdulkarṇāvadāna*, poses a similar argument in his *Vajrasūci*. Basing his arguments on the authority of the Vedas and Smṛtis, Aśvaghoṣa argues that neither the soul (*jīva*) nor the body make up a Brāhmaṇa. The soul is not a Brāhmaṇa because the gods Sūrya, Soma, and Indra were once animals. If the body were a Brāhmaṇa, then Kṣatriyas, Vaiśyas, and Śūdras, who are born from the Brahmā's body would also be Brāhmaṇas. Aśvaghoṣa argues along the same lines as the *Suttanipāta* that human beings are not of different classes, or species, just as the four sons of the same father cannot be of different races and just as fruits of the same tree cannot be of different species.[13] He states this in the following manner:

> Some fruits of an *udumbara* or a *paṇasa* [tree] grow on the branches, some on the trunk, some at the branching parts of the stem, and some on the edges. There is no difference among them as, "this is a Brāhamaṇa fruit, this is a Kṣatriya fruit, this is a Vaiśya fruit, and this is a Śūdra fruit," because they have grown on the same tree. In the same way, there is no difference among human beings as well, because they have originated from the same Man (*puruṣa*).[14]

Like the *Śārdulakarṇāvadāna*, Aśvaghoṣa's *Vajrasūci* points to the following fault of the Brāhmaṇic postulation of the origin of class division:

> If a Brāhmaṇa is born from the mouth [of Brahmā], wherefrom is a Brāhmaṇī born? If she is born from the same mouth, alas, then you are having intercourse with your sisters! Thus, you do not consider what is appropriate or inappropriate sexual intercourse, and this is extremely repugnant to the world.[15]

Although the Mahāyāna tradition advocated the equality of all social classes and their solidarity, the new Mahāyāna ideal of a Buddhist spiritual family became that of the Mahāyāna monastic and lay communities. Only those who ascended to the Mahāyāna Vehicle (*mahāyāne ārudha*) by generating the spirit of awakening (*bodhicitta*) are referred to as the sons and daughters of the noble family (*kula-putra* or *kula-duhitṛ*). Likewise, the epithets Jinaputra ("a son of the Jina") and Sugatasuta ("a child of the Sugata") apply to those who, in the words of Nāgārjuna, "drink the elixir of emptiness for themselves and others" and "who burnt the fuel of mental afflictions with the cognitive fire of emptiness (*śūnyatā-jñānāgni*)."[16] The spirit of awakening (*bodhicitta*), "the seed of all the qualities of the Buddhas,"[17] became a necessary qualification for spiritual birth into the family of the perfectly awakened Buddha (*samyaksaṃbuddha-kula*).[18] Citing the *Ratnakāraṇḍasūtra* in his *Śikṣāsamuccaya*, Śāntideva asserts that even an ordinary person (*pṛthag-jana*) may be a Bodhisattva.[19] He substantiates this assertion on the basis of the view expressed in the

Vimalakīrtinirdéśa that the spirit of awakening can arise even in a person whose belief in the true existence of the personality (*satkāya-dṛṣṭi*) is as massive as Mt. Sumeru. Thus, a prerequisite for the arising of the spirit of awakening is not one's philosophical orientation, but one's ability to be inspired and incited to generate the spirit of awakening. As the *Dharmadaśakasūtra* points out, this particular ability is the *bodhisattva-gotra*, or one's predilection for the Bodhisattva path.[20] While some Mahāyāna authors differentiated five types of *gotras*,[21] others identified *gotra* with the *dharmadhātu* and argued against its divisibility, affirming its beginningless and endless existence in all sentient beings without exception.[22] However, according to the *Kālacakratantra*, it is one who retains his semen (*bodhicitta*) by the power of meditative concentration (*samādhi*) that becomes a Bodhisattva born into the family of the Jinas.[23] The *Vimalaprabhā* comments that by being born into the family of the Jina in this way, one increases the lineage of the Sugatas. For this very reason, Māras, Rākṣasas, and other demons steal the emitted semen from those who are not well concentrated and devour it on a daily basis.

The holders of the Kālacakra tradition in India further developed the earlier Buddhist precursory notions of a socially integrated and inherently unified spiritual family and attributed to them new practical applications and soteriological implications. The *vajra*-family emerged as a new model of an ideal spiritual family. The phrase "*vajra*-family," which may be interpreted here as an "indestructible or indivisible family" (the word "*vajra*" meaning "indestructible, indivisible"), has diverse connotations and implications. First, it denotes a community of individuals initiated into the same Vajrayāna tradition, a community that is indivisible and indestructible by virtue of its spiritual, social, and ethnic integration. As will be demonstrated later, in the context of the *Kālacakratantra* tradition, the emergence of this kind of *vajra*-family has socio-political and soteriological significance. Second, the "*vajra*-family" designates the family of Bodhisattvas who by means of tantric practices have become *vajra*-sons (*vajra-putra*), born into the family of Vajrasattva, or Kālacakra, and who are endowed with an insignificant degree of obscurations (*āvaraṇa*) regarding their spirit of awakening (*bodhicitta*).[24]

The aforementioned arguments of the earlier Buddhist systems against Brāhmaṇic social discrimination were also incorporated into the social theory of the Buddhist *tantras*. There is no doubt that those arguments circulated among the Indian Buddhist communities for centuries, since they also reoccur in the Kālacakra tradition. Even though the Kālacakra tradition reiterates those arguments, setting them in the context of Buddhist tantric social theory and practice, it gives them a uniquely tantric application, which will be discussed later in this chapter. The following passage from the *Vimalaprabhā* illustrates the Kālacakra tradition's criticism of the Brāhmaṇic social theory and demonstrates the strong influence of the earlier Buddhist social critiques on this tantric system.

> They say here that Brahmā's mouth is the source of Brāhmaṇas, because they originated from there. Likewise, his two arms are the birthplace of Kṣatriyas . . . his two thighs are the birthplace of Vaiśyas, and his two feet are the birthplace of Śūdras. Thus, there are four castes. The fifth class of Caṇḍālas immediately follows these four. What is their birthplace? That much Brāhmaṇas do not know. Moreover, is it true, as they say, that Brāhmaṇas are born from the Brahmā's head? Hence, I ask: "Are

Brāhmaṇīs also born from there? If they are, then they are their sisters, because they originated from the same source. Furthermore, do Kṣatriyas and others have marital relations with their sisters? Why? If that happens, then the Barbarians' (*mleccha*) Dharma becomes prevalent. When the Barbarians' Dharma becomes prevalent, then there is an end of social classes. Due to the destruction of social classes, there is hell. . . . It has been further investigated that if there is a single creator of living beings, then why are there four castes? Just as four sons of one father are not of different castes, so is this true of castes. If the difference is due to the division of the Brahmā's head and other bodily parts, that is not logically possible. Why? Just as there is no difference between the *udumbara* fruits growing at the lowest level, in the middle or at the top, so is that the case for castes. Since one cannot perceive any distinction [among castes] in terms of the classification of the white, red, yellow, and black colors nor in terms of the elements, sense-faculties, happiness, suffering, knowledge, sacred scriptures, and the like, therefore it has been established that a caste is impermanent.[25]

This passage from the *Vimalaprabhā* parallels a passage from the *Paramārthasevā*, which is also traditionally attributed to Puṇḍarīka and included in the literary corpus of the Kālacakra tradition. According to the *Paramārthasevā*, people are born into different social classes due to the nature of their *karma* and not due to their origination from the particular parts of Brahmā's body. The following passage of the same text refutes the Brāhmaṇical characterization of social classes in terms of their colors and their inherent predilections for their inherited functions in society, which were standardized by the authors of the Indian Dharmasūtras and Dharmaśāstras.

Just as the fruits of an *udumbara* tree, growing from the lowest level, middle, and top, are of the same form, ingredients, texture, and taste, so the regions of [the Brahmā's] mouth and other parts are the same.

Whoever is born from his mouth is not bright like moon-rays. Whoever is born from his arms is not like the rising sun. One who is born from his thighs is not like yellow paint. Whoever is born from his feet is not like very dark eye-coloring.

All Twice-born are not the class of knowledge, nor are they the princely class. Those born from the Kṣatriya caste are not [necessarily] heroes. All Vaiśyas are not endowed with wealth. Śūdras are not the greatest workers in the world.

The states of happiness and suffering are due to the classification of the elements. According to the scriptures and reasoning, as people are born due to their accumulations of virtue and sin, they experience the world in the same manner. The four castes of people originate in this manner.[26]

Like their predecessors, the holders of the Kālacakra tradition viewed conceited attachment to one's own caste and family as impediments to spiritual maturation and the actualization of Buddhahood. The literature of the Kālacakra tradition frequently warns against social and moral discrimination, which is perpetuated by attachment to one's own caste and its regulations. By means of the different types of analysis, it tries to demonstrate the insubstantiality of the reasons traditionally given in support of social discrimination. To demonstrate the untenability of social discrimination, the *Kālacakratantra* at times uses a type of analysis that is similar to the one frequently applied in Buddhist refutations of the independent existence of a personal identity. The following verse exemplifies one such method:

> There are earth, water, fire, wind, space, *guṇas*, mind (*manas*), intellect (*buddhi*), self-grasping (*ahaṃkāra*), and vital breath. There are the sense objects, form and the like, the sense-faculties, the eye, and so on; and there are the five faculties of action (*karmendriya*). Among these phenomena that pervade the bodies of animals and humans, which is of the highest caste, and which is of the lowest?[27]

The Kālacakra tradition often calls attention to the detrimental effects of social discrimination for one's progress on this tantric path. It also views the absence of conceited attachment to one's social status and lineage as a prerequisite for receiving Buddhist tantric teachings and engaging in Buddhist tantric practices. The *Vimalaprabhā* confirms the assertion of the earlier *Guhyasamājatantra* that not a single Tathāgata between Dīpaṃkara and Śākyamuni taught the Mantrayāna, because people during that era were not suitable to receive the teachings on the great secrets of Mantrayāna.[28] It interprets this statement of the *Guhyasamājatantra* in terms of its own social theory, affirming that during that era, people in the land of Āryans were unsuitable for tantric teachings due to their prejudice concerning the four castes. The Kālacakra tradition sees this same social prejudice as the reason that the Buddha Śākyamuni did not initially teach the *Paramādibuddhatantra* to the people of the land of Āryans but to Sucandra, a king of Sambhala and an emanation of Vajrapāṇi, who took it with him to Sambhala, where it was preserved for centuries before it was revealed to the people of India.

This Buddhist tantric system closely links the negative soteriological implications of social prejudice to its negative socio-political implications. Its eschatological teachings relate the demise of the "Barbarian Dharma," or Islam, to the social and spiritual unification of the *vajra*-family. It sees a causal relationship between the resurgence of the Barbarian Dharma with the reoccurrence of social segregation. According to the *Vimalaprabhā*, the Buddha prophesied in the *Paramādibuddhatantra* that Yaśas, the eighth king of Sambhala in the line of Sucandra, an emanation of Mañjuśrī, will unite all social classes into a single clan (*kalka*) by means of initiation into the *Kālacakratantra*. He foretold the following:

> Due to making the four castes into a single clan within the *vajra*-family and not making them into Brahmā's family, Vāgmī Yaśas, who has a *vajra*-family, will be Kalkī.[29]

The term *kalka*, meaning, a "clan," is interpreted by the *Vimalaprabhā* as a unification of the castes and noncastes, or outcasts.[30] Since that clan will belong to King Yaśas, he will be called *kalkī*, meaning, "one who has a clan"; and his lineage (*gotra*) will be the lineage of *kalkī*.[31] His son Puṇḍarīka, who will write a commentary on the abridged version of the *Paramādibuddhatantra*, will be the second *kalkī*. He will be succeeded by twenty-three other *kalkīs*, after whose reign, Mañjuśrī Yaśas will reappear as Raudra Cakrī and engage in a fierce battle with a vicious king of the Barbarians. He will eliminate the Barbarian Dharma by converting Barbarians to his own Dharma, thereby incorporating them into his *vajra*-family. At that time, all human families will be fulfilled in terms of the three pursuits of a human life: Dharma, pleasure (*kāma*), and wealth (*artha*). His two sons, Brahmā and Sureśa, who will rule the northern and southern sections of Small Jambudvīpa, will also practice Dharma. However, upon his departure to the state of bliss, he will be succeeded by his son Brahmā, and class segregation will reoccur within Brahmā's lineage. Consequently, many divisions in the lineage of Brahmā and in other lineages will appear in the northern part of the earth, and at the end of the *kali-yuga*, the Barbarian Dharma will be propagated once again in all the regions of the earth. After eighteen hundred years, the Barbarian Dharma will be destroyed again, and the Buddhist Dharma will prevail for another eighteen thousand years.[32]

This account of the Buddha's prophecy concerning the role of Buddhist *kalkīs* in the elimination of social segregation and the subsequent eradication of the Barbarian Dharma is a Buddhist response to the Purāṇic teachings, which identify the Buddha and Kalkī as the ninth and tenth *avatāras* of Viṣṇu. The *Vimalaprabhā* urges the reader to consider the Purāṇas as nonsensical treatises, composed by corrupt sages for the sake of establishing their own social class.[33] It asserts the historical precedence of these Buddhist prophecies over those in the Purāṇas on the ground that the Purāṇic prophecies were composed by corrupt Brāhmaṇas at the time of the Buddha's appearance and are not contained in the earlier Vedic texts. Sarcastically reiterating the Purāṇic interpretation of the Buddha's identity and his association with those of low social strata, it tries to demonstrate the supremacy of Buddhist social ethics. It is worth citing here the *Vimalaprabhā*'s full account of the Purāṇic interpretation of the Buddha, since it also sheds some light on the centuries-long conflict between Hindu and Buddhist social and ethical theories.

> This Bhagavān Buddha is the ninth *avatāra* [of Viṣṇu], called Vasudeva; and Kalkī is the tenth. In the *kali-yuga*, the Buddha will vitiate the sacrificial laws by means of a great, delusive deception. He will abolish the military laws, ancestral rites, the propagation of castes, killing, lying, stealing, sexual misconduct, abusive language, slander, idle talk, avarice, malice, false views, harm to all sentient beings, the dwelling of one's own lineage, the duties of a Kṣatriya, the instructions of the great sage Vyāsa, the *Bhārata*, the teachings of the *Gīta*, and the teachings of the Vedas, which yield the fruit of heaven. Thus, having abolished them, he will teach a perverted Dharma to Śūdras and other low classes. For example, Bodhisattvas must bring to completion these ten perfections: the perfection of generosity, the perfection of ethical discipline, the perfection of patience, the perfection of zeal, the perfection of meditation, the perfection of wisdom, the perfection of skillful means (*upāya-pāramitā*), the perfection of aspiration (*praṇidhi-pāramitā*), the perfection of powers (*bala-pāramitā*), and the perfection of gnosis (*jñāna-pāramitā*). They must cultivate the spirit of loving kindness toward all sentient beings and the spirit of compassion. They must benefit all sentient beings, and they must not engage in ten unwholesome actions—namely, killing, lying, stealing, sexual misconduct, abusive language, slander, idle talk, avarice, malice, and false views.
>
> After bringing the Śūdras and other low classes to understanding by means of these perverted teachings and shaving them, he will make them monks wearing red robes. Because those who formerly stood in the army of Dānava were not killed in battle by Vasudeva, and because they must go to hell due to offending the Brāhmaṇas, Viṣṇu created this illusion of the Buddha so that Śūdras and other low classes, who stand on the side of former demons, may go to hell.[34]

The *Vimalaprabhā* also objects to the Purāṇic interpretation of Kalkī as the tenth *avatāra* of Viṣṇu, who will be born as a Brāhmaṇa, kill the Barbarians, and make the earth full of Brāhmaṇas. It once again asserts that Kalkī, who is none other than Mañjuśrī born into the Kṣatriya family of Śākyas, will make all castes into a single caste, because in the past, thirty million Brāhmaṇas in the land of Sambhala demonstrated their inclination toward the Vajrayāna. It also bases its objection to the Purāṇic interpretation of Kalkī on the reading of the *Kālacakratantra* (Ch. 1, v. 26), which prophesies both the appearance of the king Yaśas in Sambhala six hundred years after the year of the Buddha's teaching of the *Paramādibuddhatantra* and the introduction of the Barbarian Dharma into the land of Mecca eight hundred years after his appearance. The *Vimalaprabhā* argues that if Kalkī is a son of the Brāhmaṇa Yaśas, then he cannot be called Kalkī, since without a clan (*kalka*), he cannot be one who has a clan (*kalkī*), just as without wealth, one cannot be a wealthy man. It also refutes the Purāṇic prophecy of Kalkī killing the Barbarians with his arrows made of *darbha* grass, claiming that *kalkī* Yaśas will not kill them but will only eradicate their Dharma. Seeing the extreme wickedness of Barbarians, he will emanate supreme horses by means of his "*samādhi* on supreme horses" (*paramāśva-samādhi*) and will thus melt the minds of Barbarians and establish them in his own Dharma. The *Vimalaprabhā* explains the statement of the *Kālacakratantra* (Ch. 1, v. 161), which affirms that *kalkī* Yaśas will destroy the Barbarians by way of the *Kālacakratantra*'s proselytizing efforts. It interprets this as the *Kālacakratantra*'s method of attracting the evil sages to this tantric path, and it substantiates this proselytizing method on the basis that "spiritual awakening is not possible when the spirit of doubt arises first."[35]

The aforementioned eschatological passages express the Kālacakra tradition's view of social segregation as causally related to the decline of Buddhism and the rise of Islam in India. They point to social unification as a social condition necessary for securing the mundane and spiritual prosperity of the country. These passages reflect legitimate concerns of Buddhist communities in northern India during the tenth and eleventh centuries, which were provoked by the constant threat of Sultān Mahmūd's invasions and the increasing dominance of the Islamic faith. The words of Sultān Mahmūd's secretary, Al-'Utbi, which indicate that Islam or death was the only alternative that Sultān Mahmūd placed before his people,[36] attest to the political and religious crisis faced by Indian Buddhists of that period. The Kālacakra tradition expresses the concern that due to the similarity between the Vedic and Barbarian Dharmas with regard to killing, future generations of Brāhmaṇical communities may well convert to Islam, unless they join their Buddhist compatriots in the *vajra*-family. The *Vimalaprabhā*'s account of Mañjuśrī Yaśas's teaching of the *Kālacakratantra* to thirty-five million Brāhmaṇic sages in Sambhala attests to that concern. According to the *Vimalaprabhā*, the king Yaśas was aware that Brāhmaṇas in Sambhala were originally from different countries with contrary customs regarding eating meat, drinking liquor, and the like. Therefore, he deemed it necessary to unite them into a single *vajra*-family by initiating them into the *kālacakra-maṇḍala*, which he constructed in a sandalwood grove, south of the village of Kalāpa. Before leading them into the *kālacakra-maṇḍala* and giving them tantric precepts, the king Yaśas provided them with the following socio-political and soteriological reasons for consolidating them into the unified *vajra*-family:

> I must lead you here into this *maṇḍala* palace of the Bhagavān Kālacakra and give you mundane (*laukika*) and supramundane (*lokottara*) initiations. Moreover, you must eat, drink, and have marital relations with your *vajra*-family as I command you. If you do not obey my command, then leave my nine hundred and sixty million villages and go wherever you please. Otherwise, after eight hundred years have passed, your descendants will engage in the Barbarians' Dharma and will teach the Barbarians' Dharma in the ninety-six great countries of Sambhala and eleswhere. With the *mantra* of the Barbarians' deity, Vismillāh, striking animals on their necks with a cleaver, they will eat the flesh of the animals killed with the *mantra* of their own deity and condemn the eating of the flesh of animals that died due to their own *karma*. . . . There is no difference between the Barbarians' Dharma and Vedic Dharma with respect to killing. Therefore, the descendants of your family, seeing the vigor of those Barbarians and the manifestation of their deity Māra in battle, will become Barbarians in the future, after eight hundred years have passed. Once they join those Barbarian races, all the inhabitants of the nine hundred and sixty million villages, the four castes and other social classes, will become Barbarians. . . . Thus, regarding the Vedic Dharma as authoritative, they will adopt the Barbarians' Dharma. For this reason, I have given you precepts (*niyama*) so that the Barbarians' Dharma may not enter [here] in the future.[37]

On the basis of these passages, one may surmise that in the context of the Kālacakra tradition, the *vajra*-family represents a society that cannot be destroyed by foreign enemies and their religion, but is able to preserve its distinct identity because it is founded on the religious theories and practices that radically differ from those of its adversary. According to this tantric system, the reason why Buddhist teachings have not yet disappeared is that the Tathāgata, being free of social prejudice, did not dispense them to just some individuals on the basis of their high social class and hold them back from others due to their low class. Rather, he taught the diverse systems of the Buddhist Dharma for the benefit of all, in accordance with their inclinations.[38]

In light of the earlier mentioned concerns, the Kālacakra tradition admonishes Buddhist practitioners not to admire the Vaiṣṇava and Śaiva Dharmas, on the ground that these Dharmas, characterized by the arrogance of class prejudice (*jāti-vāda*) and the absence of compassion for all sentient beings, produce a false sense of self-identity (*mithyāhaṃkāra*).[39] A false sense of self-identity implies here a sense of self-identity that is based on one's social status, and determined by one's own caste, its duties, and lineage. The Kālacakra tradition, like other related Buddhist tantric traditions, distinguishes this false sense of self-identity from the valid sense of self-identity that the tantric practitioner establishes on his path of actualizing Buddhahood. For example, at the time of the self-empowerment on the stage of generation (*utpatti-krama*), the tantric adept appropriates his true self-identity by identifying himself with the body, speech, and mind of all the Tathāgatas, with the *vajra* of gnosis (*jñāna*) and emptiness (*śūnyatā*), and with the purified *dharma-dhātu*. Appropriating this self-identity, he maintains it in all of his activities.[40] Not only does he establish this self-identity for himself, but he also regards all other beings as endowed with the same identity. Thus, one may infer that in this tantric system, a valid sense of personal identity empowers the individual in his spiritual endeavors, thereby yielding a profound sense of nonduality with all living beings. This sense of nonduality with one's natural and social environment, in turn, facilitates religious and social unification, thereby empowering the entire society and enabling it to endure in perilous times. A false sense of personal identity, on the contrary, separates the individual from his natural and social environments and disempowers both the individual and the society. Consequenctly, a society that is disempowered by social and religious segregation is unable to endure in times of danger.

The author of the *Vimalaprabhā* declares that his reason for elaborately describing the characteristics of the *kālacakra-maṇḍala* in the abridged *Kālacakratantra*, as they were taught by Mañjuśrī in the *Ādibuddhatantra*, is to eliminate the self-grasping (*ahaṃkāra*) of the sages who propound class discrimination (*jāti-vādin*).[41] The bearers of the Kālacakra tradition in India considered class prejudice as most intimately related to the Hindu doctrines of a personal god and creator (Īśvara) and of an independent, inherently existent Self (*ātman*). They also saw class prejudice as creating the linguistic bias of extolling the excellence of the Sanskrit language and showing disdain for vernacular languages.[42] They were fully aware of the ways in which the *Kālacakratantra*'s theoretical, practical, and linguistic features contradicted the cultural, religious, and social norms of the mainstream Brāhmaṇical tradition. The Kālacakra literature interprets those features not only in terms of their conversionary activity and the *Kālacakratantra* soteriology but also in terms of the *Kālacakratantra*'s social theory. It explains the grammatical inaccuracies and lexical syncretism of the Sanskrit language of the *Kālacakratantra* as a: (1) skillful means of eradicating the conceit of those attached to their social class, knowledge, and proper words, and (2) skillful means of making the Buddhist tantric teachings accessible to a diverse audience, which speaks different languages and dialects. The *Vimalaprabhā* affirms that individuals who are overcome by a false sense of self-identity grasp onto the "single, parochial Sanskrit language" and teach, as attested by the *Mahābhārata*, 6, 1, 84, that a single word well-pronounced yields one's desires in heaven.[43] It accuses the Brāhmaṇic sages of writing the Dharmas of the *Bhagavadgīta*, Siddhāntas, and Purāṇas in the Sanskrit language out of greed for material things. It asserts that Brāhmaṇas wrote these scriptures in Sanskrit in order to prevent the Vaiśyas, Śūdras, and other low social classes from reading their scriptures and gaining knowledge of their Dharma and various sciences. The *Vimalaprabhā* states further that the Brāhmaṇic author of these scriptures knew that if lower classes were to gain knowledge, they would stop revering the Brāhmaṇas for their special qualities.[44] It contrasts the selfish motivation of the conceited Brāhmaṇic sages to the altruistic motivation of the Buddhas and Bodhisattvas, who are free of grasping onto social discrimination and linguistic bias. The Buddhas and Bodhisattvas do not exclusively use the Sanskrit language to teach and redact the Buddhist teachings, for they also resort to the "omniscient language" (*sarvajña-bhāṣā*), using the expressions of vernaculars and languages of different countries.[45] Relying on the meaning of the teachings, they use different vernaculars and different grammars in order to bring others to spiritual awakening. Although this characterization of the Buddhas' universal language is also found in the writings of Mahāyāna,[46] it is most emphasized in the Buddhist *tantras*.

The *Paramādibuddhatantra* also advocates the usage of a lexically syncretized language that would benefit people of all social classes, ethnic groups, and mental dispositions. According to the *Paramādibuddhatantra*, the Buddha himself expressed this sentiment in the following words:

> When one understands the meaning from regional words, what is the use of technical terms?
>
> On the earth, a jewel is called by different names from country to country, but there is no difference in the jewel itself.
>
> Likewise, the various redactors of my pure Dharma use diverse terms in accordance with the dispositions of sentient beings.[47]

In this tantric tradition, as in other related tantric systems, every stage of tantric practice is either directly or indirectly related to its social theories. Eating the flesh of an animal that died due to natural causes or an accident, drinking liquor, and engaging in sexual relations with the members of all social classes were prohibited for members of the Brāhmaṇa caste. The *Kālacakratantra* literature, however, often presents these practices as tantric pledges (*samaya*), which are designed to counteract grasping onto one's own social class and tradition.[48] The following verse from the *Paramādibuddhatantra* demonstrates this point:

> The Vajrī who perceives reality has prescribed food, drink, and unsuitable sexual intercourse in order to destroy attachment to one's own lineage.[49]

This and other explicit passages from the *Kālacakratantra* literature specify that the eradication of attachment to one's own social and spiritual lineage is a reason behind certain practices of tantric pledges, and they also explain similar but less explicit passages in other *anuttara-yoga-tantras*. The tantric pledges of all the *anuttara-yoga-tantras* equally involve the transgression of social conventions and cultural boundaries in order to cultivate a perception of one's own social environment in a nondual fashion. For example, one reads in the *Hevajratantra* that a person who has joined the *vajra*-family through initiation should eat all kinds of meat, associate with all kinds of people, and keep the company of all kinds of women. One who engages in tantric *yoga* should interact with all social groups and consider them as a unified, single caste, because he draws no distinctions among the various social classes. He may touch men of low castes and outcasts—Ḍombas, Caṇḍālas, Carmāras, Haḍḍikas, Brāhmaṇas, Kṣatriyas, Vaiśyas, and Śūdras—as readily as his own body. The tantric *yogīs* who have mastered *yoga* should neither favor nor despise other beings.[50] Likewise, the *Caṇḍamahāroṣaṇatantra*, which belongs to the literary corpus of the *Guhyasamājatantra*, admonishes the tantric practitioner never to think in terms of edible and inedible food, suitable and unsuitable work, appropriate and inappropriate people for sexual relations, nor think in terms of sin and virtue, or heaven and liberation.[51] The unique approach of the Kālacakra tradition to these tantric practices is not in its rendering of their soteriological importance but in placing them in its own historical context and giving them historical and political significance. Its distinctiveness with regard to these tantric practices also lies in its interpretation of these practices in terms of mundane convention (*loka-vyavahāra*) and in terms of supramundane gnosis (*lokottara-jñāna*), which may elucidate the observances of tantric pledges in other related *tantras*.

The *Kālacakratantra* literature reveals that a *vajrācārya* was expected to teach the required tantric pledges to tantric beginners only in terms of the mundane, conventional truth, according to the differing customs of their own countries and social groups. Just as certain practices with regard to eating, drinking, and sexual relations were prohibited in one region and for one social class and were allowed in another region or for another social class, so would the specific tantric pledges differ from one tantric beginner to another. For example, the *Vimalaprabhā* informs us that in accordance with the customs of different countries, tantric beginners in specific countries should eat beef, horse meat, dog meat, elephant meat, pork, or even human flesh, and so on. Similarly, one should follow the customs of one's own country and social class with regard to drinking liquor, as in specific countries, liquor is prescribed to Brāhmaṇas, Śūdras, or to the members of all social classes. The same principle is applied to one's sexual relations. In certain countries, when a husband dies, the mother becomes her son's wife; brother and sister may marry; one may marry a maternal uncle; members of castes are allowed to have sexual relations with outcasts; or Brāhmaṇas may have sexual relations with low-caste courtesans.[52]

The tantric beginner is advised to eat, drink, and have sexual relations according to the customs of his own country until he attains the *mantra-siddhi* or the gnosis-*siddhi* and thereby becomes a tantric *yogī*. The Kālacakra tradition offers several reasons why the tantric beginner should not transgress the customs of his country and social group for as long as he lacks the above-mentioned *siddhis*. First, if the tantric beginner, who has not attained those *siddhis*, eats the flesh of an animal that is a tutelary deity of his family and thereby offends that deity and causes it to bring misfortune to his family, he will be unable to protect his family from calamity. Similarly, if the tantric beginner violates the customs of his country by eating the flesh of animals that are the tutelary deities of other families, and by having sexual relations with prohibited castes and outcasts, the people he offends will harass him, since he lacks the *siddhis* and realizations of a *yogī*. Furthermore, as in other related tantric systems, so too in this tantric tradition, the tantric practitioner must be able to consume the substances of tantric pledges with a nonconceptual mind (*nirvikalpa-citta*); otherwise, they will not give him the *samaya-siddhi*, by means of which inedible poison can be transformed into edible food, foul smelling feces can become sweet smelling, and so on. If the tantric beginner lacks the *samaya-siddhi*, he will poison himself. Therefore, a *vajrācārya* is not to give the precepts pertaining to the consumption of these substances to those in the community who do not meditate on deities and *mantras*, for they will die as a result of eating the poisonous substances. The *Vimalaprabhā* warns that one's pollution caused by impure pledges may give rise to a disregard for the world, out of which one may commit suicide and go to hell. In light of these dangers, the *Kālacakratantra* criticizes the Śaiva tradition for leading people to hell by instructing them to eat semen and uterine blood in order to attain the bliss of Śiva.[53] Therefore, in the Kālacakra tantric system, the substances that are generally regarded as impure and poisonous are not to be prescribed by a *vajrācārya* to beginners but only to *yogīs*, who are not ordinary sentient beings (*prākṛta-sattva*) and who by the power of their *mantras* and meditative concentration are able to transmute these poisons into ambrosias (*amṛta*). By the power of his mind, an extraordinary *yogī* transforms liquor into milk, deadly poisons into elixirs of life (*rasāyana*), the bones of an animal into flowers, teeth into pearls, urine into musk, uterine blood into benzoin (*sihlaka*), semen into camphor, feces into fragrant unguent, and so on. When these substances are purified and transformed into ambrosias, they do not harm the *yogī*'s body but induce great powers and facilitate the attainment of Buddhahood. For example, purified liquor, which represents innate bliss (*sahajānanda*), facilitates the attainment of that bliss. The five types of meat symbolize the five sense-faculties; and when purified, they facilitate the purification of the senses. The five ambrosias (*amṛta*)—purified feces, semen, urine, uterine blood, and marrow—represent the five Buddhas, and their ritual consumption facilitates the attainment of the five types of gnosis, because by consuming the five ambrosias, one worships the five Buddhas.[54] However, if these substances are not transformed into ambrosias and properly understood, they will not bring forth the qualities of Buddhahood to the person who consumes them. According to the *Vimalaprabhā*, these substances are also not to be given to conceited scholars, "the hypocrites who crave after the properties of the Buddhist temples and monasteries and teach the meaning of Buddhist *tantras* incorrectly."[55] Because the minds of the conceited scholars are evil, even when the defiled substances are transformed into ambrosias, they retain their harmful qualities.

However, once a tantric adept attains the *mantra-siddhi* or the gnosis-*siddhi* (*jñāna-siddhi*), he is allowed to eat and drink and have sexual relations not just according to the customs of his country and social class but just as he pleases, because he has transcended the distinction between the allowed and prohibited, the suitable and unsuitable, and no one is able to object or harass him.[56] The supramundane gnosis (*lokottara-jñāna*), which he actualizes, does not grasp onto the edible and inedible, since for it, the edible and inedible only fill the belly and are not gates to liberation. Therefore, a tantric *yogī* is able to transform the nature of other substances into himself.

The aforementioned Kālacakra tradition's justification for conforming to the customs of one's own country and family indicates that one should behave in accordance with those customs not out of attachement to them or due to conceit in one's own social class but for the sake of protecting oneself and one's family. As the earlier-cited verse from the *Paramādibuddhatantra* attests, freedom from attachment to one's own caste and family is posited in this tantric system not only as a moral qualification for joining the unified *vajra*-family but also as one of the main goals of the *Kālacakratantra* practice. This has both sociological and soteriological significance. As indicated earlier, the sociological efficacy of detachment from one's social class and family is that it provides an indispensable condition for social and ethnic unification and the resultant prosperity of society. The soteriological efficacy of detachment from one's spiritual lineage and family relations is that it removes obstacles, which, according to the *Paramādibuddhatantra*, "Māra creates in forms of the Buddhas, Bodhisattvas, fathers, mothers, daughters, sisters, sons, brothers, and chosen wives."[57] This form of detachment is also soteriologically significant in the sense that it enables one to engage in the much commended act of generosity, namely, the offering of sensual love (*kāma-dāna*). Offering one's own courtesan, wife, daughter, or other female relative as a gift of sensual love to Buddhist tantric *yogīs* of all social classes, who seek the attainment of mundane *siddhis* and the experience of the immutable bliss, is praised as a supreme act of generosity. This form of generosity is regarded as the highest form of generosity for several reasons. First, it provides Buddhist *yogīs* with an actual consort (*karma-mudrā*) and enables them to attain various mundane *siddhis*, by means of which they can protect themselves and others from enemies, malicious spirits, and other dangers. In times of imminent foreign invasion, mundane *siddhis* such as pacification, dominance, immobilizing, bewildering, and the like may have had a special appeal for the Indian Buddhists of that period.

Likewise, detachment to one's own family and social class, expressed in the *kāma-dāna*, becomes a gift of Buddhahood to others. At the same time, it becomes a gift of Buddhahood to oneself, for it is said that one who gladly offers his wife as a gift of sensual love to others is promised to swiftly attain the ten perfections (*pāramitā*) in this very life. On the other hand, one who is attached to his wife goes to hell.[58] The soteriological efficacy of the gift of sensual love seems to exceed that of all other forms of generosity, since it increases the donor's stores of merit (*puṇya*) and knowledge (*jñāna*) more than any other form of generosity. The *Kālacakratantra* tells us that the Buddhas themselves resorted to this form of generosity for the sake of spiritual awakening.

> Long ago, for the sake of Buddhahood, the Buddhas gave their land, elephants, horses, chariots, and numerous golden objects. They gave even their own heads, blood, and flesh. Because the desired Buddhahood did not come about, they gave the gift of sensual love (*kāma-dāna*). This secret offering of men brings forth Buddhahood in the family of the progenitor of Jinas.[59]

It also points to the salvific power of the meritorious nature of the *kāma-dāna* in the following manner:

> Hatred and other faults of the best of men and gods are due to attachment, due to love for their chosen wives and others. For the sake of uprooting that [attachment], the sons of all the Jinas have given her in the gift of sensual love. Therefore, rejoicing in generosity brings forth the reward of immutable bliss. This produced accumulation of merit is a kinsman to the three worlds who always removes the peoples' fear of hell.[60]

The *Vimalaprabhā* also affirms the absolute necessity of the *kāma-dāna* in pursuing spiritual awakening on the tantric path, stating that within the system of *mantras* (*mantra-naya*), it is impossible to attain the *mahāmudrā-siddhi* without the gift of sensual love.[61] For this reason, upon receiving the initiation, the initiate, whether a householder or a monk, pledges to give one-sixth of all his possessions, including his consort, to his spiritual mentor (*guru*) so that he may not succumb to attachment to his property and family. Giving one-sixth of a consort meant offering one's own consort to the spiritual mentor for five days each month. According to the *Paramādibuddhatantra*,[62] prior to the two higher initiations (*uttarābhiṣeka*), the secret and wisdom initiations, a householder who seeks liberation is expected to offer ten attractive (*rūpiṇī*) consorts (*mudrā*) to his spiritual mentor, namely, a sister's daughter, a daughter, a sister, the mother, the mother-in-law, the maternal uncle's wife, the wife of the father's brother, a sister of the father, a sister of the mother, and his own wife. The ten offered consorts represent the ten Vidyās, beginning with Tārā and ending with

Dharmdhātubhaginī, who are the purified aspects of women belonging to ten social groups—specifically, Śūdrī, Kṣatriṇī, Brāhmiṇī, Vaiśyī, Ḍombī, Kāivartī (fisherman's wife), Nāṭikā (a dancer), Rajakī (a washerwoman), Carmakārī (the wife of a leather maker), and Caṇḍālī. They are also the manifestations of the ten perfections (*pāramitā*), ten magical powers (*vaśitā*), ten *bodhisattva-bhūmis*, and ten powers (*bala*). Thus, by offering the ten consorts to his spiritual mentor, a householder symbolically offers to others the aforementioned spiritual achievements, which are the sublimated aspects of a unified society, and he himself becomes qualified to obtain them. A householder who, being protective of his family, refuses to offer them to his spiritual mentor is considered unqualified to receive the two higher initiations. When a householder refuses to offer such consorts, the spiritual mentor initiates Buddhist monks (*bhikṣu*) and wandering ascetics (*śrāmaṇera*) into the *kālacakra-maṇḍala* with other consorts of the lower social classes, Śūdrī and Caṇḍālī. This indicates that monks and wandering ascetics who wished to engage in the *Kālacakratantra* practices depended on the householder's generosity in this way, in order to acquire a consort who would be of good family, pleasing manners, or attractive appearance. Since this generosity was not always available, those who depended on the generosity of the householder had to be free of social and other related biases in order to engage in the tantric, yogic practices. Just as the offering of one's own consort is considered soteriologically significant since it provides one with an accumulation of merit (*puṇya-saṃbhāra*), so is the respectful acceptance of the consorts of all social classes regarded as soteriologically significant. Respect for the consort involves not only a disregard for the consort's social status but also the nonemission of semen during the sexual act, which is viewed as a form of celibacy (*brahmacarya*). Respect for the consort is a requirement for the accumulation of ethical discipline (*śīla-saṃbhāra*), which, together with the accumulation of merit, provides the basis for the accumulation of knowledge (*jñāna-saṃbhāra*). According to this tantric tradition, complete and perfect Buddhahood (*samyaksaṃbuddhatva*) does not take place, except by means of these three types of accumulation.[63]

The passage from the *Paramādibuddhatantra* that clearly indicates that monks and wandering ascetics are to be given the two higher initiations is supported by passages from the *Vimalaprabhā*, describing the ritual offering of a consort to monks and wandering ascetics; but this seems to contradict the statement of Dīpaṃkara Śrījñāna (Atīśa) in his *Bodhipathapradīpa*, which asserts the following:

> A celibate (*brahmacārin*) should not receive the secret and wisdom initiations, since it is specifically prohibited in the *Ādibuddha*, the supreme *tantra*.
>
> If a celibate practices what is prohibited upon receiving those initiations, then a downfall from observing the austerity will occur.
>
> An ascetic will fall into a great sin and into an unfavorable state of existence, and men will never have the *siddhi*.[64]

Nowhere in the abridged *Kālacakratantra* nor in the *Vimalaprabhā* is there any clear reference to the statement in the *Ādibuddhatantra* that prohibits monks from receiving the two higher initiations. One passage in the *Vimalaprabhā* indicates only that a tantric initiate had to take the following vow (*praṇidhāna*) prior to receiving the first seven *Kālacakratantra* initiations: "For the sake of the accumulation of ethical discipline (*śīla-saṃbhāra*), with regard to sexual intercourse between the castes and outcasts, I will clearly observe the vow (*saṃvara*) of celibacy in the union with a lotus."[65] In the literature of this tantric tradition, celibacy is often interpreted not as abstinence from engaging in sexual tantric practice, but as the practice of retaining sexual fluids during sexual tantric practices.

In the tantric feast (*gaṇa-cakra*) following the initiation, a woman of any caste and age, whether she was lovely or filthy, crippled or facially deformed, had to be worshipped by means of sexual *yoga* for the sake of spiritual awakening. The Kālacakra tradition also acknowledges that in order to carry out this tantric precept, one must be a Bodhisattva with a compassionate heart, free of all mental afflictions and attachments, and not involved in social conflicts.[66] Thus, on the one hand, the Buddhist tantric *yogīs*' impartiality and lack of social prejudice had to be developed out of practical necessity; and on the other hand, they had to be cultivated as expressions of compassion and wisdom by means of which one perceives all phenomena as being of the same essence (*sama-rasa*), the essence of gnosis (*jñāna*). Accepting women of despised social classes and professions and women who were socially rejected due to physical deformities as their rightful consorts and partners in their spiritual pursuits, Buddhist *yogīs* made it possible for the most disempowered and disdained members of Indian society to partake in Buddhist tantric practices and to pursue their own spiritual goals. At the same time, their lack of social prejudice and impartiality to external appearances was seen as an indication of their spiritual maturity, which qualified them for receiving the most advanced tantric teachings and for engaging in the most advanced tantric practices.

The gathering of a *gaṇa-cakra* reveals yet another way in which the Kālacakra tradition envisioned a socially integrated *vajra*-family. The participants in the tantric feast were either the actual or symbolic representatives of thirty-six social classes of India,[67] whom a tantric practitioner had to view as one's own immediate family and as manifestations of enlightened awareness. The couple representing the lowest Ḍomba class had to be perceived as one's own mother and father. The representatives of the four main social classes became one's own brothers and sisters. The classes of braziers, flute-dancers, jewelers, well-diggers, weavers, liquor-makers, goldsmiths, and garland-makers became one's own sons and daughters; and all the remaining social groups became one's own grandchildren.[68] This *vajra*-family of the *gaṇa-cakra* symbolizes not only a well-integrated human family or society but also the unified nature of ultimate reality. As in the *Cakrasaṃvaratantra*, so too in this tantric system, the assembly of thirty-six social classes represents thirty-six pure families of *yoginīs*, who symbolize the thirty-seven factors of spiritual awakening (*bodhi-pākṣika-dharma*).[69] This identification of thirty-six social classes with the factors of spiritual awakening implies that the entire society is to be viewed on this tantric path as the social body of the Buddha.

The *Vimalaprabhā* asserts that apart from these families of *yoginīs*, there are no other pure families.[70] The *Kālacakratantra*'s identification of thirty-six social classes with the pure families of *yoginīs* explains why the acceptance of qualified consorts of all social groups is interpreted here as a worship of the thirty-six families of *yoginīs* of the *kālacakra-maṇḍala*. It also explains why tantric practitioners, by engaging in sexual *yoga* with representatives of the thirty-six social classes, satisfy the *yoginīs* belonging to the thirty-six families of the *kālacakra-maṇḍala* with sexual bliss. It is said that when the tantric practitioner pleases the *yoginīs* in this way, they protect him from adversities by giving him the mundane *siddhis*. This form of worshiping the *yoginīs* also facilitates the *yogīs*' attainment of the supramundane *siddhi*. Embracing qualified tantric consorts of all social classes with a proper attitude, the *yogīs* embrace the represented factors of spiritual awakening and empower themselves to attain them swiftly.

The seating arrangement of the participants of the tantric feast reveals yet another way in which this tantric tradition in India advocated social integration and envisioned the *vajra*-family. The seats of the representatives of the thirty-six social classes were arranged in accordance with the places of the thirty-six families of *yoginīs* in the *kālacakra-maṇḍala*. The couple of the Ḍomba class, which makes the gnosis-*cakra* and represents the Sahajakāya of the Buddha and the gnosis-*vajra* of the individual, was seated in the center of the human *kālacakra-maṇḍala*. In the four cardinal directions, around the Ḍomba couple, were seated the representatives of the four main castes. The Śūdra caste was in the east, the Kṣatriya caste was in the south, the Brāhmaṇa caste was in the north, and the Vaiśya caste was in the west. The second circle of the *gaṇa-cakra*, or the mind-*cakra*, which symbolizes the Dharmakāya of the Buddha and the mind-*vajra* of the individual, includes the representatives of the following eight social classes: the class of braziers in the east, the class of flute-dancers in the south, the class of jewelers in the north, the class of well-diggers in the west, the class of weavers in the southeast, the class of liquor-makers in the southwest, the class of goldsmiths in the northeast, and the class of garland-makers in the northwest. The third circle, or the speech-*cakra*, which symbolizes the Saṃbhogakāya of the Buddha and the speech-*vajra* of the individual, includes an additional eight social classes: namely, the class of butchers in the east, the class of potters in the southeast, the class of pillow-makers in the south, the class of courtesans in the southwest, the class of tailors in the west, the class of fishermen in the northwest, the class of actors in the north, and the class of washermen in the northeast. The fourth circle, or the body-*cakra*, which symbolizes the Nirmāṇakāya of the Buddha and the body-*vajra* of the individual, consists of yet another eight social classes: the class of blacksmiths in the east, the class of lac-makers in the south, the class of scabbard-makers in the west, the class of oil-pressers in the north, the class of flute-makers in the southeast, the class of carpenters in the southwest, the class of cobblers in the northwest, and the class of barbers in the northeast. Finally, outside the body-*cakra*, in the circle that represents a cemetery, which was always outside the town, are the representatives of the following outcasts and ethnic groups: Barbarians (*mleccha*) in the east, Haḍḍas, the sweepers, in the south, Mātaṅgas in the west, Tāpins in the north, Varvaras in the southeast, Pukkasas in the southwest, Bhillas in the northwest, and Śabaras in the northeast.[71] Thus, the entire assembly at the tantric feast represents a unified society, the *vajra*-family that consisted of the diverse social and ethnic groups that constituted Indian society at that time. This *vajra*-family of the *gaṇa-cakra* also represents the individual, whose unified capacities, or *vajras* of the body, speech, mind, and gnosis are understood as the internal *gaṇa-cakra*, or *vajra-family*. Likewise,

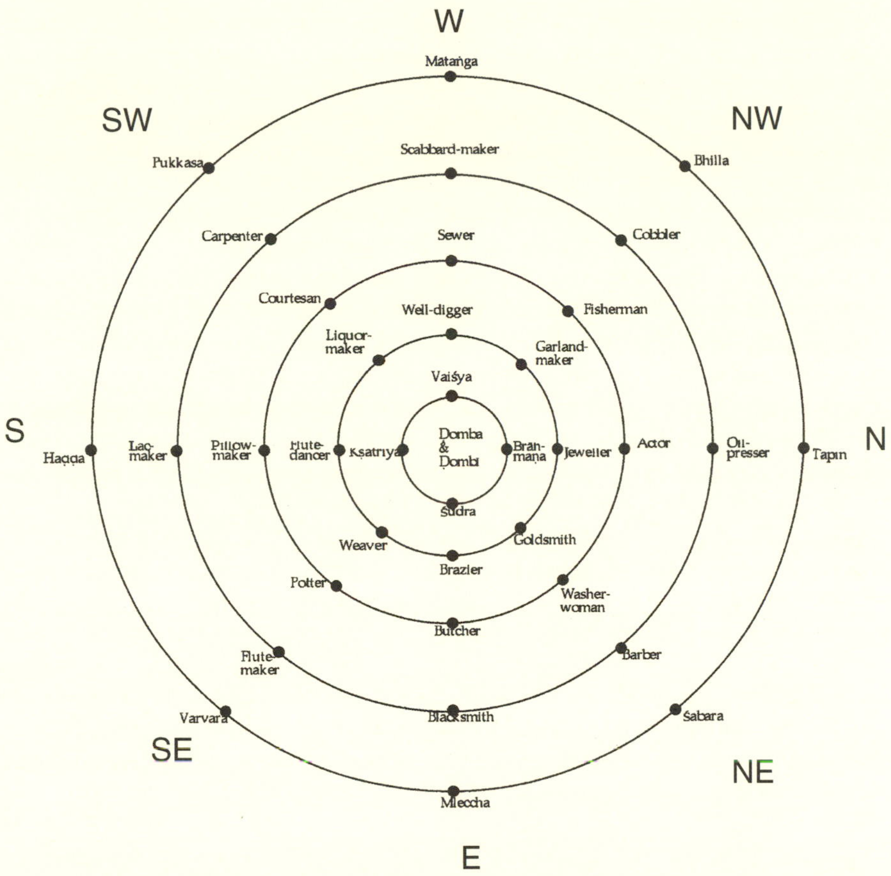

FIGURE 6.1 The *gaṇacakra-maṇḍala*

it symbolizes the enlightened *vajra*-family, or the mutual pervasiveness of the four bodies of the Buddha. In this manner, the Kālacakra tradition expresses its view of the indivisibility of the *vajra*-family in all its aspects: the individual, social, and ultimate. See figure 6.1.

As in the *gaṇa-cakra*, so too in the *kālacakra-maṇḍala*, the Ḍomba couple is identified with the presiding deities (*adhidevatā*) located at the center of the *maṇḍala*, whose nature is the pure and omniscient gnosis that emits and pervades all other inhabitants of the *maṇḍala*. In this way, the social class that was generally treated as the lowest in the mundane realm becomes here a symbol of the supreme in the spiritual realm. The class whose living areas were restricted to the outskirts of towns and villages is placed at the very center of the *gaṇa-cakra* and the *kālacakra-maṇḍala*.[72]

By identifying the Buddha Kālacakra with the Ḍomba class, the *Kālacakratantra* conveys several messages. On the one hand, if the Ḍomba class pervades all other social classes, then not a single social class can claim to be pure and unmixed. On the other hand, if the Ḍomba class is stainless, enlightened awareness, which generates all the Jinas, then even the lowest social class is ultimately pure, as are all the other classes that are permeated by it. This is one of the ways in which the Kālacakra tradition reinforces its position that all social classes are fundamentally of equal value and ultimately undifferentiated. Another reason for the *Kālacakratantra*'s identification of Kālacakra and Viśvamātā with the Ḍomba class perhaps can be inferred from other *anuttara-yoga-tantras*, which also identify their central deities with this particular class of outcasts. For example, it is stated in the literature of the *Hevajratantra* that Hevajra's consort Bhagavatī is called Ḍombī on the grounds that she is intangible, that is to say, outside the realm of sensory experience.[73] It is very likely that the Kālacakra tradition adopted this idea of identifiying the Ḍomba caste as its principal deity from the earlier Buddhist *tantras*, as it adopted many other similar ideas as well. A similar apotheosis of Ḍombī also characterizes the Buddhist Sahajayāna, which was contemporary with the Kālacakra tradition in India. For instance, two Old Bengali songs (*caryāpada*) of Kāṇhapāda (ca. the eleventh century CE) are addressed to Ḍombī, the goddess Nairātmyā,[74] who lives in the cottage outside the city—meaning, outside the world of the sense-faculties—and only touches the Brāhmaṇas and the shaven-headed but does not reveal herself to them.[75]

The unification of all social classes into one family by means of a tantric initiation is not unique to the *Kālacakratantra* and other Buddhist tantric systems of the *anuttara-yoga* class. It is also characteristic of some tantric Śaiva sects as well. For instance, Rāmānuja in his *Śrībhāṣya* (II. 2. 35–37) criticizes the sect of the Kāpālikas for their claim that even individuals belonging to the lowest classes can immediately attain the status of a Brāhmaṇa and the highest stage of life (*āśrama*) by means of initiatory rites. Similarly, a passage in the *Kulārṇavatantra* reads that the differentiation between the Śūdrahood of a Śūdra and the Brāhmaṇahood of a Brāhmaṇa has vanished for those who have received tantric initiation, since those who are consecrated by initiation do not discriminate among social classes.[76] The same text also asserts that in the circle of worship (*pūjā-cakra*), all are equal to Śiva.[77] However, the *Kulārṇavatantra* and other Śaiva sources give clear indications that the transcendence of social barriers within the Śaiva tradition took place only in a ritual context and did not extend to the everyday life. The denial and reevaluation of social classes were valid only in that circle during a secret gathering. Outside a secret gathering, each would resume his or her own social status and its prescribed rules of conduct and duties. The *Kulārṇavatantra* indicates that even the differing durations of studentship in tantric Śaivism were prescribed to the initiates according to their social class. This does not seem to have been the case in the Kālacakra tradition. Nowhere in the literature of the *Kālacakratantra* corpus can one find indications that the denial of class barriers was limited to the ritual context. The *Paramādibuddhatantra* does state that certain kinds of individuals—namely, a householder who lives off a monastery, a servant, who is under the rule of someone else, a ploughman, who kills sentient beings by ploughing the ground, a trader of weapons, a person who sells the Dharma, and a mentally dull person—are not suitable for the role of a *vajrācārya*.[78] However, this assertion does not refer to the incompatibility of their social class for the position of a *vajrācārya* but to the incompatibility of their lifestyles with the responsibilities of the *vajrācārya* and to their inadequate moral and mental capacities for that spiritual role. The *Vimalaprabhā* explicitly states that such types of activities rob one of his duty (*dharma*) of a *vajrācārya*.[79] The Kālacakra tradition differentiates *vajrācāryas* as superior, middling, and inferior not on the basis of their social classes but according to their religious status. For example, an ordained *vajrācārya* is considered to be superior; a *vajrācārya* who lives as a wandering ascetic (*śramaṇa*) is regarded as middling; and a *vajrācārya* who is a householder is regarded as an inferior *vajrācārya*, who should not be honored by an ordained *vajrācārya*.[80] This type of classification reveals that the Kālacakra tradition retained a strong, monastic orientation, which was characteristic of the earlier forms of Buddhism and which engendered a certain religious hierarchy. This often counteracted class discrimination in Buddhist communities by giving higher honor and status to a monk of a lower social class than to a householder of a higher caste. The Kālacakra tradition also classifies tantric disciples as superior, middling, and inferior. Again, it does not make the classification on the basis of their social class and lineage but on the basis of the spiritual goals that they seek. Those intent on practicing the Dharma that consists of compassion and emptiness and seeking the supramundane *siddhi* are regarded as superior disciples, who are eligible to receive all eleven initiations. Those who desire the mundane *siddhis* are regarded as middling disciples, who are eligible to receive only the first seven initiations. Whereas those who desire none of the *siddhis* but respect a spiritual mentor are characterized as inferior disciples, who do not qualify for tantric initiations and are eligible to receive only the teachings on the five ethical precepts.[81]

In the context of the *Kālacakratantra*, the Buddha Kālacakra, who is identified with Ḍomba, is portrayed as the progenitor of the four castes: Brāhmaṇa, Kṣatriya, Vaiśya, and Śūdra. The four castes originate from the four mouths of Kālacakra, which belong to his four faces, which, in turn, symbolize the four aspects in which enlightened awareness manifests in the world—namely: the meditative, peaceful, passionate, and wrathful aspects.[82] This interpretation of the four castes as the social manifestations of the four different expressions of enlightened awareness affirms the *Kālacakratantra*'s view of the fundamental equality of all castes. It can be construed as a Buddhist tantric counterpart of the Vedic *Puruṣasūkta*, which affirms the mouth of the Primordial Man (*puruṣa*) as the birthplace of the caste of Brāhmaṇas only. Thus, by presenting the four castes as the ways in which ultimate reality manifests itself in a human society, the Kālacakra tradition suggests that on this tantric path, one must reinterpret one's habituated view of one's own social environment in order to realize the nonduality of all the aspects of phenomenal existence. Likewise, if one analyzes this interpretation of the origin and manifestation of the four castes in terms of the standard Hindu view of the roles of the four castes in Indian society, other implications of this interpretation become clearer. When one examines the *Kālacakratantra*'s explanation of the four castes in light of the exposition of the *Baudhāyanadharmasūtra* (I. 18. 2–5)—which ascribes the duties of preservation of the Vedic tradition, protection of people and their properties, protection of domestic animals, and service to the other three castes to the respective duties of the four castes, respectively[83]—it suggests that the social functions of the four above-mentioned aspects of enlightened awareness are to preserve spiritual learning and to secure the physical and material well-being of the individual and society.

However, unlike the Hindu treatises that prescribe to the caste of Brāhmaṇas the duty of preserving only the Vedic tradition, the Kālacakra tradition views Kālacakra as a depository and guardian of diverse religious systems. According to the Kālacakra tradition, enlightened awareness manifests not only as the social forms of the Buddha but also as the religious body of the Buddha, which incorporates diverse Hindu and Buddhist systems of thought and practice. Different religious systems and schools are also said to arise from the four mouths of Kālacakra as their ultimate source. The Jñānakāya of Kālacakra, assuming the various forms of transmission, teaches diverse treatises, including the Vedas. Thus, the Buddha Kālacakra teaches the *Ṛg-Veda* from his western mouth, the *Yajur-Veda* from his northern mouth, the *Sāma-Veda* from his southern mouth, and the *Atharva-Veda* from his eastern mouth. He also teaches other religious systems with those same mouths. For example, he teaches the *tantra* of spirits (*bhūta-tantra*) and the Buddhist *yogānuviddha*, Madhyamaka, and the systems of Sthaviras with his western mouth. He teaches the Hindu *kaula-tantras* and the Buddhist wisdom-*tantras* (*prajñā-tantra*), the Yogācāra and Sarvāstivāda systems with his eastern mouth. With his northern mouth, he teaches the Hindu Siddhānta, the Buddhist action-*tantra* (*kriyā-tantra*), and the systems of the Vaibhāṣikas and Mahāsaṃghikas. With his southern mouth, he teaches the Dharma of Viṣṇu, the Buddhist *yoga-tantra*, Sūtrānta, and the system of Samitīyas.[84] Thus, the diverse religious systems are simply the manifestations of different aspects of the Buddha's unified mind, or integrated wisdom, taking the form of a religious body in accordance with the mental dispositions of different people.

This view of Kālacakra as the single source of the diverse religious systems implies the inherent value of the different religious traditions, and more importantly it provides a justification for the theoretical syncretism of the *Kālacakratantra* as its conversionary method. It suggests that becoming a member of the *vajra*-family does not involve completely abandoning one's prior religious tradition, but entails only a hermeneutical shift with regard to the authoritative scriptures of that tradition. This ascription serves as a conceptual basis for the reinterpretation of non-Buddhist ideas that one frequently encounters in the literature of the *Kālacakratantra*. It also explains the Kālacakra tradition's argument, already mentioned in the chapter on syncretism, that there is no distinction between Buddhists and non-Buddhists with regard to the manner in which a conventional reality appears; rather, the only difference between them is in the Buddhists' understanding of personal (*pudgala*) and phenomenal (*bhāva*) identitylessness (*nairātmya*).[85]

One example of the Kālacakra tradition's reinterpretation of non-Buddhist teachings is related to the *Kālacakratantra*'s assertion that the practice of offering the *kāma-dāna* was also taught in the Vedānta but that evil Brāhmaṇas concealed it for their own selfish reasons. The *Kālacakratantra* rejects the traditional Brāhmaṇic interpretation of Vedic sacrifice and interprets it in terms of the tantric *yoga* of gnosis (*jñāna-yoga*) in the following manner:

> At the time of sacrifice, approach the lords of bulls, rhinoceroses, horses, and elephants as the bodily sense-objects and sense-faculties. When your knife is purified, there is a cessation of those sense-objects and sense-faculties in the *yoga* of gnosis. The drink of the initiated, which is mixed with blood and *somavallī*, is in the cowhide. The nectar of semen (*soma*), gone from the tip [of sexual organ] to uterine blood in vulva, is of the nature of the all-pervading bliss.

> Brahmā is the body, Hara is speech, and Hari is the mind of living beings. They are three Vedas. They are three letters, the syllable *auṃ*. They are the moon, sun, and

fire, or three *nāḍīs*; and they are the [three] *guṇas*. An additional member of the family (*kaula*) within the body, present in the sense-objects and *guṇas*, is of the nature of the sound (*nāda*) of the fire-priest (*atharvan*). Within that [body], the *anāhata*, which is devoid of the sense-objects and *guṇas*, is the indestructible.

In old times, Brahmā told this secret to *yogīs* in the Vedānta. The sages whose knowledge became lost in the course of time taught here the killing of living beings. Humans' engagement in that [sacrificial killing] for the sake of heaven brings about a miserable hell as its result. Charcoal moistened here by the flow of milk nowhere becomes of the color of *soma*.

People who are deceived by the words of the Vedas, which are incorrect and devoid of pledges (*samaya*), guard their wives day and night for the sake of acquiring sons for themselves. Supposedly, a son gives an offering to a father who has departed to the world of the dead. Therefore, the evil Brāhmaṇas concealed this gift of sensual love (*kāma-dāna*), which brings forth the result of immutable bliss.[86]

I believe it is on the basis of this and similar interpretations of the meaning of the Vedic tradition and Vedic sacrificial rites that the *Kālacakratantra* can attribute the authorship of the Vedas to the Buddha Kālacakra without contradicting its main Buddhist principles. This view of the origin of different religious systems explains in part the previously discussed syncretism of the *Kālacakratantra*; and it is yet another way in which this *tantra* advocates religious integration by means of conversion to the Kālacakra tradition.

In addition to its social and religious aspects, the *vajra*-family reveals itself also in its temporal and cosmic aspects. For the *Kālacakratantra*, the four *yugas* ("ages") of the world and the six types of cyclic existence (*gati*) are the particular modes of the four expressions of enlightened awareness. As such, they are the temporal and cosmic correlates of the four castes. The social, religious, and temporal structures of the conventional world are the diverse and mutually pervasive manifestations of the same *vajra*-family, which manifests itself in this world as a society, expresses itself through the religious systems of that society, and transforms its social and religious aspects due to its own temporal power. Its social, religious, and temporal manifestations are a display of its powers and enlightened activities that create and destroy the phenomenal world. It is said that Kālacakra generates the six types of cyclic existence from his four mouths. Likewise, he paralyzes, bewilders, pacifies, improves, dominates, attracts, destroys, and expels this world by means of the same four mouths.[87] Finally, one could say that Kālacakra's social, religious, and temporal bodies bear the inseparable and mutually pervasive features of the conventional and ultimate realities.

Table 6.1 illustrates the *Kālacakratantra*'s presentation of the interrelationship among the four mouths, or aspects, of Kālacakra, the four castes, the four groups of religious systems, the four *yugas* of the world, and the six types of cyclic existence.

In conclusion, one may say that it is chiefly on the basis of the aforementioned perspectives on the commonality of the fundamental nature and source of different social classes and religious systems that the *Kālacakratantra* opposes social discrimination and rejects the mainstream Brāhmaṇical interpretation of the Hindu scriptures. It regards social discrimination and the interpretation of scriptures that supports such discrimination as detrimental to both the socio-political, material, and

TABLE 6.1 The Manifold Manifestations of the Four Aspects of Kālacakra

Western mouth of the yellow face	Northern mouth of the white face	Southern mouth of the red face	Eastern mouth of the dark blue face
Their Mental Aspects			
meditative	peaceful	passionate	wrathful
Their Mental Powers			
paralyzing and bewildering	pacification and prosperity	dominance and attraction	killing and expelling
Their Social Manifestations			
Vaiśya	Brāhmaṇa	Kṣatriya	Śūdra
Their Religious Manifestations			
Buddhist: Sthavira Madhyamaka *yogānuviddha*	*Buddhist*: Vaibhāṣika Mahāsaṃghika action-*tantras* (*kriyā-tantra*)	*Buddhist*: Sāmitīya Sūtrānta *yoga-tantras*	*Buddhist*: Sarvastivāda Yogācāra wisdom-*tantras* (*prajñā-tantra*)
Hindu: Ṛg-Veda spirit-*tantras* (*bhūta-tantra*)	*Hindu*: Yajur-Veda Siddhānta	*Hindu*: Sāma-Veda Vaiṣṇava	*Hindu*: Atharva-Veda *kaula-tantras*
Their Temporal Manifestations			
kṛta-yuga	*tretā-yuga*	*dvāpara-yuga*	*kali-yuga*
Six Types of Cyclic Existence as Their Manifestations			
animals	denizens of hells and *asuras*	gods and *pretas*	humans

spiritual welfare of society and to the psychological and physical well-being of the individual. The *Kālacakratantra* warns against the harms of the pernicious Hindu practices that involve suicide and other hurtful activities that result from grasping onto social discrimination in the following manner:

> He who has a caste as his standard, o king, has the Veda as his authority. He who has the Veda as his authority, has sacrifice as his standard on the earth. He who has a sacrifice as his standard, has the slaying of various animals and people as his sanction. For him who has killing as his sanction, a sin causing the fear of death will be a measure.[88]

> The monk, the wandering ascetic, the naked mendicant, the shaven-headed one, and one with clotted hair, who delight in supreme bliss, and the learned one who delights in listening and reading—they all, deprived of the path, create hardship by grasping onto the creator and the Self, by continually grasping here onto themselves and others, onto their sons and wives, onto allowed and prohibited food, and by grasping onto delight in [discriminating between] the noble and ignoble family and onto the worthy and unworthy vessel [of receiving the teaching].

> Abandoning the entire Buddha-field, which yields the fruit of immutable bliss and has a body, speech, mind, and passion, the evil-minded seeks another lord in a field, in a place of pilgrimage, and in other places by means of hundreds of vows and precepts, by means of fasting and jumping from cliffs. Attached to the pleasures of sense-objects, [one seeks another lord] in battle and in the eclipsed sun, by means of killings in fire and by means of numerous weapons.
>
> Long ago, Māras invented all this in order to drink the blood of those who had died due to fasting in places of pilgrimage for the sake of heaven, or those who were killed in a battle, who died for the sake of the liberation of a bull and the sun, who died for the sake of their home and wealth, or who died in the duty of a Brāhmaṇa.[89]

The *Kālacakratantra*'s view of all the objects of one's experience as inherently pure in nature and its underlying premise that everything within the provisional and ultimate realms of experience is a part of the nondual reality (*advaya-tattva*) is also characteristic of other *anuttara-yoga-tantras*. The *Hevajratantra* expresses it in these words:

> Whatever things there are, mobile and immobile, grass, shrubs, and creepers, they are regarded as the supreme reality having the nature that is one's own nature.[90]
>
> The Innate (*sahaja*) is the entire world. It is called own-form (*sva-rūpa*). One's own-form itself is *nirvāṇa* when the mind is in its purified form.[91]

Even though the notion that diverse religious systems and their tenets originate from a single, omniscient gnosis (*jñāna*) is suggested in other *anuttara-yoga-tantras*, it is developed at greater length and explicated in more detail in the Indian literary sources of the Kālacakra tradition than in any other *anuttara-yoga-tantra*. One of the characteristics that is specific to the Kālacakra tradition is its unique interpretation of the nature and origination of society and the social classes, which directly pertains to its soteriological paths and goals. Likewise, the socio-political reasons for social and religious integration that the Kālacakra tradition offers seem to be unique to this Buddhist tantric tradition and its socio-political climate.

The Individual as a Society

For the Kālacakra tradition, the individual is not merely a member of the *vajra*-family or the society but is the *vajra*-family and the society itself. The individual is the microcosmic manifestation of the social and religious bodies of the Buddha in both their phenomenal and ultimate aspects. The Kālacakra tradition interprets the individual as the embodiment of its society in various ways. While doing so, it utilizes a conventional classification and characterization of the social classes of India at that time and reinterprets them in the light of its broader theory of the nature and composition of the individual. It does so by addressing the following issues: (1) the transcendent and immanent aspects of a society, (2) the ways in which a society manifests and functions within the individual, (3) the interrelatedness of the transcendent and individual aspects of a society, and (4) their soteriological relevance and practical applications on the individual's path of purification.

TABLE 6.2 Castes as the Individual's Vajras and the Kāyas of the Buddha

The four castes and their colors			
Vaiśya	Brāhmaṇa	Kṣatriya	Śūdra
yellow	white	red	black
The individual			
gnosis	body, semen	speech, uterine blood	consciousness
gnosis-*vajra*	body-*vajra*	speech-*vajra*	mind-*vajra*
Kālacakra			
Jñānakāya	Nirmāṇakāya	Saṃbhogakāya	Dharmakāya

The *Kālacakratantra* indirectly correlates the four castes with the four *vajras* of the individual's body, speech, mind and gnosis and with the four bodies of the Buddha by also interpreting Kālacakra's four faces and their colors as the symbolic representations of the four *vajras* of the individual and the Kālacakra's four bodies. In this way, it explains the four castes as the four social manifestations of the capacities of the individual's body, speech, mind, and gnosis and as the social manifestations of the four bodies of the Buddha.

Table 6.2 illustrates the manner in which the Kālacakra tradition classifies and identifies the four castes with their immanent aspects manifesting in the individual and with their ultimate aspects manifesting in the four bodies of the Buddha.

The Kālacakra tradition also identifies the earlier mentioned thirty-six social classes of Indian society with the thirty-six constituents of the individual, namely: the six elements (*dhātu*), the six sense-faculties (*indriya*), the six sense-objects (*viṣaya*), the six psycho-physical aggregates (*skandha*), including the aggregate of gnosis as the sixth, the six faculties of action (*karmendriya*), and the six activities of the faculties of action. It is the father's semen and mother's uterine blood, represented in the *kālacakra-maṇḍala* by the white and red faces of Kālacakra, that give rise to the six families of the six elements. Among these six families, the three families of the water, wind, and space elements are ascertained as the father's family, since they arise from semen and become the body, speech, and mind of a male. The three families of the earth, fire, and gnosis elements are ascertained as the mother's families, for they arise from uterine blood and become the body, speech, and mind of a female. These six families of the six elements arise within the individual at the time of the origination of the element of gnosis, at the age of twelve within the female body and at the age of sixteen within the male body. They are the six families from which evolve the six sense-faculties (*indriya*), six sense-objects (*viṣaya*), six aggregates (*skandha*), six faculties of action (*karmendriya*), and six activities of the faculties of action (*karmendriya-kriyā*).[92] Each of these six families is comprised of different bodily constituents representing six different social classes. The individual's body, speech, and mind develop and function only when the bodily constituents that belong to the father's and mother's families embrace each other. Due to their union, they become of mixed social classes and become mutually indivisible. Thus, just as the thirty-six social classes in Indian society have developed from intermarriages of the four castes and outcasts, so the aforementioned thirty-six members of the individual's body develop from the integration of the six elements. The mutual interdependence and pervasiveness of these thirty-six members of the bodily *vajra*-family correspond to the interdependence and pervasiveness of the members of the social and enlightened *vajra*-families.

The inner yogic practices by means of which the tantric adept unifies his internal thirty-six social groups into a single *vajra*-family correspond to the external tantric practices by means of which the external *vajra*-family socially and spiritually unifies itself. The mutual pervasiveness of the diverse components of the individual's body, speech, and mind and the powers that result from this pervasiveness are the internal manifestations of the characteristics of the socially unified *vajra*-family.

The six classes, which give rise to the thirty-six social classes, evolve due to their intermingling and are specified in this tantric system as the six main families (*kula*): Brāhamaṇa, Kṣatriya, Viaśya, Śūdra, Ḍomba, and Caṇḍāla. In terms of the individual, these six families are the earlier-mentioned six elements; and in terms of enlightened awareness, they are the six Buddha families: namely, the families of Vairocana, Ratnasaṃbhava, Amitābha, Amoghasiddhi, Akṣobhya, and Vajrasattva. These six Buddha families are also present within the individual's six *cakras* and six *nāḍīs*. This exposition of the origination of the thirty-six social classes from the mutual pervasiveness of the six families, which, in turn, originate from a single source, is yet another way in which the Kālackara tradition subtantiates its theories of social equality and the nonduality of the different aspects of the phenomenal and ultimate realities.

Just as the previously discussed unity of the four castes is symbolicaly represented in the *kālacakra-maṇḍala* by the four faces of the Buddha, so the unity of these six social classes is depicted by the six faces of the Buddha. The two lowest social classes, Ḍomba and Caṇḍāla, are said to originate from the additional two faces of Kālacakra, the upper and lower faces. In terms of enlightened awareness, three of the six families—the Vaiśya, Kṣatriya, and Caṇḍāla families of Vairocana, Ratnasaṃbhava, and Vajrasattva—belong to the body, speech, and mind of the wisdom aspect of enlightened awareness. Whereas the other three—the Brāhmaṇa, Śūdra, and Ḍomba families of Amitābha, Amoghasiddhi, and Akṣobhya—belong to the body, speech, and mind of the compassion aspect of the same awareness. Owing to their mutual pervasiveness, they form an indivisible and therefore indestructible unitary reality, which is the ultimate *vajra*-family. This ultimate *vajra*-family is the ideal family that brings about the well-being of the world, for it is the indestructible union (*vajra-yoga*) of wisdom and compassion.

There are different ways in which the Kālacakra tradition describes the ultimate *vajra*-family, or the spiritually awakened *vajra*-society, which manifests as the social and the individual human body of the Buddha. Tables 6.3.a–f illustrate how the Kālacakra tradition in India interpreted the *vajra*-family, comprising thirty-six different social groups, as it manifests in the human being, society, *kālacakra-maṇḍala*, and Buddha Kālacakra.

With regard to the six elements within the individual and the members of the *gaṇa-cakra*, the female members of Ratnasaṃbhava's family embrace the male members of Amitābha's family, whereas the female members of Amitābha's family embrace the male members of Ratnasaṃbhava's family. Likewise, the female members

TABLE 6.3.A The Family of Vairocana

The individual	Kālacakra-*maṇḍala*	Color Taste Symbol	Social class
the form-aggregate (*rūpa-skandha*)	Vairocana	yellow salty wheel	Vaiśya
the earth-element (*pṛthivī-dhātu*)	Locanā	yellow salty wheel	Vaiśyī
skin	Viṣkambhī	yellow salty wheel	garland-maker
smell	Gandhavajrā	yellow salty wheel	female garland-maker
the anus	Stambhaka	yellow salty wheel	scabbard-maker
talking	Stambhī	yellow salty wheel	female scabbard-maker
	The *nāḍī* of excrement		
	The yellow navel-*cakra*		

TABLE 6.3.B The Family of Ratnasaṃbhava

The individual	Kālacakra-*maṇḍala*	Color Taste Symbol	Social class
the aggregate of feeling (*vedanā-skandha*)	Ratnasaṃbhava	red hot jewel	Kṣatriya
the fire-element (*tejo-dhātu*)	Pāṇḍarā	red hot jewel	Kṣatriṇī
an eye	Kṣitigarbha	red hot jewel	liquor-maker
taste	Rasavajrā	red hot jewel	female liquor-maker
the hands	Jambhaka	red hot jewel	lac-maker
walking	Jambhī	red hot jewel	female lac-maker
	The *nāḍī* of uterine blood		
	The red throat-*cakra*		

TABLE 6.3.C The Family of Amitābha

The individual	Kālacakra-*maṇḍala*	Color Taste Symbol	Social class
the aggregate of discernment (*saṃjñā-skandha*)	Amitābha	white sweet lotus	Brāhmaṇa
the water-element (*toya-dhātu*)	Māmakī	white sweet lotus	Brāhmaṇī
the tongue	Lokeśvara	white sweet lotus	goldsmith
form	Rūpavajrā	white sweet lotus	female goldsmith
the feet	Mānaka	white sweet lotus	oilman
taking	Māninī	white sweet lotus	oilwoman
	The *nāḍī* of semen The white *lalāṭa-cakra*		

TABLE 6.3.D The Family of the Amoghasiddhi

The individual	Kālacakra-*maṇḍala*	Color Taste Symbol	Social class
the aggregate of mental formations (*saṃskāra-skandha*)	Amoghasiddhi	black bitter sword	Śūdra
the wind-element (*vāyu-dhātu*)	Tārā	black bitter sword	Śūdrī
the nose	Khagarbha	black bitter sword	weaver
touch	Sparśavajrā	black bitter sword	female weaver
the speech-faculty	Atibala	black bitter sword	blacksmith
the flow of feces	Atibalā/Ananta-vīryā	black bitter sword	female blacksmith
	The *nāḍī* of urine The black heart-*cakra*		

TABLE 6.3.E The Family of Akṣobhya

The individual	Kālacakra-*maṇḍala*	Color Taste Symbol	Social class
the aggregate of consciousness (*vijñāna-skandha*)	Akṣobhya	green astringent *vajra*	Ḍomba
the space-element (*ākāśa-dhātu*)	Vajradhātvīśvarī	green astringent *vajra*	Ḍombī
the ear	Vajrapāṇi	green astringent *vajra*	jeweler
a mental object (*dharma-dhātu*)	Dharmadhātuvajrā	green astringent *vajra*	female jeweler
the vulva	Uṣṇīṣa	green astringent *vajra*	dancer
emission of semen	Raudrākṣī	green astringent *vajra*	female dancer
	The *nāḍī* of consciousness (*vijñāna*) The dark green *uṣṇīṣa-cakra*		

TABLE 6.3.F The Family of Vajrasattva

The individual	Kālacakra-*maṇḍala*	Color Taste Symbol	Social classes
the aggregate of gnosis (*jñāna-skandha*)	Vajrasattva	blue sour cleaver	Caṇḍāla
the gnosis-element (*jñāna-dhātu*)	Viśvamātā	blue sour cleaver	Caṇḍālī
the mind	Samantabhadra	blue sour cleaver	brazier
sound	Śabdavajrā	blue sour cleaver	female brazier
the male sexual organ	Sumbharāja	blue sour cleaver	washerman
the flow of urine	Atinīlā	blue sour cleaver	washerwoman
	The *nāḍī* of gnosis (*jñāna*) The blue secret-*cakra*		

of Amoghasiddhi's family embrace the male members of Vairocana's family; and the female members of Vairocana's family embrace the male members of Amoghasiddhi's family. Similarly, the female members of Akṣobhya's family embrace the male members of Vajrasattva's family; and the female members of Vajrasattva's family embrace the male members of Akṣobhya's family.[93] Due to their mutual embracing, or pervasion, the families belonging to the Buddha Kālacakra (father, compassion) and those belonging to his consort Viśvamātā (mother, wisdom) become mutually indivisible. Thus, even with regard to ultimate reality, one may say that the body of the Buddha arises from the mutual pervasion, or unification, of the different factors constituting Buddhahood. The nondual, absolute reality, which is devoid of conceptualization and atomic matter, is said to have all colors and all aspects. This implies that in social terms, ultimate reality reveals itself in every individual, in every social group, and in their functions in society.

On the ground that the thirty-six social classes are present in all the *guṇas* of *prakṛti*, the Kālacakra tradition sees the social body as nondual from the cosmic body. It even classifies the different types of soil with which one constructs the *kālacakra-maṇḍala* in terms of social classes, according to their colors, smells, and tastes. For example, white, red, yellow, and black soil represent the respective Brāhmaṇa, Kṣatriya, Vaiśya, and Śūdra castes, and green soil represents the Ḍomba outcast.[94] Thus, one may infer that in terms of conventional reality, the material body of the *kālacakra-maṇḍala* itself is symbolically made of the mixture of castes and outcasts. In this respect, it is also a symbolic representation of the socially integrated society. Likewise, the body of the Buddha Kālacakra visually depicted as the *kālacakra-maṇḍala* metaphorically consists of a mixture of social classes. The white soil of the Brāhmaṇa caste symbolizes the purity of the Buddha's body; the red soil of the Kṣatriya caste indicates the purity of his speech; the yellow soil of the Vaiśya caste represents the purity of gnosis; the black soil of the Śūdra caste represents the purity of the Buddha's mind; and the green soil of the Ḍomba class in the center of the *maṇḍala* symbolizes the source of these four types of purity.[95] As in the *gaṇa-cakra*, so in the *kālacakra-maṇḍala*, the class of disdained outcasts is ironically indicated as the source of all aspects of the individual's purification. Similarly, since the thirty-six families of the *yoginīs* of the *kālacakra-maṇḍala* represent thirty-six social classes, the *yoginīs* are also said to be of mixed breed due to the efficacy of the *guṇas* of their *prakṛti*.[96]

The thirty-six social classes that form the social body manifest as the diverse colors, smells, and tastes of the bodies of the individual and the cosmos. Like the three previously mentioned bodies of the individual, society, and enlightened awareness, the body of the cosmos is a cosmic manifestation of the *vajra*-family. The five *maṇḍalas* of the cosmos and the lotus in the center of Mt. Meru are the cosmic representations of the six social classes. Thus, the space-*maṇḍala* on which this world-system rests is of the Ḍomba class, the wind-*maṇḍala* is of the Śūdra caste, the water-*maṇḍala* is of the Brāhmaṇa caste, the fire-*maṇḍala* is of the Kṣatriya caste, the earth-*maṇḍala* is of the Vaiśya caste, and the lotus in the center of Sumeru is of the Caṇḍāla class. The nature of the six families of the cosmos corresponds to the nature of the six families of the six elements in the body of the individual. Likewise, their arrangement in the cosmic body corresponds to their arrangement in the individual's body. In this way, the cosmic and individual bodies are the macrocosmic and microcosmic features of

TABLE 6.4.A The Indivual, Cosmic, and Sublimated Aspects of Social Classes

The individual	Kālacakra-*maṇḍala*	Cosmos	Social class
The four elements and the four psycho-physical aggregates	Four Vidyās and four Buddhas	The gods of the Brahmā-world (*brahmāṇḍa*)	**Four castes**[1] Śūdras (four types) Kṣatriyas (four types) Vaiśyas (three types) Brāhmaṇas (seven types)
The six sense-objects and the six sense-faculties	Six Vajrās and Six Bodhisattvas	Six types of gods dwelling in the desire-realm	**Six social groups** braziers liquor-makers goldsmiths garland-makers weavers jewelers
The five faculties of action and their activities	Ten male and female *krodhas*	The human world	**Ten social groups** lac-makers scabbard-makers oil-pressers blacksmiths shoe-makers carpenters barbers flute-makers well-diggers flute-dancers

The gnosis and mind *maṇḍalas*
The gnosis and mind-*vajras* of the individual

The Viśuddhakāya and the Dharmakāya

[1] The *Vimalaprabhā* commentary on the *Kālacakratantra*, Ch. 3, v. 131, lists the following four types of Kṣatriyas: foot-soldiers, horsemen, elephant-riders, and charioteers. It specifies the three types of the Vaiśya caste as merchants (*vaṇij*), writers (*kāya-stha*), and physicians (*vaidya*); and it enumerates the following seven types of the Brāhmaṇa caste: four types belonging to the branches (*śākhā*) of the *Ṛg-Veda*, *Yajur-Veda*, *Sāma-Veda*, and *Atharva-Veda*, forest-dwellers (*vana-prastha*), ascetics (*yati*), and liberated ones (*mukta*).

the social body. Like other *vajra*-families, the macrocosmic *vajra*-family arises as a unitary cosmic body due to the unification of the six families. Thus, one may say that every body, or every aspect of the *vajra*-family—whether individual, social, cosmic or spiritual—stems from the union of the diverse classes that it embodies. In this way, the Kālacakra tradition indirectly refutes the disparaging view expressed by the authoritative, legal treatises of the Hindu tradition toward some mixed social classes in India.

Another way in which the Kālacakra tradition explains the nonduality of the phenomenal aspects of the Buddha's social and cosmic bodies with the body of the individual is demonstrated by tables 6.4.a–b.

TABLE 6.4.B The Individual, Cosmic, and Sublimated Aspects of Social Classes

The individual	Kālacakra-*maṇḍala*	Cosmos	Social classes
Eight *nāḍīs*	Eight male and female *pretas*	The world of *pretas*	**Eight social groups** butchers potters pillow-makers prostitutes sewers fishermen actors washermen
Eight fingers and toes	Eight *nāgas* and eight *pracaṇḍās*	The underworld (*pātāla*)	**Eight lowest social groups**[1] barbarians sweepers Mātaṅgas Tāpins Varvaras Pukkasas Bhillas Śabaras
The speech and body *maṇḍalas* The speech and body *vajras* of the individual The Saṃbhogakāya and the Nirmāṇakāya			

[1] Mātaṅgas is another name for Caṇḍālas, the outcasts. Varvaras are members of one of the non-Āryan tribes in India. Bhillas are members of a wild tribe living in the Vindhya hills, in the forests of Mālawa, Mewar, Khandesha, and Deccan. Śabaras are the members of a mountain tribe in south India.

In addition to the already mentioned aspects of the *vajra*-family, the *vajra*-family also manifests in a temporal form. Specifically, it manifests as the "wheel of time," consisting of the diverse families of the diverse units of time. Likewise, the three years of the central *nāḍī*, during which a tantric *yogī* practices the *yoga* of *nāḍīs* on the stage of completion (*sampatti-krama*) by joining the right and left *nāḍīs* in the *madhyamā*, are also viewed in this tantric tradition as a *vajra*-family. Six families of this temporal *vajra*-family are the six periods of three years, each of which consists of one hundred and eighty days. Its thirty-six families are the thirty-six months of the three years.[97] Thus, the unification of the different units of time and the yogic practice of unifying the *nāḍīs* correspond to social unification. In this way, the Kālacakra tradition indicates that in order to actualize the ultimate unification, or the ultimate *vajra*-family, which is the state of nonduality, one must first conventionally understand the ways in which the different phenomenal aspects of the *vajra*-family are already unified; and then by means of tantric *yoga*, one must consolidate the conventional *vajra*-families into the single ultimate *vajra*-family, called Kālacakra, or gnosis (*jñāna*).

In conclusion, one may say that in this tantric tradition, the interrelatedness and mutual pervasiveness of the various components of the individual's mind and body represent the social and ethnic integration of a socially and ethnically mixed society through intermarriages. Likewise, the mutual pervasiveness of the mind and body of the Buddha and the interdependence of the thirty-seven factors of awakening represent the ultimate unity of the society, which is characterized by the interdependence and pervasiveness of its thirty-six social classes. Similarly, the mutual relations and influences of the individual, the cosmos, and time parallel those in the society. Thus, the organization and functions of the different members of the social body are nondual from the structure and functions of the different members of the bodies of the individual, the cosmos, and enlightened awareness. By identifying Indian society with the individual, the cosmos, time, and ultimate reality in the above-illustrated ways, the Kālacakra tradition demonstrates its vision of the ideal society and its potential, and it provides its rationale for that vision. Just as the transformation and unification of the various components of one's own mind and body on this tantric path transform one's experience of one's natural environment, so it transforms one's experience of one's social environment. Likewise, in this tantric tradition, the unification of all the phenomenal and ultimate aspects of the *vajra*-family, which abolishes all dualities, is nothing other than the state of self-knowing: the state of knowing oneself as the cosmos, society, individual, and enlightened awareness; and that self-knowledge is what is meant by omniscience (*sarva-jñatā*) in the tradition of the *Kālacakratantra*.

The Gnostic Body

The *Kālacakratantra* as a Buddhist Gnostic System

The twentieth-century discoveries of the Nag Hammadi Codices (Upper Egypt, 1945), and the Manichean texts of Inner Asia (Taklamakan desert, 1902–1914) have given rise to the contemporary view of gnosticism as a world religion rather than a mere heretical formulation of Christianity. This new awareness of the temporal and geographical, as well as the theoretical and practical diversity of gnosticism, has aroused great interest in that tradition among contemporary scholars of religions. At present, there is a wide range of translations of gnostic texts and secondary literature on gnosticism.

Fairly recent endeavors of Buddhist scholars in preparing new editions and definitive translations of Indo-Tibetan Buddhist *tantras* are bringing to light diverse and intriguing aspects of tantric Buddhism. Some Buddhist *tantras*, especially the *tantras* of the *anuttara-yoga* class, show a strong affinity with the gnostic views of the individual and the universe and striking similarities with practices of various non-Indian gnostic groups. Likewise, due to their strong emphasis on the soteriological significance of realizing gnosis (*jñāna*), the unmediated knowledge of absolute reality, the *anuttara-yoga-tantras* can justifiably be considered as religious treatises of a Buddhist gnostic tradition in India. The interpretation of gnosis as intuitive knowledge, knowledge or a vision of oneself as a spiritual reality, and the view of the universe as the macrocosm of that reality are found equally in Jewish and Christian forms of gnosticism, in eastern Manicheism, and in the *anuttara-yoga-tantras*. Similarly, the view of gnosis as distinct from reflective knowledge, namely, wisdom that is acquired through study and investigation, is common to the aforementioned gnostic traditions. I will attempt to demonstrate here that the *Kālacakra* tradition in India is an authentic gnostic tradition of Indian Buddhism and that gnosticism manifested itself in a greater variety of forms and localities than many scholars have originally thought.

While using the term "gnosticism" as a typological category, I am fully aware that this term is a modern construct that does not accurately define all of the traditions and sources regularly classified as "gnostic." The term "gnosticism" has often been used as an umbrella term for various systems of belief and multilayered traditions of thought that were held together by gnosis. One of the most renowned scholars of gnosticism, Hans Jonas, asserts that we can speak of gnostic schools, sects, and cults, of gnostic writings and teachings, of gnostic myths and speculations in the sense that they share the following common features: (1) the emphasis on gnosis as the means for attaining liberation or as the form of liberation itself, and (2) the claim to the possession of gnosis.[1] This broad typological definition of gnosticism can most certainly be applied to the branch of tantric Buddhism that is represented in the *Kālacakratantra* and other *anuttara-yoga-tantras*.

In the *Kālacakratantra*, gnosis (*jñāna*), which is considered the ultimate reality, is the most crucial concept. As in other gnostic traditions, the main focus of the *Kālacakratantra* is on gnosis as the *source* of the individual's aspiration for enlightenment, as the *means* leading to the fulfillment of that aspiration, and as the *fulfillment* of that aspiration. When this source of aspiration for spiritual awakening is brought forth, or made fully conscious, it liberates one from cyclic existence. But when it is not brought forth, or remains unconscious, it destroys the individual and keeps him in cyclic existence. Therefore, it is said that gnosis is the source of both cyclic existence and *nirvāṇa*. In this regard, the *Kālacakratantra* fully accords with the writings of other gnostic systems, which also see gnosis as the source of sublime power, the ground of all being, and the potential for liberation or destruction, existing in a latent state within the psyche of all people. The *Gospel of Thomas* expresses it in this way:

> If you bring forth what is within you, what you bring forth will save you. If you do not bring forth what is within you, what you do not bring forth will destroy you.[2]

Likewise, the *Kālacakratantra*'s interpretation of gnosis as the ultimate support of the conceptual mind in which it expresses itself by means of thought resonates with the following passage from the Nag Hammadi text *Trimorphic Protennoia*:

> I am perception and knowledge, uttering a Voice by means of Thought. [I] am the real Voice. I cry out in everyone, and they know that the seed dwells within.[3]

Or in the poem that is included in the longer version of the *Apochryphon of John*, the Revealer says the following:

> And I entered in the midst of their prison, that is, the prison of their body. And I said, "You who hear, wake up from the heavy sleep!" And he wept and poured forth heavy tears, and then wiped them away and said, "Who is it that is calling my name? And from where does this hope come, since I am in the chains of the prison?"[4]

The Kālacakra tradition's interpretation of the presence of pure and transcendent gnosis within every sentient being and within all things as their nature, even when not being yet realized as such, also accords with interpretations of gnosis in other gnostic texts. For example, in the *Gospel of Thomas*, Jesus says to his disciples who mistake salvation, or "Kingdom," for a future event, that the Kingdom is inside them and also outside of them. He says further: "What you look forward to has already come, but you do not recognize it."[5]

Furthermore, in the same way that some Christian gnostic texts identify Jesus the teacher simply with "knowledge of the truth,"[6] so the Kālacakra tradition identifies the Buddha Kālacakra with both knowledge (*jñāna*) and truth (*tattva*). For the Kālacakra tradition as well as all other gnostic traditions, knowledge of the truth can be actualized only by looking within, for one's own gnosis is ultimately one's own teacher. The *Kālacakratantra* expresses this in the following manner:

> What mother or father, what precious sons or daughters of yours, what brother or sister, what wife, what master or group of friends, having abandoned the path of truth, can remove [your] fear of death? . . . [7]

The Christian gnostic text the *Testimony of Truth* asserts that the gnostic is a disciple of his own mind, "the father of the truth."[8] Therefore, gnosis is nothing other than self-knowledge, insight into the depths of one's own being. As for all other gnostic traditions, so too for the Kālacakra tradition, the individual who lacks this knowledge is driven by impulses that he does not comprehend. One suffers due to ignorance regarding one's own divine nature. Therefore, ignorance of oneself is a form of self-destruction. To know oneself, one must first understand the elements of one's own natural environment and of one's own body. For this very reason, the first two chapters of the *Kālacakratantra* focus on the exposition of the elemental nature of the cosmos and the individual and on the manner of their origination and destruction. In this respect, the *Kālacakratantra* also shows a great affinity with other gnostic writings. The following passage from the Christian gnostic text the *Dialogue of the Savior* perfectly accords with the Kālacakra tradition's way of understanding oneself and the world in which one lives in terms of conventional reality.

> . . . If one does not [understand] how the fire came to be, he will burn in it, because he does not know his root. If one does not first understand the water, he does not know anything. . . . If one does not understand how the wind that blows came to be, he will run with it. If one does not understand how the body that he wears came to be, he will perish with it. . . . Whoever does not understand how he came will not understand how he will go. . . .[9]

Just as in the context of Christian gnosticism, whoever achieves gnosis is no longer a Christian, but a Christ, so for the Kālacakra tradition, whoever actualizes gnosis is no longer a mere tantric Buddhist, but the Buddha Kālacakra. In other words, in these gnostic traditions, one becomes the transcendent reality that one perceives at the time of spiritual transformation. Having perceived oneself in this way, one perceives and knows all things in the same way. Likewise, just as in the *Kālacakratantra*, so too in some Christian gnostic systems, the realization of gnosis entails the transcendence of all differentiations, or dualities, for it is the final integration of the knower and the known. One reads in the *Gospel of Thomas*:

> When you make the two one, and when you make the inside like the outside and the outside like the inside, and the above like the below, and when you make the male and the female one and the same . . . then you will enter [the Kingdom].[10]

The *Kālacakratantra* speaks of this nondual perception of the world in terms of seeing all things as being of the "same taste" (*sama-rasa*), the taste of gnosis.

There are many other "gnostic" features characterizing the Kālacakra tradition and other Buddhist tantric systems in India that are also characteristic of other ancient gnostic systems. Some of their common, gnostic characteristics are the following: (1) an affinity for the nonliteral significance of language and for the usage of symbolic language, (2) the assertion that the ultimate is essentially indescribable but can be imagined as androgynous, a dyad consisting of masculine and feminine elements, the Father and Mother, (3) the claim to the possession of esoteric teachings that are not intended for the general public but only for those who have proven themselves to be spiritually mature and qualified for receiving initiation, and (4) a subversive attitude with regard to the social hierarchy and the deconstruction of established, cultural norms, which can be escaped through ritual enactments.[11] A certain ambivalence with regard to the physical body is equally found in various Nag Hammadi texts, in the *Kālacakratantra*, and in other *anuttara-yoga-tantras*. On the one hand, these texts speak of the physical body as a "prison" and a source of suffering due to its weakness and impermanence; and on the other hand, they present the human body as a domain in which the convergence of the two realms—the utterly pure, transcendent realm and the impure, material realm—takes place. Just as the *Kālacakratantra* sees the human body as a microcosmic image of the external world and spiritual reality and the universe as the body of the Buddha Kālacakra, so some Jewish and Christian gnostic groups saw the human anatomy as a kind of a map of reality and the universe as a divine body. For example, according to Hippolytus, Nassenes interpreted the biblical description of the Garden of Eden and its four rivers as the brain and the four senses, whereas Simonians interpreted the Garden as the womb, Eden as the placenta, and the river that flows out of Eden as the navel, which is divided into four channels—two arteries and two veins. Similar allegorical interpretation of the human body and anatomical interpretation of the environment are characteristic of many Buddhist and non-Buddhist *tantras*. Likewise, for many gnostic systems, as for the *Kālacakratantra* tradition, a goal is not only to transform the mind but also to transform the body itself.

There are also some commonalities regarding the methods of achieving gnosis. Even though most of the gnostic texts discovered at Nag Hammadi do not explain methods for realizing gnosis, the few texts that describe the practice of meditation and tonal recitations as the means of accessing inner gnosis show correspondences with the Kālacakra tradition and all other tantric systems.

The "Final Document" of the conference on gnosticism that was held in Messina, Italy, in 1966 proposes a working definition of gnosticism, according to which,

> not every *gnosis* is Gnosticism, but only that which involves in this perspective the idea of the divine consubstantiality of the spark that is in need of being awakened and re-integrated. This *gnosis* of Gnosticism involves the divine identity of the *knower* (the Gnostic), the *known* (the divine substance of one's transcendent self), and *the means by which one knows* that *gnosis* as an implicit divine faculty is to be awakened and actualized. This *gnosis* is a revelation tradition of a different type from the Biblical and Islamic revelation tradition.[12]

As the aforementioned parallels suggest, and as the rest of this chapter will demonstrate, the above-given definition of the gnosis of gnosticism can easily be applied to the *Kālacakratantra*, even though the Kālacakra tradition does not call itself "gnostic." Nowhere in the Kālacakra literature can one find explicit references to the tradition as a Buddhist gnosticism and to its adherents as gnostics, but this does not mean that this tantric tradition did not recognize its gnostic orientation. As the early Buddhist Pāli sources indicate, the earliest disciples of the Buddha never referred to themselves as Buddhists (*bauddha*) but as disciples (*sāvaka*), monks (*bhikhu*), novices (*sāmaṇera*), mendicants (*paribājjaka*), and so on. The absence of their self-designation as Buddhists by no means excludes their Buddhist self-identification. Moreover, one encounters in the *Vimalaprabhā* at least one implicit reference to the *Kālacakratantra* as a gnostic system. Defining the Kālacakra tradition as the Vajrayāna tradition that consists of the systems of *mantras* (*mantra-naya*) and of perfections (*pāramitā-naya*), the *Vimalaprabhā* interprets *mantra* as gnosis in the following manner: "*Mantra* is gnosis because it protects the mind."[13] In this way, the *Vimalaprabhā* implicitly defines the *Kālacakratantra* as a gnostic system (*jñāna-naya*).

The absence of the explicit self-designation "gnostic" is characteristic of most gnostic writings. Scholars of gnosticism point out that in all original gnostic writings of different gnostic traditions, the self-designation *gnostikos* nowhere appears. It is only in the works of the early Christian heresiologists, specifically, Irenaeus, Hippolytus, and Epiphanius, that we read reports of the self-designation *gnostikos*. The contemporary American scholar of gnosticism Michael A. Williams asserts: "to the extent that 'gnostic' was employed as a self-designation, it ordinarily, or perhaps always, denoted a quality rather than a sectarian or socio-traditional identity."[14] This also seems to be the manner in which the Kālacakra tradition in India understood its gnostic character.

Some scholars of gnosticism, seeing the obvious similarities between Buddhist and Judeo-Christian gnosticism, have considered the possibility of Buddhist influence on gnostic communities in Alexandria, where Buddhist missionaries had been proselytizing for generations at the time when trade routes between the Greco-Roman world and Asia were opening up and gnosticism flourished (8–200 CE).[15] Edward Conze also points to the possible influences of Buddhism on the Christian gnostic communities in South India, whose authoritative scripture was the *Gospel of Thomas*.[16] However, for the time being, the lack of conclusive evidence leaves us uncertain as to whether their commonalities are due to mutual influences or whether they are expressions of the same issues taking different forms at different times and in various regions.

Likewise, the *Kālacakratantra*'s evident gnostic orientation and affinity with non-Buddhist gnostic traditions led some German scholars to suggest that Manicheism influenced the Kālacakra tradition in India and even tantric Buddhism as a whole.[17] Their suggestions are not sufficiently substantiated, however, and need further, thorough investigation of all the relevant sources and a judicious and balanced treatment of the difficult issues pertaining to the question of the origins and historical development of the Kālacakra tradition and Manicheism.

The Manichean texts do inform us that after engaging in missionary activities in the Persian kingdom of the Sassanians, in 240 or 241, Mani visited India and the adjacent regions, known today as Beluchistan, where he converted a Buddhist king, the Tūrān Shāh. In the *Kephalaia*, 184. 12, Mani claims that during his visit to the Indus valley, he "moved the whole land of India."[18] However, there is no evidence that Manichean communities lasted in India for a long period of time or that Manicheism exerted a noticeable influence on Buddhism. On the contrary, Manichean texts, such as the *Cologne Mani Codex*, indicate that already in its earliest phase in the Parthian East Iran, where Buddhism was well established, Mani's disciples made an attempt to adopt Mahāyāna Buddhist ideas. Hans Klimkeit points out that as one looks first at the Parthian and then at the Sogdian and Turkish literature of Manicheism, one can observe the increasing adaptation of Eastern Manicheism to Buddhism. In different areas of the world, Manicheism freely adopted different symbols, myths, and languages of the coexisting traditions in those areas. For example, the Chinese Manichean source the *Hymnscroll* frequently speaks of the divine spark in man, or gnosis, as the "Buddha nature." As Mani claimed that the knowledge that he received from God embraces all wisdom contained in earlier religious traditions, the Manichean church was allowed to embrace all earlier religious communities. Mani and his missionaries thought that it was necessary to appropriate symbols and ideas from other religious traditions in order to ensure the proliferation of Manicheism in the world. Consequently, the Manichean syncretism systematically integrated itself into new cultural domains. Like the Kālacakra tradition, it was self-consciously absorbent and did not resort to just disorganized and scattered cultural borrowings and reinterpretations. There is a striking similarity between Manicheism and the Kālacakra tradition with regard to their use of syncretism as a form of proselytism. In this regard, both traditions claimed their own universality and supremacy over other religious systems, on the grounds that other systems are parochially tied to particular places and cultures. Likewise, these two gnostic systems equally see the present state of the individual as characterized by a mixture of good and evil, of gnosis and matter, which are in constant opposition to each other, with the individual as their battlefield. The second chapter of the *Kālacakratantra* depicts the individual as a battlefield, in which the war that will be waged between the Cakrī and the Barbarians in the land of Mecca is already taking place within the body of the individual. In that internal battlefield, Kalkī, who is the individual's correct knowledge (*samyag-jñāna*), with his army's four divisions[19]—the four Immeasurables—wages battle with the vicious king of the Barbarians, Kṛṇamati, who is the evil within one's own body, the path of nonvirtue (*akuśala-patha*). Kṛṇamati's fourfold army, which consists of the four classes of Māras in the body, is led by the general Aśvatthāma, who is one's own spiritual ignorance (*avidyā*). Kalkī's victory in this battle is the attainment of the path of liberation (*mokṣa-mārga*), and within the body the destruction of Aśvatthāma is the eradication of the fear of cyclic existence. The established lineages of Kalkī's sons Brahmā and Sureśa are the pure Buddhas, who have become the nature of one's psycho-physical aggregates, elements, and sense-bases.[20] Similarly, the *Kephalaia* warns that there are many powers in the body, who are its magnates that creep and walk in the body, wounding and destroying each other; however, the Mind of Light in the body acts like a soldier, releasing the body from sins and generating a new body and a new sense of self.[21] Just like the gnosis of the *Kālacakratantra*, the Manichean Mind of Light functions as the protector of the body and mind. The *Kephalaia* expresses it in this way:

> Look, then, at how much the strength and diligence of the Mind of Light is upon all the watchtowers of the body. He stands before his camp. He shuts all the reasonings of the body from the attractions of sin. He limits them, scatters them, removes them by his will.[22]

Thus, in the Kālacakra tradition and in Manicheism, the soteriological struggles in the external world are constantly being enacted in exact mimesis within one's own body. The powers in the world and within the individual are interrelated and analogous. The analogy between the microcosm and macrocosm plays an important role in both traditions. Similarly, the liberation of the mind involves its freedom from their matter, which fetters the mind to sin. Therefore, the holders of both traditions were equally concerned with their bodies as with their minds.

These and other similarities between the *Kālacakratantra* and eastern Manicheism do not constitute sufficient evidence for determining that the two traditions directly influenced each other. Rather, they suggest that their commonalities could have resulted from their independent reinterpretations of earlier Mahāyāna Buddhist concepts, which Manicheism liberally appropriated.

To determine the specific, gnostic orientation of the Kālacakra tradition, we must first understand the ways in which this tantric system interprets gnosis and its functions and delineates the practices for actualizing it.

The Individual, Gnosis, and the Individual as Gnosis

As in the case of other *anuttara-yoga-tantras*, the Kālacakra tradition's interpretation of gnosis has an earlier precedent in the Mahāyāna's interpretation of the perfection of wisdom—specifically, in the literature of the *Prajñāpāramitā* corpus. The internal evidence, however, indicates that its closest precedent is the *Mañjuśrīnāmasaṃgīti*'s presentation of the omniscient and innately pure gnosis (*jñāna*). The *Mañjuśrīnāmasaṃgīti* and the *Kālacakratantra* are intimately related in terms of their expositions of the Jñānakāya. The *Mañjuśrīnāmasaṃgīti* was traditionally included in the literary corpus of the Kālacakra tradition. Its close connection to the Kālacakra tradition is indicated by the *Vimalaprabhā* itself, which states that the *Kālacakratantra* "is embraced by the *Nāmasaṃgīti*, which clarifies the Jñānakāya, Vajradhara."[23] It asserts that the Tathāgata, having extracted the essence of the Bhagavān Vajradhara from all three Vehicles, illuminates the sublime, imperishable gnosis in the *Nāmasaṃgīti*. In this way, the *Vimalaprabhā* suggests that the essence of the Vajrayāna teachings lies at the heart of all Buddhist teachings. It also states that the Jñānakāya, which "is described by one hundred and sixty-two verses in the *Nāmasaṃgīti*," is "called the *vajra*-word in every king of *tantras* (*tantra-rāja*)"[24]—specifically, in the *Māyājāla* and in the *Samājā*, which it oddly classifies as the *kriyā* and *yoga-tantras*.[25] The *Mañjuśrīnāmasaṃgīti* itself also hints at its affiliation with the *Māyājālatantra*.[26]

The *Vimalaprabhā* frequently cites such verses from the *Mañjuśrīnāmasaṃgīti* in order to support and elucidate the *Kālacakratantra*'s theory of gnosis and the Jñānakāya. As the following analysis of the Kālacakra tradition's discussion of gnosis will demonstrate, the Kālacakra tradition's explanations of gnosis in terms of ultimate reality coincide at almost every point with the *Majñuśrīnāmasaṃgīti*'s presentation of gnosis as the gnostic being (*jñāna-sattva*), Vajrasattva, who is endowed with sublime bliss (*mahā-sukha*); as Vajradhara, who is self-arisen from space and therefore similar to space, eternal and nondual, who is thusness (*tathatā*), the completely auspicious (*samantabhadra*), great mind of the Buddhas, reality (*tattva*); and as the Ādibuddha, who is without beginning or end, the sublime breath (*mahā-śvāsa*), established within the minds of all sentient beings, and so on. Likewise, both the *Mañjuśrīnāmasaṃgīti* and the *Ādibuddhatantra* make almost identical references to the Jñānkāya as "the beginningless and endless Buddha, Ādibuddha," as "the five-syllable great emptiness (*mahā-śūnya*) and the six-syllable drop-emptiness (*bindu-śūnya*),"[27] and the like.

Gnosis as the All-Pervading Mind and as the Four Bodies of the Buddha

There are many ways in which gnosis is referred to and explained in the Indian sources of the *Kālacakratantra* tradition. It is primarily interpreted as the mind (*citta*) that brings forth immutable bliss as the desired result, and as the mind that is the result itself, namely, the mind of immutable bliss.[28] Thus, gnosis is seen as the unity (*ekatva*) of two aspects of the mind, which are the cause and result of spiritual awakening. From that vantage point, gnosis is also referred to as the supreme and indestructible *vajra-yoga* consisting of wisdom (*prajñā*) and method (*upāya*), or emptiness (*śūnyatā*) and compassion (*karuṇā*). Emptiness, which is its reflection, or form (*bimba*), is the cause; and compassion, which is indestructible bliss, is the result. Gnosis is the nondual *yoga* of these two. As such, it is identified as the unified mind that is free of momentariness and any causal relation (*niranvaya*), and lacks an inherent existence (*svabhāva*).[29] It is free of momentariness in the sense that for gnosis there is no origination, duration, or cessation of any phenomenon, although by its efficacy all worlds and everything in them arise and cease.[30] It is free of causal relations in the sense that it transcends all conceptual classifications. The *Ādibuddhatantra* describes it in the following way:

> It has passed beyond [the designations:] "It exists" and "It does not exist." It is the cessation of existence and non-existence. It is nondual. It is the *vajra-yoga* that is non-differentiated from emptiness and compassion. It is the supreme bliss.
>
> It has transcended the reality of atoms. It is devoid of empty *dharmas*. It is free of eternity and annihilation. It is the *vajra-yoga* that is without causal relations.[31]

In the Kālacakra literature, gnosis of the indivisible, supreme, and imperishable (*akṣara*) bliss is given different names in accordance with its qualities and functions. Thus, it is called the "*vajra*," and one who has it is refered to as a *vajrī* ("one who has a *vajra*"). *Vajra* is characterized as indestructible (*akṣara*) since it is imperishable and does not go anywhere. Therefore, in the literary corpus of the *Kālacakratantra*, the word "imperishable" always designates supreme, imperishable bliss and gnosis of that bliss.

Gnosis is also called a *mantra* due to its function of protecting the mind. Likewise, it is called "spiritual knowledge" (*vidyā*) of the individual and the "perfection of wisdom" (*prajñā-pāramitā*). It is termed the "the great seal" (*mahā-mudrā*), for it is believed that there is nothing beyond it. Similarly, it is referred to as the *dharma-dhātu*, the Sahajakāya ("The Innate Body"), the Jñānakāya ("Gnosis-body"), or the Viśuddhakāya ("Pure Body"). It is identified as the couple, Vajrasattva and Mātā, which evades the dependently arisen sense-faculties because it has transcended the reality of atoms (*paramāṇu-dharmatā*) and because it is like a dream or an image in a prognostic mirror. It is of the nature of the aggregates (*skandha*) and sense-bases (*āyatana*), which are free of obscurations (*āvaraṇa*) and have become of the same taste (*sama-rasa*). On that ground, they are called "supreme and indestructible" (*paramākṣara*). The supreme, indestructible is designated as the letter *a*, the Samyaksaṃbuddha, Vajrasattva, the androgynous state, the Bhagavān Kālacakra.[32]

Gnosis is the mind, radiant by nature and devoid of the impurities of habitual propensities (*vāsanā*) of transmigratory existence. This pure mind is not characterized by any form, for it is devoid of atomic particles, nor is it characterized by formlessness, for its "form" is emptiness.[33] Thus, being devoid of both form and formlessness, it is like a reflection in a prognostic mirror.

Gnosis transcends the duality of subject and object, for it is simultaneously both knowledge (*jñāna*) and the object of knowledge (*jñeya*). As the subject and the object of knowledge, it is free of conceptualizations (*vikalpa*) and atomic matter (*paramāṇu-dravya*). Although gnosis is free of conceptualizations, it is not devoid of mentation (*cintanā*) because unlike the state of deep sleep, it is self-aware (*sva-saṃvedya*).[34] But its self-awareness does not preclude the fact that gnosis is the knowledge of the absence of the inherent existence of all phenomena. Moreover, it is precisely the self-awareness and natural luminosity of the Tathāgata's gnosis that enable the Tathāgata to teach Dharma in accordance with the mental dispositions of sentient beings. This self-awareness of the Tathāgata is not affected by the sense-faculties, so it is partless, all-pervasive, free of obscurations, and aware of the nature of all *dharmas*, which are themselves unconscious due to lacking self-awareness. The independence of self-awareness from the sense-faculties implies that one does not requre a physical body in order to remove mental obscurations and experience the self-awareness of the gnosis of sublime, imperishable bliss due to the unification of one's own mind with the appearances (*pratibhāsa*) of that mind. According to this tantric system, gnosis can become self-aware through the mind alone, due to the efficacy of the adventitious (*āgantuka*), habitual propensities of the mind (*citta-vāsanā*). The adventitious, habitual propensities of the mind are the so-called psycho-physical aggregates, elements, and sense-bases. Under their influence, feelings of happiness and suffering enter the mind. Experiences in the dreaming state attest to the fact that the mind can become self-aware in the absence of a physical body in the dream. In the dreaming state, a dream body, which consists of the habitual propensities of the mind and is devoid of agglomerations of atoms, suffers injury or experiences great pleasure, and consequently, feelings of suffering or pleasure enter the mind of the dreamer, and self-awareness as knowledge of one's own suffering or happiness takes place. But this all occurs without the dreamer's actual body experiencing injury or pleasure. The *Vimalaprabhā* refers to this ability of the mind as a "great miracle," which even the learned cannot fathom. It comments that if this limited knowledge is difficult to grasp for the learned, then how much more difficult it is for foolish people to understand "the completely auspicious (*samantabhadra*) gnosis of sublime, imperishable bliss, the *yogī*'s self-awareness, which arises from the habitual propensities that are free of obscurations and which transcends the habitual propensities of transmigratory existence." To those who may assert that the mind's ability for self-awareness entails the presence of a physical body, claiming that dreaming, waking, and deep sleep arise in dependence upon the inhalations and exhalations in the body, the *Vimalaprabhā* poses the following questions and arguments:

> If the dreaming state does not arise in the mind without inhalations and exhalations, then how is it possible that without inhalations and exhalations, the appearance of the mind occurs up to one watch of the day in the unconscious state of death? How is it possible that the body, which is being led to the city of Yama by the messengers of Yama, in accordance with the injunction of king Yama, comes into existence? How is it that king Yama also appears in the city of Yama; and how is it that Yama examines the sins and virtues of the body that has been brought? Upon examining [the sins and virtues], he says: "Because the life of this one has not yet been exhausted, swiftly take this person to the world of mortals so that his body may not perish! This is the task of Yama's messengers. In accordance with their task, the messengers of Yama throw that body into the world of mortals. Once it is thrown there, then due to the power of the habitual propensities of the mind, the inhalations and exhalations of that body reoccur. Afterwards, due to the efficacy of a different habitual propensity, the waking state occurs. After the mind's awakening into the waking state, that [person] informs his relatives about king Yama. Therefore, without the body and without the inhalations and exhalations, the adventitious, habitual propensities of the mind arise due to the power of rebirths, and they are not inherent to sentient beings. . . . Thus, due to the power of the habitual propensities of the mind and not due to acquiring a body of atoms, the gnosis of wisdom (*prajñā-jñāna*) becomes self-awareness.[35]

As the last line of this passage indicates, in this tantric tradition, the Buddha's self-awareness is also understood as the gnosis (*jñāna*), or awareness, of his own wisdom (*prajñā*) that perceives the empty nature of all phenomena.

The *Vimalaprabhā* also criticizes those who argue that because during the experience of sexual bliss in a dream, it is the dreamer's physical body that emits semen and not the dream body, the self-awareness of the mind arises due to the capacity of the physical body and not due to the capacity of the mind. It rebuts their argument by asserting that even formless beings, whose bodies are composed of the space-element alone, also emit semen (which consists of the space-element) under the influence of the habitual propensities of their minds. It argues that if the emission of semen could not occur without a physical body, then formless beings would not emit semen, and thus would not be subject to the cycle of transmigration. Since formless beings are subject to the cycle of transmigration, they must experience the gnosis of bliss and seminal emission, and thus, seminal emission must arise due to the capacity of the mind and not the physical body.[36]

For this tantric system, gnosis is Buddhahood, the ultimate reality (*paramārtha*) of the Buddhas, thusness (*tathatā*), which is directly perceived[37] and whose nature is supreme, immutable bliss. That reality is a life-principle, or a sublime *prāṇa* (*mahā-prāṇa*), which pervades the entire universe, manifesting itself in different forms. As such, it is said to be present within the heart of every sentient being.[38] As a sublime *prāṇa*, it is recognized as the source of all utterances, even though it is unutterable itself.

As the pervader of everything, gnosis is recognized as the sixth element, the element of gnosis (*jñāna-dhātu*), or *dharma-dhātu*, which exists in the other five elements—earth, water, fire, wind, and space—and is also their beginning (*ādi*). The Kālacakra tradition views the gnosis-element as the birthplace (*yoni*) of all phenomena on the ground that it is primordially unoriginated. This view has its precedent in the Mahāyāna view of the *dharma-dhātu*, as presented in the *Mahāyānābhidharmasūtra*, which reads:

> The beginningless *dhātu* is the common basis of all phenomena. Because it exists, there is every state of existence and the attainment of *nirvāṇa* as well.[39]

The aforementioned explanation of the gnosis-element in the Kālacakra tradition indicates that the word *dhātu* in the compounds *jñāna-dhātu* and *dharma-dhātu* is understood in three ways—as the ingredient, as the cause, and as the locus; whereas, in the *Mahāyānābhidharmasūtra*, the word *dhātu* seems to be understood in just two ways—as the locus and as the cause. The gnosis-element as the component of phenomenal existence has two aspects: atemporal and temporal. Although the gnosis-element as the beginningless source of phenomenal existence is atemporal, it appears as temporal when it arises in the impermanent body of the individual. In its temporal appearance, the gnosis-element, like the other five elements, originates in the body from one of the six flavors—specifically from the sour flavor, provided by the embryo's nourishment through the mother's food and drink.[40] From that temporal gnosis-element within the body arise sexual bliss, which is a phenomenal aspect of gnosis, the individual's mental faculty (*mano-indriya*), and sound (*śabda*). These three are identified with the gnosis-element from which they originate. As the mental faculty, the gnosis-element apprehends the *dharma-dhātu*, which arises from the space-element (*ākāśa-dhātu*); and as sound, it is apprehended by the auditory sense-faculty, which also arises from the space-element.[41] In light of this, one may infer that within the body of the individual, the gnosis-element, being the apprehending subject (*grāhaka*) of the space-element and the apprehended object (*grāhya*) of the space-element, bears the characteristics of the space-element. Thus, being like the space-element, gnosis is indestructible and eternal. However, one does not experience one's own gnosis-element as such until one's own "gnosis merges with the form of emptiness (*śūnyatā-bimba*)," meaning, until the mind as the apprehending subject (*grāhaka*) merges into the appearance of the mind as the apprehended object (*grāhya*) and "becomes of the same taste (*sama-rasa*)—imperishable and eternal."[42] The merging of gnosis into space, which is an empty *dharma* from which all phenomena arise just as a sprout arises from a seed,[43] is understood here as emptiness. This awareness of the ultimate absence of the origination and cessation of all phenomena is the appearance of one's own mind. It is gnosis, the indestructible bliss. Thus, when one's own gnosis merges into its own appearance, which is nothing other than the absence of the origination and cessation of all phenomena, it becomes of the same taste, due not to a causal, or generative, relation with regard to its own reflection, but due to being unified in the appearance of one's own mind.[44]

The *Vimalaprabhā* interprets the *Kālacakratantra*'s characterization of gnosis as eternal (*śāśvata*) in terms of its freedom from obscurations (*nirāvaraṇa*).[45] In this way, it points to the lack of contradiction of this characterization of gnosis with the earlier quoted statement from the *Ādibuddhatantra*, which defines gnosis as "free of eternity (*śāśvata*) and annihilation (*uccheda*)" in terms of eluding any categorization.

Gnosis also transcends all classifications with regard to its grounding, for it does not abide in *nirvāṇa* or *saṃsāra*. A closer look at the *Kālacakratantra*'s interpretation of gnosis reveals that for this tantric tradition, gnosis is not grounded in either one of these two because in its empty aspect, it is devoid of *nirvāṇa* and in its blissful aspect, it transcends *saṃsāra*. This interpetation of the manner in which gnosis abides neither in *nirvāṇa* nor in *saṃsāra* is also expressed by the following verse from the *Sekoddeśa*, which states:

> Its form (*bimba*) is devoid of *nirvāṇa*, and indestructible [bliss] transcends *saṃsāra*. The union of these two, which is devoid of eternalism (*śāśvata*) and nihilism (*uccheda*), is nondual and without parallel.[46]

The same text explains further that this interpretation does not imply that the form of emptiness (*śūnyatā-bimba*) enters *saṃsāra* and indestructible bliss enters *nirvāṇa*. Instead, these two aspects of gnosis are "mutually embraced and peaceful, the supreme state of androgyny."[47]

Although gnosis itself is not grounded in *saṃsāra* or *nirvāṇa*, it is called *saṃsāra* when it manifests as the universe with its atoms, stars, planets, mountains, rivers, sentient beings, and so forth; and it is called *nirvāṇa* when it appears as complete knowledge (*parijñāna*) of cyclic existence. The complete knowledge of cyclic existence is the perception of the three realms—the desire, form, and formless realms—as they are within the three times: past, present, and future.[48]

This view of gnosis as the omnipresent mind of the Buddha, which simultaneously transcends the cycle of transmigration and is immanent within it, is similar to panentheism, the view that the finite universe lies within God, who is unbounded and infinite. However, the Kālacakra tradition goes beyond panentheism by interpreting gnosis not only as being *immanent* within the inanimate universe and within every sentient being, but also as *manifested* in the form of the phenomenal existence. It asserts that the three realms of cyclic existence are the form (*rūpa*) of Vajrasattva because gnosis dwells with great bliss within the nature of all things.[49] Likewise, the *Vimalaprabhā* asserts that "conventional reality has the form of emptiness and emptiness has the form of conventional reality,"[50] since gnosis is free of atoms and yet it is found in emptiness. This conviction that the entire cosmos is a manifestation of gnosis underlies the *Kālacakratantra*'s theory of the cosmos as the macrocosmic aspect of the individual and its presence within the body of the individual.

One may ask here: If gnosis is the source and ontological reality of everything, what are the implications for Buddhist claims about identitylessness (*nairātmya*) and emptiness (*śūnyatā*)? The *Kālacakratantra* indirectly addresses this question in a number of ways, which will be indicated later. Primarily, though, it addresses this question by identifying gnosis with the blissful aspect of the mind, which is nondual from the emptiness of inherent existence of that mind, and it thereby evades reification. It asserts that there is neither a Buddha nor enlightenment, since "the entire universe is empty, devoid of reality and of the nature of the appearances of things."[51] In this way, the *Kālacakratantra*'s theory of gnosis as the reality that transcends all conceptual constructs, including those of existence and nonexistence, in no way contradicts the Madhyamaka themes of identitylessness and emptiness. The *Vimalaprabhā* explicitly states that gnosis lacks inherent existence since gnosis is endowed with all aspects (*sarvākāra*), just as it lacks shape and yet it gives rise to all manners of shapes.[52] Likewise, as in the *Mañjuśrīnāmasaṃgīti*, so in this tantric system, gnosis is interpreted as the awareness that transcends the reality of consciousness (*vijñāna-dharmatā*), which is ascertained by the Yogācāra school.[53]

According to this tantric system, gnosis is not only the ontological reality of everything there is, but it is also "the supreme goal" (*mahārtha*) to be realized by the tantric adept. It is the Buddha Kālacakra,[54] who is seen as both "the self (*ātman*) of one's own body, speech, mind, and passion"[55] and as "the supreme, immutable bliss characterized by perfect awakening in a single moment" (*eka-kṣaṇābhisambodhi*).[56] Perfect awakening in a single moment is interpreted here as the mind that is free of momentary phenomena (*ksaṇa-dharma*) and is designated as "the lack of inherent existence" (*niḥsvabhāva*).[57] It is gnosis called "reality" (*tattva*) that is devoid of one or many moments.[58]

As supreme, immutable bliss, gnosis is also the means by which the tantric adept realizes that goal. The tantric adept attains perfect awakening in a single moment by bringing forth 21,600 moments of supreme, immutable bliss. For this reason, the Kālacakra literature also defines gnosis as "the path of the Jina"[59] and as "the path of liberation, which, embraced by wisdom, or emptiness, is one's own mind that has entered innate bliss."[60]

Furthermore, the Kālacakra tradition presents gnosis not only as the goal to be attained and as the path to that goal, but also as the discourse of the *Kālacakratantra* and as its original teacher. Such an interpretation of gnosis reminds one of Dignāga's explanation of the perfection of wisdom (*prajñā-pāramitā*), given in the *Prajñāpāramitāpiṇḍārtha*. According to Dignāga, the perfection of wisdom is nondual knowledge, the Tathāgata, the text of the *Prajñāpāramitā sūtras*, and the path toward that nondual knowledge.[61] The Kālacakra tradition's identification of gnosis with the perfection of wisdom indicates that its presentation of gnosis as the enlightened teacher and teaching is most intimately related to the aforementioned Mahāyāna's interpretation of the perfection of wisdom.

In this tantric system, gnosis is described not only in terms of the mind but also in terms of the body. The *Vimalaprabhā* asserts that apart from the body, there is no other Buddha who is the pervader (*vyāpaka*) and the bestower of liberation. The elements of the body that are free of obscurations (*nirāvaraṇa*) are the bestowers of Buddhahood and liberation.[62]

For this and other related tantric systems, due to the mental dispositions of sentient beings, gnosis, the bliss of ultimate reality, manifests in sentient beings born from a womb as the four types of bliss—namely, bliss (*ānanda*), supreme bliss (*paramānanda*), extraordinary bliss (*viramānanda*), and innate bliss (*sahajānanda*).[63] Each of these four types of bliss has four aspects: a bodily, verbal, mental, and gnostic aspect. For this reason, gnosis manifests with sixteen aspects of bliss altogether. These sixteen aspects of gnosis are none other than the body, speech, mind, and gnosis of the four bodies of the Buddha: namely, the Sahajakāya, Dharmakāya, Saṃbhogakāya, and Nirmāṇakāya. The sixteen aspects of bliss are said to appear in these four bodies according to the superior aspirations (*adhimukti*) of sentient beings. Thus, the aspect in which this unified and indivisible reality, named gnosis, will appear to the individual is determined by the individual's own dispositions and degree of spiritual maturation. Although the four bodies of the Buddha manifest and function in different ways, they are of the same nature and are mutually pervasive.

The Kālacakra tradition's theory of the manifestation of the sixteen aspects of gnosis in terms of both conventional (*saṃvṛti-satya*) and ultimate realities (*paramārtha-satya*) is schematically presented in table 7.1.

The sixteen facets of the four bodies of the Buddha (listed in the second column of the following table) arise when the sixteen types of bliss that characterize the body of the individual cease. Thus, the sixteen types of bliss of the individual are the impure, or perishable, aspects of the sixteen facets of the sublime, imperishable bliss (*mahākṣara-sukha*) of the Sahajakāya. They become purified due to the cessation of bodily semen having sixteen parts, which are the internal sixteen digits of the moon. Due to the purification of semen, one becomes the Buddha Kālacakra, whom the *Vimalaprabhā* characterizes in this respect as "the stainless light of the *vajra*-moon," using the words of the *Mañjuśrīnāmasaṃgīti*'s eulogy of the gnostic being, Mañjuśrī.[64] The *Vimalaprabhā* indicates that this classification of the gnostic *vajra* of the Buddha, which has sixteen types of bliss, has its precedent in the *Nāmasaṃgīti*'s characterization of Mañjuśrī as one who "knows the reality with sixteen aspects."[65] However, as indicated in the introductory chapter, the *Nāmasaṃgītivṛtti* (182. 5. 2) interprets these sixteen aspects of reality not in terms of bliss but in terms of emptiness.

With regard to the spiritually awakened ones, the sixteen facets of the four bodies of the Buddha are seen as the four types of unions (*yoga*), due to the classification of the four bodies of the Buddha. In terms of ordinary human beings, the aforementioned sixteen types of bliss are also characterized as the four *yogas*—the *yogas* of the body, speech, mind, and gnosis—in accordance with the classification of the waking, dreaming, sleeping, and the fourth state of the mind.[66]

In order to understand the Kālacakra tradition's concept of gnosis in terms of ultimate reality, one needs to look first at its most unmediated aspects and functions as expressed in the four bodies of the Buddha. Emphasizing the indestructibility of the four bodies of the Buddha, the Kālacakra tradition often depicts them as the four *vajras*—specifically, as the gnosis-*vajra*, the mind-*vajra*, speech-*vajra*, and the body-*vajra*. The *Kālacakratantra* demarcates the four *vajras* in the following way:

> The body-*vajra* of the Jina, which has all aspects, is inconceivable in terms of sense-objects and sense-faculties. The speech-*vajra* accomplishes Dharma by means of utterances in the hearts of all sentient beings. The mind-*vajra* of the Vajrī, which is the nature of the minds of sentient beings, is present throughout the entire earth. That which, like a pure gem, apprehends phenomena is the gnosis-*vajra*.[67]

On the premise that gnosis is constantly present in every sentient being born from the womb, the *Kālacakratantra* asserts that those four *vajras* are perpetually present in all such sentient beings, but not in a fully manifested form. Their presence in every individual is attested by one's capacities of the body, speech, mind, and gnosis,

TABLE 7.1 The Sixteen Aspects (*ṣoḍaśākārā*) of Gnosis (*jñāna*)

The sixteen aspects of gnosis in terms of conventional reality	The sixteen aspects of gnosis in terms of the ultimate reality
The Four Types of Bliss (*ānanda*)	**The Four Aspects of the Sahajakāya**
the bliss of the mind (*cittānanda*)	the Sahaja-Body (*sahaja-kāya*)
the bliss of the body (*kāyānanda*)	the Sahaja-Mind (*sahaja-citta*)
the bliss of speech (*vāg-ānanda*)	the Sahaja-Speech (*sahaja-vāc*)
the bliss of gnosis (*jñānānanda*)	the Sahaja-Gnosis (*sahaja-jñāna*)
The Four Types of Supreme Bliss (*paramānanda*)	**The Four Aspects of the Dharmakāya**
the supreme bliss of the body (*kāya-paramānanda*)	the Dharma-body (*dharma-kāya*)
the supreme bliss of the mind (*citta-paramānanda*)	the Dharma-mind (*dharma-citta*)
the supreme bliss of speech (*vāc-paramānanda*)	the Dharma-speech (*dharma-vāc*)
the supreme bliss of gnosis (*jñāna-paramānanda*)	the Dharma-gnosis (*dharma-jñāna*)
The Four Types of Extraordinary Bliss (*viramānanda*)	**The Four Aspects of the Saṃbhogakāya**
the extraordinary bliss of the body (*kāya-viramānanda*)	the Saṃbhoga-body (*sambhoga-kāya*)
the extraordinary bliss of the mind (*citta-viramānanda*)	the Saṃbhoga-mind (*sambhoga-citta*)
the extraordinary bliss of speech (*vāg-viramānanda*)	the Saṃbhoga-speech (*sambhoga-vāc*)
the extraordinary bliss of gnosis (*jñāna-viramānanda*)	the Saṃbhoga-gnosis (*sambhoga-jñāna*)
The Four Types of Innate Bliss (*sahajānanda*)	**The Four Aspects of the Nirmāṇakāya**
the innate bliss of the body (*kāya-sahajānanda*)	the Nirmāṇa-body (*nirmāṇa-kāya*)
the innate bliss of the mind (*citta-sahajānanda*)	the Nirmāṇa-mind (*nirmāṇa-citta*)
the innate bliss of speech (*vāc-sahajānanda*)	the Nirmāṇa-speech (*nirmāṇa-vāc*)
the innate bliss of gnosis (*jñāna-sahajānanda*)	the Nirmāṇa-gnosis (*nirmāṇa-jñāna*)

in the four states of the mind—waking, dreaming, deep sleep, and the fourth state, the state of sexual bliss—and in the classification of the four limbs of the individual. Within the ordinary human being, the four *vajras* are located within the four respective *cakras* in the navel, heart, throat, and forehead. The four *vajras* are the seats of the twelve links of dependent origination (*pratītyasamutpāda*). Thus, spiritual ignorance (*avidyā*), karmic formations (*saṃskāra*), and consciousness (*vijñāna*) are in the gnosis-*vajra*. The mind-and-body (*nāma-rūpa*), six sense-bases (*ṣaḍ-āyatana*), and sensory contacts (*sparśa*) are in the body-*vajra*. Feeling (*vedanā*), craving (*tṛṣṇā*), and grasping onto existence (*upādāna*) are in the speech-*vajra*. Becoming (*bhava*), birth (*jāti*), aging (*jarā*), and death (*maraṇa*) are in the mind-*vajra*. In this way, the twelve links of dependent origination are the twelve impure aspects of the four *vajras*. When the twelve links of dependent origination, the bodily *prāṇas*, and uterine blood cease, that is to say, when they become the twelve facets of perfect awakening, the four *vajras* of the individual manifest as the four purified *vajras*, or the four bodies, of the Buddha Kālacakra. In this regard, the *Vimalaprabhā* resorts again to the *Mañjuśrīnāmasaṃgīti*'s description of Majñuśrī, by characterizing the Buddha Kālacakra as "the *vajra*-sun, the supreme light."[68] These twelve aspects of the individual's and the Buddha's four *vajras* are considered to be the twelve conventional aspects of the supreme, indestructible bliss of sentient beings and Buddhas.[69]

On the basis of the belief that the gnostic *vajra* generates sexual bliss, it is considered as the "progenitor" of the twelve links of dependent origination. This view of the gnosis-*vajra* as the fundamental cause of the twelve links of dependent origination indicates that all other *vajras* of the individual's body are simply different manifestations of a single gnosis-*vajra*, which has the twelve links of dependent origination as its twelve phenomenal aspects.[70] This fourfold classification of the gnosis-*vajra* corresponds to the Kālacakra tradition's identification of the Jñānakāya with the other three bodies of the Buddha.

Furthermore, it is also believed that the efficacy of the four drops (*bindu*) generates the twelve links of dependent origination. The four drops are physical composites of the size of a small seed, which consist of red and white drops of the semen and uterine blood. They are pervaded by very subtle *prāṇas* and located within the four earlier-mentioned *cakras*. Each of the four *bindus* has its own specific capacities that may manifest differently, depending on whether or not they are affected by the habitual propensities of spiritual ignorance (*avidyā-vāsanā*). For example, the drop in the *lalāṭa* has the capacity to bring forth appearances to the mind. When this drop is affected by the habitual propensities of spiritual ignorance, it brings forth impure appearances of phenomena to the mind, and it produces the waking state when most of the *prāṇas* converge in the *lalāṭa*. When this drop becomes purified, it manifests as nonconceptual gnosis. The drop at the throat-*cakra* has the capacity to bring forth verbal expression. When this drop is affected by the habitual propensities of spiritual ignorance, it brings forth improper speech, and it produces the dreaming state when most of the *prāṇas* converge in the throat-*cakra*. When this drop becomes purified, it brings forth the Buddha's all-faceted speech. Similarly, the drop at the heart-*cakra* has a dual capacity. In its impure form, this drop induces confusion, and it produces the state of deep sleep when most of the *prāṇas* converge in the heart-*cakra*. When purified, it manifests as the nonconceptual mind. Finally, the drop at the navel-*cakra* has the capacity to bring forth innate bliss. In its impure aspect, this drop brings forth the experience of sexual bliss when most of the *prāṇas* converge in the navel-*cakra*. When this drop is purified, it induces the supreme, immutable bliss of *nirvāṇa*.

The four bodies of the Buddha, which are latently present within the individual, are located within the six *cakras* of the individual's body due to the *guṇas* of those *cakras*. Thus, the Sahajakāya, which is free of ideation and is similar to a prognostic mirror, is in the secret *cakra*, in the *uṣṇīṣa*, and in the navel-*cakra*, which arise from the elements of gnosis, space, and earth, respectively. The Dharmakāya is located in the heart-*cakra*, which arises from the wind-element. The Saṃbhogakāya is in the

TABLE 7.2 The Four Kāyas of the Buddha in the Body of the Individual

Sahajakāya	Dharmakāya	Saṃbhogakāya	Nirmāṇakāya
the secret-*cakra* the navel-*cakra* the forehead-*cakra*	the heart-*cakra*	the throat-*cakra*	the forehead-*cakra*
the gnosis-element the space-element the earth-element	the wind-element	the fire-element	the water-element
the gnosis-vajra	**the mind-vajra**	**the speech-vajra**	**the body-vajra**
spiritual ignorance (*avidyā*)	becoming (*bhava*)	feeling (*vedanā*)	mind and body (*nāma-rūpa*)
karmic formations (*saṃskāra*)	birth (*jāti*)	craving (*tṛṣṇā*)	six sense-bases (*āyatana*)
consciousness (*vijñāna*)	aging (*jarā*) and death (*maraṇa*)	grasping (*upādāna*)	contact (*sparśa*)

throat-*cakra*, which arises from the fire-element. The Nirmāṇakāya is in the *lalāṭa*, which arises from the water-element.[71] Table 7.2. illustrates the manner in which the Kālacakra tradition delineates the four bodies of the Buddha with regard to the body of the individual.

The four *vajras* that are present within the bodily *cakras* manifest as the four bodies of the Buddha only at the attainment of full and perfect awakening (*samyak-saṃbodhi*). When the individual reaches full and perfect enlightenment, the individual's gnosis-*vajra* that has been purified by the liberation through emptiness (*śūnyatā-vimokṣa*) becomes the Sahajakāya. The individual's mind-*vajra* that has been purified by the liberation through signlessness (*animitta-vimokṣa*) manifests as the Dharmakāya. The individual's speech-*vajra* that has been purified by the liberation through desirelessness (*apraṇihita-vimokṣa*) appears as the Saṃbhogakāya. The individual's body-*vajra* that has been purified by liberation through non-compositeness (*anabhisaṃskāra-vimokṣa*) manifests as the Nirmāṇakāya.[72]

It is interesting to note the Kālacakra tradition's interpretation of the phrase "liberation through non-compositeness." A textual study of the literature of the Kālacakra tradition in India reveals that in the context of this tantric system, the term "non-compositeness" refers to both freedom from the accumulation of *karma* and to freedom from atomic matter. In all other *anuttara-yoga-tantras*, however, it is explained chiefly in terms of the Buddha's freedom from the accumulation of *karma*. For the Kālacakra tradition, the eradication of the fine atomic particles that constitute the transmigratory mind and body—which are the material repositories of afflictive and cognitive obscurations and the internal objects of one's actions—includes the eradication of all *karma*.

The Kālacakra tradition's interpretation of the four bodies of the Buddha as the four purified *vajras* has a direct bearing on its classification of the four gates of liberation (*vimokṣa-mukha*) as opposed to the more common classification of the three gates of liberation, which is characteristic of Mahāyāna literature in general. In terms of the four gates of liberation, the *Kālacakratantra* views the four bodies of the Buddha as the four immediate manifestations of the Buddha's fourfold perfect awakening: namely (1) perfect awakening in a single moment (*ekakṣaṇābhisaṃbodhi*), (2) perfect awakening with five aspects (*pañcākārābhisaṃbodhi*), (3) perfect awakening with twenty aspects (*viṃśatyākārābhisaṃbodhi*), and (4) perfect awakening with the net of illusions (*māyājālābhisaṃbodhi*).

1. Perfect awakening in a single moment refers here to enlightenment attained in a single moment of supreme, immutable bliss. It is the spiritual awakening that arises from bliss and that, in turn, generates immutable bliss. Thus, it is "of the nature of bliss and not of some other *karma*."[73] The moment of supreme, immutable bliss is the moment after which there is no origination, duration, or cessation of any phenomena. The moment of perfect awakening in a single moment of bliss (*sukha-kṣaṇa*) signifies an absence of all moments, and that moment of bliss is the means by which the ten powers (*daśa-bala*) of enlightened awareness descend to earth from space. The purified aggregates that are produced by that moment of bliss, in turn, generate that bliss. Thus, from the Sahajakāya, which is the gnosis of innate bliss, arises the Dharmakāya; from the Dharmakāya arises the Saṃbhogakāya; from the Saṃbhogakāya arises the Nirmāṇakāya; and from the Nirmāṇakāya arises the Sahajakāya.[74] This innate bliss, or gnosis, is like a seed from which first arise the roots, then the branches and flowers, and lastly the fruits, which, in turn, produce the seed. This interpretation of the arising of the four bodies of the Buddha in dependence upon each other implies that even the four bodies of the Buddha, like everything else in the world, do not arise of their own nature. Their mutually dependent arising further implies their absence of inherent existence.

The *Sekoddeśaṭīkā*'s interpretation of perfect awakening in a single moment suggests that the perfect awakening in a single moment is analogous to the experience of the single moment of bliss characterizing the consciousness that desires a birth and that has become of the same taste (*sama-rasa*) as the mother's and father's drops that are in the mother's secret *cakra*. It also indicates that in terms of the body belonging to the consciousness that is in the mother's womb, the perfect awakening in a single moment is analogous to the body that, like a red fish, has only one aspect, meaning, one body without limbs. In terms of enlightened awareness, the *Sekoddeśaṭīkā* describes the perfect awakening in a single moment as a nonemitted (*acyuta*) drop that is of the nature of the pure gnosis and consciousness (*śuddha-jñāna-vijñāna*), a *vajra-yoga* of the gnosis of the Svabhāvikakāya, and as Vajrasattva, who perceives all things due to being enlightened in a single moment due to the cessation of the ordinary sense-faculties and arising of the divine sense-faculties, which result from the eradication of the circulation of breaths and from establishing the mind in sublime *prāṇa* (*mahā-prāṇa*).[75]

2. Perfect awakening with five aspects refers to enlightenment that is characterized by the five types of gnosis of the Buddha: namely, the mirror-like gnosis (*ādarśa-jñāna*), the gnosis of equality (*samatā-jñāna*), the discriminating gnosis (*pratyavekṣaṇā-jñāna*), the accomplishing gnosis (*kṛtyānuṣṭhāna-jñāna*), and the gnosis of the sphere of reality (*dharmadhātu-jñāna*). These five types of gnosis are understood here as one's purified psycho-physical aggregates, sense objects and sense-fac-

ulties, Māras, and five types of spiritual ignorance. They are the mutually indivisible *vajras* that have all the aspects.

According to the *Sekoddeśaṭīkā*, the perfect awakening with the five aspects is analogous to the five types of knowledge that are of the nature of the habitual propensities (*vāsanā*) of the form and other aggregates (*skandha*), which the fetus acquires, having the indication of the five limbs, like a tortoise. With regard to the enlightened awareness, it interprets the perfect awakening with five aspects as the Dharmakāya, the *vajra-yoga* of the mind, a sublime being (*mahā-sattva*) that has the supreme, imperishable bliss due to being enlightened with five aspects. The characteristics of the five types of gnosis are of the nature of the wisdom and method of the elements and psycho-physical aggregates due to the cessation of the five *maṇḍalas*.[76]

The Kālacakra tradition defines these five types of gnosis in a number of ways. In its eulogy to gnosis with five aspects, the *Ādibuddhatantra* describes each aspect in terms of supramundane truth with the following five verses. With regard to the mirror-like gnosis, or the purified form-aggregate, it says:

> This collection of phenomena in space, which is devoid of the form of ideation (*kalpanā*), is seen like a prognostic image (*pratisenā*) in the mirror of a young maiden.

With regard to the gnosis of equality, or the purified aggregate of feeling, it states:

> Having become identical to all phenomena, it abides as a single, indestructible phenomenon. Arisen from the imperishable gnosis, it is neither nihilism nor eternalism.

With regard to the discriminating gnosis, or the purified aggregate of discernment, it says:

> Letters, having all designations, have their origin in the family of the letter *a*. Having reached the sublime, imperishable state, they are neither the designation nor the designated.

As for the accomplishing gnosis, or the purified aggregate of mental formations, it states:

> Among non-originated *dharmas*, which are devoid of mental formations (*saṃskāra*), there is neither spiritual awakening nor Buddhahood, neither a sentient being nor life.

Lastly, with regard to the gnosis of the *dharma-dhātu*, or the purified aggregate of consciousness, it says:

> The *dharmas* that have transcended the reality of consciousness, that are purified in gnosis, transparent and luminous by nature, are present on the path of the *dharma-dhātu*.[77]

In terms of the relation of the five types of gnosis to cyclic existence, the *Kālacakratantra* characterizes them in the following manner:

> That in which the form of birth reaches its culmination is called the sublime form. That in which the suffering of transmigratory existence reaches its culmination is called the sublime feeling. That in which a discernment of transmigratory existence

> reaches its culmination is the sublime, *vajra* discernment. That in which the expansion of transmigratory existence reaches its culmination is called the *vajra* mental formation.
>
> That in which waking and other states reach their culmination is called consciousness. That in which the existence of spiritual ignorance reaches its culmination is the Sage's gnosis. . . .[78]

According to this tantric tradition, these five aspects of gnosis, entering the earth and other elements, become the Nirmāṇakāyas, by means of which the single Buddha Kālacakra displays his supernatural power (*ṛddhi*) among the humans, *asuras*, and gods that live within the desire realm. Even though the Buddha is free of obscurations (*āvaraṇa*) and mental afflictions (*kleśa*), he enters the human realm by descending into a woman's womb and taking on the five psycho-physical aggregates and birth for the sake of bringing ordinary people (*prākṛta-jana*) to spiritual maturation. He leads those who have acquired nonvirtue and are devoid of precepts to the realization of the impermanence of all composite phenomena. By taking birth, he demonstrates that even the Nirmāṇakāyas of the Buddhas, which are essentially the Vajrakāya, are of an impermanent nature. In this way, he seeks to liberate ordinary people from constant concern for their own bodies, which are, in comparison to the Vajrakāya, like the pith of a plantain tree. The *Kālacakratantra* asserts that the illusion (*māyā*) of the Buddha's emanations, which has immeasurable qualities, is inconceivable even to the Buddhas themselves. That illusion, seeing itself within the three worlds, divided in accordance with the diverse mental states of sentient beings, enters the individual minds of the Buddhas, gods, and men. It takes on their originated nature. However, it does not truly arise in the mass of atoms due to the absence of a previous body, and therefore it is not truly subject to origination and cessation. Its origination gives a false impression, like the reflection of the sky in water.[79] The Buddha is an appearance of the minds of virtuous beings, since in reality, he neither originates nor ceases. His body and speech that appear to sentient beings are like the body and speech that appear in a dream. The *Vimalaprabhā* likens the appearance of the Buddha to the dream experience of a student who, asking his teacher about some dubious subject, receives clarification from the teacher, while in reality there is no actual teacher in the dream, but merely an appearance of the habitual propensities of the student's mind.[80] Thus, when the Nirmāṇakāya appears to the individual, in reality, it has neither arisen from somewhere other than one's own mind nor will it cease in some place other than one's own mind.

The *Vimalaprabhā* contests the view of those who assert that the Nirmāṇakāya of the Buddha is his Rūpakāya, in the sense of a material body, and argue that if the Buddha does not become embodied (*rūpin*), then none of his activities on earth would come into existence nor would his bodily constituents arise, which are worshipped as relics by the inhabitants of the three worlds. It refutes this view of the Buddha as becoming truly embodied with the following arguments:

> Furthermore, if the Bhagavān became embodied here, then due to being a Rūpakāya, while dwelling in one place, he would be unable to perform activities that benefit sentient beings as numerous as the dust of the immeasurable mountain ranges within

> the [limitless] world systems and as the [grains of] sand of the river Ganges. The words of the simple-minded people are: "Upon going to a single world system by means of his Rūpakāya and performing actions that benefit sentient beings dwelling there, he goes to another world system, and after that, he goes elsewhere." This does not stand logically. Why? Because world systems do not have a measure with regard to the division of directions. Repeatedly going by means of the Rūpakāya [in the form of] limitless sentient beings to world systems that are located in the ten directions, he would not be able to benefit sentient beings even in the course of limitless eons.[81]

Likewise, the *Vimalaprabhā* rejects the belief that the Buddha attracts sentient beings who dwell in the world systems of innumerable Buddha-fields by the power of his meditation and *mantra*, places them in front of himself and teaches them Dharma, establishes them on the Buddhist path, and sends them back to their world systems. It rebuts this notion on the basis that the Buddha cannot simultaneously abide with a body of atoms in the presence of limitless sentient beings who dwell in the numerous world systems that are present throughout space. It asserts:

> According to the words of simple-minded people, by means of his Rūpakāya, he engages in activities that benefit sentient beings dwelling in the triple chiliocosm within a single Buddha-field. When this statement is investigated logically and in terms of ultimate truth, it is [found to be] meaningless, just like the words of Īśvara, which are established by means of authority (*ājñā*) and are devoid of verifying cognition (*pramāṇa*) and logic. According to the received Āgamas, Īśvara is a partless creator of all. Not taking into consideration the effect, he creates and destroys the world for the sake of play, as it pleases him. In the same way, because of this heterodoxy, the Bhagavān Rūpakāya, who brings about the benefit of all sentient beings, is established by means of authority. Thus, due to the absence of wisdom among Buddhist heterodox groups (*tīrthika*), there is nothing special even about their *paṇḍitas*. Therefore, these words that are uncritical (*parīkṣa*) are not the words of the Bhagavān. . . . According to the Bhagavān's words, the Buddha who is investigated in the *Nāmasaṃgīti* is not the Rūpakāya. Why? Since he has arisen in space, he is self-arisen (*svayaṃbhū*), has all aspects (*sarvākāra*) and is without aspects (*nirākāra*), holds the four *bindus*, transcends the state of having parts and is partless, holds the tens of millions [moments] of the fourth bliss, is detachment and supreme attachment, is free of possessiveness (*mamatva*) and self-grasping (*ahaṃ-kāratva*), generates the meanings of all *mantras*, is the supreme *bindu*, indestructible, the sublime emptiness (*mahā-śūnyatā*) of the five indestructibles,[82] is the indestructibility of the space *bindu*, and is similar to space. Thus, the Bhagavān Buddha explained the Vajradharakāya of Vajrapāṇi in terms of both truths by means of one hundred and sixty-two verses of the *Nāmasaṃgīti*, beginning with: "Now, the glorious Vajradhara" and ending with: "Homage to you, the Jñānakāya." . . . Thus, according to the Bhagavān's words, the Bhagavān is not the Rūpakāya, because he is the assembly (*samāja*) of all the Buddhas. If the Rūpakāyas were the Buddhas, then the [Rūpakāyas] would not come together in the form of atoms. Even after hearing the Bhagavān's words in this manner and investigating the deep and profound Dharma that was taught by the Bhagavān, sentient beings do not understand it. Not testing a spiritual mentor for the sake of Buddhahood, they do not honor him. Great fools, overcome by greed, think: "In this life, our putrid bodies are the bodies of the Buddha."[83]

Thus, for the sake of eradicating the self-grasping (*ahaṃ-kāra*) of the Śrāvakas in heaven, and for the sake of helping them understand that the state of a god is one of great suffering, the physically nonembodied Tathāgata displays his supernatural power among them by means of his Saṃbhogakāyas. By means of his Dharmakāyas, he reveals his supernatural power among the Bodhisattvas, Subhūti, Maitreya, and others who abide in the realization of emptiness, for the sake of establishing them in the highest, perfect awakening by teaching them about the four bodies of the Buddha.[84]

3. Perfect awakening with twenty aspects is not explicitly described in the *Kālacakratantra* or the *Vimalaprabhā*. Nevertheless, Mañjuśrīmitra's *Nāmasaṃgītivṛtti*,[85] commenting on v. 133 of the *Mañjuśrīnāmasaṃgīti*, that is cited in the *Vimalaprabhā*, enumerates the twenty aspects of the Buddha's mind.[86] According to the *Nāmasaṃgītivṛtti*, the twenty aspects of perfect awakening include the sixteenfold knowledge of the sixteen types of emptiness and the first four of the aforementioned five types of the Buddha's gnosis. According to the *Sekoddeśaṭīkā*, the perfect awakening with twenty aspects should be known as being due to the cessation of the five sense-faculties, the five sense-objects, the five faculties of action (*karmendriya*), and the activities of the five faculties of action that are with obscurations. The same text also indicates that the perfect awakening with twenty aspects is analogous to the classification of the habitual propensities of the four elements, earth and the like, and to the body of the fetus that has twenty fingers. In terms of enlightened awareness, it explains the perfect awakening with twenty aspects as the *vajra-yoga* of speech of the Saṃbhogakāya and as a Bodhisattva who assists other Bodhisattvas and teaches Dharma by means of the utterances of all sentient beings due to being enlightened with twenty aspects.[87]

4. According to the *Vimalaprabhā*, perfect awakening with the net of illusions refers to the Buddha's Nirmāṇakāya, which manifests in innumerable forms, like an endless net of illusions, and knows the reality that has sixteen aspects.[88] The *Sekoddeśaṭīkā* describes it in a similar fashion but adds that the perfect awakening with the net of illusions is the bodily *vajra-yoga*, a pledge being (*samaya-sattva*) who is the foremost assistant to sentient beings due to his knowledge of the reality with sixteen aspects. For Naḍapāda, this type of awakening is due to the cessation of the drops of the sixteen types of bodily bliss (*kāyānanda*). He also sees it as analogous to the knowledge of the limitless phenomena that are like a net of illusions, which is acquired by being born from the womb.[89]

Just as the Buddha's mind is characterized by the four types of spiritual awakening, so are the four bodies of the Buddha characterized by the four different types of knowledge and their functions. The Sahajakāya is characterized by omniscience (*sarvajñatā*) on the ground that it sees everything. The Dharmakāya is characterized by knowledge of the aspects of the path (*mārgākāra-jñatā*), because it is saturated by supreme, immutable bliss. The Saṃbhogakāya is characterized by knowledge of the path (*mārga-jñatā*), for it simultaneously teaches the mundane (*laukika*) and supramundane (*lokottara*) Dharmas, using the different modes of expression of countless sentient beings. Finally, the Nirmāṇakāya is characterized by knowledge of all aspects (*sarvākāra-jñatā*), since it simultaneously spreads its powers and manifestations by means of limitless Nirmāṇakāyas.[90]

Each of these four bodies of the Buddha represents a particular type of union (*yoga*). For example, the Sahajakāya represents the union of purity and gnosis; therefore, it is also called the pure *yoga* (*śuddha-yoga*). The Dharmakāya is the union of the Dharma and the mind; hence, it is also referred to as the *dharma-yoga*. The Saṃbhogakāya is the union of speech and enjoyment, for that reason, it is also identified as the *mantra-yoga*; and the Nirmāṇakāya is the union of the body and its emanation, therefore, it is also designated as the form-*yoga* (*saṃsthāna-yoga*).[91] This perspective on the four bodies of the Buddha as the four types of *yogas* explicates the Kālacakra tradition's definition of gnosis as the *vajra-yoga*. As alluded earlier, these four types of *yogas*, which purify Kālacakra, are the four gates of liberation (*mokṣa*): a liberation through emptiness (*śūnyatā-vimokṣa*), a liberation through signlessness (*animitta-vimokṣa*), a liberation through wishlessness (*apraṇihita-vimokṣa*), and a liberation through non-compositeness (*anabhisaṃskāra-vimokṣa*). According to the *Sekoddeśaṭīkā*, a liberation through emptiness is the gnosis that is characterized by its condition of being empty and by apprehending that the past and future are empty. Due to that gnosis, the purified, imperishable, sublime bliss (*mahā-sukha*) arises form the eradication of the fourth state of the mind (*turyā*). This liberation through emptiness is nothing else than the *vajra-yoga* consisting of compassion, the Shajakāya, or the purified *yoga*. A liberation through signlessness is the gnosis that is without a sign (*nimitta*), or a cause (*hetu*), which is a mind with conceptualizations such as the "Buddha," "enlightenment," and so on. Due to this absence of a cause, the mind of the deep sleep vanishes and the mind-*vajra* that consists of loving kindness (*maitrī*), which is the Dharmakāya, arises. Since its nature is Dharma, it is also called the *dharma-yoga*. A liberation through wishlessness is a freedom from reasoning (*tarka*) that manifests in thinking: "I am the fully awakened one," and so on. The absence of such reasoning results from the absence of the earlier mentioned sign, or cause. In liberation through wishlessness, the sleeping state is destroyed, and on account of that, arises the indestructible voice that is characterized by *mantras* and sympathetic joy (*muditā*). That voice is the speech-*vajra*, the Saṃbhogakāya. It is a *mantra* because it protects (*trāṇa*) and gladdens (*modana*) the minds with the expressions of all sentient beings. Therefore, it also called the *mantra-yoga*. A liberation through non-compositeness, which results from the absence of wish (*praṇidhāna*) is the form-*yoga*. It is the body-*vajra* that consists of equanimity (*upekṣā*) and that manifests with all forms: ferocius, passionate, peaceful, and so on, leading others to the path of opposition to mental afflictions by means of limitless Nirmāṇakāyas. This liberation is said to be pure due to the destruction of the waking state.[92]

Just as there is one gnosis that manifests as various types of cognition, so too there is one Sahajakāya, which becomes of four kinds. According to the Kālacakra tradition's interpretation of the four bodies of the Buddha as the four facets of enlightened awareness, which are the purified aspects of the four states of the individual's mind, the Sahajakāya is also of four kinds. First of all, the Sahajakāya is the facet of the Buddha's mind that is devoid of the fourth state of the mind (*turya*), and thereby it is not affected by the sense-faculties nor is it polluted by attachment. For that reason, it is seen as the attainment of one's own well-being. The Sahajakāya is said to be neither wisdom nor compassion, nor of the nature of both. Due to the eradication of the state of deep sleep, it becomes the Dharmakāya for the sake of others' well-being. Due to freedom from the state of deep sleep, the Dharmakāya is never saturated by darkness. It is of the nature of both wisdom and compassion due to the distinction between gnosis (*jñāna*) and consciousness (*vijñāna*). Gnosis is understood in this context as the apprehending mind (*grāhaka-citta*), the mind that is the subject; and consciousness is taken to mean the apprehended (*grāhya*) knowledge of others' minds, minds that are objects of knowledge (*jñeya*). Gnosis, or the apprehending mind, is wisdom (*prajñā*) because it is devoid of ideation (*kalpanā*); and the apprehended mind—namely, enlightened awareness as it manifests as the world—is method (*upāya*), which is conceptually fabricated (*parikalpita*) and has the characteristic of compassion. Likewise, the Saṃbhogakāya is the mind that is free of the dreaming state, which is invariably produced by *prāṇas*. It is also of the nature of wisdom and compassion. By means of the divine eye (*divya-cakṣu*), its divine consciousness (*divya-vijñāna*) perceives past and future forms like transparent reflections in a mirror; and by means of the divine ear, it apprehends sounds that arise in those transparent forms as echoes. It knows past and future times, as well as certain events that have happened or will happen. The Saṃbhogakāya becomes the Nirmāṇakāya for spiritually mature sentient beings. The Nirmāṇakāya is the mind that is free of the waking state, and therefore it is not characterized by false notions arising from conceptualization. It also consists of wisdom and compassion. Even though it is one, it becomes many, because sentient beings see its various emanations. Ultimately, the unity of one and many Nirmāṇakāyas is the unity of wisdom and compassion, even though conventionally there is an obvious contradiction in the concept of one and many Nirmāṇakāyas. The illusion of the Buddha's emanations, which have immeasurable qualities, is said to be inconceivable even to the Buddhas themselves.[93]

Table 7.3. illustrates the Kālacakra tradition's characterization of the four bodies of the Buddha as the four types of spiritual awakening and the four facets of the Buddha's mind.

As was indicated earlier, these four bodies of the Buddha collectively and individually are understood to be nothing other than the four different manifestations of the Jñānakāya ("Gnosis-body"). The Kālacakra tradition's characterization of the Jñānakāya is based on the *Mañjuśrīnāmasaṃgīti*'s characterization of Mañjuśrī, who is identified there with the Jñānakāya. Likewise, as the main topic of the *Kālacakratantra*'s discourse, the Jñānakāya is referred to as the "*vajra*-word" that is also taught in other "kings of *tantras*"—specifically, in the method-*tantras* such as the *Guhyasamāja*, and in the wisdom-*tantras* such as the *Cakrasaṃvara*.[94] Thus, in this tantric system, the Jñānakāya is the unity of the speaker, who is the Ādibuddha, and his teaching, the *vajra*-word.

In the *Kālacakratantra*, the Jñānakāya is discussed in terms of both conventional and ultimate realities. In terms of ultimate reality, it is taught in the above way as the four bodies of the Buddha, or as the clear light of the mind (*citta-pratibhāsa*), appearing in space and being directly perceived through the yogic practices of unifying the left and right *nāḍīs* in the *madhyamā*. In terms of conventional reality, it is presented as the body that is mentally fabricated by the *yogī*'s own mind as being endowed with form, various colors, and other attributes.

With regard to the impure manifestations of the four bodies of the Buddha within the individual, the Kālacakra tradition correlates the four bodies of the Bud-

TABLE 7.3 The Four Kāyas of the Buddha as the Four Aspects of Enlightenment

Sahajakāya	Dharmakāya	Saṃbhogakāya	Nirmāṇakāya
the gnosis-*vajra*	the mind-*vajra*	the speech-*vajra*	the body-*vajra*
purified in liberation through emptiness (*śūnyatā-vimokṣa*)	purified in liberation through signlessness (*animitta-vimokṣa*)	purified in liberation through desirelessness (*apraṇihita-vimokṣa*)	purified in liberation through noncompositeness (*anabhisaṃskāra-vimokṣa*)
perfect awakening in a single moment (*eka-kṣaṇābhi-sambodhi*)	perfect awakening with five aspects (*pañcākārābhisaṃ-bodhi*)	perfect awakening with twenty aspects (*viṃśatyākārābhi-saṃbodhi*)	perfect awakening with the net of illusions (*māyā-jālābhisaṃ-bodhi*)
omniscience (*sarvākāra-jñatā*)	knowledge of the aspects of the path (*mārgākārā-jñatā*)	knowledge of the path (*mārga-jñatā*)	knowledge of all aspects (*sarvākārā-jñatā*)
the purified *yoga*	the *dharma-yoga*	the *mantra-yoga*	the form-*yoga*
the absence of the fourth state	the absence of the deep sleep state	the absence of the dreaming state	the absence of the waking state
in the navel-*cakra*	in the heart-*cakra*	in the throat-*cakra*	in the *lalāṭa*

dha with the four stages of development of a fetus in the womb and with the four phases of one's life outside the womb. Thus, at the moment of conception, consciousness, gnosis, semen, and uterine blood constitute the impure, or obscured, phenomenal aspect of the Sahajakāya. The fetus consisting of the psycho-physical aggregates and elements corresponds to the Dharmakāya. The fetus at the stage of developing the sense-bases (*āyatana*) corresponds to the Saṃbhogakāya; and the fetus that at the time of birth is completely endowed with arms, legs, hair, and the other bodily parts corresponds to the Nirmāṇakāya.[95]

With regard to the individual who is outside the womb, a newborn infant, whose *prāṇas* first begin to flow from the navel-*cakra*, corresponds to the Sahajakāya. The newborn child, though, corresponds to the Sahajakāya only for the period of sixty breaths during which the infant's *prāṇas* flow in the central *nāḍī*. The child, in the phase of life in which its limbs begin to move due to the circulation of *prāṇas*, in which its first teeth begin to grow and its indistinct speech arises, corresponds to the Dharmakāya. From the time that the child's first teeth fall out until the age of eight, when its new teeth grow and its speech becomes clear, the child corresponds to the Saṃbhogakāya. Lastly, in the phase of life from the growth of new teeth until death, the individual represents the impure aspect of the Nirmāṇakāya.[96] This categorization of the four bodies of the Buddha as the individual in the four phases of life is based on the Kālacakra tradition's view of the manner in which the individual's *prāṇas*, speech, and mind interact.

Even though the Kālacakra tradition often speaks of gnosis as the ultimate nature of all sentient beings and of the four bodies of the Buddha as present in the body of every individual, the *Vimalaprabhā* emphasizes that this does not imply that all sentient beings are already Nirmāṇakāyas of the Buddha. It criticizes those who mistakenly conclude that the bodies of sentient beings are the Buddha's Nirmāṇakāyas simply because all the kings of *tantras* (*tantra-rāja*) identify the five psycho-physical aggregates with the five Buddhas, the bodily elements with the consorts of the five Buddhas, and so on. It argues that if sentient beings within the three realms of cyclic existence are already Nirmāṇakāyas of the Buddha, then this implies that they have previously become Samyaksaṃbuddhas. However, the fact that sentient beings lack the powers and qualities of the Buddha and are still subject to the origination, cessation, and all the other sufferings of transmigratory existence indicates that they are not perfectly awakened but deeply entrenched in *saṃsāra*. It also argues that if sentient beings have already attained Buddhahood, then the practices of generosity, meditation, reflection, listening to Dharma teachings and the like would be useless. This, it says, "has not been seen, heard, inferred, or predicted by the Tathāgata."[97] Likewise, it claims that the *Kālacakratantra*'s identification of the bodily components—specifically, the male and female sexual organs, feces, urine, uterine blood, and semen—with the five Buddhas does not imply that these impure bodily constituents are actually the five Buddhas. Such identification, it says, is to be understood in terms of the language of tantric pledges (*samaya-bhāṣā*) and not in terms of definitive language, which employs words that explicitly designate their referents. It also argues that a localized (*prādeśika*) body of the individual cannot be taken as the all-pervasive body of the Buddha.

The *Kālacakratantra*'s fourfold categorization of the Buddha's body has its precedent in the earlier Mahāyāna classification of the Buddha's body into the Svābhāvikakāya ("Essential Body"), Dharmakāya, Saṃbhogakāya, and Nirmāṇakāya. The *Kālacakratantra* itself never mentions the Svabhāvikakāya; it mentions only the Sahajakāya, the Viśuddhakāya ("Pure Body"), and the Jñānakāya as synonymous. However, the *Vimalaprabhā* comments that in the system of perfections, which has the characteristic of the cause, the mind of gnosis (*jñāna-citta*) is designated as the "Svabhāvikakāya of the perfection of wisdom (*prajñāpāramitā*)," or as the "Prajñāpāramitākāya" ("Body of the Perfection of Wisdom").[98] Whereas in the system of *mantras*, which has the characteristic of the result, it is called "innate bliss" (*sahajānanda*), or the "Sahajakāya."[99] For this reason, the terms "Svābhāvikakāya" and "Sahajakāya" are sometimes used interchangeably in the commentarial literature of the Kālacakra tradition.[100]

The *Vimalaprabhā*, cites the *Abhisamayālaṃkāra* (Ch. 1, v. 18), to support this view of the close relation between the Svābhāvikakāya and the Sahajakāya; and it suggests that its classification of the four bodies of the Buddha has precedents in the interpretations of some Mahāyāna authors. The cited verse from the *Abhisamayālaṃkāra* reads:

> The Dharmakāya, which is with activity, is said to be of four kinds: the Svābhāvikakāya, together with the Saṃbhogakāya, and the Nirmāṇakāya.[101]

The Kālacakra tradition interprets the Sahajakāya similarly to some Indian Mahāyāna authors' interpretation of the *Abhisamayālaṃkāra*'s reading of the Svābhāvikakāya.[102] Just as in the *Abhisamayālaṃkāra*, the Svābhāvikakāya is just another way of characterizing the essential nature (*svabhāva*, *prakṛti*) of undefiled Buddha *dharmas*, so in the *Kālacakratantra*, the Sahajakāya is the defining essence of Buddhahood, which is indivisible from the Dharmakāya. Furthermore, just as in the *Abhisamayālaṃkāra*, the Svābhāvikakāya designates the emptiness of the Buddha's nonconceptual mind, characterized by the freedom from defilements (*nirāsrava*) and the purity of all aspects (*sarvākārā viśuddhi*),[103] so according to the Kālacakra tradition,

> the mind that is devoid of the habitual propensities of transmigratory existence is called Buddhahood. Likewise, the Bhagavān stated in the *Prajñāpāramitā*, "That mind, which is the mind, is not the mind." That very mind that is devoid of the habitual propensities of transmigratory existence is luminous by nature (*prakṛti-prabhāsvara*). Therefore, Māra is the mind that has impurities (*mala*), and the Buddha is the mind that is without impurities (*amala*).[104]

In another place, the *Vimalaprabhā* asserts:

> That which is taught in terms of ultimate reality for the sake of attaining the supramundane *mahāmudrā-siddhi*, which is endowed with the best of all forms, is the luminosity (*pratibhāsa*) of the *yogīs*' own mind, which can be directly perceived, which is devoid of the characteristics of the ideation of one's own mind, which shines in the sky and is similar to the reflection in a young maiden's mirror.[105]

Thus, with respect to the essential purity of the Buddha's mind, the *Abhisamayālaṃkāra*'s interpretations of the Svābhāvikakāya accord with the Kālacakra tradition's interpretation of the Sahajakāya. There are also other points of agreement between the Mādhyamika interpretation of the *Abhisamayālaṃkāra*'s presentation of the Svābhāvikakāya and the Kālacakra tradition's interpretation of the Sahajakāya. For example, references to the Svābhāvikakāya and the Sahajakāya as the mirrorlike gnosis (*ādarśa-jñāna*) are found in both Buddhajñānapāda's (eighth century) *Saṃcayagāthāpañjikā* commentary on the *Abhisamayālaṃkāra* and in the *Vimalaprabhā*.[106] Likewise, identifications of the Svābhāvikakāya and the Sahajakāya with a Samantabhadra, pure luminosity, the *dharma-dhātu*, which is ultimately the sole body of the Buddha, are encountered in both Dharmamitra's *Prasputapadā* (late eighth–early ninth century) and in the *Kālacakratantra* and the *Vimalaprabhā*.[107]

Furthermore, the *Vimalaprabhā* defines the Dharmakāya and the Svābhāvikakāya in the following way:

> [The body] that is neither impermanent nor permanent, neither single nor has the characteristic of many, neither substance (*dravya*) nor non-substance (*adravya*), is the Dharmakāya, which is without basis (*nirāśraya*).
>
> [The body] that is indivisible from emptiness and compassion, free of attachment and non-attachment, that is neither wisdom nor method, is the additional Svābhāvikakāya.[108]

This description of the Dharmakāya and the Svābhāvikakāya suggests that the Dharmakāya characterizes here enlightened awareness, which transcends the reality of atoms and yet exists in terms of emptiness, and which lacks a basis for superimpositions such as permanence and impermanence, existence and non-existence. Whereas the Svābhāvikakāya represents the empty nature of the enlightened awareness, which ultimately is neither the apprehending mind nor the apprehended mind. Thus, the Svābhāvikakāya does not designate here some independent component of Buddhahood, but the essential nature of all the aspects of the enlightened mind. In this respect, the Kālacakra tradition's interpretation of the fourth body accords with the Mādhyamika interpretation of the Svābhāvikakāya.

On the basis of textual evidence, one could infer that in the *Kālacakratantra* tradition, which claims to consist of both the system of perfections and the system of *mantras*, the Prajñāpāramitākāya, or the Sahajakāya, represents the unity of the two aspects of the Buddha's mind—namely, the empty nature of the Buddha's mind, which is the cause, and the blissful aspect of the Buddha's mind, which is the result. On the grounds that the empty and blissful natures of the Buddha's mind are essentially nondual, the Kālacakra tradition attends to them as a single fact, as a form (*bimba*) of emptiness and compassion. More than the literature of Mahāyāna, the Kālacakra tradition, in addition to emptiness, strongly emphasizes the blissful aspect of Buddhahood, which is seen as ultimately nondual from emptiness. One reads in the *Ādibuddhatantra*: "this Vajrasattva is the foundation of the bliss of all Buddhas due to the union of the body, speech, and mind."[109] It is in this regard that the Kālacakra tradition's interpetation of the blissful aspect of Buddhahood and the ways of achieving it diverge from the Mahāyāna's interpretation of the Svābhāvikakāya and consequently from Mahāyāna forms of practice. Thus, in the Kālacakra tradition, the Sahajakāya designates the two aspects of the essential nature of the Buddha's mind: emptiness and bliss. Considering that for this tantric system, those two aspects are nondual from each other and indivisible from all other bodies of the Buddha, one may further infer that ultimately there is only one body of the Buddha, the Gnostic Body.

The primary purpose of the *Kālacakratantra*'s classification of the four bodies of the Buddha is to provide a model for *Kālacakratantra* practice that will accord with its goal. In this tantric system, the fourfold classification of the Buddha's body outlines the essential components of spiritual awakening, which are meticulously correlated to the contemplative's psycho-physical constituents and their functions. Thus, the Sahajakāya is a representation of both the basis of purification, which is the individual's psycho-physical constituents and their functions, and the result of purification, which is the components of Buddhahood and their activities.

This concept of the Sahajakāya is common to all *anuttara-yoga-tantras*. The *Vimalaprabhā* denies that the realization of the Sahajakāya, or Jñānakāya, is ever found among Śrāvakas, Pratyekabuddhas, and Vijñānavādins, for the Sahajakāya is free from all residues (*upadhi*) and transcends the reality of consciousness (*vijñāna-dharmatā*).[110] This claim not only supports the *Kālacakratantra*'s openly stated affiliation with the philosophical views of the Mādhyamikas,[111] but it also indirectly expresses the Kālacakra tradition's interpretation of other *anuttara-yoga-tantras* as being based on the Mādhyamika philosophy.

Gnosis and Mental Afflictions

The Kālacakra tradition's theory of the Jñānakāya is most intimately connected with the *Kālacakratantra*'s view that "sentient beings are Buddhas and that there is not some other great Buddha in the universe apart from sentient beings."[112] It is by means of sentient beings' prayers and their elimination of conceptualizations (*vikalpa*) that cyclic existence ceases.[113] As indicated earlier, this view of gnosis as innately present in all sentient beings was already expressed in the *Mañjuśrīnāmasaṃgīti*, which affirms it in the following manner:

> Present within the minds of all beings, he attained equality with their minds. Gladdening the minds of all sentient beings, he is the joy of the minds of all sentient beings.[114]

This view of sentient beings is not unique to the *Kālacakratantra*, as it is also found in the earlier *anuttara-yoga-tantras*. For example, one reads in the *Hevajratantra* that the Buddha cannot be found elsewhere in some other world-system (*loka-dhātu*), for the mind itself is the perfect Buddha. It asserts that all species of sentient beings, from gods to worms, are innately endowed with a blissful nature.[115] Likewise, in the root *tantra* of the *Saṃvara* literary corpus, the *Lakṣābhidhāna*, it is stated that Vajrasattva, the sublime bliss, is within the self of sentient beings.[116] Similarly, in the root *tantra* of the *Yamāntaka* literature, the *Yogānuviddhatantra*, cited in the *Vimalaprabhā*, states that a unique, principal deity abides in the self of the three worlds with the nature of innate bliss.[117]

The view that the Buddha's mind is present in all sentient beings has its earliest precursor in the early Buddhist notion of the innate luminosity, or purity, of the mind. The *Aṅguttara Nikāya*, I. 10, expresses this view in the following manner: "Monks, the mind is luminous (*prabhassara*), but it is contaminated by adventitious defilements." Its later precursors can be traced to the Mādhyamika view of the mind and the *tathāgata-garbha* theory. One reads in the *Bodhicaryāvatāra* (Ch. 9, v. 103) that sentient beings are by nature liberated. The *Pañjikā* commentary interpets this statement in light of the Madhyamaka view of the absence of inherent existence of the transmigratory mind and of *nirvāṇa*. It asserts that natural *nirvāṇa* (*prākṛta-nirvāṇa*), which is characterized by the absence of inherent existence, is always present in the streams of consciousness of all sentient beings.[118] According to the *Tathāgatagarbhasūtra*, which identifies all sentient beings with the embryo (*garbha*) of the Tathāgata, the Buddha sees with his divine eye that all sentient beings are endowed with the Buddha's knowledge (*buddha-jñāna*), Buddha's eyes (*buddha-cakṣu*), and Buddha's body (*buddha-kāya*).[119] Likewise, the "Ṣaṭvimatsāhasra-sarvadharma-samuccaya" chapter of the *Saddharmalaṅkāvatārasūtra* asserts that the *tathāgata-garbha*, which is inherently pure clear light and primordial purity itself, is present within the bodies of all sentient beings, covered over by the psycho-physical aggregates, elements, and sense-bases.[120] Statements similar to these can also be found throughout the *Ratnagotravibhāga* and other writings of the *tathāgata-garbha* tradition. This identification of all sentient beings with the essence of the Buddha is also characteristic of some other Mahāyāna texts. For example, the *Mahāyānasūtrālaṃkāra* states that all embodied beings are the embryos of Tathāgatahood.[121] Likewise, according to the *Mahāparinirvāṇasūtra*, the essence of the Buddha (*buddha-dhātu*) is found within all sentient beings.[122]

This view of all sentient beings as being endowed with the embryo of the Tathāgata has lent itself to two different interpretations. One is that the *tathāgata-garbha* refers only to sentient beings' *potential* for spiritual awakening; and the other is that the presence of the *tathāgata-garbha* in every sentient being implies that all sentient beings are *fundamentally enlightened* but need to recognize it. As in the case of other *anuttara-yoga-tantras*,[123] the *Kālacakratantra*'s view of sentient beings as Buddhas largely accords with the second interpretation. The *Kālacakratantra* explains that enlightened awareness is innately present within an ordinary individual's body in the following way:

> Just as space does not disappear [from a jar] when water is poured into the jar, in the same way, the sky-*vajrī*, who is the pervader of the universe and devoid of sense-objects, is within the body.[124]

Even though enlightened awareness is innate to each individual, it is not actualized as long as one does not ascertain one's innate gnosis as such. However, the ascertainment of one's own gnosis as enlightened awareness entails the absence of afflictive and cognitive obscurations, which impede one's self-recognition. Their absence is conditioned by the path of purification that aims at manifesting this self-awareness of gnosis. The *Kālacakratantra* asserts that due to the power of unwholesome actions, a sinful person does not see that the wish-fulfilling gem is present in his own mind; but when purification takes place, that person becomes the Lord of Jinas (*jinendra*) and has no use for some other Jina.[125]

Thus, even though sentient beings are innately Buddhas, they are not manifestly Buddhas, and their spiritual awakening needs to manifest as a nondual gnosis that is directly aware of its own blissful and empty nature. That nondual gnosis is the mind that is essentially pure and unfettered by the obscurations of mental afflictions (*kleśāvaraṇa*), even if it is veiled by them. Therefore, that nondual gnosis is effective in the elimination of mental afflictions. The mind of a sentient being that supports the habitual propensities of *karma* (*karma-vāsanā*) and brings about suffering and happiness is the omnipresent mind that transcends transmigratory suffering and happiness and that cannot be destroyed by conceptualizations (*vikalpa*).

Like the texts of the *tathāgata-garbha* tradition, the Kālacakra tradition offers explicit reasons why one's innate gnosis, although underlying mental afflictions, remains untainted by them. However, its explanations differ from those of the *tathāgata-garbha* tradition in several ways. According to the *Ratnagotravibhāga*, the innately pure mind remains untainted by mental afflictions because mental afflictions that obscure the mind are adventitious (*āgantuka*) and are not connected with the mind, whereas the purifying elements present in the mind are innate to the mind and are indivisible from it.[126] Likewise, according to another text of the *tathāgata-garbha* tradition, the *Śrīmālādevī*, the momentary mind (*kṣaṇika-citta*), whether it is wholesome (*kuśala*) or unwholesome (*akuśala*), remains unaffected by mental afflictions because those afflictions neither touch the mind nor are touched by the mind.[127]

In contrast, a text of the Kālacakra corpus, the *Sekoddeśa*, explains the relationship between the mental afflictions and the mind in the following way:

> An adventitious stain is not in the mind nor is it prior to the mind. It does not arise without the mind nor does it stay immutable in the mind.
>
> If it were only adventitious, then the mind would be formerly stainless. If it is prior to the mind, then from where has it originated?

> If it is arisen without the mind, then it is like a sky-flower. If it is always present in the mind, then it could never vanish.
>
> Just as the impurity of copper disappears due to the prepared mixtures, its natural property, which remains in the stainless state, does not vanish.
>
> So a stain of the mind disappears due to the *yoga* of emptiness, but its state of gnosis, which remains in the stainless state, does not vanish.[128]

Even though the *Sekoddeśa* agrees that human beings are already endowed with the immutable bliss that characterizes Buddhahood, it stresses the necessity for mental purification in this way:

> Just as one must completely refine iron that is melted by intense fire, even though a precious substance is already present in one part of the iron, in the same way, one must completely refine the mind that is heated by the fire of desire, even though immutable bliss is already present in one part [of the mind].[129]

The *Vimalaprabhā* asserts that habitual propensities of the mind arise and cease due to the same cause, the power of the individual's rebirths. If the habitual propensities were inherent to the mind, then sentient beings could never reach Buddhahood, because Buddhahood comes about due to the eradication of the habitual propensities of transmigratory existence. If one examines transmigratory existence in various ways, one finds that *saṃsāra* is nothing other than the degree of one's own habitual propensities of the mind. A habitual propensity of *saṃsāra* is the moment (*kṣaṇa*) of bliss that is characterized by the emission of semen, and so it is perishable. A habitual propensity of *nirvāṇa* is the moment of bliss that is characterized by non-emission of semen, and therefore it is imperishable.[130]

The perfection of wisdom is the inconceivable gnosis of the Buddha because it consists of both attachment (*rāga*) and aversion (*virāga*). When sentient beings start thinking, attachment to desirable things and aversion to disagreeable things begin to arise. These two, attachment and aversion, are the mental causes of transmigratory existence. However, when gnosis, which is free of thinking, becomes actualized, there is no longer any attachment to desirable things or aversion to undesirable things. The absence of both results in freedom from transmigratory existence, and freedom from transmigratory existence results in full and perfect awakening.[131]

The *Kālacakratantra* itself offers only an implicit explanation. Its repeated assertion that the nature of gnosis is free of the elements of earth, water, fire, wind, and semen and their modifications implies that gnosis is free of mental afflictions, which arise from those elements. Moreover, the *Kālacakratantra*'s fundamental idea that mental afflictions, lacking inherent existence, are ultimately unreal implies that mental afflictions exist only from the perspective of the dualistic mind in which they arise. However, they neither exist nor not exist in relation to innately pure gnosis, which is beyond every perspective. This seems to be supported by the *Vimalaprabhā*, which maintains that "the nirvāṇic mind, which has transcended *saṃsāra* and is present in every body, is neither bound nor liberated by anything."[132] It further asserts that "the *vajrī*, the purified mind, is the [mind] that does not have the two—eternal existence and non-existence, or annihilation."[133]

Furthermore, according to the *tathāgata-garbha* tradition and other Indian Mahāyāna schools, mental afflictions arise from the habitual propensities of spiritual ignorance (*avidyā-vāsanā*), which manifests as erroneous views. Thus, these traditions see spiritual ignorance as the primary cause of mental afflictions, and they see the erroneous views that arise from that ignorance as the indirect cause of mental afflictions.[134] For example, for Vijñānavādins, the direct cause of mental afflictions is the view of objectification (*viṣaya-dṛṣṭi*), and for Mādhyamikas, it is any view that stands as a dogmatic position (*pakṣa*). The Kālacakra tradition, however, does not explicitly speak of any particular view as the immediate cause of mental afflictions. Although the *Kālacakratantra* often implies that applying any view contrary to that of identitylessness (*nairātmya*) or emptiness (*śūnyatā*) is detrimental to one's liberation, it clearly stresses the nature and function of *prāṇas* as the immediate cause of mental afflictions and their elimination.[135] In the *Kālacakratantra* system, mental afflictions are also referred to as impurities (*kaluṣa*) and are described as the perturbations or deformations (*vikāra*) of the mind, which are most intimately connected with the psycho-physiological constitution and processes of the individual.[136] According to the *Kālacakratantra*, the *prāṇas* are closely related to the mental states of an individual and are thus at the basis of both *saṃsāra* and *nirvāṇa*. *Prāṇas* give rise to mental afflictions by conveying the six elements through the *nāḍīs* in the body. However, it is due to the efficacy of the six elements that constitute the *prāṇas*—namely, gnosis, air, wind, fire, water, and earth—that avarice (*mātsarya*), hatred (*dveṣa*), jealousy (*īrṣyā*), attachment (*rāga*), pride (*māna*), and confusion (*moha*) respectively arise.[137] Thus, the same gnosis-element, which is identified as the cause of the Sahajakāya, which is present in the individual's secret *cakra*, also functions as the direct cause of the three kinds of the *apāna* wind, which give rise to avarice.

According to the *Kālacakratantra*, as long as a sentient being remains in the mother's womb, the *prāṇas* stay motionless in the navel-*cakra*, and mental afflictions do not arise. With the first breath at the time of birth, the *prāṇas* begin to move, carrying the five elements and thereby mental afflictions along with them. The first breath, which begins in the central *nāḍī*, is said to be devoid of the three *guṇas*; whereas the second breath takes place either in the left or or the right *nāḍī* that carries the ten *maṇḍalas*, due to the power of the *sattva-guṇa*; the third breath takes place due to the power of *rajas*, the fourth breath due to the power of *tamas*, and so on. Each of these breaths that are of the nature of *sattva*, *rajas*, and *tamas* become the five kinds due to the classification of the *guṇas* of the five sense-objects. Then, due to the threefold classification of the body, speech, and mind, they become forty-five. Then, due to the further classification of the two feet and and two arms, they become one hundred and eighty breaths; and afterward, due to the nature of wisdom and method, they, multiplied by two, become three hundred and sixty breaths.[138]

In this way, the *prāṇas* sustain mental afflictions and consequently perpetuate the cycle of rebirth. When the *prāṇas* are purified, that is, when the six elements constituting the *prāṇas* are transformed into pure gnosis, they obliterate all causes of mental afflictions and secure the bliss of liberation. Likewise, when all the bodily constituents—consisting of the elements and manifesting with the natures of *sattva*, *rajas*, and *tamas*—become purified from the afflictive and cognitive obscurations, they manifest as the ten *bodhisattva-bhūmis* and bring about Buddhahood. Thus, the bodily hair and the hair of the head become the first *bodhisattva-bhūmi*, Pramuditā, the skin and flesh become Vimalā, the two types of blood manifest as Prabhākarī, sweat and urine as Arciṣmatī, the bones and marrow as Sudurjayā, the *nāḍīs* and *prāṇas* as Abhimukhī, the gnosis-*vajra* and the element of passion (*rāga-dhātu*) as Dūraṅgamā, the mind-*vajra* as Acalā, the uterine blood as Sādhumatī, and semen as Dharmameghā. In light of this view, the *Vimalaprabhā* asserts that apart from the body, there is no other Buddha who is the pervader (*vyāpaka*) and bestower of liberation.[139]

Being the direct causes of mental afflictions and the immediate causes of their elimination, the bodily *prāṇas* are said to be supported by volition (*cetanā*).[140] Volition is understood here as the mind (*citta*), which under the influence of *sattva*, *rajas*, and *tamas*, has the waking, dreaming, and sleeping states. That mind is comprised of the five elements (*dhātu*), the mental faculty (*manas*), intellect (*buddhi*), and self-grasping (*ahaṃkāra*). Hence, in this tantric system, volition, being the transmigratory mind, is both a mental and a physical phenomenon. This transmigratory mind is further supported by innate gnosis, which is free of the five elements and thereby free of conceptualizations and mental afflictions. Being free of conceptualizations and mental afflictions, gnosis is beyond happiness and suffering, and yet it is active in bringing about the eradication of happiness and suffering.[141] This is yet another way in which the Kālacakra tradition attempts to explain why omnipresent gnosis cannot be defiled by mental afflictions despite being covered by them. One may infer here that innately pure gnosis, being the ultimate and indirect support of *prāṇas*, also functions as the ultimate factor in sustaining and eliminating mental afflictions. This understanding of the relationship between the innately pure gnosis and mental afflictions underpins the *Kālacakratantra*'s view of gnosis as the primary basis of both *saṃsāra* and *nirvāṇa*.

Furthermore, spiritual ignorance (*avidyā*) is explained in the Kālacakra tradition simply as a modification (*pratyaya*) of the elements, which are contained in the mother's blood and the father's semen and are grasped by consciousness at the moment of conception.[142] The very idea that spiritual ignorance never arises in the absence of the elements precludes the role of spiritual ignorance as the direct cause of mental afflictions. But the *Vimalaprabhā* does, on the other hand, define spiritual ignorance as a mental affliction, which consists of attachment, hatred, and delusion, and it presents it as a primary cause of these mental afflictions. It describes it as a habitual propensity of beginningless attachment, but because attachment is perishable, it gives rise to aversion (*virāga*), or hatred (*dveṣa*), which is of the nature of confusion (*mūrcchā*), or delusion (*moha*).

The *Vimalaprabhā* defines these and other mental obscurations as mental stains, which are nothing other than the mind of Māra.[143] On the ground that both the innately pure gnosis and afflictive and cognitive obscurations are present in the body of the individual, the *Kālacakratantra* asserts that both minds—the mind of Māras, which causes fear and agitation, and the blissful mind of the Buddhas—are present in the hearts of sentient beings.[144] Whereas gnosis aspires and incites one to venture for liberation from cyclic existence, the mind of Māra is said to be forever devoid of such aspiration and venturing.[145] Thus, it is due to the presence of both minds in the hearts of sentient beings that the three realms of cyclic existence endlessly revolve by the power of the Buddha within. Likewise, when the Buddha crushes the four

Māras, it is one's own innately pure gnosis that crushes the internal Māras, who are the habitual propensities of one's own body, speech, mind, and spiritual ignorance and who are not some external entities.[146] The mind of Māra and the mind of the Buddha do not exist simultaneously in the body of the individual. The moment in which the mind of Māra arises is the moment that is devoid of Buddhahood, because the mind is obscured; and the moment in which Buddhahood arises is the moment that is devoid of Māra because of the absence of obscurations. It is on this ground that the *Vimalaprabhā* asserts that Buddhahood does not precede the Buddha's destruction of Māras nor does the eradication of Māras precede Buddhahood.[147] If Buddhahood were to precede the destruction of Māras as external entities, then the Buddha's assault on Māras would imply his lack of freedom from obscurations. But if the destruction of Māras were to precede Buddhahood, then it would be unclear why ordinary sentient beings were unable to destroy Māras at any time.

According to this tantric system, the spiritual ignorance of those who delight in mundane pleasures arises due to the words of the internal Devaputra Māra. When one refuses to conform to the words of Devaputra Māra by not manifesting spiritual ignorance, the habitual propensities of one's own mind become Vajrasattva. Therefore, like Māras, Vajrasattva, who is the mind, is one's own self-imposed (*sva-kṛta*) experience. The form of Vajrasattva is a *mantra* because it is by means of *mantras* that one guards one's own mind from Māras.

That which begets all of the internal Māras is said to be a moment of perishable bliss, which is called here "Cupid" (*kāma-deva*). Eliminating one's inner Cupid by actualizing the moment of supreme, imperishable bliss, one destroys Māras, which have the form of one's own afflictive and cognitive obscurations.[148] However, it is said that out of compassion for others, one intentionally does not destroy all of one's afflictive obscurations, but retains just a trace of them "that are of the nature of the activities (*kriyā*) for the benefit of sentient beings," in order to show that path of liberation to others.[149]

Gnosis and Karma

Even though the Kālacakra tradition's philosophical explanation of *karma* is akin to the Mādhyamika view of *karma*, as being caused by mental afflictions and thereby being of the nature of mental afflictions,[150] its explanation of *karma* in terms of human physiology takes on another slant. According to the Kālacakra tradition, *karma* originates from the same elements from which mental afflictions arise. Thus, one can say here that *karma* is of the nature of mental afflictions, because they both originate from a common source. Since *karma* originates from the six elements, it is characterized by origination and cessation and therefore by conceptualization. In this way, *karma* induces and perpetuates the dualistic mind in relation to which mental afflictions arise. For the elimination of both mental afflictions and *karma*, purification takes place by melting away the fine atomic particles of the bodily *prāṇas*, which induce a dualistic vision of reality and carry the habitual propensities of *karma*. It is due to the dissolution of the atomic structure of one's body and mind that the tantric adept realizes the emptiness of all phenomena, which transcends the materiality of atoms, and thereby becomes free of *karma*.

Moreover, in terms of conventional reality, the agent (*kartṛ*) of *karma* is identified here as consciousness, or innate bliss, which appropriates the elements in the mother's womb. Eventually, when the body is formed, the six sense-faculties and the faculties of action become its means of action. However, that very consciousness is also recognized here as the agent of the elimination of *karma*, which at the time of death gradually leaves the five elements within the navel, heart, throat, forehead, and crown-*cakra*.[151] In terms of ultimate reality, the agent of *karma* is not an agent but a "a sky-pervader, a *vajrī* in the sky, free of sense-objects," the Sahajakāya without physical constituents.[152] Thus, in terms of conventional reality, gnosis is the source, originator, and destroyer of *karma*; and in terms of ultimate reality, it is none of the above, since the mind of gnosis is neither a derivative of the five elements nor does it perceive itself or anything else as an agent.[153]

Gnosis and Sexual Bliss

In the Kālacakra tradition supreme imperishable bliss is defined as tranquillity (*śānta*), which pervades the elements of every sentient being's mind and body and of the entire inanimate world. Thus, the body of every sentient being is the abode of immutable bliss[154] and contains the four bodies of the Buddha. In beings who are bound to transmigratory existence, the blissful nature of the Buddha's mind manifests in the form of sexual bliss, in which the mind, for a brief time, becomes nondual and free of conceptualization. However, since the experience of sexual bliss is mutable, it creates habitual propensities of mutable sexual desire (*kāma-vāsanā*) and induces the further emergence of that desire. In this way, it reinforces mental afflictions by binding the experiencer to sensual pleasures. For that very reason, mutable bliss is viewed in the Kālacakra tradition as being characterized by transmigratory existence.

Nevertheless, the Kālacakra tradition stresses the importance of not avoiding sensual bliss but implementing it on the path as a condition that generates mental joy, which in turn brings forth the subtle mind that counteracts conceptualizations and directly perceives the empty nature of phenomena. Thus, by refining the mind, innate bliss secures freedom from cyclic existence. The *Sekoddeśa* affirms the refining power of bliss in the following manner:

> Just as copper, refined by chemical solutions, does not become copper again, so the mind, refined by bliss, does not enter suffering again.[155]

Due to the purifying power of bliss, the experience of innate bliss is regarded as an indispensable condition for attaining Buddhahood. The *Kālacakratantra* speaks of its soteriological significance in this way:

> For one who abandons that [moment of bliss]—which is the cause of the Buddhas, by means of which the Lords of Jinas have originated and come out of the womb by the efficacy of days, and by means of which Siddhas, not emitting semen, have pulsation (*spanda*) and non-pulsation (*niḥspanda*)—and who meditates on another empty Buddhahood devoid of immutable bliss, he will not experience innate bliss for tens of millions of eons.[156]

Likewise, with regard to the soteriological efficacy of sexual bliss, one reads in the *Vimalaprabhā*:

> Bliss that is produced by two sexual organs is the reality (*tattva*) that brings forth the result of Buddhahood. Men are the aspects of Vajradhara, and women are the *vajra*-women.[157]

Since sexual bliss cannot arise without passion (*rāga*), the inducement and nurturing of passion are viewed as central components of the *Kālacakratantra* path to spiritual awakening. One reads in the *Vimalaprabhā*:

> Sin is due to the elimination of passion, on account of which, hatred toward the most loved one arises. Due to hatred there is delusion; and on account of this, the mind always becomes stupified due to the descent of one's own *vajra*.[158]

The *Sekoddeśa* also speaks of the absence of passion as sin. It states:

> There is no greater sin than dispassion (*virāga*), and there is no greater virtue than bliss. Therefore, o king, the mind should always dwell in imperishable bliss.[159]

Passion here means sexual desire (*kāma*). As indicated in chapter 5 on the "Cosmic Body," the *Kālacakratantra* identifies sexual desire with gnosis and its fire with the fire of gnosis.[160] The fire of sexual desire incinerates the impurities of the mind. Therefore, in this tantric system, to eliminate passion means to prevent virtue from arising. The tantric adept retains passion by retaining semen during sexual union, whereas the emission of semen results in dispassion, or aversion, and subsequent mental afflictions. It impedes the emergence of imperishable bliss and creates a condition for the further emergence of repeated desire for transitory bliss and all its unfavorable consequences.

The *Sekoddeśa* cautions against the deadly power of seminal emission in these words:

> It has been known that emission arouses dispassion, and dispassion arouses suffering. Due to suffering the men's elements are destroyed, and due to that destruction there is death.
>
> Due to death there is rebirth, and due to rebirth there are repeated deaths and seminal emissions. Thus, the rebirth of sentient beings is due to the arising of dispassion and not due to anything else.[161]

Whether seminal emission occurs occasionally or frequently, the consequences of seminal emission are equally detrimental with regard to one's liberation from cyclic existence. The *Vimalaprabhā* expresses it in these words:

> A lion, who feeds on deer, occasionally engages in the pleasure of sexual union at the end of the year. A pigeon, who feeds on gravel, constantly engages in the pleasure of sexual union.
>
> But just as neither one [of them] has supreme bliss, due to emitting semen either once or at all times, so too an ascetic and a lustful man do not have it because of emission in sleep and in the waking state.

> Just as a sleeping man who is bitten by a snake does not live, so too an ascetic is ruined by the vulva of a base woman, due to not retaining his semen.[162]

The *Kālacakratantra* also asserts the adverse affects of the habitual propensities of seminal emission on one's ability to actualize imperishable bliss, for perishable bliss is as antithetical to imperishable bliss as poison is to ambrosia. It asserts that imperishable bliss does not arise from the mind that is not purified from the perishable bliss of seminal emission, just as grapes do not come from the *nimba* tree and lotus flowers do not blossom from the *udumbara* tree.[163] Whereas the passion that is characterized by seminal emission brings destruction, or death, the passion that is characterized by nonemission becomes the supreme and imperishable moment of bliss, by means of which sentient beings are liberated. In this regard, it is said that the Buddhas guard the bliss, present in their hearts, which sentient beings release.[164] For this reason, the tantric *yogī* must learn to retain his semen for the sake of the *sādhana* on imperishable bliss, which is taught as a meditation on bliss through sexual union without seminal emission. It is by means of such a *sādhana* that one is able to eliminate the habitual propensities of the perishable bliss of seminal emission. One's habitual propensity for seminal emission (*cyuti-vāsanā*) is said to be an adventitious stain (*āgantuka-mala*), which has characterized the minds of sentient beings since beginningless time,[165] and it is said to be a cause of transmigratory existence. However, just as sexual union creates a condition for the arising of the habitual propensity of seminal emission, so too does it create a condition for the arising of the habitual propensity of seminal retention.[166] In light of this, the *Kālacakratantra* likens the transformative power of sexual union with regard to semen to the power of fire with regard to mercury. It states:

> Fire is an enemy of mercury. The cohesiveness (*bandha*) of mercury never occurs without fire. When it is not cohesive, it does not produce gold. Without gold, it does not give pleasure to alchemists. Likewise, the cohesiveness of men's semen (*bodhicitta*) never occurs without union with a woman. If it is not cohesive, it does not transmute the body; and the non-transmuted body does not give supreme bliss.[167]

Thus, just as mercury, which escapes due to its contact with fire, can also be made cohesive by that fire, so too semen, which escapes due to sexual contact, can be made cohesive by that contact. Likewise, just as cohesive mercury is exceptionally potent in purifying ordinary metal and transforming it into gold, so too cohesive semen has the power to purify one's psycho-physical aggregates from obscurations. Therefore, in this tantric tradition, meditation on a deity during sexual union, including the union with an actual consort (*karma-mudrā*), in which the *yogī*'s semen becomes motionless, is considered to be analogous to the processes of calcination (*jāraṇa*) and trituration (*svedana*) of mercury. Just as the process of making mercury cohesive is of two kinds—one involving the trituration and the other involving calcination—so too the process of making one's own semen cohesive and motionless has two aspects—dispassion (*virāga*) for a consort and passion (*rāga*) for a consort. It consists of passion and dispassion, because the *yogī* focuses his mind on a deity and on the personal identitylessness of himself and his consort, which induces dispassion, while engaged in sexual union with a consort, which induces passion. Likewise, just as the twofold process of making mercury cohesive and thermostable induces the different states of mercury, from vaporous to motionless,[168] due to its different powers of consuming metals, so too, the habitual practice of this twofold process of making one's own semen cohesive induces different states of semen, from soft, moderate, excessive, to the most excessive, due to meditation on the impermanence of the individual, different *kṛtsnas*, and due to the destruction of the inanimate (*jaḍa*) aggregates, elements, and sense-bases.[169]

Although the *Kālacakratantra* identifies sexual bliss with the blissful nature of gnosis, the experience of sexual bliss is seen only as a *facsimile* of the manifestation of self-aware gnosis, because, while experiencing that bliss in sexual union, one is unable to ascertain it as gnosis. Similarly, although the nonconceptual state of the mind that is induced by sexual bliss is identical to the direct realization of emptiness, the experience of that state is only a *facsimile* of the realization of emptiness, because, while being in that state of nonconceptuality, one is unable to ascertain it as such. Nevertheless, the experience of the *facsimiles* of the manifestation of gnosis and of the realization of emptiness can facilitate the *actual* manifestation of gnosis and the realization of emptiness. When the experience of the facsimiles of immutable bliss and emptiness is utilized as the essence out of which a tantric adept mentally creates *maṇḍalas* and their deities in the stage of generation, it diminishes the habitual propensities that impel one to grasp onto ordinary experiences as truly existent. When the experience of mutable bliss is implemented in this way, it induces one's mental perception of the world as a mere illusion, and consequently, diminishes one's attachment to the world.

Thus, in the Kālacakra tradition, the transformation of mutable bliss into immutable bliss is contingent upon one's motivation and one's mode of engaging in sexual practices. Those who engage in sexual practices merely for the pleasure of mutable bliss or while grasping onto such concepts as the Self (*ātman*) and creator are said to be incapable of actualizing imperishable bliss.

Thus, one may conclude that it is not the nature of gnosis itself that sustains and eliminates one's mental obscurations but one's mode of experiencing it. As long as one's experience of gnosis as innate bliss is mutable, the cycle of transmigration is perpetuated. When one's experience of innate bliss becomes immutable, Buddhahood is realized. The mode of one's experience of innate bliss directly depends upon the presence or absence of mental obscurations, and the presence of those obscurations proceeds from the fusion of consciousness and matter. The *Kālacakratantra*'s view that one's gross, physical body is a mere hindrance to Buddhahood is supported by the earlier-mentioned theory that mental afflictions and *karma* arise from the elements that form the human body.

From the premise that one's psycho-physical factors are the source of one's mental obscurations arises the necessity of transforming the ordinary physical nature of one's body and mind. The *Kālacakratantra* considers that transformation as the most direct means leading to the state in which one's own body, speech, and the mind of immutable bliss become mutually pervasive and unified. The result of that transformation is none other than the actualization of the four bodies of the Buddha, the four aspects of gnosis and bliss.

Within the context of *Kālacakratantra* soteriology, to *actualize* the four bodies of the Buddha means to bring one's own gnosis into conscious experience. One reason for this is that the *presence* of the gnosis of imperishable bliss in sentient beings does not imply that it is *fully manifest in their experience*. When nondual gnosis becomes fully manifest, an ordinary sentient being becomes the Bhagavān Kālacakra, who, according to the *Vimalaprabhā*, "is praised by the Jinas in all the *tantras* as Vajrasattva, the word *evaṃ*."[170] The Kālacakra tradition's interpretation of Vajrasattva, which is based on the definition given in the *Ādibuddhatantra*, is almost identical to that of the *Hevajratantra*. It states:

> Gnosis that is entirely indivisible (*abhedya*) is called the "*vajra*." A being (*sattva*) who is the unity of the three worlds is called "Vajrasattva."[171]

Likewise, according to the *Vimalaprabhā*, the word *evaṃ* designates Vajrasattva in this way: the letter *e* denotes the space-element, which is the *vajra* throne occupied by syllable *vaṃ*, which denotes the body, speech, mind, and gnosis.[172] In light of these interpretations of Buddhahood, one may say in conclusion that in this tantric system, the actualization of the innate gnosis of imperishable bliss involves the realization of the unitary nature of all forms of existence, which manifests in the four aspects that are, like space, all-pervading and empty of inherent existence.

The Transformative Body

The Path of Actualizing Gnosis, the Individual, and the Path as the Individual

The *Kālacakratantra*'s theory of the nature of gnosis, *prāṇas*, spiritual ignorance, and mental afflictions, as well as the relationship among them, provides the rationale for the *Kālacakratantra* practices for eliminating mental afflictions and actualizing the four bodies of the Buddha. Among the *Kālacakratantra*'s multifaceted approach to the eradication of mental afflictions, several are especially significant. First, the path of *eliminating* mental afflictions is the path of sublimating the afflictive nature of mental afflictions into the peaceful and pure nature of the enlightened beings who are the pure aspects of the elements from which mental afflictions arise. Second, the path of *sublimating* mental afflictions in the Kālacakra tradition is the path of recognizing the ultimate nature of one's own mental afflictions, which is gnosis. This path is comprised of two methods. One is a conceptual method of familiarizing oneself with the ultimate nature of one's own mind by means of autosuggestion, specifically by means of generating oneself in the form of the deities of the *kālacakra-maṇḍala*. The other method is a nonconceptual method of spontaneous and direct recognition of gnosis as the ultimate nature of one's own mind. The first method, which is characteristic of the stage of generation (*utpatti-krama*), is contrived and based on one's faith in the innately pure nature of one's own mind, and it uses primarily one's powers of imagination. Even though it is characterized by freedom from grasping onto one's own ordinary psycho-physical aggregates, or one's self-identity as an ordinary being, it is still characterized by holding onto the imagined self-identity. The second method, which is characteristic of the stage of completion (*saṃpatti-krama*), draws upon the experience of imperishable bliss and the direct perception of the innately pure nature of one's own mind, which is devoid of grasping onto any identity. Thus, on the path of sublimating mental afflictions, the *Kālacakratantra* adept starts the purificatory practices using one type of conceptualization in order to eliminate another type of conceptualization, and concludes with the eradication of all conceptualization. In this tantric tradition then, mental afflictions are nothing other than conceptualizations that obstruct the unmediated perception of the empty and blissful nature of one's own mind.

In the *anuttara-yoga-tantras* other than the *Kālacakratantra*, the primary goal of the path of sublimating mental afflictions is the purification of their immediate causes, beginning with the *prāṇas*. In those *tantras*, the purified *prāṇas* eventually become a purified material substance of the mind of clear light, and one's pure illusory body arises from this substance. In the *Kālacakratantra*, on the other hand, the primary goal of sublimating mental afflictions is the complete eradication of all present and future *prāṇas*. It is upon such complete eradication that the body of empty form, called "the form of emptiness" (*śūnyatā-bimba*), and the mind of immutable bliss arise. Since the cessation of the circulation of the *prāṇas* induces the actualization of Buddhahood in the form of Kālacakra, Buddhahood is characterized here as the "windless state" (*avāta*) that one attains by means of wind. Similarly, the nonabiding *nirvāṇa* (*apratiṣṭhita-nirvāṇa*) of the Buddha is also explained in terms of the absence of the wind of the *prāṇas*.[1] The eradication of the *prāṇas* is characterized by two conditions of the mind. First, due to the destruction of the *prāṇas*, one's dualistic mind becomes unified, and it becomes both the apprehending subject and the apprehended object. In this way, one's own mind becomes a form of emptiness (*śūnyatā-bimba*), in which conceptualizations cannot arise. Second, the destruction of the *prāṇas* and the elements that they carry eradicates the five psycho-physical aggregates and, in their absence, imperishable bliss arises.

Thus, in the context of the *Kālacakratantra*, by completely extinguishing one's own psycho-physiological constitution and processes, one extinguishes the source of one's own cycle of rebirth and attains the state of the eternal manifestation of the gnosis of supreme, immutable bliss. From the premise that one's ordinary psycho-physical factors, which are composed of atomic particles, are the source of one's mental obscurations, arises the necessity of transforming the ordinary, physical nature of one's body and mind into their blissful nature. The Kālacakra tradition considers that process of transformation as the most direct means to the state of the mutual pervasiveness and unification of one's own body, speech, and the mind of immutable bliss.

The diverse aspects of this tantric path of actualizing the gnosis of immutable bliss are closely related to the previously described views of the Kālacakra tradition on the ways in which the four bodies of the Buddha are present within the individual and on the manners in which their powers manifest in the bodily, verbal, and mental capacities of the human being. In light of the Kālacakra tradition's identification of the individual with the four bodies of the Buddha, the path of actualizing the gnosis of immutable bliss can be seen as the path of bringing forth the true nature of one's own bodily, verbal, and mental capacities. The path of actualizing the four bodies of the Buddha is the path of the purification of the previously mentioned four bodily drops from the habitual propensities of spiritual ignorance, which are sustained by *prāṇas*. Therefore, in the Kālacakra tradition, the path of actualizing the fourfold mind of the Buddha is inseparable from the path of the sublimation, or transformation, of the *prāṇas* and *nāḍīs* in the body. In that regard, the phenomenal forms of the four bodies of the Buddha and the manners in which they manifest within every individual are most intimately related through their common causal relationship to the *prāṇas*. Their interrelation is even more clearly demonstrated in the *Kālacakratantra*'s multifaceted, practical approach to the actualization of the four bodies of the Buddha.

With regard to this, one may say that in this tantric system, the transformative body of the path of actualizing blissful gnosis is the path of the mind's self-discovery through the elimination of its inessential ingredients with which the mind falsely identifies itself. Thus, the transformative body of the *Kālacakratantra* path is nothing else than the gnostic body revealing itself in the process of elimination until there is nothing left to be identified with, until the basis for self-affirmation, or self-identification, ceases and nondual self-awareness arises.

As in other related tantric systems, here too, the transformative path of actualizing the gnosis of immutable bliss consists of the three main stages of practice: the initiation (*abhiṣeka*), the stage of generation, and the stage of completion. However, the contents of these three main stages of *Kālacakratantra* practice differ from those in the other *anuttara-yoga-tantras*, since the form of Buddhahood that is sought in this tantric tradition differs from those in the other related *tantras*.

In this tantric tradition, the actualization of the four bodies of the Buddha as the four aspects of the Jñānakāya is instantaneous, but the path of purifying the four drops, which are the inner supports of the four types of the Jñānakāya, is gradual. The process of sublimating the four drops is characterized by the *Kālacakratantra*'s unique path consisting of three types of accumulations: the accumulations of merit (*puṇya*), ethical discipline (*śīla*), and knowledge (*jñāna*). For this tantric system, the accumulation of merit results in the attainment of the first seven *bodhisattva-bhūmis*, and the accumulation of ethical discipline leads to the attainment of the eighth, ninth, and tenth *bodhisattva-bhūmis*. The accumulation of ethical discipline is defined here as meditation on reality (*tattva*),[2] and it is said to result from observing the tantric vows (*vrata*) and pledges (*niyama*), especially those related to the practices with a consort. Lastly, the accumulation of knowledge results in the attainment of the eleventh and twelfth *bodhisattva-bhūmis*, which are characterized by the actualization of the gnosis of imperishable bliss and by the unification of one's own mind and body. Consisting of not two but three types of accumulations, this tantric path is closely related to the yogic practices that are specific to the *anuttara-yoga-tantras* and to the relevant schema of the twelve *bodhisattva-bhūmis*.

Likewise, this entire tantric path of spiritual transformation is seen as being of two kinds, mundane and supramundane, due to the differing qualities of tantric disciples. Thus, the stage of initiation is said to be of two kinds: mundane (*laukika*) and unexcelled (*anuttara*). The mundane initiations are those that involve the generation of bliss by means of sexual union with an actual consort (*karma-mudrā*). Due to their involvment with union with an actual consort, these mundane initiations are considered ineffective in bringing forth nondual gnosis, without which there is no Buddhahood; and their inefficacy is explained as follows. If in the union of the tantric couple, the bliss of the male consort that has arisen due to the female consort is the gnosis of the female consort, then the bliss of the female consort that has arisen due to the male consort is the gnosis of the male consort. In that case, there are two types of gnosis between the two consorts, which means that there is an absence of nonduality. Accordingly, the *Vimalaprabhā* asserts that the mundane initiations are taught not for the sake of bringing about the experience of nonduality but for converting people to this tantric path.[3] The unexcelled initiations, on the other hand, do not involve the union of two sexual organs but are practiced by means of the *mahāmudrā*-consort, or the empty form consort, and these initations do give rise to the nondual gnosis of imperishable bliss.

Similarly, the stage of generation, in which one meditates on the sexual union of oneself and an imagined consort (*jñāna-mudrā*) is regarded as a mundane *sādhana*, for it brings about only mundane results, such as the perishable experience of innate bliss and the mundane *siddhis*. The stage of completion, on the other hand, in which one meditates by means of the *mahāmudrā*-consort, is seen as the supramundane path to Buddhahood, for it induces the realization of the supramundane gnosis.

Thus, the transformative body of the path takes on first a mundane form that is accessible to the tantric practitioner who is new to the *Kālacakratantra* theory and practice; and it gradually evolves into the supramundane form by means of which the mundane person is transformed into a supramundane being.

The Transformative Body of the Path of Initiation

This tantric path of the accumulation of merit, ethical discipline, and knowledge begins with the sevenfold initiation into the *kālacakra-maṇḍala*, and this is seen as the first step in enabling the individual's four *vajras* to eventually arise as the four bodies of the Buddha. It ends with two sets of the four higher initiations, intended for the advanced Buddhist practitioners. The first seven initiations authorize the initiate to engage in the meditations on *mantras*, *mudrās*, and *maṇḍalas* that will facilitate the elimination of mental afflictions and the consequent accumulation of merit. According to the Kālacakra tradition, they are given for the sake of converting sentient beings to this body of the path and for providing the initiate with an understanding of this tantric path. The four higher initiations authorize the initiate to engage in the meditation on emptiness that has the best of all aspects, which facilitates the accumulation of knowledge;[4] and the four highest initiations authorize the initiate to become a tantric master, a *vajrācārya*.

The initial method of manifesting the four bodies of the Buddha is characterized by the initiate's entrance into the *kālacakra-maṇḍala* through the four gateways of the *maṇḍala*-palace, which symbolize the four gates of liberation corresponding to the four bodies of the Buddha, and by the initiate's visualization of his own psycho-physical constituents in the form of deities. This visualization during the stages of initiation of one's entire psycho-physical makeup in the form of deities is unique to *Kālacakratantra* practice.

1. The first two initiations, the Water (*udaka*) and Crown (*mukuṭa*) initiations, are designed to induce the initial eradication of the obscurations of the drop in the *lalāṭa cakra* by sublimating the initiate's elements and psycho-physical aggregates, respectively. Thus, these two initiations, during which the initiate is led into the *maṇḍala* through the northern gate, are said to facilitate the transformation of the initiate's body and the eventual actualization of the five Tathāgatas. Thus, this initial purification of the drop in the *lalāṭa* is believed to empower the initiate to actualize the Nirmāṇakāya of the Buddha.[5]

The other two initiations, the Crown-pendant (*paṭṭa*) and the Vajra-and-Bell (*vajra-ghaṇṭā*) initiations, are designed to purify the drop in the throat-*cakra* by purifying the right and left *nāḍīs*. In doing so, these two initiations, which are performed at the southern gate of the *kālacakra-maṇḍala*, are said to facilitate the purification of the initiate's speech-*vajra* and the actualization of the Saṃbhogakāya. The Crown-pendant initiation is said to empower the initiate to attain the ten powers that are for the sake of attaining the ten perfections; whereas the Vajra-and-Bell initiation is said to empower the initiate to attain imperishable bliss by purifying the semen and uterine blood.[6]

Likewise, the Vajra-Conduct (*vajra-vrata*) and Name (*nāma*) initiations, which are performed at the eastern gate of the *kālacakra-maṇḍala*, are designed to facilitate the purification of the drop at the heart-*cakra*, which is the mind-*vajra*, and the actualization of the Dharmakāya. The Vajra-Conduct initiation is said to induce the initial sublimation of the sense-faculties and their objects and to empower the initiate to attain the divine eye (*divya-cakṣu*) and other divine faculties. The Name initiation is believed to purify the faculties of action (*karmendriya*) and their activities and to empower the initiate to attain the four Immeasurables (*brahma-vihāra*).[7]

Lastly, the Permission (*anujñā*) initiation, which is performed at the western gate of the *kālacakra-maṇḍala*, is designed to remove the defilements of the drop at the navel-*cakra* and to facilitate the actualization of the Jñānakāya. It is said to empower the initiate to set the Wheel of Dharma in motion.

In this tantric system, the initiate who has undertaken this initial purification of the body, speech, mind, and gnosis by means of the seven initiations is considered authorized to practice the *sādhanas* for the sake of the mundane *siddhis* (*laukika-siddhi*).[8] While receiving these seven initiations, the initiate takes the twenty-five tantric vows (*vrata*) and the pledges to avoid the fourteen root downfalls (*mūlāpatti*). In this manner, he increases his store of merit.[9] The power of merit that the initiate accumulates by means of the first seven initiations is considered effective in facilitating the attainment of the first seven *bodhisattva-bhūmis*, either in this life or in a future rebirth. If the initiate visualizes the *kālacakra-maṇḍala* while he is being initiated into it, then he accumulates enough merit to empower him to attain mastery over the seven *bodhisattva-bhūmis* in his present life. But, if the initiate who is free of the ten nonvirtues dies, he attains mastery over the seven *bodhisattva-bhūmis* in the next life.[10]

2. The two higher initiations, the Vase (*kumbha*) and Secret (*guhya*) initiations, are designed to increase the initiate's ethical discipline that qualifies him to eventually attain permanent mastery over the other two *bodhisattva-bhūmis*, Acalā and Sādhumatī. In terms of the sexual *yoga* of *Kālacakratantra* practice, attaining Acalā ("Immovable") entails the immovability, or nonemission, of semen; and attaining Sādhumatī ("Good") entails the attainment of the mind of sublime bliss (*mahā-sukha-citta*) during sexual intercourse.[11] Likewise, the other two higher initiations, the Wisdom and Gnosis initiations, are believed to facilitate the attainment of the tenth *bodhisattva-bhūmi*, Dharmameghā, which is described in this tradition as "the rain of sublime bliss that brings forth one's own well-being and the well-being of others," "the state of Mañjuśrī that removes the fear of cyclic existence."[12] These empowerments are said to be effective due to the power of the ethical discipline that the initiate accumulated during the two earlier higher initiations.

The four higher initiations are believed to empower the initiate to attain the remaining *bodhisattva-bhūmis* by further purifying the habitual propensities of the previously accumulated impurities. In the course of these four higher initiations, the initiate engages in sexual union with an actual consort (*karma-mudrā*), experiences sexual bliss, and at the same time meditates on emptiness. At the same time, the initiate identifies himself with the Buddha's four *vajras*—the *vajras* of the body, speech, mind, and gnosis, respectively. Thus, in the Vase initiation, the initiate identifies himself with the body-*vajra*, and he mentally offers to his spiritual mentor the young consort, the *maṇḍala*, and prayers. When the offered consort returns, the initiate gazes at the imagined consort, whom he visualizes as Viśvamātā, and imagines caressing her breasts. By doing so, the initiate brings forth the experience of bliss (*ānanda*), and while experiencing that bliss, he meditates on emptiness. This unified manner of experiencing bliss and cognizing emptiness during the Vase initiation is believed to facilitate the purification of the drop at the forehead-*cakra* and to further empower the initiate to attain the Nirmāṇakāya.

During the Secret initiation, the initiate identifies himself with the speech-*vajra* and visualizes his spiritual mentor engaging in sexual union with his own consort. Subsequently, he visualizes that rays of light, which are emitted from the spiritual mentor's heart, bring all the deities of the *kālacakra-maṇḍala* into the spiritual mentor's mouth. Those deities descend into the spiritual mentor's heart, and from there they arrive at the tip of his sexual organ, at which point, the initiate imagines the spiritual mentor placing a drop of purified semen into the initiate's mouth. The initiate gazes at the sexual organ of the consort and experiences sexual bliss, due to which the drop of *bodhicitta* from the throat-*cakra* descends into the initiate's heart-*cakra* and causes the initiate to experience supreme bliss (*paramānanda*). While experiencing supreme bliss, the initiate meditates on emptiness. Thus, by unifying the initiate's experience of great bliss with his cognition of emptiness, the Secret initiation facilitates the purification of the drop in the throat-*cakra* and further empowers the initiate to attain the Saṃbhogakāya.

During the Wisdom initiation, the initiate identifies himself with the mind-*vajra*. Here, the initiate enters into sexual union with the imagined consort (*prajñā-mudrā*) whom he offered to his spiritual mentor during the Vase initiation. During the imagined sexual union, the initiate visualizes his sexual organ as a five-pointed *vajra* and the organ of his consort as light out of which arises a red lotus with three petals, with the yellow syllable *phaṭ* in its center. Due to this sexual union, the initiate experiences innate bliss (*sahajānanda*) as the drop of *bodhicitta* descends from the heart-*cakra* into the navel-*cakra*. While experiencing this innate bliss, the initiate meditates on emptiness. Unifying the initiate's experience of bliss with his cognition of emptiness in this manner, the Wisdom initiation is said to facilitate the purification of the drop in the heart-*cakra* and to empower the initiate to attain the Dharmakāya.

During the Gnosis initiation, the initiate identifies himself with the gnosis-*vajra*, and he identifies his consort with Viśvamātā. He enters into sexual union with the consort and experiences supreme, immutable bliss (*parama-sama-sukha*). Due to the experience of this bliss, a drop of *bodhicitta* descends from the navel-*cakra* to the tip of his sexual organ and remains there without being emitted. While experiencing the moment of supreme, immutable bliss, the initiate meditates on emptiness. In this manner, the Gnosis initiation facilitates the purification of the drop in the navel-*cakra* and empowers the initiate to attain the Jñānakāya.

Thus, one may say that in the four higher initiations, it is the initiate's experience of the four types of bliss[13] and emptiness that induces the further purification of the four drops. In the Vase initiation, it is the experience of sexual bliss induced by the imagined caressing of the body and breasts of the consort; in the Secret initiation, it is the experience of sexual bliss induced by the imagined sexual union; in the Wisdom initiation, it is the experience of sexual bliss induced by the pulsation (*spanda*) of the tip of the sexual organ; and in the Gnosis initiation, it is the experience of sexual bliss induced by nonpulsation (*niḥspanda*) that is caused by passion for the *mahāmudrā* consort. In light of this, the four higher initiations themselves can be classified into the two types of path. The first two higher initiations can be characterized as the mundane, or conceptual, path, and the other two as the supramundane, or nonconceptual path. The four types of blissful experiences then are seen as the means by which these four initiations contribute to the removal of the habitual propensities of former mental obscurations and counteract their further emergence.

The initiate's progress through the eleven initiations is seen in the Kālacakra tradition as a symbolic representation of one's spiritual progress on the Buddhist path from a lay person to a monastic novice, to a fully ordained monk, and finally, to a Buddha. This symbolic progression is considered to be related to the initiate's empowerment to eventually attain the twelve *bodhisattva-bhūmis*. Thus, one who is initiated in the first seven initiations is referred to as a "lay Buddhist" (*upāsaka*), for he is predicted to attain the first seven *bodhisattva-bhūmis*. One who is initiated in the higher Vase initiation is referred to as a "novice" (*śrāmaṇera*), a "Buddha's son" (*buddha-putra*), or a "youth," since he is predicted to attain the eighth *bodhisattva-bhūmi*. Similarly, one who is initiated in the higher Secret initiation is referred to as a "fully ordained monk" (*bhikṣu*), "an elder" (*sthavira*), or "a crown-prince (*yuva-rāja*) of the Buddha," for he is predicted to attain the ninth *bodhisattva-bhūmi*. One who is initiated in the higher Wisdom and Gnosis initiations is referred to as a "Buddha," or "a teacher of the Dharma," since he is predicted to attain the tenth *bodhisattva-bhūmi*.[14] The four highest initiations empower the initiate to attain the remaining two *bodhisttava-bhūmis*.

This analogy of the progression through the eleven initiations to the progression from a Buddhist lay life to Buddhahood is one of many internal indications of the Kālacakra tradition's strong monastic orientation. This analogy is similar to the *Sekoddeśa*'s analogy of the four higher initiations to the four stages of life—childhood, adulthood, old age, and Buddhahood. However, the *Sekoddeśa* draws its analogy on the basis of the experience of the four types of bliss during the four higher initiations, whereas the *Kālacakratantra*'s analogy is based on the predicted attainment of the *bodhisattva-bhūmis*. Therefore, in the *Sekkodeśa*, one who is initiated in the higher Vase initiation is called a "child" (*bāla*), since he attains sexual bliss merely by touching the consort. One who is initiated in the higher Secret initiation is called an "adult" (*prauḍha*), for he experiences his bliss due to the imagined sexual union. One who is initiated in the higher Wisdom initiation is called an "old person" (*vṛddha*), for he experiences bliss caused by *bodhicitta* touching the tip of his sexual organ. Lastly, one who is initiated in the higher Gnosis initiation is called "the progenitor of all Protectors," "Vajrasattva," "a great being" (*mahā-sattva*), "Bodhisattva," "the nondual," "the indestructible," "the fourfold *vajra-yoga*," "Kālacakra," and so on, since his experience of bliss is caused by his passion for the *mahā-mudrā* consort.[15]

The four highest initiations (*uttarottarābhiṣeka*) have the same names as the four higher initiations. They are said to induce the further purification of the four drops from their obscurations. In the four highest initiations, the initiate is given ten consorts, representing the ten powers (*śakti*), or ten perfections. As in the earlier Vase initiation, here too the initiate experiences sexual bliss by arousing sexual desire due to mentally gazing and caressing the breasts of a consort who is chosen from among the ten. Due to the aroused desire, a drop of *bodhicitta* descends from his *uṣṇīṣa* into the *lalāṭa* and gives rise to bliss (*ānanda*). During the other three highest initiations, due to the imagined sexual union with the remaining nine of the ten consorts and due to the retention of semen, he sequentially experiences supreme bliss (*paramānanda*), extraordinary bliss (*viramānanda*), and innate bliss (*sahajānanda*). As in the four higher initiations, which came earlier, here too the experience of the four types of bliss is accompanied by meditation on emptiness. Due to this, the experience is believed to further facilitate the transformation of the *vajras* of the body, speech, mind, and gnosis into the four bodies of the Buddha.[16] As with the preceding path of the four higher initiations, due to the experience of the four types of bliss, this fourfold path of initiation has both aspects: mundane and supramundane. In this way, the four highest initiations are the preliminary practices for the stage of completion.

In the four higher and the four highest initiations, the experience of the four types of bliss becomes the means of purifying one's own mental obscurations and facilitating the nondual vision of reality. As indicated earlier, the experience of sexual bliss is thought to exert its purifying power only when it is accompanied by both the retention of semen and meditation on emptiness. The following verses from the *Ādibuddhatantra* express this in the following manner:

> In the union with an actual consort (*karma-mudrā*) and in desiring a gnosis-consort (*jñāna-mudrā*), those who firmly hold the vows should guard their semen (*bodhicitta*), the great bliss.
>
> Upon placing one's own sexual organ into the vulva, one should not emit *bodhicitta*. Rather, one should meditate on the entire three worlds as the body of the Buddha.
>
> Due solely to that guarded [*bodhicitta*], Buddhahood, which is completely filled with the accumulation of ethical discipline and is fully endowed with merit and knowledge, comes about in this lifetime.
>
> The Samyaksaṃbuddhas, who have attained the ten perfections, abide in the three times. By means of this [guarded *bodhicitta*], all Samyaksaṃbuddhas turn the Wheel of Dharma.
>
> There is no greater gnosis than this, which is the lord of the three worlds and is not devoid of emptiness and compassion for the sake of accomplishing its own well-being and the well-being of others.[17]

Thus, already in the stage of initiation, one's own gnosis that manifests as both sexual bliss, or passion, characterized by seminal nonemission, and as the cognition of emptiness, or dispassion, acts as the means for actualizing the gnosis of imperishable bliss.

The Transformative Body of the Path of the Stage of Generation

The second phase of the transformative body of the path of actualizing the four bodies of the Buddha is the stage of generation (*utpatti-krama*). It consists of four main phases of practice, which are classified as the four types of *sādhanas*:

1. the generation of the body, or the supreme king of *maṇḍalas* (*maṇḍala-rājāgrī*), which is specified as the "phase of worship" (*sevāṅ(ga)*,
2. the generation of the speech, or the supreme king of actions (*karma-rājāgrī*), which is specified as the "auxiliary *sādhana*" (*upasādhana*),
3. the *yoga* of the drops (*bindu-yoga*), which is characterized by the generation of the drops of semen and is specified as a "*sādhana*,"
4. and the subtle *yoga* (*sūkṣma-yoga*), which is characterized by the arising of bliss and is specified as the "sublime *sādhana*" (*mahā-sādhana*).[18]

This fourfold classification of the stage of generation corresponds to the fourfold classification of the Buddha's bodies, and it delineates the body of the path which is made up of progressively more subtle forms of tantric practice. The first two types of *sādhana*, which involve meditation on the fourfold *kālacakra-maṇḍala* and all its indwelling deities, are based on intricate mental imagery, which cannot be maintained without adequate meditative quiescence (*śamatha*). Moreover, the symbolic implications of the mental imagery sustained by meditative quiescence facilitate the contemplative's insight (*vipaśyanā*) into the empty and blissful nature of that imagery and its referents. Investigating the impermanent nature of the imagined deities of the *kālacakra-maṇḍala*, and thereby realizing his own impermanence and the impermanence of all sentient beings abiding within the triple world, the tantric contemplative realizes that nothing in the *kālacakra-maṇḍala* or in the three worlds is of enduring essence. Therefore, on the stage of generation, the path of the purification of the four drops is uniquely characterized by the simultaneous development of quiescence and insight. This path is complemented by the practice of the meditator's self-identification with the visualized deities, or the cultivation of divine pride, which is necessarily based on some conceptual understanding of the emptiness of inherent existence of the deities with whom the contemplative identifies himself.

The visual formation of the *kālacakra-maṇḍala* is called "the supreme sovereign *maṇḍala*" because it corresponds to the generation of the four bodies of the Buddha.[19] When this mentally created, supreme, sovereign *maṇḍala* is conceived as the visual representation of the pure aspects of the contemplative's own gnosis, mind, speech, and body, it acts as the purifying agent of the meditator's four drops. The transformative power of the visualized *kālacakra-maṇḍala* is believed to lie in its efficacy to partially eradicate the obscurations of conventional reality (*saṃvṛty-āvaraṇa*), by allowing ultimate reality to manifest itself through the generated *maṇḍala*. However, as indicated earlier, its purifying efficacy is believed to be contingent upon the contemplative's own understanding of emptiness. The *Kālacakratantra* asserts that one should engage in meditation on the *kālacakra-maṇḍala* only after one has understood that "the entire world is empty," that ultimately "there is neither a Buddha nor spiritual awakening."[20] The transformative power of this practice is also said to lie in the contemplative's understanding that the entire *kālacakra-maṇḍala*, which is a mere illusion (*māyā*) and an ideation (*kalpanā*), is nothing other than the manifestation of one's own mind. Accordingly, the contemplative must understand that in order to free his mind from ideation, he must eventually leave behind this form of practice and, in order to transform his mind into the actual Kālacakra, the unity of bliss and emptiness, he must engage in nonconceptual meditation. In light of this, the *Kālacakratantra* states:

> Because the entire *sādhana* of a *vajrī* is an illusion, o king, one should make one's own mind free of impurities; one should make it the lord of the *maṇḍala*.[21]

On the grounds that the visualized *kālacakra-maṇḍala* is a mere mental construct that arises nondually with the meditator's own mind, one may say further that in this stage of practice the transformative agent of the meditator's four drops is his own mind.

1. In the first phase of the stage of generation, the method of purifying the four drops is characterized by the visualization of the *kālacakra-maṇḍala* and its diverse classes of deities, who represent the enlightened aspects of the meditator's body and of the cosmic body. As in the case of many Buddhist Mahāyāna meditational practices, here too, the confession of sins, rejoicing in virtue, taking refuge, and arousing the spirit of awakening (*bodhicitta*) precede the practice of meditative visualization.

The path of the actualization of the four bodies of the Buddha on the stage of generation involves meditative practices during which the tantric adept imaginatively dies as an ordinary person and arises as the Buddha Kālacakra. For that reason, the stage of generation begins with a meditation in which the tantric adept mentally casts off his transmigratory psycho-physical aggregates in order to obtain the supramundane aggregates (*lokottara-skandha*). In this phase of practice, prior to visualizing the *kālacakra-maṇḍala* as the sublimated aspect of his own body and of the cosmic body, the tantric adept imaginatively dissolves the atomic structure of his own body and the body of the universe. In order to relinquish his habituated sense of self-identity and establish his new identity, the meditator mentally disintegrates his body in the same manner that the body dissolves by itself during the dying process. By meditating on the water-element, he eliminates first the fire-element; then when the earth-element has lost its solidity due to the absence of fire and it becomes liquid, he dries it up by meditating on the wind-element, which he disperses afterward into space. After that, he meditates on the space-element as the reflection of emptiness, or as empty form, which transcends the reality of atoms.[22] This manner of settling one's own mind on empty form and establishing it as one's true identity is a prerequisite for adequate meditative practice of generating oneself in the form of the deities of the *kālacakra-maṇḍala*.

Whereas the first phase of the stage of generation is analogous to the stage of dying and the dissolution of the cosmos, the second phase of the stage of generation is analogous to conception in the womb and to the formation of the cosmos. It entails the mental generation of the four divisions of the *kālacakra-maṇḍala* as the mother's body and as the cosmic body. In this phase of practice, the tantric practitioner visualizes first the mind-*maṇḍala*, at the center of which is gnosis, which has the form of a lotus within the tetrahedral source of wisdom (*prajñā-dharmodaya*). In this way, he symbolically generates the Dharmakāya and the Jñānakāya of the Buddha, the sublimated aspects of the wind and earth *maṇḍalas* of the universe and of the mother's forehead and navel *cakras*. After mentally generating the mind-*maṇḍala*, the tantric contemplative visualizes the speech-*maṇḍala* encircling the mind-*maṇḍala*. By visualizing the speech-*maṇḍala*, he generates the Saṃbhogakāya of the Buddha, the sublimated aspect of the fire-*maṇḍala* of the universe and of the mother's throat-*cakra*. He further visualizes the body-*maṇḍala* encircling the speech-*maṇḍala*, and in this way, he generates the Nirmāṇakāya of the Buddha, the sublimated aspect of the water-*maṇḍala* of the cosmic body and of the mother's heart-*cakra*. Visualizing these four *maṇḍalas* of the gnosis, mind, speech, and body, together with their individual sets of four gates, portals, and the like, the tantric *yogī* mentally generates the sublimated universe and the mother's body, as well as his transformed environment, in which he will arise as the Buddha Kālacakra in the next phase of the stage of generation practice. (See figure 8.1.)

The following verses from the *Ādibuddhatantra* indicate the manner in which a tantric adept should understand that the *maṇḍalas* that he generates as the purified aspects of the mother's body and the cosmos are the symbolic representations of the Buddhahood into which he will arise as the Śuddhakāya:

> The *maṇḍalas* of the mind, speech, and body correspond to the Buddha, Dharma, and sublime Saṅgha. The four *vajra*-lines correspond to the four divine abidings (*brahma-vihāra*).
>
> A quandrangular [form within the *maṇḍala*] entirely corresponds to the four applications of mindfulness (*smṛtyupasthāna*),[23] and the twelve gates correspond to the cessation of the twelve links [of dependent origination].
>
> Likewise, the exquisite portals correspond to the twelve *bhūmis*, and the cremation grounds in the eight directions correspond to the Noble Eightfold Path.
>
> The sixteen pillars are [sixteenfold] emptiness, and the upper floors correspond to the elements. The crests correspond to the eight liberations, to the eight corporeals (*rūpin*),[24] and to the eight qualities.[25]
>
> The face and the sides [of the gates] accord with the classification of the mind, speech, and body. The five pure colors correspond to the five: ethical discipline (*śīla*), and the like.
>
> The three fences in the *maṇḍalas* of the mind, speech, and body correspond to the three Vehicles, to the five faculties of faith, and the like, and to the five powers (*bala*) of faith, and so on.
>
> The pavilions in the three *maṇḍalas* correspond to the *samādhis* and *dhāraṇīs*. The variegated jeweled strips of fabric correspond to all of the ten perfections.

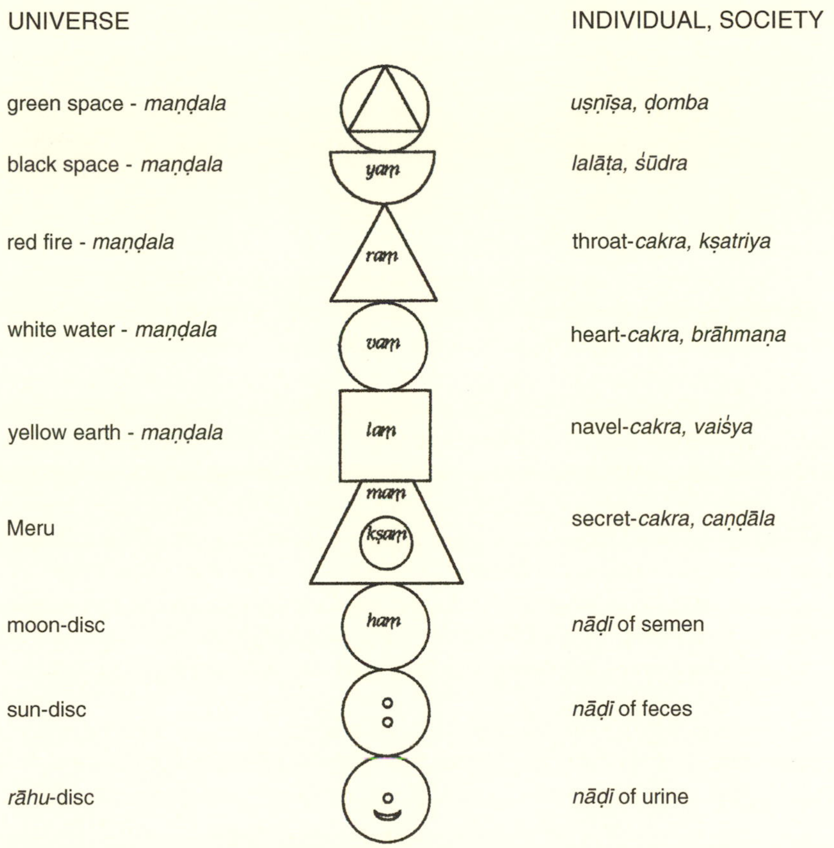

FIGURE 8.1 The body of the seed-syllables

The pearl-garlands and the half [pearl-garlands] correspond to the eighteen unique qualities [of the Buddha] (*āveṇikā-dharma*). *Bakulī* flowers correspond to the [ten] powers.[26] The balconies correspond to virtues.

[Balconies] filled with the sounds of bells and the like correspond to liberation through emptiness, and so on. Their state of being full of victory-banners corresponds to the [four] bases of supernatural powers (*ṛddhi-pāda*), and their glistening with mirrors corresponds to the [four] exertions (*prahāṇa*).

The vibration of their yak-tail whisk corresponds to the [seven] limbs of enlightenment, and their decorative garlands correspond to the nine divisions [of the Buddha's teaching]. The corners that are adorned with variegated *vajras* correspond to the four means of assembly (*saṃgraha*).

Their being studded with the four jewels of [the Four Noble] Truths at the junctures between the gates and crests and always being surrounded by five great circles [symbolizes] the five extrasensory perceptions (*abhijñā*).

> They are surrounded by the *vajra*-chain of the constituents of enlightenment (*bodhyaṅga*) of one who knows all aspects, by a single wall of bliss, and by the light-rays of the gnosis-*vajra*.
>
> The ever-risen moon and sun are in accordance with the division of wisdom and method. The pure mind, speech, and body are the Wheel of Dharma, the great pitcher, drum, tree of spiritual awakening, its wish-fulfilling jewels, and the like. This is a *maṇḍala* of splendid Kālacakra, which is the *dharma-dhātu*.[27]

After purifying one's own perception and conception of the environment in this way, the tantric practitioner enters the next phase of the stage of generation, in which he imagines himself as an enlightened being arising in a pure environment. Therefore, this phase of the stage of generation is analogous to the individual's development in the mother's womb and to the origination of cosmic time. At this phase of practice, the tantric *yogī* generates the body of the Buddha Kālacakra as the sublimated form of the universe and of his own body by visualizing Kālacakra standing on the discs of the sun, moon, and Rāhu and emanating the five rays of light. This phase of visualization is analogous to the moment of conception in the womb. Thus, the sun, moon, and Rāhu represent the purified aspects of the mother's uterine blood, the father's semen, and the meditator's consciousness, which are joined in the purified mother's body that was generated earlier as the four *maṇḍalas*. The five rays of light symbolize the five types of gnosis, the purified aspects of the meditator's psycho-physical aggregates.

The next phase of visualization, which is analogous to the third month in the womb, represents the sublimation of the three links of dependent origination. In that phase, the meditator visualizes the Buddha Kālacakra standing in the *ālīḍha* posture,[28] which symbolizes the flow of the *prāṇas* in the meditator's right *nāḍī* and their retraction in his left *nāḍī*. With his feet, the Buddha Kālacakra crushes the hearts of Rudra and Māra, the meditator's mental defilements. Here the tantric contemplative visualizes Kālacakra in union with Viśvamātā, the personified representation of the perfection of wisdom, or gnosis, who is standing in the *pratyālīḍha* posture,[29] which symbolizes the flow of the *prāṇas* in the contemplative's left *nāḍī* and their retraction in his right *nāḍī*. By visualizing Kālacakra and Viśvamātā, the tantric adept mentally generates the two aspects of the Buddha's mind: bliss and emptiness. According to the *Vimalaprabhā*, Kālacakra represents innate bliss (*sahajānanda*), or supreme, imperishable bliss (*akṣara-sukha*); and Viśvamātā represents the gnosis of the emptiness that has all aspects (*sarvākāra-śūnyatā-jñāna*), which perceives the three times and is "purified by the elimination of the obscurations of conceptualizations (*vikalpa*) and the bliss of seminal flow (*cyavana-sukha*)."[30] Their sexual union within the pericarp of the lotus of the *maṇḍala* symbolizes the union of these two aspects of the Buddha's mind. The presence of these two deities in the heart of the *kālacakra-maṇḍala* is to remind the meditator that gnosis, characterized by bliss and emptiness, is the ultimate nature of all other deities in the *maṇḍala*, that is to say, of all other aspects of Buddhahood and of the meditator's own psycho-physical constituents. In other words, all other deities in the *maṇḍala* are to be understood as the emanations of the two principal deities. For example, Viśvamātā, who is the perfection of wisdom, becomes Vajradhātvīśvarī for the sake of destroying ordinary hatred (*prākṛta-dveṣa*) and bringing forth sublime hatred (*mahā-dveṣa*), which is the absence of hatred. She becomes Locanā for the sake of destroying ordinary delusion. Due to her sublime compassion, she becomes Māmakī for the sake of destroying ordinary pride, Pāṇḍarā for the sake of destroying ordinary attachment, and Tārā for the sake of eradicating ordinary envy, and so on. Likewise, Vajrasattva becomes Vairocana for the sake of illuminating the minds of deluded people, Amitābha for the sake of those afflicted by attachment, Ratnasambhava for the sake of generosity toward suffering beings, Amoghasiddhi for the sake of removing obstacles, and so on.[31] In this way, unified bliss and emptiness, symbolized here by the two principal deities in sexual union, free the mind from its obscurations by sublimating the elements that give rise to mental obscurations.

At times, the two principal deities are also identified with the contemplative's aggregate of gnosis (*jñāna-skandha*) and the element of gnosis (*jñāna-dhātu*), respectively; and at other times, they are both referred to as the element of gnosis that gives rise to the individual's mental sense-faculty (*mano-indriya*). For this reason, they are also called "the gnostic deities" (*jñāna-devatā*).[32]

The subsequent phases of the visualization of the deities accompanying Kālacakra and Viśvamātā are viewed as analogous to the further development of the fetus in the womb and to the sublimation of the remaining links of dependent origination. Thus, the tantric adept further visualizes the two principal deities surrounded by the eight goddesses who stand on the eight petals of the lotus and represent eight perfections. As he visualizes the other deities of the mind-*maṇḍala*—the four Buddhas and their consorts, the Vidyās, the deities with a tree and a pitcher (*sataru-sakalaśā*), the male and female Bodhisattvas, and the five male and female wrathful deities (*krodhendra*)—the tantric adept generates the sublimated aspects of his elements, sense-bases (*āyatana*), and other bodily constituents. The generation of the four Buddhas and their consorts and the male and female wrathful deities within the mind-*maṇḍala* is said to be analogous to the fourth month in the womb and to the sublimation of the fourth link of dependent origination.[33] Whereas the generation of the male Bodhisattvas is seen as analogous to the fifth month in the womb and to the sublimation of the fifth link of dependent origination or the six sense-faculties. The generation of their female consorts is analogous to the sixth month in the womb and to the sublimation of the sixth link of dependent origination.

In the schema of the fourfold *kālacakra-maṇḍala*, the gnostic couple, Kālacakra and Viśvamātā, who are the meditator's sublimated gnosis-aggregate and element, represent the Sahajakāya of the Buddha; all other deities of the mind-*maṇḍala* represent the Dharmakāya of the Buddha. The sequential visualization of the deities of the gnosis and mind-*maṇḍalas* illustrates the Kālacakra tradition's view of the Dharmakāya arising from the Sahajakāya as analogous to the arising of the sense-faculties and their objects from the elements. Accordingly, the Kālacakra tradition views the mental generation of the mind-*maṇḍala* as the sublimation of the meditator's conceptual and perceptual types of awareness. Every deity in the *kālacakra-maṇḍala* corresponds to the specific component of the human body or to its functions. Table 8.1 illustrates the manner in which the Kālacakra tradition identifies the six Buddhas and their consorts with the six elements, and the six male and female Bodhisattvas with the twelve sense-bases that arise from the six elements, respectively.[34]

Upon generating this mind-*maṇḍala*, the contemplative generates the goddesses

TABLE 8.1 Buddhas and Bodhisattvas within the Human Body

Six male buddhas and bodhisattvas	Six female buddhas and bodhisattvas
Amoghasiddhi = the wind-element	Tārā = the wind element
Vaigarbha = the nose	Sparśavajrā = touch
Ratnasaṃbhava = the fire-element	Pāṇḍarā = the fire element
Kṣitigarbha = the eye	Rasavajrā = taste
Vairocana = the earth-element	Locanā = the earth-element
Sarvanīvaraṇaviṣkambhī = the body	Gandhavajrā = smell
Amitābha = the water-element	Māmakī = the water-element
Lokeśvara = the tongue	Rūpavajrā = form
Kālacakra = the gnosis-element	Viśvamātā = the gnosis-element
Samantabhadra = the mind	Śabdavajrā = sound
Akṣobhya = the space-element	Dharmadhātvīśvarī = the space-element
Vajrapāṇi = the ear	Dharmadhātuvajrā = a mental object

of the *nāḍīs* of time (*kāla-nāḍī*) within the speech-*maṇḍala*, in addition to the eight goddesses (*devī*) and their attending sixty-four *yoginīs* as standing on the eight petals of the speech-*maṇḍala*. The visualization of the eight principal goddesses and their retinue of *yoginīs* of the speech-*maṇḍala* is analogous to the seventh month in the womb and to the sublimation of the seventh link of dependent origination. By visualizing the goddesses of the speech-*maṇḍala*, the tantric adept generates the Saṃbhogakāya of the Buddha.[35]

After visualizing the speech-*maṇḍala*, the meditator visualizes the diverse classes of deities of the body-*maṇḍala*: namely, the *nairṛtyas*, *sūryadevās*, *nāgas*, and *pracaṇḍās*. Visualizing the twelve *nairṛtyas*, the tantric practitioner generates the sublimated aspects of the twelve main *nāḍīs* of his body; and visualizing the twelve lotuses on which they are standing, he generates the twelve purified aspects of the *cakras* within the twelve joints of his arms and legs, which are called the action-*cakras* (*karma-cakra*) and the activity-*cakras* (*kriyā-cakra*). Similarly, mentally creating the *sūryadevas*, the contemplative generates the purified aspects of the *nāḍīs* of his hands, feet, crown-*cakra*, and anus. The generation of these two classes of deities, *nairṛtyas* and *sūryadevas*, is viewed as analogous to the eighth month in the womb and to the sublimation of the eighth link of dependent origination. Visualizing the ten *nāgas* and ten *pracaṇḍās* within the body-*maṇḍala*, the *yogī* generates the sublimated *nāḍīs* of his ten fingers and ten toes. This visualization is said to be analogous to the ninth month in the womb and to the sublimation of the ninth link of dependent origination. Visualizing the deities of the body-*maṇḍala* in this way, the contemplative generates the Nirmāṇakāya of the Buddha.

Just as all of the aforementioned deities of the four *maṇḍalas* symbolize the purified aspects of the four bodies of the Buddha that are latently present in the body of the fetus, so do they symbolize the purified aspects of the four bodies of the Buddha that are latent in the body of the individual born from the womb. The deities of the gnosis and mind *maṇḍalas* symbolize the four bodies of the Buddha latently present in the body of a young child; and the deities of the speech and body *maṇḍalas* symbolize the actualized aspects of the four bodies of the Buddha that are present in the

TABLE 8.2.A The Gnosis and Mind Maṇḍalas within the Individual

		Gnosis-*maṇḍala*			
Sahajakāya			Sahajakāya		
Kālacakra Viśvamātā *divyās* *satarusakalaśās*			consciousness gnosis semen uterine blood		
		Mind-*maṇḍala*			
Dharmakāya		Saṃbhogakāya		Nirmāṇakāya	
Buddhas *vidyās*	aggregates elements	Bodhisattvas	sense-bases	*krodhas*	arms legs hair, etc.

body of the individual.[36] Thus, by mentally generating the deities of the four *maṇḍalas*, the tantric adept imaginatively transmutes his entire life, from the time of conception until death, into the state of Buddhahood.

Tables 8.2.a–b show the correspondences among the deities of the fourfold *maṇḍala*, the four bodies of the Buddha, and one's bodily constituents.

The Kālacakra tradition sees this entire phase of the generation of the body of Kālacakra as the fourfold *kālacakra-maṇḍala* as a meditation on perfect awakening with five aspects (*pañcākāra-saṃbodhi*); and it considers the following phase of *upasādhana* to be a meditation on perfect awakening with twenty aspects.[37]

2. The *upasādhana* phase of the stage of generation practice involves a *sādhana* on the enlightened activities of the deities of the *kālacakra-maṇḍala*, that is, the activities of the four bodies of the Buddha. In this phase of practice, the tantric contemplative imaginatively awakens his consciousness, which has fallen into stupor and is unaware of its true nature, and he stimulates it to engage in enlightened activities. For example, he imagines the female consorts of the four Buddhas, who symbolize the four Immeasurables, the pure aspects of the four bodily elements, as stand-

TABLE 8.2.B The Speech and Body Maṇḍalas within the Individual

		Speech-*maṇḍala*			
Sahajakāya			Sahajakāya		
devīs *yoginīs*			flow of *prāṇas* from the navel-*cakra*		
		Body-*maṇḍala*			
Dharmakāya		Saṃbhogakāya		Nirmāṇakāya	
sūryadevas	contraction of the limbs and indistinct speech	*nāgas*	growth of the first teeth and distinct speech	*pracaṇḍās*	falling of the first teeth, growth of the new teeth, and the period until death

ing in his four *cakras* and sexually inciting the Buddha Kālacakra, that is, his own mind-*vajra*, with these songs:

> I am Locanā, the mother of the world, present in the *yogī*'s seminal emission. O Kālacakra, arise with the nature of my *maṇḍala* and desire me.
>
> I am Māmakī, a sister, present in the *yogīs*' spiritual maturation. O Kālacakra, arise with the nature of my *maṇḍala* and desire me.
>
> I am Pāṇḍarā, a daughter, present in any man among the *yogīs*. O Kālacakra, arise with the nature of my *maṇḍala* and desire me.
>
> I am Tāriṇī, a wife, present in the *yogīs*' purity. O Kālacakra, arise with the nature of my *maṇḍala* and desire me.
>
> Protector of the world, whose intention is the deliverance of the world, upon perceiving the empty *maṇḍala*, expand the *maṇḍalas* of the body, speech, and mind.[38]

Hearing their songs, one's own mind—the Buddha Kālacakra who is absorbed in emptiness—awakes, perceives that the entire world is like an illusion, and engages in activities for the benefit of all sentient beings.[39] This arousing of one's own awareness to engage in enlightened activities is closely related to the mutual union of the *kālacakra-maṇḍala*'s female and male deities, which are the wisdom and method aspects, or the mind and body aspects, of the Buddha. The sexual union of the male and female deities, who belong to different families, is pertinent to the Kālacakra tradition's view of the ways in which the mutual pervasion of the four bodies of the Buddha gives rise to their enlightened activities. For example, the union of the deities comprising the Sahajakāya and the body-*vajra* gives rise to Kālacakra's body, just as their phenomenal aspects give rise to the body of the fetus. Likewise, the mutual pervasion of the deities representing the Dharmakāya and the speech-*vajra* is for the sake of teaching the Dharma, just as their phenomenal aspects within the body of the individual give rise to the prattling of a child. The union of the deities symbolizing the Saṃbhogakāya and the mind-*vajra* acts for the well-being of all sentient beings. The union of the deities who comprise the Nirmāṇakāya and the gnosis-*vajra* is said to bring about the liberation of sentient beings, just as their phenomenal aspects in the body of the individual give rise to the capacity for sexual bliss at the age of sixteen.[40]

Upon generating the *kālacakra-maṇḍala* and all its deities in this way, the tantric adept performs a self-empowerment. He first purifies his bodily and mental constituents by invoking the deities that represent the *vajras* of the enlightened body, speech, and mind, and he requests the initiation from the goddess who belongs to the *maṇḍalas* of the body, speech, and mind. This imagined initiation is said to further purify the contemplative's *cakras* and facilitate the actualization of the four bodies of the Buddha. Thus, the eight *divyās* purify his eight-spoked heart-*cakra* and facilitate its transmutation into the Dharmakāya of the Buddha. The four Buddhas and their consorts, who are collectively multiplied by two due to being classified in terms of body and mind, purify the sixteen-spoked *lalāṭa* and facilitate its transmutation into the Sahajakāya. The six Bodhisattvas, their consorts, and the four *krodhas*, who become thirty-two when multiplied by two due to being classified in terms of wisdom and method, purify the thirty-two spoked throat-*cakra* and facilitate its transformation into the Saṃbhogakāya. Similarly, the sixty-four *yoginīs* purify the sixty-four spoked navel-*cakra* and facilitate its transformation into the Nirmāṇakāya. All other *cakras* in the joints of the contemplative's arms and legs, all the *nāḍīs* in the body, and the psycho-physical aggregates are purified by other deities of the *kālacakra-maṇḍala*.[41] Upon imagining himself being initiated and purified in this manner, the tantric adept identifies himself with the body, speech, mind, and gnosis of all the Buddhas in order to further diminish his grasping onto his ordinary psycho-physical aggregates.

The two aforementioned phases of the stage of generation, the *sevāṅga* and *upasādhana*, constitute the *Kālacakratantra*'s deity-*yoga* (*devatā-yoga*), which is believed to give mundane *siddhis*. Therefore, in this tantric system, a *sādhana* on the *kālacakra-maṇḍala* is referred to as "a mundane *sādhana*" (*laukika-sādhana*). In light of the fact that meditation on the *kālacakra-maṇḍala* is a conceptual meditation that involves mental visualization and imagination, the *Vimalaprabhā* speaks of the first two types of *sādhanas* of the stage of generation as the *sādhanas* in which the object of meditation lacks duration, for it is characterized by origination and cessation. The *kālacakra-maṇḍala* as the object of a *sādhana* is understood to lack duration in the sense that in the moment in which the tantric contemplative concentrates on the principal deity in the center of the *maṇḍala*, he is no longer aware of the other deities in the *maṇḍala*. Likewise, when the *yogī* concentrates on the blue face of Kālacakra, he is not cognizant of Kālacakra's red, white, and yellow faces, and so on. Since meditation on the *kālacakra-maṇḍala* is characterized by limited and momentary cognition, it is considered ineffective in directly inducing the state of nonconceptual and imperishable gnosis. From this vantage point, the *Vimalaprabhā* speaks of the *sādhanas* of the stage of generation as inferior *sādhanas*, which are designed for spiritually less mature practitioners. It comments in this regard:

> The Bhagavān, who knows reality, upon resorting to conventional truth in accordance with the power of sentient beings' inclinations, taught this truth as dependently originated gnosis—which is the domain of the dependently originated sense-faculties and is limited and capable of limited functions—to simple-minded people who are lacking in courage, who do not seek ultimate reality, whose minds are intimidated by deep and profound gnosis, who are satisfied with *sādhanas* for pacification and other such acts, who are attached to the pleasures of sense-objects and delight in the *sādhanas* for mundane *siddhis*, alchemy, eye-ointment, pills, and the magic daggers.[42]

On the one hand, the *Vimalaprabhā* acknowledges that there are inconceivable powers in this limited, conceptual meditation, along with the *mantras*, gems, pills, magical daggers, alchemical substances, and similar objects that are of limited functions. On the other hand, it affirms that the mundane knowledge and mundane *siddhis* that one acquires through the practice of conceptual meditation cannot perform the limitless functions of supramundane omniscience and the supramundane *siddhi*.[43] The limited knowledge and mundane *siddhis* do not bring about the omniscient language or supernatural powers (*ṛddhi*), because they are not free of mental obscurations. Therefore, the *yogī* who practices conceptual meditation is thought to be unable to bring about the well-being of all limitless sentient beings in the way that the

Jñānakāya, which is free of coneptualizations, is able to do. Since the imagined *kālacakra-maṇḍala* is a reflection of the contemplative's own mind, which is shrouded with obscurations, then the *kālacakra-maṇḍala* is also a manifestation of the contemplative's mental obscurations. The *Vimalaprabhā* explains this in the following manner:

> When a phenomenon (*dharma*) that is with obscurations is made manifest, the *yogī* does not become omniscient; when a phenomenon that is free of obscurations becomes manifest, the *yogī* becomes omniscient. The omniscient one has the divine eye and ear, knowledge of others' minds, recollection of former lives, omnipresent, supernatural powers, the destruction of defilements (*āsrava*), ten powers, twelve *bhūmis*, and the like. He who meditates on the *maṇḍala-cakra*, on the other hand, does not become Vajrasattva who has ten powers, but destroying his path to omniscience and being overcome by false self-grasping, he thinks: "I am Vajrasattva who has ten powers."[44]

This assertion not only reveals the *Vimalaprabhā*'s view of the stage of generation practice as inferior to that of the stage of completion, but it also suggests that the stage of generation can be detrimental to the realization of the ultimate goal of *Kālacakratantra* practice. Further analysis of the text indicates that this is the Kālacakra tradition's reaction to some people's belief that due to the power of the *sādhana* using the *maṇḍala*, the contemplative's psycho-physical aggregates will actually become transformed into the aspects of the *maṇḍala* and will thereby directly cause Buddhahood. Therefore, the *Vimalaprabhā* also asserts that the contemplative cannot become a Buddha by the power of the generation stage practice alone and without the accumulation of merit and knowledge, just as a pauper who is devoid of merit cannot become a king by merely imagining that he is the king.[45] Although it denies the efficacy of the *sādhana* on the *kālacakra-maṇḍala* for eliminating all of one's mental obscurations, it never denies that it has certain purificatory powers, if practiced with the understanding that the imagined deities are not ultimate truth and that one's own impure body is not manifestly the pure body of the deity.

The deity-*yoga* of the stage of generation is followed by two yogic practices: the *yoga* of drops (*bindu-yoga*) and the subtle *yoga* (*sūkṣma-yoga*). The *yoga* of drops and the subtle *yoga* are designed to facilitate the purification of the four drops by inducing an experience of the four types of bliss. The *yoga* of drops directly induces the emergence of the drops of semen, and the subtle *yoga* induces the attainment of bliss caused by the flow of semen. The *Ādibuddhatantra* defines these two types of *yogas* in this manner:

> That which makes the ambrosia that is of the nature of semen flow in the form of a drop and that holds the four drops is called the "*yoga* of drops."
>
> That which, transcending any partition, is partless and holds the highest point of the four *dhyānas* is called the "subtle *yoga*," because it transcends [seminal] emission.[46]

The practice of the two *yogas* involves a *sādhana* on sexual bliss with a consort who in this stage of practice is commonly an imagined consort, also called a "gnosis-consort" (*jñāna-mudrā*). According to the *Vimalaprabhā*, an actual consort is prescribed for simple-minded practitioners, an imagined consort for medially mature *yogīs*, and the *mahāmudrā* consort, who is implemented in the stage of completion, is prescribed for superior *yogīs*.[47]

3. In the *yoga* of drops, during union with a consort, the contemplative visualizes himself as Vajradhara and meditates on the three worlds as being a reflection of the Buddha. Not emitting semen, he generates heat, called "*caṇḍālī*," in his navel-*cakra*. Upon generating *caṇḍālī*, the contemplative imagines that in the left *nāḍī* of his navel-*cakra*, it incinerates the five *maṇḍalas* of the *prāṇas*, which are the phenomenal aspects of the five Tathāgatas, and that in the right *nāḍī* of the same *cakra*, it incinerates the *prāṇas* of the sense-faculties and their objects, which are the phenomenal aspects of the consorts of the five Tathāgatas. The incineration of the consorts of the five Tathāgatas implies here the cessation of activity of the sense-faculties, because the mind apprehends the *dharma-dhātu*. When *caṇḍālī* incinerates the consorts of the five Tathāgatas, semen begins to flow in the form of a drop. The drop of semen (*bodhicitta*) flows to the top of the head, and from there it sequentially flows into the throat, heart, navel, and secret *cakras*, bringing forth the experience of the four types of bliss: bliss (*ānanda*), supreme bliss (*paramānanda*), extraordinary bliss (*viramānanda*), and innate bliss (*sahajānanda*), respectively. When a drop of *bodhicitta* descends into the throat and melts there, it becomes the purified drop of speech (*vāg-bindu*); when it melts in the heart, it becomes the purified drop of the mind (*citta-bindu*); when it melts in the navel, it becomes the purified drop of gnosis (*jñāna-bindu*); and when it melts in the secret-*cakra*, it becomes the purified drop of the body (*kāya-bindu*).

4. In the practice of subtle *yoga*, the drop of purified *bodhicitta* that descends into the secret *cakra* during the practice of the *yoga* of drops, now sequentially ascends into the navel, heart, throat, and *uṣṇīṣa*, bringing forth the experience of the aforementioned four types of bliss, which melt the atomic nature of the four drops and facilitate their transformation into the four bodies of the Buddha.[48] Thus, in the practice of these last two *yogas*, the path of the sublimation of the four drops is the path of the generation of sexual bliss, and the agent of sublimation is that very bliss. It is said that as the tantric adept purifies the drops of the body, speech, and mind in this manner, he also purifies the desire, form, and formless realms, which he previously imagined as the reflection of the Buddha. Mentally retracting the purified three realms with the light rays of his gnosis, or sexual bliss characterized by seminal non-emission, the tantric contemplative brings forth the gnosis of the three times (*trikālya-jñāna*).[49]

The Transformative Body of the Path of the Stage of Completion

The deity-*sādhana* of the stage of generation is viewed in this tantric system as characterized by ideation or imagination (*kalpanā*). As such, it is considered to induce directly the attainment of mundane *siddhis* and only indirectly to induce the attainment of spiritual awakening as the supramundane *siddhi* (*lokottara-siddhi*) or the *mahāmudrā-siddhi*. The preceding practices of the *yoga* of drops and the subtle *yoga* mark a transitional process from the stage of generation and its conceptualized *sādhana* to the stage of completion and its nonconceptualized *sādhanas*. The practice of the stage of completion is seen as the most pertinent to the attainment of spiritual awakening, for it is free of ideation and is uncontrived. It is free of ideation because it entails meditation on the form of emptiness (*śūnyatā-bimba*), or empty form, in which one does not imagine the deity's bodily form. Thus, due to the absence of the *yogī*'s imagination of the bodily form, there is no appearance of empty form; and since the tantric *yogī* meditates on the empty form, it cannot be said that there is an absence of appearance of empty form. In this regard, the meditation on empty form is meditation on the nonduality of existence and nonexistence and on cyclic existence as devoid of inherent existence. In light of this, the *Vimalaprabhā* characterizes meditation on empty form as a nonlocal, or nonlimited (*apradeśika*), meditation since it is devoid of all mundane conventions. It also interprets this form of meditation as a tantric implementation of the Mādhyamika doctrine.[50] Therefore, it is considered here inappropriate for one who wishes to attain the supramundane *siddhi* to imagine the empty form—which is the universal form that has all aspects and holds all illusions—in terms of limited shapes, colors, symbols, and the like. In contrast to the *sādhana* on the *kālacakra-maṇḍala*, due to the absence of all conceptualizations, meditation on empty form is not characterized by the origination or cessation but by the absence of everything. Just as it excludes the visualization of Kālacakra and other deities, so does it exclude one's self-identification with Kālacakra.[51] Due to these characteristics, meditation on empty form is called the "*sādhana* of supramundane reality" (*lokottara-tattva-sādhana*), the "gnosis-*sādhana*," or the "*sādhana* on the form of emptiness" (*śūnyatā-bimba-sādhana*).[52]

Contrary to the *sādhana* on the *kālacakra-maṇḍala*, the gnosis-*sādhana* of the stage of completion is believed to lead to achieving the *mahāmudrā-siddhi*. The *mahāmudrā* is understood here as the perfection of wisdom, characterized by the absence of inherent existence of all phenomena, the source of all phenomena (*dharmodaya*), which is the Buddha-field, the place of joy (*rati-sthāna*), and the place of birth (*janma-sthāna*). It is not a field of the transmigratory beings' attachment and aversion, nor is it an outlet of the ordinary bodily constituents, because it is the mind of imperishable time (*akṣara-kāla*), free of origination and cessation, embraced by the body that is free of obscurations as its wheel (*cakra*). It is said that whoever frequently and steadily meditates on this sublime emptiness, "the mother of innate bliss, who is a measure of the manifestation of one's own mind and is devoid of ideation with regard to all phenomena, and whoever embraces her, is called the omniscient Bhagavān who has attained the *mahāmudrā-siddhi*."[53] Thus, by practicing a *sādhana* on the *mahāmudrā*, one practices a *sādhana* on the ultimate nature of one's own mind; whereas by practicing the *sādhana* on the *kālacakra-maṇḍala*, one meditates on the conventional nature of one's own mind. These defining characteristics of conceptual and nonconceptual types of meditative practices are the most crucial factor in determining their soteriological efficacy with regard to their ability to provide one with the adequate accumulations of merit and knowledge. The Kālacakra tradition strongly affirms that just as the accumulation of merit does not take place without service to sentient beings, so the accumulation of knowledge does not take place without meditation on supreme, imperishable gnosis.

The practice of the stage of completion entails abandoning conceptual meditation, as well as sexual practices with the actual and imagined consorts. The union with either one of these two consorts is believed to induce perishable bliss only, the bliss characterized by pulsation (*spanda*). In contrast, union with the *mahāmudrā* consort, or the "empty form-consort, who is of the nature of a prognostic mirror and is not imagined,"[54] is believed to induce supreme, imperishable bliss that is devoid of puslation (*niḥspanda*).[55]

The gnosis-*sādhana* is divided into four main phases: worship (*sevā*), the auxiliary *sādhana* (*upasādhana*), the *sādhana*, and the supreme *sādhana* (*mahā-sādhana*). This four-phased *sādhana* describes the six-phased *yoga* (*ṣaḍ-aṅga-yoga*) of the *Kālacakratantra*, which consists of the following six phases: retraction (*pratyāhāra*), meditative stabilization (*dhyāna*), *prāṇāyāma*, retention (*dhāraṇā*), recollection (*anusmṛti*), and concentration (*samādhi*).

The first two phases of the six-phased *yoga*, retraction and meditative stabilization, constitute the worship phase of the gnosis-*sādhana*. They are also called the "tenfold *yoga*," since by means of these two phases, the contemplative mentally apprehends the ten signs, including smoke, and so on. The subsequent phases of *prāṇāyāma* and retention constitute the *upasādhana*, which is characterized by perception of the subtle prāṇic body. The recollection phase constitutes the *sādhana* stage and is characterized by the experience of the three imperishable moments of bliss within the secret, navel, and heart *cakras*. Finally, the concentration phase of the six-phased *yoga* constitutes the *mahā-sādhana*, which is characterized by the unity of gnosis and its object and is accompanied by imperishable mental bliss.[56] These four categories of the six-phased *yoga* are said to correspond to the body, speech, mind, and gnosis *vajras* of the Buddha, or to his four faces in the *kālacakra-maṇḍala*, for they bring forth the manifestation of the four bodies of the Buddha.

On the stage of completion, the path of the purification of the four drops is characterized by meditation on the four drops. The final purification of the four drops takes place in the final phase of the six-phased *yoga*. Since the practice of the six *yogas* is believed to bring about the purification of the six aggregates—the aggregates of gnosis, consciousness, feeling, mental formations, discernment, and the body—it is interpreted in this tantric tradition as the way of actualizing the six Tathāgatas: namely, Vajrasattva, Akṣobhya, Amoghasiddhi, Ratnasaṃbhava, Amitābha, and Vairocana.

The Six-Phased Yoga

The *Kālacakratantra*'s *ṣaḍ-aṅga-yoga* begins with the manifestation of the mentally nonconstructed appearances of one's own mind, that is to say, the nighttime and daytime signs, and ends with the manifestation of one's universal form (*viśva-bimba*). In this way, the whole process of the *ṣaḍ-aṅga-yoga* is a meditative process of bringing into manifestation the successively more subtle and more encompassing aspects of one's own mind.

1. The *yoga* of retraction (*pratyāhāra*) involves the meditative practice of retracting the *prāṇas* from the right and left *nāḍīs* and bringing them into the central *nāḍī*. In this phase of practice, the contemplative stabilizes his mind by concentrating on the aperture of the central *nāḍī* in the *lalāṭa*, having the eyes opened with an upward gaze called the gaze of the ferocious deity, Uṣṇīṣacakrī. As a result of that,

the *prāṇas* cease to flow in the left and right *nāḍīs* and begin to flow in the central *nāḍī*. The cessation of the *prāṇa*'s flow within the left and right *nāḍīs* severs the connections between the five sense-faculties and their objects. Consequently, the five sense-faculties and their objects become inactive, meaning, the six types of consciousness cease to engage with their corresponding objects, and bodily craving for material things diminishes. This disregard for the pleasures of the body, speech, mind, and sexual bliss is what is meant here by worship. As the ordinary sense-faculties disengage, the extraordinary sense-faculties arise. Due to that, the ten sequential signs—the signs of smoke, a mirage, fire-flies, a lamp, a flame, the moon, the sun, the supreme form, and a drop—spontaneously appear; but these images are none other than appearances of one's own mind. As the contemplative's mind becomes more stabilized, the ten signs appear more vividly, and the contemplative's perception of external appearances diminishes. Wisdom and gnosis become the apprehending mind, and the ten signs, which are like an image in a prognostic mirror, become the apprehended objects. Thus, gnosis apprehends itself in the same way that the eye sees its own reflection in a mirror. This entering of the apprehending mind (*grāhaka-citta*) into the apprehended mind (*grāhya-citta*) constitutes its nonengagement with external objects.

The first four signs appear during the practice of retraction at nighttime or in a dark and closed space. Their appearance indicates that the *prāṇas* within the *nāḍīs* in the intermediate directions of the heart-*cakra* have entered the *madhyamā*. The other six signs appear during the practice of retraction-*yoga* during the daytime and in open space.[57] A drop appears as the tenth sign with the form of the Buddha in its center. This Buddha is the Nirmāṇakāya, which is devoid of sense-objects due to its freedom from matter and ideation (*kalpanā*). Afterward, the *yogī* hears a sound that is not produced by any impact (*anāhata-dhvani*), which is the Saṃbhogakāya. The appearance of the first four of the six daytime signs indicates that the *prāṇas* within the *nāḍīs* in the cardinal directions of the heart-*cakra* have entered the central *nāḍī*; and the appearance of the last two signs indicates that the winds of *prāṇa* and *apāna* have been dissolved. Due to the spontaneity of this arising of the ten signs, the purified aggregate of gnosis (*jñāna-skandha*) is considered to be uncontrived or nonconceptualized (*avikalpita*).[58]

The *yoga* of retraction is said to induce the state of Kālacakra and lead to the attainment of the body of Kālacakra by purifying the aggregate of gnosis (*jñāna-skandha*). In terms of mundane results, such a *yoga* can accomplish a *siddhi* by which all one's words come true. This occurs due to the inactivity of the ordinary sense-faculties, which empowers the contemplative's speech with *mantras*.

2. The *yoga* of meditative stabilization (*dhyāna*) refers here to a meditative absorption on the all-pervading form (*viśva-bimba*), which is also practiced with the gaze of Uṣṇīṣacakrī. It is designed to unify the five sense-faculties and their objects. Due to the tenfold classification of the sense-faculties and their objects as the apprehending subjects and the apprehended objects, meditative stabilization is considered here to be of ten kinds. It is also interpreted as a mind that has become unified with empty form as its meditative object and is characterized by the five factors of wisdom (*prajñā*), investigation (*tarka*), analysis (*vicāra*), joy (*rati*), and immutable

bliss (*acala-sukha*). According to the *Vimalaprabhā*, wisdom here means observing the empty form; investigation means apprehending its existence; analysis implies ascertainment of that empty form; joy means absorption into the empty form; and immutable bliss is the factor that unifies the mind with empty form.[59] During the initial practice of the *yoga* of meditative stabilization, the ten signs, which appeared earlier during the retraction phase, spontaneously reappear. During the daytime *yoga*, the tantric *yogī* gazes at the cloudless sky either during the morning or afternoon, with his back turned to the sun, until a shining, black line appears in the center of the drop. Within the central *nāḍī*, the body of the Buddha, which is the entire three worlds, appears. It looks clear like the sun in water, and it has all aspects and colors. It is identified as one's own mind that is free of the sense-objects and not as someone else's mind, because it lacks knowledge of other beings' minds. Thus, in the six-phased *yoga*, one first perceives the appearance of one's own mind with the physical eye (*māṃsa-cakṣu*) of the Buddha, and at the culmination of the *yoga*, one perceives the minds of others with the divine eye of the Buddha.

The *yoga* of meditative stabilization is said to induce the state of Akṣobhya, for it purifies the aggregate of consciousness (*vijñāna-skandha*), and to induce the actualization of the five kinds of extrasensory perception (*abhijñā*). In terms of mundane results, it is believed to induce the experience of mental and physical well-being.

3. The *yoga* of *prāṇāyāma* is thought to be effective in unifying the ten right and left *maṇḍalas* by bringing the *prāṇas* into the central *nāḍī*. For this reason, it is said to be of ten kinds. In the practice of this *yoga*, the contemplative stabilizes the *prāṇas* within his navel-*cakra* by concentrating on the center of that *cakra*, which is regarded as the seat of the drop associated with the fourth state of the mind (*turīya*). In this phase of the *yoga*, the tantric adept practices the gaze of the ferocious being Vighnāntaka, directing his gaze toward the *lalāṭa*. During inhalation, the contemplative apprehends the arisen form of the Kālacakra's Saṃbhogakāya and brings it from his nostril into the navel, where Kālacakra and his consort merge with the drop. As the Saṃbhogakāya descends into the navel and merges into the drop there, the drop disappears, but Kālacakra and his consort remain in the navel-*cakra*. During exhalation, Kālacakra and Viśvamātā rise above the level of the drop that has reappeared and ascend along the central *nāḍī*. When they ascend during *pūraka*,[60] the tantric adept concentrates first on the lower aperture of the *madhyamā*, wherefrom Kālacakra is brought into the navel; during *recaka*,[61] he brings it down into the lower *cakra*. Practicing in this way, the tantric contemplative brings the *prāṇas* into the navel-*cakra* and stabilizes them there. As a result of this, the external breath ceases, and the contemplative engages in the practice of *kumbhaka*.[62] After perceiving the Saṃbhogakāya, by means of *kumbhaka*, in the drop of the navel-*cakra*, he unifies the wind of the *prāṇa* that flows above the navel with the wind of the *apāna* that flows below the navel until a circle of the rays of light appears surrounded by his own body. After the contemplative stabilizes his mind on that drop in the navel-*cakra*, the abdominal heat (*caṇḍālī*) arises, melts the drop at the top of the *uṣṇīṣa*, and induces the experience of the previously mentioned four types of bliss. When the drop reaches the throat-*cakra*, the tantric adept experiences bliss (*ānanda*); when it reaches the heart-*cakra*, he experiences the sublime bliss (*mahānanda*); when it reaches the

navel-*cakra*, he experiences the extraordinary bliss (*viramānanda*); and when it reaches the secret-*cakra*, he experiences the innate bliss (*sahajānanda*). By melting the four drops, the *caṇḍālī* melts the afflictive and cognitive obscurations.

The *yoga* of *prāṇāyāma* is said to induce the state of Amoghasiddhi, for it purifies the aggregate of mental formations (*saṃskāra-skandha*); and in terms of mundane benefits, it is believed to purify the right and left *nāḍīs* by conveying the *prāṇas* into the central *nāḍī*, and it makes the tantric adept worthy of being praised by Bodhisattvas.

4. The *yoga* of retention (*dhāraṇā*) is also considered to be of ten kinds due to the tenfold classification of the *prāṇa*'s leaving from and arriving to the *cakras* of the navel, heart, throat, *lalāṭa*, and *uṣṇīṣa*. The *yoga* of retention entails the unification of the winds of *prāṇa* and *apāna* in the navel-*cakra* and the practice of the gaze of Vighnāntaka. The unification of these two winds is accompanied by the manifestation of Kālacakra and his consort. In the subsequent stages of this *yoga*, the contemplative continues this practice by sequentially concentrating on the *cakras* of the heart, throat, *lalāṭa*, and *uṣṇīṣa*, which are associated with the elements of water, fire, wind, and space, respectively. As a result of this practice, the four elements sequentially dissolve into one another, and the *yogī* experiences the four types of bliss. As the contemplative's concentration gradually moves from the navel-*cakra* to the upper *cakras*, he experiences the four types of ascending bliss; and as his concentration shifts from the *uṣṇīṣa* to the lower *cakras*, he experiences the four types of descending bliss. After experiencing these types of bliss, due to the cessation of the *prāṇa*'s movements, the contemplative's mind becomes unified, and he apprehends the form of emptiness (*śūnyatā-bimba*), the spontaneously arisen appearance of Kālacakra and Viśvamātā.

The *yoga* of retention is said to induce the state of Ratnasaṃbhava, since it purifies the aggregate of feeling (*vedanā-skandha*). Due to the power of this *yoga*, it is said that the tantric adept attains the ten powers (*bala*) and is purified of Māras and mental afflictions, due to unifying his mind and destroying the flow of *prāṇa*.

5. The *yoga* of recollection (*anusmṛti*) implies here the union of the mind with empty form, the state of freedom from all conceptualizations.[63] In the *yoga* of recollection, the contemplative perceives in his navel-*cakra* the form of Kālacakra and Viśvamātā as innumerable rays of light consisting of five colors. The *yoga* of recollection is said to induce the state of Amitābha, since it purifies the aggregate of discernment (*saṃjñā-skandha*). In terms of immediate results, it is said to induce the realization of the form of gnosis (*jñāna-bimba*), or the empty form. Due to the power of that form, one is purified to the point that one appears as a stainless disc of light.

6. The *yoga* of *samādhi* is also classified into ten kinds, due to the cessation of the ten winds of *prāṇa*.[64] It is said to induce the state of Vairocana, since it purifies the aggregate of form (*rūpa-skandha*). According to the *Vimalaprabhā*, the contemplative who becomes purified by the *yoga* of *samādhi* attains the Sahajakāya within a period of three years and three fortnights.[65]

In the *samādhi* phase, the object of gnosis (*jñeya*) and gnosis (*jñāna*) itself become unified and give rise to supreme, imperishable bliss. For that reason, the *samādhi* that is practiced here is defined as "a meditative concentration on the form of gnosis (*jñāna-bimba*)."[66] It is also interpreted as the imperishable bliss that arises from the union of the apprehended object (*grāhya*) and the apprehending subject (*grāhaka*).[67] This sixth phase of *yoga* is characterized by the simultaneous stacking of red and white drops in inverted order within the individual *cakras* and by the resultant experience of the 21,600 moments of immutable bliss. In this phase of the *yoga*, the tantric adept stacks 3,600 white drops of *bodhicitta*, starting at the tip of the sexual organ and ending at the *uṣṇīṣa*; and he stacks the same number of red drops of *bodhicitta*, beginning at the *lalāṭa* and ending at the tip of the sexual organ. As the bliss courses through the six *cakras* during the 3,600 moments, it manifests two *bodhisattva-bhūmis* within each of the six *cakras*, due to the destruction of *prāṇas*. This stacking of 3,600 drops within the six *cakras* brings about the experience of 21,600 moments of immutable bliss. By the efficacy of these moments of immutable bliss, 21,600 *karmic prāṇas* cease; and consequently, 21,600 material elements of the *yogī's* body transform into a body having the aspect of emptiness (*śūnyatākāra*). Accordingly, the material aspects of the four drops also vanish, together with a cessation of the states of the mind of waking, dreaming, deep sleep, and the fourth state; for the drops are the supports of *bodhicitta*, which is this fourfold mind of transmigratory beings. Due to the melting of the material nature of the four drops, which is their obscuration (*āvaraṇa*), pure gnosis, or the self-awareness of imperishable bliss, arises, and it becomes of four kinds, corresponding to the four bodies of the Buddha. The manner in which imperishable bliss transforms the elements of the body is likened to the manner in which a stainless jewel transforms stone and other elementary substances into a gem by merely touching them, without shattering them.[68] It is said that from the moment that one's material nature becomes transformed into empty form, its earth aspect is not perceived as solid, its water aspect is not perceived as liquid, its fire aspect is not fiery, nor does its wind aspect move anywhere. Because of the absence of matter, it has an empty aspect, the aspect of space. Likewise, although endowed with colors, it is colorless, due to the absence of matter; and though endowed with all aspects, it is invisible to the foolish.[69] As one's own body transforms into empty form, one's mind pervades space and abides in the gnosis of the minds of others; the body pervades the mind, and speech pervades the body. In this way, the four mutually pervading aspects of the Buddha become actualized as the four bodies of the Buddha that dwell in all sentient beings who are born from the womb. It is said that from that point on, being compelled by supreme compassion, the Śuddhakāya of the Buddha enters the realm of *karma* (*karma-bhūmi*) for the sake of liberating sentient beings, is conceived in the womb, teaches Dharma, and creates the limitless illusions of his Nirmāṇakāya.[70]

One may conclude here that within the methodological framework of the Kālacakra system, meditative concentration (*samādhi*) is given special attention in every stage of practice. It is in meditative concentration that the tantric adept finally attains the supramundane psycho-physical aggregates and supreme, imperishable bliss. As in the stage of generation, so too in the stage of completion, meditative concentration is characterized by the union of quiescence (*śamatha*), or bliss, and insight (*vipaśyanā*), or gnosis of that bliss.

The path of actualizing the four bodies of the Buddha in all stages of *Kālacakratantra* practice—initiation, generation, and completion—is the path of utilizing one's own bliss and gnosis in order to completely and permanently manifest these two aspects of one's own mind. Thus, in this tantric tradition, the innate purity and blissfulness of one's own mind is the transformative agent, the transformative means as the body of the path, and the transformed body of Buddhahood. That is to say, the empty and blissful gnosis is both the *agent* that actualizes gnosis and the *object*, the actualized gnosis itself. This perspective on the gnosis of imperishable bliss as the cause and result of Buddhahood is based on the previously discussed view of the *Kālacakratantra* on gnosis as the essential nature (*tattva*) and the support (*ādhāra*) of all phenomena. For as soon as gnosis is asserted to be the ground of reality, it inevitably plays a central role in the soteriology of the *Kālacakratantra*.

The role of gnosis in the *Kālacakratantra*'s soteriology parallels the salvific role of the *tathāgata-garbha* in the *tathāgata-garbha* tradition. For example, one reads in the *Śrīmālāsūtra* that the *tathāgata-garbha* is the support (*ādhāra*) of all conditioned (*saṃskṛta*) and unconditioned (*asaṃskṛta*) phenomena; and "if the *tathāgata-garbha* would not exist, there would be neither aversion to suffering nor longing, earnestness, and aspiration for *nirvāṇa*."[71] This and other previously discussed parallels between the *tathāgata-garbha* tradition and the *Kālacakratantra* tradition point to the influences of the earlier Mahāyāna interpretations of the inherent purity of the mind and its role in the path of the individual's spiritual awakening on the formulations of gnosis in the Kālacakra tradition and other tantric systems of the *anuttara-yoga* class.

As demonstrated earlier, in *Kālacakratantra* practice, the process of bringing forth the pure and blissful nature of gnosis starts with inducing many moments of immutable bliss, or the bliss of seminal nonemission, and ends with the actualization of a single moment of supreme, immutable bliss. Thus, the mind of bliss that is characterized by nonemission purifies itself from its adventitious defilements by means of its own bliss; and due to the absence of defilements, it cognizes itself as such. It is in light of this view of the nonduality of gnosis and bliss, of the cause and effect of spiritual awakening, that the Kālacakra system identifies supreme, imperishable bliss as the gnostic *yoga* (*jñāna-yoga*), a unique peace.[72] Therefore, in the context of the *Kālacakratantra*, the multifaceted process of actualizing the gnosis of imperishable bliss, or Kālacakra, is seen as the nondual transformative body of the path of gnosis. This transformative body, which is characterized by the nonduality of the basis, agent, means, and result of transformation is Kālacakra, the nondual *tantra* of the wheel of time.

Appendix

Table B.1 illustrates the *Kālacakratantra*'s fourfold classification of the deities of the *kālacakra-maṇḍala.*

TABLE B.1 Deities of the Kālacakra-maṇḍala as the Four Bodies of the Buddha

Gnosis-maṇḍala	Mind-maṇḍala	Speech-maṇḍala	Body-maṇḍala
Sahajakāya	Dharmakāya	Saṃbhogakāya	Nirmāṇakāya
Kālacakra &	*Buddhas*:	*Devīs*:	*Nairtyas*:
Viśvamātā	Amoghasiddhi	Carcikā	Danuka, or Nairtya
	Ratnasaṃbhava	Khagapatigamanā,	Cala, or Vāyu
	Amitābha	or Vaiṣṇavī	Yama
	Vairocana	Śūkarī, or Vārāhī	Pāvaka
		Ṣaṇmukhī, or	Ṣaṇmukha
		Kaumārī	Yakṣa
		Vajrahastā, or	Śakra
		Aindrī	Brahmā
		Abdhivaktrā, or	Rudra
		Brahmāṇī	Samudra
		Raudrī	Gaṇapati
		Mahālakṣmī	Viṣṇu
Divyās:	*Vidyās*:	*Sixty-four Yoginīs*:	*Sūryadevās*:
Dhūmā	Tārā	Bhīmā	Mārīci
Mārīci	Pāṇḍarā	Ugrā	Bhṛkuṭī
Khadyotā	Māmakī	Kāladaṃṣṭrā	Śṛṅkhalā
Pradīpā	Locanā	Jvaladanalamukhā	Cundā
Pītadīptā		Vāyuvegā	Raudrekṣaṇā
Śvetadīptā		Pracaṇḍā	Atinilā
Kṛṣṇadīptā		Raudrākṣī	
Śaśikalā		Sthūlanāsā	Nīladaṇḍa
			Acala
			Anantavīrya
			Takkirāja
			Sumbha
			Uṣṇīṣa
	Satarusakalaśās:	Śrī	*Nāgas*:
	goddesses with	Māyā	Padma
	wish-fulfilling trees	Kīrti	Karkoṭaka
	and pitchers filled	Lakṣmī	Vāsuki
	with feces, urine,	Suparamavijayā	Śaṅkhapāla
	blood, and marrow	Śrījayā	Kulika
		Śrījayantī	Ananta
		Śrīcakrī	Takṣaka
		Kaṅkālī	Mahābja
		Kālamatrī	Jaya
		Prakupitavadanā	Vijaya
		Kālajihvā	
		Karālī	

(continued)

TABLE B.1 (continued)

Gnosis-maṇḍala	Mind-maṇḍala	Speech-maṇḍala	Body-maṇḍala
	Krodhendras:	Kālī	*Pracaṇḍās*:
	Atibala	Ghorā	Śvānavakatrā
	Jambhaka	Virūpā	Śūkarāsyā
	Stambhaka	Padmā	Vyāghravaktrā
	Māṇaka	Anaṅgā	Jambhukāsyā
	Uṣṇīṣa	Kumārī	Kākavaktrā
		Mṛgapatigamanā	Gṛdhravaktrā
	Krodhinīs:	Ratnamālā	Khagapativadanā
	Stambhakī	Sunetrā	Ulūkavaktrā
	Mānī	Klīnā	Vajrākṣī
	Jambhakī	Bhadrā	Atinīlā
	Anantavīryā	Vajrābhā	
		Vajragātrā	
		Kanakavatī	
		Urvaśī	
		Citralekhā	
		Rambhā	
		Ahalyā	
		Sutārā	
		Savitrī	
		Padmanetrā	
		Jalajavatī	
		Buddhi	
		Vāgīśvarī	
		Gāyatrī	
		Vidyut	
		Smṛti	
		Gaurī	
		Gaṅgā	
		Nityā	
		Turitā	
		Totalā	
		Lakṣmaṇā	
		Piṅgalā	
		Kṛṣṇā	
		Śvetā	
		Candralekhā	
		Śaśadharadhavanā	
		Haṃsavarṇā	
		Dhṛti	
		Padmeśā	
		Tāranetrā	
		Vimalaśaśadharā	

TABLE B.1 (continued)

Gnosis-maṇḍala	Mind-maṇḍala	Speech-maṇḍala	Body-maṇḍala
	Bodhisattvas:	*Icchās*:	*Pratīcchās*
	Vajrapāṇi	Vidveṣecchā	
	Khagarbha	Stobhanecchā	
	Kṣitigarbha	Pauṣṭikecchā	
	Lokeśvara	Stambhanecchā	
	Viṣkambhī	Māraṇecchā	
	Samantabhadra	Utpādanecchā	
		Vādyecchā	
	Vajrās:	Bhūṣaṇecchā	
	Śabdavajrā	Bhojanecchā	
	Sparśavajrā	Gandhecchā	
	Rūpavajrā	Aṅśukecchā	
	Rasavajrā	Maithunecchā	
	Gandhavajrā	Kaṇḍūyanecchā	
	Dharmadhātuvajrā	Vadanagataka-photsarjanecchā	
	Pūjadevīs:	Malecchā	
	Gandhā	Nṛtyecchā	
	Mālā	Āsanecchā	
	Dhūpā	Plāvanecchā	
	Dīpā	Majjanecchā	
	Lāsyā	Saṃtāpecchā	
	Hāsyā	Bandhanecchā	
	Vādyā	Mṛduvacanecchā	
	Nṛtyā	Śoṣanecchā	
	Gītā	Uccātanecchā	
	Kāmā	Sparṣecchā	
	Naivedyā	Ākṛṣṭecchā	
	Amṛtaphalā	Bandhecchā	
		Sarvāṅgakṣodha-necchā	
		Mūtraviṭsrāva-necchā	
		Vañcanecchā	
		Bahukalahecchā	
		Ucchiṣṭabhakt-ecchā	
		Saṃgrāmecchā	
		Ahibandhecchā	
		Dārakākrośa-necchā	

Table B.2 demonstrates the manner in which the Kālacakra tradition identifies the thirty-seven *yoginīs* of the *kālacakra-maṇḍala* as the sublimated aspects of the bodily constituents.

TABLE B.2 Yoginīs of the Kālacakra-maṇḍala and the Bodily Constituents

Vidyās	**Bodily constituents**
Locanā	the left and right sides of the back, and
Pāṇḍarā	
Māmakī	the female and male sexual organs
Tārā	
Viśvamātā	the spine (*kula-pīṭha*)
Vajrās	
Śabdavajrā	the joints of the right upper arm and
Sparśavajrā	the right hip,
Rūpavajrā	the six sense-bases (*āyatana*) of men
Gandhavajrā	the joints of the left upper arm and the
Rasavajrā	left hip,
Dharmadhātuvajrā	the six sense-bases (*āyatana*) of women
Devīs	
Carcikā	the joints of the right lower arm and
Vaiṣṇavī	the right knee,
Māheśvarī	the eight *samāna*-winds of men
Mahālakṣmī	
Brahmāṇī	the joints of the left lower arm and the
Aindrī	left knee,
Vārāhī	the eight *samāna*-winds of women
Kaumārī	
Sūryadevās and ***Krodhinīs***	
Atinīlā	the joints of the right hand and the
Atibalā	right foot,
Vajraśṛṅkhalā	the men's base of the tongue, the two
Mānī	hands and feet, the right and left
Cundā	*nāḍīs* of the anus, and the *nāḍīs*
	of urine and feces
Stambhī	
Marīcī	the joints of the left hand and the left
Jambhī	foot,
Bhṛkuṭī	the women's base of the tongue, the
Raudrākṣī	two hands and feet, the right and left
	the *nāḍīs* of the anus, and the *nāḍīs*
	of urine and feces
Pracaṇḍās	
Śvānāsyā	the nails of the right and left fingers,
Kākāsyā	the eight bodily apertures
Vyāghrāsyā	
Ulūkāsyā	
Jambukāsyā	
Garuḍāsyā	
Śūkarāsyā	
Gṛdhrāsyā	

Tables B.3 illustrates the Kālacakra tradition's identification of the aforementioned thirty-seven *yoginīs* with the thirty-seven factors of spiritual awakening *(bodhipākṣika-dharma)*. On this tantric path of sublimation, the bodily constituents that are represented by the following thirty-seven *yoginīs* become transformed into the thirty-seven factors of spiritual awakening. Thus, once the purification takes place, these bodily constituents are said to bear the characteristics of the Dharmakāya.[1]

TABLE B.3 Yoginīs of the Kālacakra-maṇḍala and the Factors of Enlightenment

Yoginis	Factors
Vidyās	**The four applications of mindfulness** (*smṛtyupaspthāna*)
Locanā	the mindfulness of body (*kāyānusmṛtyupasthāna*)
Pāṇḍarā	the mindfulness of feeling (*vedanānusmṛtyupasthāna*)
Māmakī	the mindfulness of the mind (*cittānusmṛtyupasthāna*)
Tārā	the mindfulness of *dharmas* (*dharmānusmṛtyupasthāna*)
Viśvamātā and Vajrās	**The seven limbs of enlightenment** (*saṃbodhyaṅga*)
Viśvamātā, 'or Rūpavajrā	equanimity (*upekṣāsaṃbodhyaṅga*)
Śabdavajrā	mindfulness (*smṛtisaṃbodhyaṅga*)
Sparśavajrā	the investigation of Dharma (*dharmapravicayasaṃbodhyaṅga*)
Rūpavajrā	enthusiasm (*vīryasaṃbodhyaṅga*)
Gandhavajrā	love (*prītisaṃbodhyaṅga*)
Rasavajrā	repose (*praśrabdhisaṁbodhyaṅga*)
Dharmadhātuvajrā	meditative concentration (*samādhisaṃbodhyaṅga*)
Devīs	**The four abandonments** (*prahāṇa*)
Carcikā	the abandonment of nonarisen nonvirtues (*anutpannānāṃ pāpānāṃ prahāṇa*)
Vaiṣṇavī	the abandonment of arisen nonvirtues (*utpannānāṃ pāpānāṃ prahāṇa*)
Maheśvarī	a generation of virtues as the abandonment of nonarisen nonvirtues (*kuśalotpādana*)
Mahālakṣmī	a transformation into Buddhahood as the abandonment of arisen nonvirtues (*buddhatvaparināmanā*)
Devīs	**The four bases of extraordinary powers** (*ṛddhipāda*)
Brahmāṇī	the basis of the extraordinary power of aspiration (*chandharddhipāda*)
Aindrī	the basis of the extraordinary power of enthusiasm (*vīryarddhipāda*)
Vārāhī	the basis of the extraordinary power of the mind (*cittarddhipāda*)
Kaumārī	the basis of the extraordinary power of analysis (*mimāṃsarddhipāda*)

(continued)

TABLE B.3 (continued)

Yoginis	Factors
Sūryadevās* and *Krodhinīs	**The five powers**
Atinīlā	the power of faith (*śraddhābala*)
Atibalā	the power of enthusiasm (*vīryabala*)
Vajraśṛṅkhalā	the power of mindfulness (*smṛtibala*)
Mānī	the power of meditative concentration (*samādhibala*)
Cundā	the power of wisdom (*prajñābala*)
Sūryadvās* and *Krodhinīs	**The five faculties** (*indriya*)
Stambhī	the faculty of faith (*śraddhendriya*)
Marīcī	the faculty of enthusiasm (*vīryendriya*)
Jambhī	the faculty of mindfulness (*smṛtīndriya*)
Bhṛkuṭī	the faculty of meditative concentration (*samādhīndriya*)
Raudrākṣī	the faculty of wisdom (*prajñendriya*)
Pracaṇḍās	**The eightfold noble path** (*aṣtāryāṅga-mārga*)
Śvānāsyā	the right view (*samyagdṛṣṭi*)
Kākāsyā	the right thought (*samyaksaṃkalpa*)
Vyāghrāsyā	the right speech (*samyagvāc*)
Ulūkāsyā	the right action (*samyakkarmānta*)
Jambukāsyā	the right livelihood (*samyagājīva*)
Garuḍāsyā	the right effort (*samyagvyāma*)
Śūkarāsyā	the right concentration (*samyaksamādhi*)

Table B.4 illustrates the manner in which the Kālacakra tradition identifies the universe with the fetus. This form of identification is characteristic of the stage of the generation practice, in which one visualizes the origination of the universe as the mother's body.

TABLE B.4 The Universe and the Fetus

The universe	The fetus
the wind-*maṇḍala*	the *lalāṭa*
the fire-*maṇḍala*	the throat-*cakra*
the water-*maṇḍala*	the heart-*cakra*
the earth-*maṇḍala*	the navel-*cakra*
Mt. Meru	from the navel-*cakra* to the secret *cakra*
sun, moon, and Rāhu	the *nāḍīs* carrying feces, urine, and semen

Conclusion

We have seen that the *Kālacakratantra* incorporates several literary genres, for its various parts display the distinctive features of tantric yogic, gnostic, prophetic, and medical literature. Its inclusion of different genres can be seen as yet another expression of a Buddhist tantric interpretation of a *tantra* as an expansion.

As a prophetic literary work, the *Kālacakratantra* shows features that are characteristic of prophetic literature in general. As we have seen in chapter 6 on the "Social Body," the *Kālacakratantra*'s eschatological prophecies serve as a political justification for tantric practices that defy the prescribed norms of social conduct. Their function also lies in supporting and legitimizing the power of a future universal monarch (*cakravartin*). The *Kālacakratantra*'s prophecies are concerned with both religious and sociopolitical legitimations. Since their audience consists not only of monastic and lay Buddhist communities but also of all other religious and political communities existing in India at that time, their religious and political functions are not entirely separated.

Like other Buddhist tantric and gnostic literary works, the *Kālacakratantra* engages in the reformulation of some common Indian Buddhist tenets. However, its reformulation cannot be accused of having no boundaries. In fact, one can clearly see that in all of the *anuttara-yoga-tantras* there is some consensus with regard to the boundaries of tantric reformulation. For example, in all such *tantras*, the radical break with the conventional rules of monastic celibacy, which is expressed in tantric hermeneutics and in tantric yogic practices, is seen as ascetic for as long as one's engagement in sexual tantric practices complies with the given guidelines for practice.

The reformulation of common Mahāyāna Buddhist tenets in the *Kālacakratantra* is based on exegesis. Accordingly, exegetical issues form the basis for the *Kālacakratantra*'s refutation of certain Mahāyāna interpretations of Buddhist teachings. Like gnostic and tantric texts of other religious traditions, the *Kālacakratantra* resorts to historical realism, pointing to the proximity of the earliest holders and practitioners of this tantric tradition to Buddha Śākyamuni as evidence of the validity of its reformulation of the conventional interpretations of Buddha's teachings. We have also seen that the *Kālacakratantra*'s reformulation that undermines conventional readings threatened to reshape social relations. The described fragility and impermanence of the human body, which is a psychophysiological map of society, suggests the fragility of society and the impermanence of the existing social order. Escape from the constraints of society is indispensable for achieving the spiritual unification of society, which reflects the unity of enlightened awareness. The *gaṇa-cakra* is a ritual community, in which ritual imagery is dominated by gnosis. Entry into such a community ensures protection from negative forces that abide inside and outside the individual. It is the initial birth into the Buddha's spiritual family that is protected by gnosis, which is invoked through initiation consisting of outer and inner offerings to external and internal deities.

The yogic practices of the *Kālacakratantra* are a form of inner sacrifice, in which regenerative fluids, sometimes called *soma*, are the inner offering to the deities dwelling within one's own body. Likewise, in this rite of inner sacrifice, *caṇḍāli*, or the fire of gnosis, is a purifying fire to which all of one's imperfections are offered. Being the inner sacrifice, it is the most powerful and expedient means to spiritual realization.

The cosmos is a universal sacrifice, in which the negative *karma* of all sentient beings inhabiting the universe is offered to the purifying *kālāgni*, the fire that incinerates the universe at the end of time. Similarly to a Vedic sacrifice, these sacrifices lead the fragmentation of the individual and universe, respectively, back to Kālacakra, also referred to as Prajāpati. Thus, the practices of the *Kālacakraratantra* can be seen as forms of a sacrificial reconstruction of Kālacakra, which provide a blueprint for tracing the ultimate source of all existence.

Notes

Introduction

1. This number of verses is given in the *Vimalaprabhā* commentary on the *Kālacakratantra*, Ch, 1. v. 9. The *sradgharā* meter consists of four lines (*pada*) of twenty-one syllables each.

2. See *Sekoddeśaṭīkā* of Naḍapāda, 1941, pp. 4–5: *uddeśa-nirdeśau dvāv eva tantra-saṃgītiḥ. tatroddeśanā-saṃgītiḥ samasta-laghu-tantram.*

3. For more detailed information on the Tibetan historical accounts of the history of the *Kālacakratantra* in India, see G. N. Roerich, tr., *Blue Annals*, 1988, pp. 753–766. For a well-systematized presentation of the Tibetan accounts, see John Newman, "A Brief History of the Kālachakra," in *The Wheel of Time: The Kalachakra in Context*, 1985, pp. 51–84. See also Giacomella Orofino, *Sekoddeśa*, 1994, pp. 15–24.

4. The *Kālacakrānusāriganita*, or the *Kālacakraganitopadeśa*, National Archives in Kathmandu, no. 152 VI, 22, Mf. B22/22. According to the *Kālacakrānusāriganita*, the Kālacakra era (*dhruvaka*) corresponds to the nineteenth year of the Jupiter cycle, which, according to G. Orofino, falls forty-one years before the end of the sexagenary cycle. On this basis, Orofino, 1994, p. 16, presumes that the astronomical era of the *Kālacakratantra*'s *laghu-karaṇa* corresponds to 805 CE of the Gregorian calendar.

5. See G. Orofino, 1994, p. 15 and fn. 27.

6. G. Grönbold, 1991, p. 393; D. Schuh, 1973, p. 20.

7. The *anuṣṭubh* meter consists of the four lines (*pada*) of eight syllables each.

8. The *Vimalaprabhā* commentary on the *Kālacakratantra*, Ch. 2, v. 99, citing v. 86 from the *Sekoddeśa*, states that the verse was taught by the Bhagavān in the *Sekoddeśa* in the root-*tantra* (*mūla-tantra*). Likewise, the *Vimalaprabhā* commentary on the *Kālacakratantra*, Ch. 2, v. 107, asserts the same, citing verses 51–52*b*.

9. The *Sekoddeśaṭippanī* of Sādhuputra, Asiatic Society of Bengal, Calcutta, MS. #10744, folio 1b/3–5. Tib.

10. *Paramārthasaṃgrahanāmasekoddeśaṭīkā* of Nāropā, 1941, pp. 3–4.

11. The *Ārya-ḍākinī-vajrapañjara-mahātantrarājakalpa-nāma* of the unknown author is extant only in Tibetan translation, Derge edition, *rgyud* #419. G. Orofino, 1994, p. 14, points out that according to Bu ston's *Tantra Catalogue*, it is associated with the literary corpus of the *Hevajratantra*. However, this is not the case according to the Nyingma edition of the *sDe-dge bKa'-'gyur/bsTan-'gyur*.

12. The *Hevajrapiṇḍārthaṭīkā* of Vajragarbhadaśabhūmīśvara, National Archives, Kathmandu, C 128, Mf., C 12/6.

13. See the *Vajrapādasārasaṃgrahapañjikā* of Nāḍapāda (Nāropā), Peking ed. of *The Tibetan Tripiṭaka*, #2070, p. 148, 4b/1.

14. See G. Orofino, 1994, p. 23, and J. Newman, "Outer Wheel of Time," 1987, p. 112.

15. *Tāranātha's History of Buddhism in India*, 1990, p. 440.

16. *Blue Annals*, p. 797.

1. *The Broader Theoretical Framework of the* Kālacakratantra

1. The *Vimalaprabhā* commentary on the *Kālacakratantra*, Ch. 4, v. 234, and 1986, Ch. 1, p. 19.

2. The *Vimalaprabhā* commentary on the *Kālacakratantra*, 1986, Ch. 1, p. 19.

3. Ibid. *Sekoddeśa*, 1994, vs. 3–6.

4. The *Kālacakratantra*, Ch. 5, v. 243.

5. The *Vimalaprabhā* commentary on the *Kālacakratantra*, 1986, Ch. 1, p. 18.

6. The *Vimalaprabhā* commentary on the *Kālacakratantra*, 1986, Ch. 1, p. 19.

7. The *Vimalaprabhā* commentary on the *Kālacakratantra*, Ch. 5, v. 127.

8. The *Ādibuddhatantra*, cited in the *Vimalaprabhā* commentary on the *Kālacakratantra*, Ch. 5, v. 127.

9. Ibid.

10. See the *Kālacakratantra*, Ch. 5, vs. 238–240, and the *Vimalaprabhā*.

11. The *Vimalaprabhā* commentary on the *Kālacakratantra*, Ch. 3, v. 2.

12. The *Kālacakratantra*, Ch. 3, v. 2.

13. Aśvaghoṣa's *Gurupañcāśikā* and the *Ḍākārṇavayoginītantra* give similar characterizations of a bad spiritual mentor.

14. See the *Kālacakratantra*, Ch. 3, v. 3, and the *Vimalaprabhā*.

15. A list of the ten principles, which is given in the last chapter of the *Vajrahṛdayālaṃkāratantra*, includes the ten inner and ten outer principles. The ten inner principles are: two rituals of warding off danger, the secret and wisdom empowerments, the ritual of separating the enemies form their protectors, the offering cake (*bali*) and *vajra*-recitation, the ritual of wrathful accomplishment, blessing the images, and establishing *maṇḍalas*. The ten outer principles are: the *maṇḍala*, meditative concentration (*samādhi*), *mudrā*, standing posture, sitting posture, recitation, fire ritual, applying activities, and conclusion. For the explanation of the ten outer principles, see Praśāntamitra's *Māyājālatantrapañjikā*.

16. The *Gurupañcāśikā*, also known as the *Gurusevādharmapañcāṣaḍgāthā*, traditionally ascribed to Aśvaghoṣa, vs. 7–9, cited in the *Vimalaprabhā* commentary on the *Kālacakratantra*, Ch. 3, v. 3. The Sanskrit version of the *Gurupañcāśikā* was published in the *Journal Asiatique*, Paris, 1929, vol. 215: 255–263.

17. The *Ācāryaparīkṣā*, cited in the *Vimalaprabhā* commentary on the *Kālacakratantra*, Ch. 3, v. 3:

> Due to his complete knowledge (*parijñāna*) of the ten truths (*daśa-tattva*), among the three, a fully ordained monk (*bhikṣu*) is superior (*uttama*). A wondering ascetic (*śrāmaṇera*) is said to be middling (*madhyama*); and a householder (*gṛhastha*) is inferior (*adhama*) to the two.

Cf. the *Gurupañcāśikā*, vs. 4–5.

18. The *Vimalaprabhā* commentary on the *Kālacakratantra*, Ch. 3, v. 3.

19. Cf. the *Vajramālā-guhyasamāja-vyākhyā-tantra*, which also distinguishes three types of *vajrācāryas*, asserting that the best *vajrācārya* is a fully ordained monk, the middling *vajrācārya* is a Buddhist novice, and the lowest one is a householder who took tantric vows.

20. The *Vimalaprabhā* commentary on the *Kālacakratantra*, Ch. 1, v. 4.
21. The *Kālacakratantra*, Ch. 3, v. 4, and the *Vimalaprabhā*.
22. The *Kālacakratantra*, Ch. 4, v. 214. See also Bu ston's annotations [201].
23. The *Kālacakratantra*, Ch. 4, v. 216.
24. See the *Vimalaprabhā* commentary on the *Kālacakratantra*, Ch. 3, v. 2, and Ch. 2. v. 13.
25. Ibid.
26. Ibid.
27. The *Vimalaprabhā* commentary on the *Kālacakratantra*, Ch, 2. v. 13.
28. See the *Vimalaprabhā* commentary on the *Kālacakratantra*, Ch. 3, v. 4.
29. See the *Vimalaprabhā* commentary on the *Kālacakratantra*, 1986, Ch. 1, p. 43.
30. See the *Kālacakratantra*, 1986, Ch. 1, v. 4, and the *Vimalaprabhā* commentary.
31. See the *Vimalaprabhā* commentary on the *Kālacakratantra*, 1986, Ch. 1, p. 18.
32. The *Vimalaprabhā* commentary on the *Kālacakratantra*, Ch. 5, v. 127.
33. Ibid.
34. Cf. the *Hevajratantra*, part 2, Ch. 4, vs. 97–99, and the *Guhyasamājatantra*, Ch. 18, v. 36.
35. Cf. the *Hevajratantra*, part 1, Ch. 5, vs. 2–7, and part 2, Ch. 11, vs. 5–7.
36. For the sixfold classification in the *Hevajratantra*, see Snellgrove, *Hevajra Tantra: A Critical Study*, 1976, p. 38.
37. The *Kālacakratantra*, Ch. 2, v. 1.
38. See the *Kālacakratantra*, Ch. 2, vs. 166–167, and the *Vimalaprabhā* commentary.
39. The *Kālacakratantra*, Ch. 2, vs. 168–169, and the *Vimalaprabhā* commentary.
40. The *Kālacakratantra*, Ch. 2, v. 170.
41. The *Kālacakratantra*, Ch. 2, v. 171.
42. The *Kālacakratantra*, Ch. 2, v. 172.
43. The *Kālacakratantra*, Ch. 2, v. 174, and the *Vimalaprabhā* commentary.
44. The *Kālacakratantra*, Ch. 2, v. 175.
45. The *Kālacakratantra*, Ch. 3, v. 176, and the *Vimalaprabhā* commentary.
46. The *Jñānasārasamuccaya*, cited in the *Vimalaprabhā* commentary on the *Kālacakratantra*, Ch. 2, v. 173.
47. See the *Kālacakratantra*, Ch. 2, v. 173, and the *Vimalaprabhā* commentary.
48. The *Kālacakratantra*, Ch. 4, v. 200.
49. See the *Kālacakratantra*, Ch. 2, v. 178.
50. The *Kālacakratantra*, Ch. 2, v. 179.
51. The *Vimalaprabhā* commentary on the *Kālacakratantra*, Ch. 1, v. 1.
52. The *Vimalaprabhā* commentary on the *Kālacakratantra*, 1986, Ch. 1, p. 18.
53. The *Vimalaprabhā* commentary on the *Kālacakratantra*, Ch. 5, v. 127.
54. The *Vimalaprabhā* commentary on the *Kālacakratantra*, 1986, Ch. 1, p. 18.
55. *Sekoddeśaṭīkā of Naḍapāda*, 1941, p. 7, states: "The word "ādi" means without beginning or end (*ādi-śabdo 'nādinidhanārthaḥ*). The Buddha means one who perceives all true phenomena (*aviparītān sarva-dharmān buddhavān iti buddhaḥ*); and this Buddha is promordial, the Primordial Buddha. He is devoid of origination and cessation, meaning, he is omniscient (*utpādāvyaya-rahitaḥ savajña ity arthaḥ*)."
56. The *Vimalaprabhā* commentary on the *Kālacakratantra*, 1986, Ch. 1, p. 18 and the *Sekoddeśaṭīkā*, 1941, p. 7, cite this line from the *Mañjuśrīnāmasaṃgīti* in order to substantiate their interpretation of the Ādibuddha.
57. The *Vimalaprabhā* commentary on the *Kālacakratantra*, Ch. 4, v. 234.
58. The *Kālacakratantra*, Ch. 4, v. 234.
59. The *Vimalaprabhā* commentary on the *Kālacakratantra*, Ch. 1, v. 2.
60. The *Vimalaprabhā* commentary on the *Kālacakratantra*, 1986, Ch. 1, p. 19.

61. The *Vimalaprabhā* commentary on the *Kālacakratantra*, Ch. 1, v. 1.

62. The *Nāmasaṃgīti*, v. 54:

saṃsārapārakoṭisthaḥ kṛtakṛtyaḥ sthale sthitaḥ
kaivalyajñānaniṣṭhyūtaḥ prajñāśastro vidāranaḥ.

63. The *Vimalaprabhā* commentary on the *Kālacakratantra*, Ch. 5, v. 127.

64. The *Vimalaprabhā* commentary on the *Kālacakratantra*, Ch. 1, v. 1, and Ch. 5, v. 127.

65. See the *Vimalaprabhā* commentary on the *Kālacakratantra*, Ch. 5, v. 127.

66. See the *Kālacakratantra*, Ch, 1. v. 5, and the *Vimalaprabhā* commentary.

67. The *Ṇāmasaṃgītivṛtti*, 176. 1. 7, 176. 2. 8, Taishō, 2532, from the *Peking Tibetan Tripiṭaka*, vol. 74, pp. 171. 1. 1–184. 4. 8. For the complete list of the ten truths, see Ronald Davidson, 1981, p. 24, fn. 69.

68. The *Ārya-nāmasaṃgīti-ṭīkā-mantrārthāvalokinī-nāma*, 196. 5. 5., 197. 2. 1, Taishō 2533, from the *Peking Tibetan Tripiṭaka*, vol. 47, pp. 184. 4. 8-226. 2. 1.

69. The *Vimalaprabhā* commentary on the *Kālacakratantra*, Ch. 5, v. 114.

70. The *Vimalaprabhā* commentary on the *Kālacakratantra*, Ch. 1, v. 1.

71. Ibid.

72. Ibid.

73. The *Vimalaprabhā* commentary on the *Kālacakratantra*, Ch. 4, v. 133.

74. See the *Kālacakratantra*, Ch. 4, v. 51, Ch. 5. v. 127, and the *Vimalaprabhā* commentary.

75. The *Vimalaprabhā* commentary on the *Kālacakratantra*, Ch. 5, v. 127.

76. See the *Kālacakratantra*, Ch. 3, v. 105, and the *Vimalaprabhā* commentary.

77. The *Kālacakratantra*, Ch, 2, v. 5; the *Āyuṣmannandagarbhāvakrāntinirdeśanāmamatrāyānasūtra*, Peking ed. of the *Tibetan Tripiṭaka*, vol. 23, #760.

78. See Bu ston's annotation [315] on the *Kālacakratantra*, Ch, 2. v. 8.

79. The *Kālacakratantra*, Ch. 2, v. 8. For the *Amṛtahṛdayāṣṭaṅgaguhyopadeśatantra*'s assertion, see the *Encyclopaedia of Tibetan Medicine*, vol. 2, 1994, p. 17.

80. The *Āyuṣparyantasūtra*, Peking ed. of the *Tibetan Tripiṭaka*, vol. 39, #973.

81. The *Nandagarbhāvasthā* (Tib. *dga' bo mngal gnas*), cited in Bu ston's annotation [313] on the *Kālacakratantra*, Ch. 2, v. 4.

2. *A History of the ṣaḍ-aṅga-yoga of the* Kālacakratantra *and Its Relation to Other Religious Traditions of India*

1. The *Maitrāyaṇīya Upaniṣad*, Ch, 6. v. 18: *tathā tatprayogakalpaḥ prāṇāyāmaḥ pratyāhāro dhyānaṃ dhāraṇā tarkaḥ samādhiḥ ṣaḍaṅgā ity ucyate.*

2. See Günter Grönbold, *The Yoga of Six Limbs: An Introduction to the History of Ṣaḍaṅgayoga*, 1996, p. 11.

3. See Mircea Eliade, *Yoga: Immortality and Freedom*, 1969, p. 125.

4. The *Vāyu Purāṇa*, Ch. 10, v. 76 reads:

prāṇāyāmas tathā dhyānaṃ pratyāhāro 'tha dhāraṇā
smaraṇaṃ caiva yoge 'smin pañcadharmāḥ prakīrtitaḥ.

5. A six-phased *yoga* that contains contemplative inquiry (*tarka*) as the fifth phase is also mentioned in the *Dakṣasmṛti*, Ch. 7, v. 3; the *Atrismṛti*, Ch. 9., v. 6; the *Mṛgendrāgama*, Ch. 7, v. 5; Abhinavagupta's *Tantrāloka*, Ch. 4, v. 15, etc.

6. The *Kālacakratantra*, Ch. 4, v. 116.

7. The *Vimalaprabhā* commentary on the *Kālacakratantra*, Ch. 4, v. 116.

8. See Abhinavagupta, *A Trident of Wisdom*, tr. by Jaideva Singh, 1988, p. 196.

9. See N. Rastogi, *The Krama Tantricism of Kashmir*, 1996, pp. 59–60. Cf. the *Mālinīvijayottaratantra*, Ch. 17, v. 16, 1922, p. 114, which reads: "contemplative inquiry is the highest phase of *yoga*" (*tarko yogāṅgam uttaram*).

10. For the explanation of *niyama* in the context of the *Kālacakratantra*, see the *Vimalaprabhā*, 1986, Ch. 1, p. 117, the *Kālacakratantra*, Ch. 3, vs. 70, 138, and 147, together with the *Vimalaprabhā* commentary.

11. The *Vimalaprabhā* commentary on the *Kālacakratantra*, Ch. 3, v. 70.

12. G. N. Roerich, tr., *Blue Annals*, 1988, p. 764.

13. The *Ṣaḍaṅgayogaṭīkā* was translated into Tibetan by Vibhūticandra and included in the Peking edition of the Tibetan *Bstan 'gyur*, vol. 47, #2084: 238.2.5.–242.4.2. It has been translated into German by Günter Grönbold, 1969. See also the *Guṇabharaṇīnāma-ṣaḍaṅgayoga-ṭippaṇī*, half of which was initially translated into Tibetan by Vibhūticandra and is included in the Peking edition of the Tibetan *Bstan 'gyur*, vol. 47, #2103: 283.1.5–294.4.8.

14. Roerich, *Blue Annals*, p. 764; *Tāranātha's History of Buddhism in India*, 1990, pp. 307–308; Padma dkar po's *'Brug pa'i chos 'byung* and *Dpe med 'tsho'i lugs kyi rnal 'byor yan lag drug pa'i khrid rdo rje'i tshig 'byed* in the *Collected Works of Padma dkar po*, vols. 2 (*kha*) and 17 (*tsa*); and Bu ston's *Sbyor ba yan lag drug gi sngon 'gro'i rim pa* in the *Collected Works of Bu ston*, pt. 3 (*ga*), 1965, p. 348.

15. Several Tibetan authors such as Nag tsho, Sum pa, and others mention Vikramapura in Bengal as the birthplace of Atīśa. They speak of Vikramapura as a prosperous city with a large population. For more details see Alaka Chattopadhyaya, *Atīśa and Tibet*, 1996, pp. 57–66.

16. *Tāranātha's History of Buddhism in India*, 1990, p. 316.

17. Ibid., pp. 307–308.

18. See Roerich, tr., *Blue Annals*, 1988, p. 764.

19. Anupamarakṣita's *Ṣaḍaṅgayoga* is preserved in Tibetan translations and included in the *Tibetan Tripiṭaka*, Peking edition of the Tibetan *Bstan 'gyur* (Vibhūticandra's and Gnyal Lotsaba Mi myam zang po's translation), vol. 47, #2083:234.2.4.–238.2.5; (Dpang Lo tsa ba Dpal ldan blo gros brtan pa's translation), vol. 47, #2102:274.3.7.–283.1.5.

20. Roerich, tr., *Blue Annals*, p. 800.

21. Several works belonging to the Kālacakra corpus are ascribed to Śrīdharanandana, known also as Sādhuputra. See the Derge edition of Tibetan *Bstan 'gyur, rgyud* section: the *Sekoddeśaṭippanī*, #1352, the *Śrīkālacakrasādhananāma*, #1356, and the *Śrīkālacakramaṇḍalavidhi*, # 1359.

22. *Collected Works of Padma dkar po*, vol. 17 (*tsa*), 1974, p. 213.

23. *Collected Works of Bu ston*, vol. 16 (*ma*), 1965, p. 4.

24. Padma gar dbang's *Zab chos sbas pa mig 'byed kyi chos bskor las paṇ che sha wa dbang phyung gi snyan rgyud rdo rje sum gyi bla ma rgyud pa'i rnam that dad pa'i rnga chen*, 24 a. For the full reference, see Cyrus Stearns, "The Life and Tibetan Legacy of the Indian *Mahā-paṇḍita* Vibhūticandra," *Journal of the International Association of Buddhist Studies* 19.1, 1996, pp. 129, fn. 9, and 169.

25. Śākyaśrībhadra wrote several commentarial works on the *Kālacakratantra*, which are preserved in Tibetan. The Derge edition of the Tibetan *Bstan 'gyur, rgyud* section, contains the following works: the *Śrīkālacakra-gaṇanopadeśa-nāma*, #1384, the *Sūryacandragrahaṇagaṇita*, #1385, and the *Pañcagraha-pṛthaggaṇanopadeśa-nāma*, #1386.

26. Padma gar dbang's *Zab chos sbas pa mig 'byed kyi chos bskor las pan che sha wa dbang phyug gi snyan rgyud rdo rje sum gyi bla ma rgyud pa'i rnam thar dad pa'i rnga chen*, 24a.

27. The *Ṣaḍaṅgayoganāma* is preserved in the Tibetan translation. See the *Tibetan Tripiṭaka*, vol. 47, #2091, 258.4.2–258.5.1.

28. Tāranātha, *Rdo rje'i rnal 'byor gyi 'khrid yig mthong ba don ldan gyi lhan thabs 'od brgya 'bar*, 707.5–6, 456. See Stearns, "The Life and Tibetan Legacy of the Indian *mahā-paṇḍita* Vibhūticandra," *Journal of the International Association of Buddhist Studies* 19.1, 1996, p. 139. For a biographical sketch of Śavaripa, see ibid., pp. 139–141, fn. 46.

29. Tshong kha pa, *Collected Works*, vol. 17, 1976, pp. 49–50.

3. *The Nature of Syncretism in the* Kālacakratantra

1. The *Paramādibuddhatantra*, cited in the *Vimalaprabhā*, 1986, Ch. 1, p. 24.
2. The *Kālacakratantra*, Ch. 2, v. 177, lines *a–b*.
3. Ibid., lines *c–d*. This analogy of the mind's impressionability to that of a crystal is most likely borrowed from the *Yoginīsaṃcāratantra*, Ch. 11, v. 2, which is cited in a different context in the *Vimalaprabhā* commentary on the *Kālacakratantra*, Ch. 5, v. 47:

yena yena hi bhāvena manaḥ saṃyujyate nṛṇām
tena tanmanyatāṃ yāti viśvarūpo maṇir yathā.

4. The *Vimalaprabhā* commentary on the *Kālacakratantra*, Ch. 2, v. 176.
5. The *Kālacakratantra*, Ch. 5, v. 66.
6. The *Kālacakratantra*, Ch. 5, v. 86.
7. The *Vimalaprabhā* commentary on the *Kālacakratantra*, Ch. 5, v. 86.
8. The *Vimalaprabhā* commentary on the *Kālacakratantra*, Ch. 5, v. 127.
9. Ibid.
10. Ibid.
11. Ibid.
12. Ibid.
13. The *Kālacakratantra*, Ch. 2, v. 161, and the *Vimalaprabhā*.
14. The *Kālacakratantra*, Ch. 2, v. 85, and the *Vimalaprabhā*.
15. The *Kālacakratantra*, Ch. 2, v. 86, and the *Vimalaprabhā*.
16. The *Sāṃkhyakārikā*, vs. 22, 28.
17. The *Kālacakratantra*, Ch. 2, v. 83, and the *Vimalaprabhā*.
18. See *Sāṃkhyakārikā*, v. 23.
19. According to Sāṃkhya, the functions of the mind (*manas*) are: analyses and conceptualization (*vikalpa*), and decision and determination (*saṃkalpa*).
20. One can encounter a similar procedure in the *Bhagavad Gīta*'s exposition of the universal validity of the Kṛṣṇa doctrine, where it often uses its terms with overlapping meanings. Cf. Edgerton's essay (Ch. 10), accompanying his translation to *The Bhagavad Gīta*, 1972, p. 179.
21. The *Kālacakratantra*, Ch. 2, vs. 83, 85.
22. The *Kālacakratantra*, Ch. 2, v. 93.
23. See M. Dyczkowski, tr., *The Aphorisms of Śiva: The Śiva Sūtra with Bhāskara's Commentary, the Vārttika*, 1992, Ch. 1, v. 11.
24. The *Kālacakratantra*, Ch. 2, v. 86, and the *Vimalaprabhā*.
25. The *Vimalaprabhā* commentary on the *Kālacakratantra*, Ch. 2, vs. 61, 65, 86.
26. See Dyczkowski, tr., *The Aphorisms of Śiva*, pp. 43, 138, 140; J. Singh, tr., *The Yoga of Delight, Wonder, and Astonishment: A Translation of the Vijñāna-Bhairava*, 1991, pp. 71, 79–80.
27. The *Kālacakratantra*, Ch. 2, v. 7, and the *Vimalaprabhā*.
28. See the *Vimalaprabhā* commentary on the *Kālacakratantra*, Ch. 2, v. 8.
29. See the *Vimalaprabhā* commentary on the *Kālacakratantra*, Ch. 5, v. 127.
30. Ibid.
31. For further information on the *Kālacakratantra* cosmology, see chapter 5 on the "Cosmic Body."

32. The *Kālacakratantra*, Ch. 3, v. 169.
33. See the *Vimalaprabhā* commentary on the *Kālacakratantra*, Ch. 3, v. 169.
34. See the *Vimalaprabhā* commentary on the *Kālacakratantra*, Ch. 3, vs. 167–168.
35. Ibid.
36. The *Vimalaprabhā* commentary on the *Kālacakratantra*, Ch. 5, v. 127.
37. See the *Kālacakratantra*, Ch. 4, v. 5.
38. The *Vimalaprabhā* commentary on the *Kālacakratantra*, Ch. 4, v. 48.
39. The *Vimalaprabhā* commentary on the *Kālacakratantra*, 1986, Ch. 1, p. 40.
40. Ibid., p. 34.
41. See the *Vimalaprabhā* commentary on the *Kālacakratantra*, Ch. 2, v. 173.

4. *The Concept of Science in the Kālacakra Tradition*

1. See Romila Thapar, *A History of India*, vol. 1, 1966, 253–254.

2. Verses 128–147 of the first chapter of the *Kālacakratantra* give a detailed instruction on building the different types of weapons that should be used by the Kalkī's army in the final battle with the Barbarians in the land of Mecca.

3. This view of theological knowledge and scientific learning as complementary is dominant in the Vajrayāna, whereas in the writings of Mahāyāna they are simply compatible rather than complementary.

4. See the *Samaññaphalasutta* of the *Dīghanikāya*, *Thus Have I Heard*, 1987, pp. 68–91.

5. *Bodhicaryāvatāra*, 1995, Ch. 5, v. 100.

6. The *Mahāyānasūtrālaṃkāra*, 1970, Ch. 11, v. 60.

7. See E. Obermiller, *The Jewelry of Scripture by Bu-ston*, 1987, p. 29.

8. The *Mahāyānasūtrālaṃkāra*, Ch. 12, v. 3.

9. This is not unique to the *Kālacakratantra*. The earlier medical treatises of Āyurveda—the *Suśrutasaṃhitā* (first to second centuries CE) and the *Carakasaṃhitā* (c. fourth century CE)—assert that the five elements that are present in the body—earth, water, fire, wind, and space—form the entire universe.

10. See the *Vimalaprabhā* commentary on the *Kālacakratantra*, 1986, p. 43.

11. The *Nettipakaraṇa*, 1962, [76].

12. If one were to ask, "How is introspection scientific in the context of Buddhism?" an answer would be that just as physical phenomena are to be scientifically studied for as far as possible by means of direct observation, similarly, it is true for the first-person mental phenomena. Introspection is widely recognized in Buddhism as the sole means of observing one's own conscious states.

13. The *Vimalaprabhā* commentary on the *Kālacakratantra*, Ch. 5, v. 127.

14. Ibid.

15. The *Vimalaprabhā* commentary on the *Kālacakratantra*, Ch. 5, v. 192.

16. The *Vimalaprabhā* commentary on the *Kālacakratantra*, 1986, Ch. 1, p. 44.

17. The *Vimalaprabhā* commentary on the *Kālacakratantra*, Ch. 5, v. 88.

18. The *Vimalaprabhā* commentary on the *Kālacakratantra*, Ch. 2, v. 96.

19. Ibid.

20. Already in the early Buddhist Pāli literature, the Buddhist Dhamma was referred to as the verifiable teaching, as the Dhamma that involves one's "coming and seeing" (*ehipassika*).

21. The *Kālacakratantra*, Ch. 2, vs. 48–50.

22. See the *Kālacakratantra*, Ch. 2, v. 96, with the *Vimalaprabhā* commentary.

23. The *Discourses of Gotama Buddha: Middle Collection*, 1992, "With Māgandiya," "Major Discourse on the Destruction of Craving."

24. The *Kālacakratantra*, Ch. 2, v. 107, lines *a–b*.

25. For more information see Kenneth G. Zysk, *Asceticism and Healing in Ancient India*, 1991, and the *Encyclopaedia of Buddhism*, 1963, vol. 1, p. 447.

26. According to the *Encyclopaedia of Buddhism*, 1963, p. 478, some Indian manuscripts ascribe the *Yogaśataka* to Vararuci instead of Nāgārjuna.

27. These five Buddhist medical treatises are included among the twenty-two Āyurvedic works that are incorporated in the Tibetan *Tengyur*, where they are ascribed to Nāgārjuna. Apart from the *Yogaśataka*, the Sanskrit originals of the other four treatises are lost.

28. According to the *Encyclopaedia of Buddhism*, 1963, vol. 1, p. 478, an alternative attribution of the *Kakṣapuṭa*, or the *Kacchapuṭa*, is to Nityanāthasiddha.

29. See the *Vimalaprabhā* commentary on the *Kālacakratantra*, 1986, Ch. 2, v. 141.

30. Cf. Śāntideva, *Śikṣāsamuccaya*, 1961, pp. 77–78, where Śāntideva advises Bodhisattvas to counteract diseases with the recitation of *mantras*, along with the usage of medications and water and the offerings of flowers to the image of the Buddha.

31. Cf. Maurice Walshe, tr. *Thus I Have Heard: The Long Discourses of the Buddha: Dīgha Nikāya*: "*Aṭānāṭiya Sutta: The Aṭānāṭā Protective Verses*," 1987, pp. 471–478; the *Vinayapiṭaka*, vol. 4, 1879–1883. Cf. Śāntideva, *Śikṣāsamuccaya*, 77, where the author cites the *mantras* that are set forth in the *Trisamayarāja* as the *mantras* to be used for the protection of Bodhisattvas against the Māras and other evil entities.

32. See the *Kālacakratantra*, Ch. 5, v. 187, and the *Vimalaprabhā*.

33. *Kālacakratantra*, Ch. 2, vs. 154–160.

34. According to the *Kālacakratantra*, Ch. 2, v. 153, the symptoms of irrevocable death are the following: the entire body becomes white, very subtle boils appear, the neck is bent together with the body, blood drips into the mouth, sexual organ, or the rectum.

35. The *Kālacakratantra* Ch. 2, vs. 152–153.

36. See the *Kālacakratantra*, Ch. 2, v. 146, and the *Vimalaprabhā*.

37. See the *Kālacakratantra*, Ch. 2, v. 159, and the *Vimalaprabhā*.

38. The fragrant root of *Andropogon Muricatus*.

39. *Valeriana jatamansi*.

40. The *Kālacakratantra*, Ch. 2, v. 149, and the *Vimalaprabhā*.

41. The *Kālacakratantra*, Ch. 2, v. 152.

42. The name of a medicinal plant with a bitter root.

43. *Methonia Superba*.

44. *Cucumis Colocynthis*, a wild bitter gourd.

45. The *Kālacakratantra*, Ch. 2, vs. 124, 126–127.

46. The *Vimalaprabhā* commentary on the *Kālacakratantra*, Ch. 2, v. 128.

47. Ibid., v. 130, reads: *oṃ phre Viśvamāte vajrakaṇṭakān nāśaya nāśaya mama śāntiṃ kuru kuru svāhā*.

48. The *Vimalaprabhā* commentary on the *Kālacakratantra*, Ch. 2, v. 149 reads: *oṃ āḥ huṃ amukāyā garbhaśūlaṃ hara hara svāhā*.

49. See the *Kālacakratantra* Ch. 2, v. 129, with the *Vimalaprabhā* commentary.

50. See the *Vimalaprabhā* commentary on the *Kālacakratantra*, Ch. 4, v. 109.

51. The *Vimalaprabhā* commentary on the *Kālacakratantra*, Ch. 4, v. 56.

52. See the *Vimalaprabhā* commentary on the *Kālacakratantra*, Ch. 3, v. 1.

53. The *Vimalaprabhā* commentary on the *Kālacakratantra*, Ch. 5, v. 127.

54. The *Vimalaprabhā* commentary on the *Kālacakratantra*, Ch. 2, v. 112, describes the *vajra* posture in the following way: "The *vajra* posture entails the left leg on the right thigh, and the right leg on the left thigh. Those two legs have the *vajra*-connection with the arms being on the top. The right foot is held by the left hand, and the left foot is held by the right hand."

55. The Sanskrit word *kuṣṭharoga*, or "leprosy," is a general term for the eighteen types of leprosy. Neither the *Kālacakratantra* nor the *Vimalaprabhā* specifies whether the term *kuṣṭharoga* here refers to all of the eighteen types of leprosy or to a specific type of leprosy.

56. The *Kālacakratantra*, Ch. 2, v. 122.

57. See the *Kālacakratantra*, Ch. 2, v. 128, and the *Vimalaprabhā*.

58. Three *kaṭukas* are three spices: black and long peppers and dry ginger.

59. The *Kālacakratantra*, Ch. 2, v. 124.

60. *Arka* is a tropical and subtropical milky plant that grows in the dry, plain areas. It is also known as *Calotropis gigantea*, linn., or the milky weed plant.

61. The *Kālacakratantra*, Ch. 2, v. 114.

62. The *Kālacakratantra*, Ch. 5, v. 186, and the *Vimalaprabhā*.

63. The *Vimalaprabhā* commentary on the *Kālacakratantra*, Ch. 2, v. 135.

64. See the *Āyuṣparirakṣānāma*, which is preserved in Tibetan translation under the title *Tshe bsgrub pa'i gdams ngag ces bya ba* and is included in the Tantra commentary (*rgyud 'grel*) section of the *Tengyur* (Peking edition of the *Tibetan Tripiṭaka*, edited by D. T. Suzuki, vol. 69, no. 3236, Tokyo-Kyoto: Tibetan Tripiṭaka Research Foundation, 1955–1961); the *Āyuḥsādhana*, which is existent only in Tibetan translation under the title *Tshe sgrub pa'i thabs* and occurs in the Tantra commentary section of the *Tengyur* (Peking edition of the *Tibetan Tripiṭaka*, edited by D. T. Suzuki, vol. 86, no. 4863, Tokyo-Kyoto: Tibetan Tripiṭaka Research Foundation, 1955–61); the *Āyurbuddhānusmṛti*, which is also extant only in its Tibetan translation under the title *'Phags pa sngas rgyas rjes su dran pa* and is included in the Tantra commentary section of the *Tengyur* (P. Cordier, ed. *Catalogue du Fonds Tibétain*, vol. 2, p. 371, no. 4); the *Āyurvardhanīvidhi* which is attributed to Candragomin is preserved only in Tibetan translation under the title *Tshe 'phel ba'i cho ga* in the Tantra commentary section of the *Tengyur* (*Tōhoku-Teikoku-Daigaku Hōbun-gakubu Tibet-Daizōkyō-So-Mokuroku*. Sendai 1932, no. 3666).

65. According to the *Kālacakratantra*, Ch. 2, v. 125, and the *Vimalaprabhā*, the five internal *amṛtas*—feces, urine, semen, blood, and marrow—when combined with the equal portions of the five external *amṛtas*—sulfur, nectar from black bees, talk, quicksilver, and three myrobalans—soaked for seven days, dried on the heat, and ingested with ghee and honey every day for up to six months, have a life-giving power because they release energy, acid, oil, and salt.

66. According to the *Kālacakratantra*, Ch. 2, v. 111, and the *Vimalaprabhā*, the maladies of liver, spleen, and hemorrhoids are considered abdominal ailments.

67. See the *Vimalaprabhā* commentary on the *Kālacakratantra*, Ch. 2, v. 11.

5. *The Cosmic Body*

1. In its most restricted meaning, the Sanskrit term *loka-dhātu* designates a single world-sphere, but its meaning also extends to the variably numbered sets of the world-spheres.

2. See the *Vimalaprabhā* commentary on the *Kālacakratantra*, Ch. 1, v. 2.

3. The *Vimalaprabhā* commentary on the *Kālacakratantra*, Ch. 1, v. 4

4. The *Kālacakratantra*, Ch. 1, v. 4, and the *Vimalaprabhā*.

5. See The *Kālacakratantra*, Ch. 1, v. 4 , Ch. 2, v. 3, and the *Vimalaprabhā*.

6. The *Kālacakratantra*, Ch. 5, v. 63.

7. The *Kālacakratantra*, Ch. 5, v. 165, and the *Vimalaprabhā*.

8. The *Kālacakratantra*, Ch, 5. v. 167, and the *Vimalaprabhā*.

9. The ten winds are: *prāṇa*, *apāna*, *udāna*, *samāna*, *vyāna*, *nāga*, *kūrma*, *kṛkara*, *devadatta*, and *dhanaṃjaya*.

10. The *Kālacakratantra*, Ch. 2, v. 85.

11. See the *Kālacakratantra*, Ch. 2, v. 24.

12. See the *Kālacakratantra*, Ch. 2, vs. 85–86, and the *Vimalaprabhā*.

13. The *Kālacakratantra*, Ch. 5, v. 168, and the *Vimalaprabhā*.

14. The *Vimalaprabhā* commentary on the *Kālacakratantra*, Ch. 1, v. 4.

15. The name Caṇḍālī is etymologically derived from the adjective *caṇḍa*, meaning "violent," "hot," "passionate," "angry," etc. All these adjectives can also be applied to Kālāgni.

16. See the *Kālacakratantra*, Ch. 4, v. 125, and the *Vimalaprabhā*.

17. According to the *Vimalaprabhā* commentary on the *Kālacakratantra*, Ch. 2, v. 26, the thumb or big toe arises from the earth-element, the forefinger arises from the water-element, the middle finger arises from the fire-element, the ring-finger arises from the wind-element, and the little finger from the space-element.

18. See the *Kālacakratantra*, Ch. 5, v. 236, and the *Vimalaprabhā*.

19. The *prāṇas* stop carrying the earth-element in the navel, the water-element in the heart, the fire-element in the throat, the wind-element in the *lalāṭa*, and the space-element in the *uṣṇīṣa*.

20. The *Vimalaprabhā* commentary on the *Kālacakratantra*, Ch. 5, v. 127.

21. Ibid.

22. See the *Vimalaprabhā* commentary on the *Kālacakratantra*, Ch. 5, v. 184.

23. The *Ādibuddhatantra*, cited in the *Vimalaprabhā* commentary on the *Kālacakratantra*, Ch. 3, v. 53.

24. For example, with regard to linear measurements, the *Kālacakratantra*, Ch. 1, v. 13 and the *Vimalaprabhā* state that eight subtle (*sūkṣma*) atoms (*aṇu*), placed in line, make one atom; eight atoms make up the tip of a human hair, and so on. Whereas the *Abhidharmakośa*, 85*d*–88*a*, states that seven *paramāṇus* make one atom (*aṇu*); and seven atoms make one gold dust mote (*loha-rajas*). According to the same *Kālacakratantra* text, eight lice make up a measurement of one barley kernel, but in the *Abhidharmakośa*, it is said that seven lice make up a measurement of one barley kernel. Likewise, the *Kālacakratantra* states that two thousand *dhanus* ("bow") make up the measurement of one *krośa*, and four *krośas* make up one *yojana* ("league"). Whereas the *Abhidharmakośa* states that five hundred *dhanus* make one *krośa*, and eight *krośas* make one *yojana*. Cf. the *Śārdulakarṇāvadāna* and the *Lalitavistara*, Ch. 12, which state that one thousand *dhanus* make one *krośa*, and four *krośas* make one *yojana*.

25. The *Vimalaprabhā* commentary on the *Kālacakratantra*, Ch. 1, v. 10.

26. The *Kālacakratantra*, Ch. 5, v. 69.

27. The *Paramādibuddhatantra*, cited in the *Vimalaprabhā* commentary on the *Kālacakratantra*, Ch. 1, v. 10.

28. The *Kālacakratantra*, Ch. 5, v. 129.

29. The *Vimalaprabhā* commentary on the *Kālacakratantra*, Ch. 1, v. 10.

30. The *Kālacakratantra*, Ch. 5, v. 166.

31. The *Vimalaprabhā* commentary on the *Kālacakratantra*, Ch. 5, v. 166.

32. See the *Abhidharmakośa*, Ch. 3, vs. 47–48a, and the *Vimalaprabhā* commentary on the *Kālacakratantra*, Ch. 1, v. 10.

33. The *Kālacakratantra*, Ch. 2, v. 18, *padas c–d*, which describes the elements in the body, reads:

> The support of earth is water; the support of water is fire; the support of fire is wind; and the support of wind is space. O king, the support, which in turn needs to be supported, arises in this manner.

34. See the *Vimalaprabhā* commentary on the *Kālacakratantra*, Ch. 1, v. 10.

35. See the *Tattvārthasūtra*, Ch. 3, v. 1.

36. In both traditions, the third and fourth hells are characterized as extremely cold hells, whereas the fifth hell is characterized as a very hot hell. Different commentaries on the

Tattvārthasūtra give different measurements of the hells. According to Siddhasenagaṇi's *Svopajñabhāṣyaṭīkā*, belonging to the Śvetāmbara sect, from the uppermost hell downward, their widths are as follows: 1, 2.5, 4, 5, 6, and 7 *rajjus* ("rope"), respectively. Their heights are 180,000, 132,000, 128,000, 120,000, 118,000, 116,000, and 108,000 leagues. According to Pūjapāda Devanandi's commentary, the *Sarvārthasiddhi*, belonging to the Digambara sect, their heights are 180,000, 32,000, 28,000, 24,000, 20,000, 16,000, and 8,000 leagues, respectively. In the Jaina tradition, the shape of hells is quadrangular, thus corresponding in shape to the hells described in the *Abhidharmakośa*. For a more detailed description of the hells, see the *Tattvārthasūtra*: *That Which Is*, Umāsvāti, 1994, pp. 69–73.

37. According to the *Abhidharmakośa*, Ch. 3, vs. 58–59, the hot and cold hells are not located within the *maṇḍalas* as they are in the Kālacakra tradition. The hot hells are below the Jambudvīpa island, under the layers of white clay and mud, in between the surface of the earth and the golden earth-*maṇḍala*. The eight hot hells are located one beneath the other and are quadrangular in shape. Starting from the top downward, they are Saṃjīva, Kālasūtra, Saṃghāta, Raurava, Mahāraurava, Tāpana, Pratāpana, and the Avīci hell. Each of the first seven hot hells measures five thousand leagues in width and height. Avīci is the largest of the hot hells, measuring twenty thousand leagues in width. Its upper surface measures twenty thousand leagues, and its bottom surface is forty thousand leagues. The eight cold hells are located next to the eight hot hells below Jambudvīpa. Their names are: Arbuda, Nirarbuda, Aṭaṭa, Hahava, Huhuva, Utpala, Padma, and Mahāpadma.

38. See the *Ādibuddhatantra* cited in the *Vimalaprabhā* commentary on the *Kālacakratantra*, Ch. 1, v. 10, and the *Vimalaprabhā* commentary on the Kālacakratantra, Ch. 2, v. 94.

39. The *Vimalaprabhā* commentary on the *Kālacakratantra*, Ch. 2, v. 94.

40. In some of the *anuttara-yoga-tantras* such as the *Hevajratantra*, Part I, Ch. 6, v. 22, Part II, Ch. 2, v. 12, one finds the names of the Avīci and Raurava hells corresponding to those mentioned in the *Abhidharmakośa*.

41. For the description of the disintegration of the elements in the body of the individual at the time of death, see the *Kālacakratantra*, Ch. 2, v. 106, and the *Vimalaprabhā* commentary.

42. Cf. the *Visuddhimagga*, Ch. 7: 40–41, which gives the same measurement for the circumference of this world-system (*cakravāla*) and the measurement of 1,203,450 leagues for breadth and width.

43. The *Abhidharmakośabhāṣya*, Ch. 3, vs. 45–48*a*.

44. The *Kālacakratantra*, Ch. 1, v. 16, and the *Vimalaprabhā* commentary on the *Kālacakratantra*, Ch. 1, vs. 11, 16.

45. The *bhoga-bhūmi* is a land in which one enjoys the results of one's actions performed in previous lives and does not accumulate new *karma*. The term *bhoga-bhūmi* appears also in the *Viṣṇu Purāṇa*, Book 2, Ch. 3, v. 22, where it designates all other countries of Jambudvīpa, except the Bhāratavarṣa, which is said to be the land of *karma* (*karma-bhūmi*).

46. The *Vimalaprabhā* commentary on the *Kālacakratantra*, Ch. 1, vs. 11, 16.

47. The comparison of rivers to bodily veins occurs already in the Upaniṣads. See the *Chandogya Upaniṣ.ad*, Ch. 6, vs. 332–333.

48. According to the *Vimalaprabhā* commentary on the *Kālacakratantra*, Ch. 1, v. 11, Meru here does not refer to Mandara, which is in some cases implied by the word Meru. Cf. Kirfel's *Kosmographie der Inder*, 1920, p. 129, which indicates that in early Jaina cosmological texts, Mandara is another name for Mt. Meru and the name of various mountains in Brāhmaṇical literature.

49. Tibetan translation and some Sanskrit mss. read Niṣaṭa.

50. See the *Kālacakratantra*, Ch. 1, v. 10.

51. The *Tattvārthasūtra*: *That Which Is*, 1994, p. 75.

52. More precisely, each of the six continents, oceans, and mountains measures 888.89 leagues in diameter.

53. See the *Kālacakratantra*, Ch. 1, vs. 18–19, and the *Vimalaprabhā*.

54. The seven continents listed in the *Viṣṇu Purāṇa*, Book 2, Ch. 2, v. 5, as Jambu, Plakṣa, Śālmali, Kuśa, Krauñca, Śāka, and Puṣkara are also found in the *Bhāgavata*, *Garuḍa*, *Mārkaṇḍeya*, and other Purāṇas. The seven oceans mentioned in the *Viṣṇu Purāṇa*, Book 2, Ch. 2, v. 6 are the salty ocean and the oceans of sugar cane, of wine, of clarified butter, of curd, of milk, and of fresh water. According to S. M. Ali, 1966, 27, although the notion of the seven continents and seven oceans is very old, it appears for the first time in the *Rāmāyāṇa* and the *Mahābhārata*, 6.11.4.

55. For example, the *Viṣṇu Purāṇa*, Book 2, Ch. 3, v. 28, mentions one hundred thousand leagues as the measure of Jambudvīpa's diameter.

56. Cf. the *Abhidharmakośabhāṣya*, Ch. 3, vs. 51c–52c, which states that the salty ocean measures 322,000 leagues in diameter.

57. The *Abhidharmakośa*, Ch. 3, vs. 48*b*–49c, mentions only four continents: Jambudvīpa, Pūrvavideha, Godanīya, and Uttarakuru. It describes Jambudvīpa as having the shape of a trapezoid whose three sides measure 2,000 leagues and whose short side measures three and a half leagues.

58. See the *Kālacakratantra*, Ch. 1, v. 17, and the *Vimalaprabhā*.

59. According to the Tibetan commentator Mkhas grub rje it is 25,000 leagues long from the south to the north. See J. Newman, 1987, p. 581. Cf. the *Sumaṅgalavilāsinī*, II, 423, in which Jambudvīpa is said to be ten thousand leagues in size, and the *Abhidharmakośabhāṣya*, Ch. 3, vs. 53b–55d, in which three sides of Jambudvīpa are 2,000 leagues long, and one side is three and a half leagues long.

60. Cf. the *Abhidharmakośabhāṣya*, Ch. 3, vs. 53b–55d, where Pūrvavideha is also described as semicircular but as having two sides of 2,000 leagues and one side of 350 leagues in length. Uttarakuru is quadrangular and extends 2,000 leagues on each side, thus measuring 8,000 leagues in circumference; and Godanīya is round like the moon and is 7,500 leagues in circumference.

61. The *Kālacakratantra*, Ch. 1, vs. 150–151.

62. The *Kālacakratantra*, Ch. 1, v. 24, and the *Vimalaprabhā*.

63. The *Kālacakratantra*, Ch. 1, vs. 22–23, and the *Vimalaprabhā*.

64. See the *Vimalaprabhā* commentary on the *Kālacakratantra*, Ch. 3, v. 165.

65. See Snellgrove, the *Hevajra Tantra*: *A Critical Study*, 1959, p. 69, fn. 2.

66. The *Vimalaprabhā* commentary on the *Kālacakratantra*, Ch. 3, v. 165.

67. Saraha, *Dohākoṣa*, edited by Bagchi, v. 25, line *d*.

68. Within the eight outer petals of the lotus there are eight Vajraḍākinīs; and within the inner eight petals there are skull-cups (*kapāla*) filled with ambrosia. Outside the lotus, in each of the eight directions, the earth-*maṇḍala* extends for twenty-five thousand leagues.

69. Cf. the *Hevajratantra*, Part 1, Ch. 7, vs. 12–18, which lists only twenty-four pilgrimage sites. Cf. the commentaries on the *Hevajratantra*, the *Netravibhaṅga*, Ch. 17, 336*a*–423*a*, and the *Padminī*, Ch. 15, 142*a*–194*b*, which specify thirty-two pilgrimage sites.

70. The *Vimalaprabhā* commentary on the *Kālacakratantra*, Ch. 3, vs. 162–166, gives different lists of the pilgrimage sites in the body of the individual. The given lists have these numberings: thirty-six, sixty-four, and twenty-four. The *Ādibuddhatantra*, cited in the *Vimalaprabhā* commentary on the *Kālacakratantra*, Ch. 5, v. 35, mentions forty-eight sites. The *Hevajratantra*, part 1, Ch. 7, vs. 12–18, names twenty-four pilgrimage sites, whereas, its commentaries, Dharmakīrti's *Netravibhaṅga* (XVII. 365*b* 7–366*a* 1), Saroruha's *Padminī* (XV. 165*b* 1–2), and Vajragarbha's *Hevajrapiṇḍārthaṭīkā* (XV. 61*b* 3–4), speak of thirty-two places, corresponding to the thirty-two *nāḍīs* in the body.

71. See the *Vimalaprabhā* commentary on the *Kālacakratantra*, Ch. 5, v. 35.

72. See the *Kālacakratantra*, Ch. 1, v. 10, and the *Vimalaprabhā*.

73. The Kālacakra tradition offers several other models of identifying pilgrimage sites with the bodily joints. These are illustrated in the appendix.

74. The *Kālacakratantra* Ch. 3, vs. 162–165, and the *Vimalaprabhā*.

75. The *Kālacakratantra*, Ch. 5, v. 61.

76. See the *Kālacakratantra*, Ch. 2, v. 93, and the *Vimalaprabhā*.

77. See the *Kālacakratantra*, Ch. 2, v. 34, and the *Vimalaprabhā*. Cf. the *Abhidharmakoṣa*, Ch, 3, v. 8*c–d*, where the following four origins are mentioned: the egg, womb, moisture, and apparitional beings (*upapāduka*).

78. According to the *Kālacakratantra*, Ch. 1, v. 21, Śakra is in the east, Agni is in the southeast, Yama is in the south, Danu is in the southwest, Varuṇa is in the west, Vāyu is in the northwest, Yakṣa is in the north, Hara is in the northeast, Brahmā is in the upper region, and Viṣṇu is below.

79. In the Jaina cosmology, Saudharma is the first of twelve heavens below the nine Graiveyaka heavens that are on the neck of the cosmic man. The Jaina notion of Saudharma corresponds to the *Kālacakratantra*'s notion of Saudharma only in name but not in terms of its location in the universe or in any other respect.

80. According to the *Vimalaprabhā* commentary on the *Kālacakratantra*, Ch. 1, v. 15, the measurement of the medium eon (*madhyama-kalpa*) is the shortest eon (*adhama-kalpa*) multiplied hundred times. The duration of an extended eon (*utkṛṣṭa-kalpa*) is a medium eon multiplied by one hundred.

81. The *Vimalaprabhā* on the *Kālacakratantra*, Ch. 1, v. 25: *śatāyur vai puruṣaḥ śatendriyaḥ*.

82. They are also said to equal 4,320,000 breaths of a god of the Akaniṣṭha heaven. See the *Kālacakratantra*, Ch. 5, v. 150 and the *Vimalaprabhā*. This number of the years of the four *yugas* corresponds to the number given in the *Viṣṇu Purāṇa* and in the *Manusmṛti*.

83. The *Kālacakratantra*, Ch. 5, v. 120.

84. Ibid.

85. The *Vimalaprabhā* on the *Kālacakratantra*, 1986, Ch. 1, p. 20.

86. The *Vimalaprabhā* on the *Kālacakratantra*, Ch. 4, v. 2.

87. Cf. the *Śatapatha Brāhmaṇa*, X.4.3.1, which states that a year is he, referring to Prajāpati, or Time, who by means of a day and a night destroys the life of mortal beings. Likewise, one reads in the *Cakrasaṃvaratantra* that a day is called the "Bhagavān Vajrī," and a night is called "wisdom."

88. Cited in the *Vimalaprabhā* on the *Kālacakratantra*, Ch. 4, v. 2.

89. The *Vimalaprabhā* on the *Kālacakratantra*, Ch. 4, v. 2.

90. The *Vimalaprabhā*, 1986, Ch. 1, p. 11.

91. The *Vimalaprabhā*, 1986, Ch. 1, p. 21.

92. The *Kālacakratantra*, Ch, 5, v. 89, and the *Vimalaprabhā*.

93. The *Vimalaprabhā*, 1986, Ch. 1, p. 17; Ch. 5, v. 127.

94. Naḍapāda, *Sekoddeśaṭīkā*, Carelli, 1941, p. 3.

95. The *Ādibuddhatantra*, cited in the *Vimalaprabhā*, 1986, Ch. 1, p. 11. The *Ādibuddhatantra*, cited in the *Vimalaprabhā*, 1986, Ch. 1, p; the *Vimalaprabhā* on the *Kālacakratantra*, Ch. 5, v. 127.

96. The *Vimalaprabhā* on the *Kālacakratantra*, Ch. 5, v. 127.

97. The *Ādibuddhatantra*, cited in the *Vimalaprabhā*, 1986, Ch. 1, p. 8.

98. The *Kālacakratantra*, Ch. 5, vs. 244–245.

99. The *Ādibuddhatantra*, cited in the *Vimalaprabhā*, 1986, Ch. 1, p. 17.

100. See the *Atharva Veda*, XIX. 53. 1–10; XIX. 54. 1–5. The *Bṛhat-saṃhitā*, I. 7. reads: Some say that time is a cause (*kāraṇa*), some say it is the inherent nature (*svabhāva*), and yet others say it is a sacrificial ritual (*karma*)."

101. See the *Śatapatha Brāhmaṇa*, IV. 2. 4. 11, X. 4. 1. 7, X. 4. 3. 1, III. 2. 2. 4, etc.

102. Cf. the *Śatapatha Brāhmaṇa*, X. 4. 1. 17, where two of each of the hair, skin, blood, flat, sinews, bones, and marrow of Prajāpati are identified with the sixteen digits of the moon, with the table illustrating the same type of identification, given later in this chapter.

103. See the *Sekoddeśa*, 1994, vs. 22–23.

104. The *Maitrī Upaniṣad*, VI. 14–16, See also the *Taittirīya Upaniṣad*, III. 1, which speaks of time as Brahma, the *Mahānārāyaṇa Upaniṣad*, XI. 14, in which time is identified with Nārāyaṇa.

105. The *Mahābhārata*, Ādiparvan, I. 248–250, and the *Kūrma Purāṇa*, II. 3. 16: *Kālaḥ sṛjati bhūtāni kālaḥ saṃharate prajāḥ*. Cf. the *Vāyu Purāṇa*, 32. 29–30.

106. See the *Viṣṇu Purāṇa*, I. 2. 25., I. 72. 1–7.

107. See the *Bhagavadgīta*, Ch. 10, vs. 30, 33, Ch. 11, v. 32,

108. For example, six breaths, or six pairs of inhalations and exhalations, make up one *pāṇipala*, or *liptā*. Three hundred and sixty breaths make up sixty *pāṇipalas*, or one *ghaṭikā*, or *daṇḍa* (twenty-four minutes). Twenty-one thousand and six hundred breaths make up sixty *ghaṭikās*, or one solar day (*dina*). Thus, 7,776,000 breaths make up three hundred and sixty solar days, or a year; and 77,760,000 breaths make up a human life span of one hundred years. See the *Kālacakratantra*, Ch. 1, v. 24 and the *Vimalaprabhā*.

109. The *Vimalaprabhā* commentary on the *Kālacakratantra*, Ch. 2, v. 9.

110. The *Kālacakratantra*, Ch. 2, v. 38, and the *Vimalaprabhā*.

111. Aries and the like.

112. Taurus and the like.

113. The *Kālacakratantra*, Ch, 2, v. 40, and the *Vimalaprabhā*.

114. According to the *Vimalaprabhā* commentary on the *Kālacakratantra*, Ch. 2, v. 2, one visualizes the Kālacakra's body as consisting of the twelve zodiacs. Likewise, each of his two feet consists of the six zodiacs, each of his three throats consists of four zodiacs, each of his four faces consists of three zodiacs, each of his six shoulders consists of two zodiacs, his twelve upper arms consist of twelve lunar months, making up the twelve zodiacs, and each of his twenty-four hands consists of a half of a zodiac. In the *Vimalaprabhā* commentary on the *Kālacakratantra*, Ch. 5, v. 44, Capricorn, Aquarius, and Pisces are the black, red, and white faces, respectively, due to the classification of the *tamas*, *rajas*, and *sattva* of the mind-*vajra*. Aries, Taurus, and Gemini are the red, white, and black faces, respectively, due to the classification of the *rajas*, *sattva*, and *tamas* of the speech-*vajra*. Cancer, Leo, and Virgo are the white, black, and red faces due to the classification of the *sattva*, *tamas*, and *rajas* of the body-*vajra*. Libra, Scorpio, and Sagittarius are the yellow, red, and white faces, respectively, due to the classificationof the *tamas*, *rajas*, and *sattva* of the gnosis-*vajra*.

115. The *Abhidharmakośa*, the *Daśabhūmikasūtra*, Nāgārjuna's *Pratītyasamutpādahṛdayakārikā*, etc.

116. Ch. Lindtner, *Nagarjuniana*, 1982, p. 171.

117. The *Kālacakratantra*, Ch. 1, vs. 114–115, and the *Vimalaprabhā*. In the schema that is presented in the *Vimalaprabhā*, there seems to be a discrepancy in the correlation among the solar months, or zodiacs, and lunar months, unless in this case, the lunar months are intentionally calculated in a different way. See also the *Vimalaprabhā* commentary on the *Kālacakratantra*, Ch, 5. v. 127.

118. The *Kālacakratantra*, Ch. 5, v. 137, and the *Vimalaprabhā*.

119. The *Vimalaprabhā* commentary on the *Kālacakratantra*, Ch. 5, v. 127, cites v. 170 from the "Chapter on Gnosis," from the *tantra-rāja*, but it does not specify which *tantra-rāja*. The verse is not from the *Laghukālacakratantra*, the *Guhyasamājatantra*, or the *Hevajratantra*.

120. Lindtner's *Nagarjuniana*, p. 203.

121. The *Mūlamadhyamakakārikā*, Ch. 24, vs. 18–19.

122. The sixteen hundred and twenty *nāḍīs* of the wheel of time in the body correspond to the total number of sixteen hundred and twenty deities of the *kālacakra-maṇḍala*. Of these sixteen hundred and twenty deities, eight hundred and ten are male deities, who are days, and eight hundred and ten are female deities, who are nights. Each group of eight hundred and ten deities has eight hundred and ten *daṇḍas* and thirteen and a half constellations. See the *Kālacakratantra*, Ch. 2, vs. 57–59, and the *Vimalaprabhā*.

123. According to the *Kālacakratantra*, Ch. 2, v. 59, four *nāḍīs* of the *uṣṇīṣa* and sixteen *nāḍīs* of the heart-*cakra* become disturbed by phlegm (*kapha*); thirty-two *nāḍīs* in the throat-*cakra* and eight *nāḍīs* in the heart become disturbed by bile (*pitta*); and sixty-four *nāḍīs* in the navel and secret *cakras* become disturbed by the wind.

124. The *Kālacakratantra*, Ch. 5, v. 190, and the *Vimalaprabhā*.

125. The *Kālacakratantra*, Ch. 5, v. 139, and the *Vimalaprabhā*.

126. The *Vimalaprabhā* commentary on the *Kālacakratantra*, Ch. 5, v. 138.

127. In light of this, the *Vimalaprabhā* commentary on the *Kālacakratantra*, Ch. 5, v. 92, describes emptiness, which is here referred to as the "wheel," in this way: "It is deep (*gambhīra*) because of the absence of the past and future, and it is profound (*udāra*) because of perceiving the past and future."

Appendix

1. See the *Kālacakratantra*, Ch. 3, v. 166, and the *Vimalaprabhā*. The *Vimalaprabhā* offers another alternative to this model by correlating the joints of both upper arms to the *kṣetras* and the joints of both thighs to the *upakṣetras*, and so on.

2. See the *Kālacakratantra*, Ch. 2, v. 47, and the *Vimalaprabhā*.

3. Spring, rainy season, autumn, and winter.

6. The Social Body

1. For example, according to the *Manusmṛti*, I. 98, Brāhmaṇa is the eternal, physical form of Dharma, fit to become one with Brahman.

2. The *Vāseṭṭha Sutta* of *The Suttanipāta*, translated by Saddhatissa, 1985, vs. 14–18 (607–611); the *Śārdulakarṇāvadāna* of the *Divyāvadāna*, 1970, XXXIII, pp. 625–630.

3. The *Vāseṭṭha Sutta* of *The Suttanipāta*, vs. 27, 28, 36, 39.

4. The *Thera and Therī-gāthā*, Dvādasanipāto, 1966, v. 631, p. 64.

5. The *Mahāvagga* of the *Aṅguttara Nikāya*, XIX. 14.

6. The *Majjhima Nikāya*, II. 84. 4.

7. The *Puggalapaññati*, 1969, I.10, p, 19; the *Visuddhimagga*, 1950, IV. 74; the *Majjhimanikāya*, III. 256.

8. The *Puggalapaññati*, 1969, pp. 4–5, fn. 5 and the *Puggalapaññatyatthakathā*. The *Atthasālinī*, III. 109, p. 43: "Does a *gotra-bhū* first see *nirvāṇa*? Just as when a man who has arrived to the king's presence with some task and has seen the king on the elephant's back leaving toward the road was asked: 'Have you seen a king?', since he has not accomplished the task that ought to be accomplished, he answers: 'I have not seen him,' in the same way, upon seen *nirvāṇa*, one says: 'Even though I have seen *nirvāṇa*, it is not a seeing, because of the absence of the eradication of mental afflictions, which is a task to be accomplished."

9. The *Śārdulakarṇāvadāna*, XXXIII, p. 625: "There is only one universal caste in the world and not separate [castes] (*ekaiva jātir 'smin loke sāmānyā na pṛthagvidhā*)." The *Vajrasūci of Aśvaghoṣa*, 1950 (Aśvaghoṣa), vs. 22–30. The *Paramārthaseva*, cited in Bu ston's annotations to the *Kālacakratantra* and the *Vimalaprabhā*, Ch. 2, v. 167.

10. The *Śārdūlakārṇāvadāna* of the *Divyāvadāna*, XXXIII, p. 625: *ekaiva jātir 'smin loke sāmānyā na pṛthagvidhā*, and p. 630: *ekam idaṃ sarvam idam ekam*.

11. The *Divyāvadānam*, 1959, p. 325.

12. *The Divyāvadāna: A Collection of Early Buddhist Legends*, 1970, p. 636.

13. The *Vajrasūci of Aśvaghoṣa*, 1950, pp. 1–3, 9.

14. Ibid., p. 9.

15. Ibid.

16. The *Bodhicittavivaraṇa*, vs. 103, 90, in C. Lindtner, *Nagarjuniana: Studies in the Writings and Philosophy of Nāgārjuna*, 1982, pp. 211, 215.

17. The *Gaṇḍavyūha*, cited in Śāntideva's *Śikṣāsamuccaya*, 1961, Ch. 1. pp. 6–7: "O son the noble family (*kula-putra*), the spirit of awakening is a seed (*bīja*) of all the qualities (*dharma*) of the Buddha. It is a field (*kṣetra*), since it makes the pure qualities (*śukla-dharma*) of the entire world grow. It is soil (*dharaṇi*), since it supports the entire world. It is the father (*pitṛ*), since it protects *bodhisattvas*. . . . It is Vaiśravaṇa, since it eradicates all poverty. It is a king of wish-fulfilling gems (*cintāmaṇi-rājan*), since it accomplishes all goals. It is a lottery vase (*bhadra-ghaṭa*), since it fulfills all expectations. It is power (*śakti*) for the victory over the enemy, mental afflictions (*kleśa*). It is Dharma, since it completely eradicates the fundamental mental engagement (*yoniśo-manaskāra*). It is a sword (*khaḍga*), since it makes the heads of mental afflictions fall. It is an ax (*kuṭhāra*), since it completely cuts off the tree of suffering. It is a weapon (*praharaṇa*), since it defends from all misfortunes. It is a fish-hook (*baḍiśa*), since it pulls out those who live in the waters of *saṃsāra*. It is a whirl-wind (*vāta-maṇḍalī*), since it scatters the grass of all obscurations (*āvaraṇa*) and hindrances (*nīvaraṇa*). It is a summary (*uddāna*), since it compiles all of the aspirations and conducts of a *bodhisattva*. It is a shrine of the worlds of gods, men, and *asuras*. Thus, o son of the noble family, the spirit of awakening is endowed with these and other immeasurable, diverse good qualities."

18. The *Ratnolkadhāraṇī*, cited in Śāntideva's *Śikṣāsamuccaya*, 1961, Ch. 1., p. 5:

> Those who generate the spirit of awakening are engaged in the virtues of great sages (*ṛṣi*). Those who engage in the virtues of great sages are born (*anujāta*) into the Buddha-family for life.

19. The *Śikṣāsamuccaya*, Ch. 1, p. 7: "Furthermore, how can one know that [the statement:] 'the spirit of awakening arises even in the case of an ordinary person' is not a mere phrase? Because it has been demonstrated in many *sūtras*. . . . It is known from the *Ratnakāraṇḍasūtra* that even an ordinary person is a *bodhisattva* (*pṛthagjano 'pi bodhisattvo iti jñāyate*)."

20. The *Dharmadaśakasūtra*, cited in the *Śikṣāsamuccaya*, Ch. 1, p. 8: "Here, o son of the noble family, one who has not yet generated the spirit of awakening but being aroused, taught, and instigated, will generate the spirit of awakening with regard to the supreme, full awakening, dwells in the *bodhisattva-gotra*. This is the first cause for the generation of *bodhicitta*."

21. The *Mahāvyutpatti* (*Buddhist Terminological Dictionary*), 1995, Ch. 58, 1260–1265, p. 100, enumerates the following five *gotras*: the *śrāvakayānābhisamaya-gotra*, *pratyekabuddhayāna-gotra*, *tathāgatayāna-gotra*, *aniyata-gotra*, and *agotra*. The *Saddharmalaṅkāvatārasūtra*, 1963, Ch. 2, 63.2–5, pp. 27–28, also mentions these five *gotras* and describes their characteristics. The *Mahāyānasūtrālaṃkāra*, 1970, Ch. 3, distinguishes (1) the inherent (*prakṛtyā*) and acquired (*paripuṣṭa*) *gotras*, one being the support and the other being the supported; (2) true and unreal *gotras*, one being the cause and the other being the result; (3) the definite (*niyata*) and indefinite (*aniyata*) *gotras*, one that cannot be destroyed by conditions and the other that can be destroyed; and (4) *agotra*, which is devoid of the characteristics of *nirvāṇa*.

22. The *Abhisamayālaṃkāra*, 1992, I, 38–39:

> *Gotra* is the basis of the uniqueness of disciples, of the practice of the ultimate truth, of knowledge and effortless activity.

> A division of *gotra* is inappropriate due to the indivisibility of the *dharma-dhātu*. But its division is mentioned due to the differentiation of its attributed characteristics.

Likewise, Haribhadra in the *Abhisamayālaṃkārāloka* equates the *gotra* with the *dharma-dhātu* and states that the *gotra*, which exists in every individual, is the beginningless outflow of *dharmatā*. See also the *Ratnakūṭa* (cited in the Gser-phreng, I. 246b4–5), and the *Ratnagotravibhāga* E. H. Johnston, ed. and tr.

23. The *Kālacakratantra*, Ch. 5, v. 83, and the *Vimalaprabhā*.

24. The *Kālacakratantra*, Ch. 5, v. 166, and the *Vimalaprabhā*.

25. The *Vimalaprabhā* commentary on the *Kālacakratantra*, Ch. 2, v. 167. See also the *Kālacakratantra*, Ch. 2, v. 162.

26. The *Paramārthaseva*, cited in Bu ston's annotation to the *Vimalaprabhā* commentary on the *Kālacakratantra*, Ch. 2, v. 167.

27. The *Kālacakratantra*, Ch. 5, v. 200, *pada a–c*.

28. The *Vimalaprabhā* commentary on the *Kālacakratantra*, 1986, Ch. 1, p. 19. Cf. the *Guhyasamājatantra*, 1965, p. 116.

29. The *Ādibuddhatantra* cited in the *Vimalaprabhā* commentary on the *Kālacakratantra*, Ch. 1, p. 24.

30. The *Vimalaprabhā* commentary on the *Kālacakratantra*, Ch. 5, v. 127.

31. The *Vimalaprabhā* commentary on the *Kālacakratantra*, Ch. 1, pp. 22, 24.

32. The *Kālacakratantra*, Ch. 1, vs. 159–169.

33. The *Vimalaprabhā* commentary on the *Kālacakratantra*, Ch. 5, v. 127.

34. Ibid.

35. Ibid.

36. See R. C. Majmudar, *The History and Culture of the Indian People: The Struggle for Empire*, 1966, pp. 499–500.

37. The *Vimalaprabhā* commentary on the *Kālacakratantra*, Ch. 1, pp. 24–28.

38. The *Vimalaprabhā* commentary on the *Kālacakratantra*, Ch. 1, p. 41.

39. Ibid.

40. See the *Kālacakratantra*, Ch. 4, v. 100, and the *Vimalaprabhā* commentary. During the process of empowering his own body, mind, and speech, the tantric adept appropriates his true identity by reciting the following: "Oṃ, I consist of the nature of the body, speech, and mind of all the Tathāgatas" (*oṃ sarva-tathāgata-kāya-vāc-citta-svabhāvātmako 'ham*); "Oṃ, I consist of the nature of the *vajra* of gnosis and emptiness" (*oṃ śūnyatā-jñāna-vajra-svabhāvātmako 'ham*); and "Oṃ, I consist of the purified sphere of reality" (*oṃ viśuddha-dharma-dhātu-svabhāvātmako 'ham*).

41. The *Vimalaprabhā* commentary on the *Kālacakratantra*, Ch. 3, v. 36.

42. See the *Vimalaprabhā* commentary on the *Kālacakratantra*, Ch. 5, v. 127.

43. The *Vimalaprabhā* commentary on the *Kālacakratantra*, Ch. 1, v. 1, p. 40.

44. Ibid.

45. Ibid., p. 34.

46. Cf. the *Vyākhyāyukti*, cited in E. Obermiller, *The Jewelry of the Scripture By Bu-ston*, 1987, p. 28, which states that the word of the Buddha is fit for all the forms of verbal expression, because it accommodates itself to the forms and character of every kind of grammar (*sarva-śabdānupraviṣṭā sarva-vyākaraṇa-sarvākāra-lakṣaṇānupraviṣṭāt*).

47. The *Paramādibuddhatantra*, cited in the *Vimalaprabhā* commentary on the *Kālacakratantra*, 1986, Ch. 1, pp. 24–25.

48. See the *Vimalaprabhā* commentary on the *Kālacakratantra*, 1986, Ch. 1, pp. 15–16.

49. Ibid., p. 16.

50. The *Hevajratantra*, 1976, Part 2, Ch. 3, vs. 46–48, Ch. 11, v. 8; Part 1, Ch. 6, v. 4.

51. The *Caṇḍamahāroṣaṇatantra*, 1974, Ch. 7, pp. 32, 79. Cf. the *Guhyasamājatantra*, Ch. 5, vs. 2–3, 6–7.

52. The *Vimalaprabhā* commentary on the *Kālacakratantra*, Ch. 5, v. 127.

53. The *Kālacakratantra*, Ch. 3, v. 83.

54. See the *Kālacakratantra*, Ch. 3, v. 98, together with the *Vimalaprabhā*.

55. The *Vimalaprabhā* commentary on the *Kālacakratantra*, Ch. 5, v. 127.

56. Ibid.

57. The *Paramādibuddhatantra*, cited in the *Vimalaprabhā* commentary on the *Kālacakratantra*, 1986, Ch. 1, p. 7.

58. The *Kālacakratantra*, Ch. 4, v. 221.

59. The *Kālacakratantra*, Ch. 4, v. 208.

60. The *Kālacakratantra*, Ch. 5, v. 118.

61. The *Vimalaprabhā* commentary on the *Kālacakratantra*, Ch. 3, v. 198.

62. The *Paramādibuddhatantra*, cited in the *Vimalaprabhā* commentary on the *Kālacakratantra*, Ch. 3, v. 119.

63. The *Vimalaprabhā* commentary on the *Kālacakratantra*, Ch. 3, v. 98.

64. See the *Bodhipathapradīpa of Dīpaṃkara Śrījñāna*, 1995, vs. 63–65, p. 98.

65. The *Vimalaprabhā* commentary on the *Kālacakratantra*, Ch. 3, v. 86.

66. The *Kālacakratantra*, Ch. 3, v. 138, and the *Vimalaprabhā*.

67. The *Bṛhaddharma Purāṇa*, II. 13–14, also mentions thirty-six mixed castes in India.

68. See the *Kālacakratantra*, Ch. 3, vs. 125–127, and the *Vimalaprabhā*.

69. See Ibid., vs. 157–168, and the *Vimalaprabhā*.

70. The *Vimalaprabhā* commentary on the *Kālacakratantra*, Ch. 3, v. 154.

71. According to the *Vedavyāsasmṛti*, among others, the cobblers (*carmakara*), Bhillas, washermen (*rajaka*), dancers and actors (*naṭas*), and Caṇḍālas, which are included in the *Kālacakratantra*'s *gaṇa-cakra*, are listed as outcasts (*antyaja*). See Kane, *The History of Dharmaśāstra*, vol. 1, part 1, p. 71.

72. Ḍombas and Caṇḍālas are used interchangeably in the *Vimalaprabhā*. According to Albiruni's (1020 CE) report from his travels in India, Ḍombas and Caṇḍālas were considered as a single social class and were distinguished only by their occupations.

73. See the *Hevajratantra*, Part 1, Ch. 5, v. 18, and the *Yogaratnamālā*.

74. In the *Hevajratantra*, Nairātmyā, or the Bhagavatī, the principal female deity is identified as Ḍombī.

75. For the translation of Kāṇha's songs, see Sh. Bh. Dasgupta, *Obscure Religious Cults*, 1962, pp. 96–106.

76. The *Kulārṇavatantra*, Ch. 14, v. 91.

77. Ibid., Ch. 8, v. 101.

78. The *Paramādibuddhatantra*, cited in the *Vimalaprabhā* commentary on the *Kālacakratantra*, Ch. 3, v. 3.

79. The *Vimalaprabhā* commentary on the *Kālacakratantra*, Ch. 3, v. 105.

80. The *Vimalaprabhā* commentary on the *Kālacakratantra*, Ch. 3, v. 3, cites the *Ācāryaparīkṣā*, which states:

> Owing to the complete knowledge of ten principles, among the three, a monk is superior, a so-called wandering ascetic is middling, and a householder is inferior to these two.

81. The *Kālacakratantra*, Ch. 3, v. 4, and the *Vimalaprabhā*. The five ethical precepts refer to the first five Buddhist precepts common for all Buddhists, lay and monastic, namely, abstinence from killing, from stealing, from sexual misconduct, from false speech, and from taking intoxicants.

82. The *Kālacakratantra*, Ch. 5, vs. 50–51.
83. See also R. Lingat, *The Classical Law of India*, 1973, p. 30.
84. The *Kālacakratantra*, Ch. 4, v. 156, Ch. 5, vs. 48–49, 52.
85. The *Kālacakratantra*, Ch. 2, v. 161, and the *Vimalaprabhā*.
86. The *Kālacakratantra*, Ch. 4, vs. 201–204.
87. See the *Kālacakratantra*, Ch. 4, vs. 129–130.
88. The *Kālacakratantra*, Ch. 4, v. 211.
89. The *Kālacakratantra*, Ch. 4, vs. 217–219.
90. The *Hevajratantra*, Part 2, Ch. 8, v. 45.
91. Ibid., Ch. 2, v. 44.
92. The *Vimalaprabhā* commentary on the *Kālacakratantra*, Ch. 1, vs. 1–2.
93. The *Kālacakratantra*, Ch. 5, v. 47, and the *Vimalaprabhā*.
94. According to the *Kālacakratantra*, Ch. 3, v. 7, and the *Vimalaprabhā*, the white soil of the Brāhmaṇa class has a divine smell, the red soil of the Kṣatriya class has a lotus-scent and a hot taste, the yellow soil of the Vaiśya class has a pungent smell and a sweet and saline taste, the black soil of the Śūdra class has a putrid smell and a sour taste, and the green soil of the Ḍomba class incorporates all colors, smells, and tastes.
95. The *Kālacakratantra*, Ch. 3, v. 43, and the *Vimalaprabhā*.
96. For the classification of the *yoginīs* of the *kālacakra-maṇḍala* in terms of social groups, see the *Kālacakratantra*, Ch. 3, vs. 144–147.
97. See the *Kālacakratantra*, Ch. 2, v. 51, and the *Vimalaprabhā*.

7. The Gnostic Body

1. Hans Jonas, *The Gnostic Religion: The Message of the Alien God and the Beginnings of Christianity*, 1963, p. 32.
2. The *Gospel of Thomas*, 45. 30–33, cited in Elaine Pagels, *The Gnostic Gospels*, 1979, p. 126.
3. The *Trimorphic Protennoia*, 36. 12–16, cited in Pagels, *The Gnostic Gospels*, p. 55.
4. The *Apocryphon of John*, II 31, 3–9, cited Michael A. Williams, *Rethinking "Gnosticism": An Argument for Dismantling a Dubious Category*, 1996, p. 121.
5. The *Gospel of Thomas*, 42. 7–51, cited in Pagels, *The Gnostic Gospels*, p. 128.
6. *Book of Thomas the Contender*, 138. 13, cited in ibid., p. 131.
7. The *Kālacakratantra*, Ch. 5, v. 196.
8. *The Testimony of Truth*, 44. 2, 43. 26, cited in Pagels, *The Gnostic Gospels*, p. 132.
9. The *Dialogue of the Savior*, 134. 1–2, in Nag Hammadi Library 234, cited in Pagels, *The Gnostic Gospels*, p. 126.
10. The *Gospel of Thomas*, 37. 20–35, cited in ibid., p. 129.
11. For example, in the *Adversus Haereses*, 1.24.4–5, Irenaeus accuses Basilideans of eating meat that was offered to idols, of treating all sorts of behavior as morally neutral, and of resorting to magic, incantations and other occult practices.
12. Ugo Bianchi, ed., *Le Origini Dello Gnosticismo: Colloquio de Messina, 13–18 Aprile 1966*, Studies in the History of Religions (Supplements to *Numen*), vol. 12, 1970, p. 27.
13. The *Vimalaprabhā* commentary on the *Kālacakratantra*, Ch. 2, v. 13, Ch. 3, v. 1: *mantraṃ jñānam iti manastrāṇabhūtatvāt*. Cf. the *Guhyasamājatantra*, 1965, vs. 69cd–70ab.
14. Williams, *Rethinking "Gnosticism,"* p. 41.
15. Pagels, *The Gnostic Gospels*, p. xxi.
16. See E. Conze, "Buddhism and Gnosis," 1996.
17. Helmut Hoffmann, "*Kālacakra* Studies I: Manicheism, Christianity and Islam in the *Kālacakratantra*," *Central Asiatic Journal* (13: 52–73, 1969). H. Hoffmann, *Tibet: A Handbook*, 1975.

18. See Hans-Joachim Klimkeit, *Gnosis on the Silk Road: Gnostic Texts from Central Asia*, 1993, p. 3.

19. The army's four divisions are: the elephants, horses, chariots, and footmen.

20. See the *Kālacakratantra*, Ch. 2, vs. 48–50 and the *Vimalaprabhā*.

21. See the *Kephalaia*, 70, 175. 6–14, 38, 96. 13–27, 96. 27–97. 22, cited in Jason Beduhn, "Metabolism of Salvation: The Manichean Body in Ascesis and Ritual," 1995, pp. 203, 206–207.

22. The *Kephalaia*, 38, 100. 1–6, cited in ibid., p. 207.

23. The *Vimalaprabhā*, 1986, Ch. 1, pp. 18, 19: *vajradharajñānakāyasākṣibhūtayā nāmasaṃgityāliṅgitam iti.*

24. The *Vimalaprabhā* commentary on the *Kālacakratantra*, Ch. 4, v. 234.

25. See the *Vimalaprabhā* commentary on the *Kālacakratantra*, Ch. 2, vs. 51–52, which indicates that the male and female deities of the *Māyājālatantra* and the *Samājatantra* are included in the *kālacakra-maṇḍala*. It also categorizes the *Māyājālatantra* as being of three kinds and the *Samājatantra* as being of six kinds.

26. The *Mañjuśrīnāmasaṃgīti*, vs. 7, 13.

27. The *Mañjuśrīnāmasaṃgīti*, v. 144, line *b*: *pañcākṣaro mahāśūnyo binduśūnyaḥ ṣaḍakṣaraḥ*. Ronald Davidson's edition of the *Mañjuśrīnāmasaṃgīti* incorrectly reads the "one hundred syllable" (*śatākṣaraḥ*) instead of the "six syllable" (*ṣaḍakṣaraḥ*). The *Ādibuddhatantra*, cited in the *Vimalaprabhā* commentary on the *Kālacakratantra*, 1986, Ch. 1, p. 33: *pañcākṣaraṃ mahāśūnyaṃ binduśūnyaṃ ṣaḍakṣaram.*

28. The *Vimalaprabhā* commentary on the *Kālacakratantra*, 1986, Ch. 1, p. 42: *iṣṭārthaphaladaḥ phalam akṣarasukhaṃ jñānacittam.*

29. The *Vimalaprabhā* commentary on the *Kālacakratantra*, 1986, Ch. 1, p. 44. Cf. the *Mañjuśrīnāmasaṃgīti*, v. 100, where the Ādibuddha is said to be without partiality (*niranvaya*). Ronald Davidson translates the term *niranvaya* as "without causal connection" on the basis of the explanation of the term in commentaries on this verse of the *Mañjuśrīnāmasaṃgīti* and the Tibetan translation of it as "causeless" (*rgyu med*).

30. Ibid.

31. The *Ādibuddhatantra*, cited in the *Vimalaprabhā* commentary on the *Kālacakratantra*, 1986, Ch. 1, p. 44.

32. The *Vimalaprabhā* commentary on the *Kālacakratantra*, Ch. 5, v. 127.

33. The *Vimalaprabhā* commentary on the *Kālacakratantra*, 1986, Ch. 1, p. 43.

34. The *Vimalaprabhā* commentary on the *Kālacakratantra*, Ch. 5, v. 127, supports this view of gnosis as self-aware with verse 155 of the *Mañjuśrīnāmasaṃgīti*, which describes Vajrasattva as self-knowing (*ātma-vid*) and knowing others (*para-vid*). Cf. the *Hevajratantra*, Part 1, Ch. 8, v. 46, which characterizes the supreme bliss (*mahā-sukha*) as self-aware (*sva-saṃvedya*), and v. 51, line *a*, which states: "Self-awareness is this gnosis, which is beyond the scope of words." The *Yogaratnamālā*, 1976, p. 129, commenting on this line from the *Hevajratantra*, explains that self-awareness implies that gnosis cannot be described by someone else, but that it is to be known by oneself.

35. The *Vimalaprabhā* commentary on the *Kālacakratantra*, Ch. 5, v. 127.

36. Ibid.

37. The *Vimalaprabhā* commentary on the *Kālacakratantra*, 1986, Ch. 1, p. 43.

38. The *Vimalaprabhā* commentary on the *Kālacakratantra*, Ch. 4, v. 55.

39. This is a translation of the Sanskrit text cited in Matsumoto Shirō's article, "The Doctrine of *Tathāgata-garbha* is not Buddhist," in *Pruning the Bodhi Tree: The Storm over Critical Buddhism*, 1997, p. 171:

anādikāliko dhātuḥ sarvadharmasamāśrayaḥ
tasmin sati gatiḥ sarvā nirvāṇādhigamo 'pi ca.

40. The *Kālacakratantra*, Ch. 2, v. 3, and the *Vimalaprabhā*.

41. The *Kālacakratantra*, Ch. 2, v. 20, and the *Vimalaprabhā*.

42. The *Kālacakratantra*, Ch. 2, v. 3-c: *śūnye jñānaṃ vimiśraṃ bhavati samarasaṃ cākṣaraṃ śāśvataṃ ca*.

43. According to the *Vimalaprabhā* commentary on the *Kālacakratantra*, Ch. 5, v. 127, a sprout does not arise from a nonperished seed nor does it arise from a perished seed. Likewise, it neither arises from abandoning its own nature, nor from the unconscious element, nor from the absence of annihilation.

44. The *Vimalaprabhā* commentary on the *Kālacakratantra*, Ch. 5, v. 127.

45. The *Vimalaprabhā* commentary on the *Kālacakratantra*, Ch. 2, v. 3.

46. The *Sekoddeśa*, 1994, v. 148.

47. Ibid., v. 151, line *b*.

48. The *Vimalaprabhā* commentary on the *Kālacakratantra*, Ch. 4, v. 106.

49. The *Kālacakratantra*, Ch. 2, v. 2, and the *Vimalaprabhā*.

50. The *Vimalaprabhā* commentary on the *Kālacakratantra*, 1986, Ch. 1, p. 43: *ataḥ saṃvṛtiḥ śūnyatārūpiṇī śūnyatā saṃvṛtirūpiṇī*.

51. The *Kālacakratantra*, Ch. 4, v. 6, lines *a–b*.

52. See the *Vimalaprabhā* commentary on the *Kālacakratantra*, Ch. 5, v. 47.

53. The *Vimalaprabhā* commentary on the *Kālacakratantra*, Ch. 1, p. 43. Cf. The *Mañjuśrīnāmasaṃgīti*, v. 99, line *a*: *vijñānadharmatātīto jñānam advayarūpadhṛk*.

54. The *Paramādibuddha* cited in the *Vimalaprabhā*, 1986, Ch. 1, pp. 17, 32, 43.

55. The *Paramādibuddha* cited in the *Vimalaprabhā*, Ch. 1, p. 32: *kāyavākcittarāgātmā vajrasattvo adhidevatā*. Cf. the *Mañjuśrīnāmasaṃgīti*, v. 166, line *a*:

> Foremost as the inherent nature of all phenomena, he maintains the inherent nature of all phenomena.

56. The *Vimalaprabhā* commentary on the *Kālacakratantra*, 1986, Ch. 1, p. 17: *paramādibuddhaḥ ekakṣaṇapañcākāraviṃśatyākāramāyājālābhisaṃbodhilakṣaṇo 'kṣarasukhaḥ paramaḥ*.

57. Ibid., Ch. 1, p. 44: *yadā kṣaṇadharmarahitaṃ cittaṃ niḥsvabhāvam ity ucyate*.

58. Ibid., Ch. 1, p. 45: *ekānekakṣaṇarahitaṃ jñānaṃ tattvam ity ucyate jinaiḥ*.

59. The *Kālacakratantra*, Ch. 4, v. 223.

60. Ibid., Ch. 4, v. 228.

61. The *Prajñāpāramitāpiṇḍārtha* (Tangyur, *mdo*, vol. 14), v. 1:

> *prajñāpāramitā jñānam advayaṃ sa tathāgataḥ*
> *sādhyatādārthyayogena tācchabdyaṃ granthamārgayoḥ*.

The Sanskrit version of the verse is taken from Th. Stcherbatsky and E. Obermiller, eds., *Abhisamayālaṃkāra-Prajñāpāramitā-Upadeśa-Śāstra: The Work of Bodhisattva Maitreya*, Bibliotheca Indo-Buddhica Series, vol. 99, 1992: vi.

62. The *Vimalaprabhā* commentary on the *Kālacakratantra*, Ch. 5, v. 65.

63. The *Vimalaprabhā* commentary on the *Kālacakratantra*, 1986, Ch. 1, p. 45.

64. The *Mañjuśrīnāmasaṃgīti*, v. 109: *vajrendu-vimala-prabha*.

65. See the *Vimalaprabhā* commentary on the *Kālacakratantra*, Ch. 5, v. 124. The cited description of Mañjuśrī as one who knows the reality with sixteen aspects (*ṣoḍaśākāra-tattvavid*) is given in v. 133 of the *Mañjuśrīnāmasaṃgīti*.

66. See the *Kālacakratantra*, Ch. 3, vs. 123–124, and the *Vimalaprabhā*.

67. The *Kālacakratantra*, Ch. 5, v. 99.

68. The *Mañjuśrīnāmasaṃgīti*, v. 109: *vajra-sūryo mahālokaḥ*.

69. The *Vimalaprabhā* commentary on the *Kālacakratantra*, Ch. 5, v. 124.

70. The *Vimalaprabhā* commentary on the *Kālacakratantra*, Ch. 4, v. 56.

71. The *Kālacakratantra*, Ch. 2, v. 27, and the *Vimalaprabhā*.

72. The *Vimalaprabhā* commentary on the *Kālacakratantra*, 1986, Ch. 1, p. 45.

73. See the *Kālacakratantra*, Ch. 5, v. 62.

74. Ibid., Ch. 5, vs. 56–57.

75. Naḍapāda, *Sekoddeśaṭīkā*, 1941, pp. 6–7.

76. Ibid.

77. The *Ādibuddhatantra*, cited in the *Vimalaprabhā* commentary on the *Kālacakratantra*, Ch. 5, v. 127.

78. The *Kālacakratantra*, Ch. 5, vs. 102–103.

79. Ibid., Ch. 5, v. 98.

80. The *Vimalaprabhā* commentary on the *Kālacakratantra*, Ch. 5, v. 127.

81. Ibid.

82. The five indestructibles (*pañcākṣara*) refer to the five Buddhas.

83. The *Vimalaprabhā* commentary on the *Kālacakratantra*, Ch. 5, v. 127.

84. The *Kālacakratantra*, Ch, 5, vs. 60–61. The *Vimalaprabhā* commentary on the *Kālacakratantra*, Ch. 5, v. 92 and the cited *Ādibuddhatantra*.

85. See the *Nāmasaṃgītivṛtti*, Peking ed. of the *Tibetan Tripiṭaka* 1956, ed. by D. T. Suzuki, vol. 74, pp. 171.1.1–184.4.8. The sixteen types of emptiness are listed in the *Vimalaprabhā* commentary on the *Kālacakratantra*, 1986, Ch. 1, p. 21, as the emptiness of the five aggregates (*skandha*), which is classified under the category of *śūnyatā*; the emptiness of the five elements (*dhātu*), which is classified under the category of *mahāśūnyatā*; the emptiness of the five sense-faculties, which is classified under the category of *paramārthaśūnyatā*; and as emptiness having all aspects (*sarvākāra*), which is the sixteenth emptiness.

86. The *Vimalaprabhā* commentary on the *Kālacakratantra*, Ch. 4, v. 114. Verse 133 of the *Mañjuśrīnāmasaṃgīti* speaks of the omniscient Buddha knowing the reality with twelve aspects, the reality with sixteen aspects, and the reality with twenty aspects.

87. Naḍapāda, *Sekoddeśaṭīkā*, 1941, pp. 6–7.

88. The *Vimalaprabhā* commentary on the *Kālacakratantra*, 1986, Ch, 1, p. 45.

89. Naḍapāda, *Sekoddeśaṭīkā*, 1941, pp. 6–7.

90. The *Vimalaprabhā* commentary on the *Kālacakratantra*, 1986, Ch, 1, p. 45.

91. Ibid.

92. Naḍapāda, *Sekoddeśaṭīkā*, 1941, pp. 5–6.

93. The *Vimalaprabhā* commentary on the *Kālacakratantra*, 1986, Ch. 1, p. 46; the *Kālacakratantra*, Ch. 5, v. 98.

94. The *Vimalaprabhā* commentary on the *Kālacakratantra*, Ch. 4, v. 234.

95. The *Vimalaprabhā* commentary on the *Kālacakratantra*, Ch. 4, v, 97; Ch. 2, v. 15.

96. The *Kālacakratantra*, Ch. 2, vs. 14–16 with the *Vimalaprabhā* commentary. The *Vimalaprabhā* commentary on the *Kālacakratantra*, Ch. 4, v. 97.

97. The *Vimalaprabhā* commentary on the *Kālacakratantra*, Ch. 5, v. 127.

98. The *Vimalaprabhā* commentary on the *Kālacakratantra*, 1986, Ch. 1, p. 43.

99. Ibid.

100. See the *Vimalaprabhā* commentary on the *Kālacakratantra*, 1986, Ch. 1, p. 46; Ch. 3, p. 80; Ch. 4, p. 149.

101. The *Abhisamayālaṃkāraprajñāpāramitopadeśaśāstra*, 1992, Ch. 1, v. 18.

102. For the excellent discussion on the Yogācāra's and Abhidharma's interpretations of the Svābhāvikakāya of the *Abhisamayālaṃkāra*, see John Makransky's *Buddhahood Embodied: Sources of Controversy in India and Tibet*, 1997.

103. The *Abhisamayālaṃkāra*, Ch. 8, v. 1.

104. The *Vimalaprabhā* commentary on the *Kālacakratantra*, 1986, Ch. 1, p. 23: *buddhatvaṃ nāma saṃsāravāsanārahitaṃ cittam/ tathā ca bhagavān āha prajñāpāramitāyām asti tac citaṃ*

yac citam acittam iti/ prakṛtiprabhāsvaraṃ tad eva saṃsāravāsanārahitam ato māraḥ samalaṃ cittaṃ buddho vigatamalaṃ cittam.

105. The *Vimalaprabhā* commentary on the *Kālacakratantra*, 1986, Ch. 1, p. 42.

106. See Makransky, *Buddhahood Embodied*, p. 261. The *Vimalaprabhā* commentary on the *Kālacakratantra*, 1986, Ch. 1, p. 39.

107. See Makransky, *Buddhahood Embodied*, p. 266.

108. The *Vimalaprabhā* commentary on the *Kālacakratantra*, 1986, Ch. 1, p. 149.

109. Ibid., Ch. 1, p. 35.

110. Ibid., Ch. 1, p. 39.

111. See the *Kālacakratantra*, Ch. 2, v. 173 with the *Vimalaprabhā* commentary.

112. The *Kālacakratantra*, Ch. 5, v. 66, line *a*:

sattvā buddhā na buddhas tv apara iha mahān vidyate lokadhātau.

113. The *Kālacakratantra*, Ch. 5, v. 66.

114. The *Mañjuśrīnāmasaṃgīti*, v. 138:

sarvasattvamano'ntasthas taccittasamatāṃ gataḥ
sarvasattvamanohlādī sarvasattvamanoratiḥ.

115. The *Hevajratantra*, 1976, Part 2, Ch. 4, vs. 74–75.

116. The *Lakṣābhidhāna*, cited in the *Vimalaprabhā* commentary on the *Kālacakratantra*, Ch. 1, v. 1:

rahasye sarvadūtīnāṃ sarvasattvātmani sthitaḥ
sarvadūtīmayaḥ sattvo vajrasattvo mahāsukhaḥ.

117. The *Yogānuviddhatantra*, cited in the *Vimalaprabhā* commentary on the *Kālacakratantra*, Ch, 1, v. 1, has a somewhat corrupt reading:

ḍākinīvajrapadmasta eko 'asāv adhidevatā
sahajānandarūpeṇa saṃsthitās tribhavātmani.

118. See *A Guide to the Bodhisattva Way of Life*, 1997, p. 127, or the *Bodhicaryāvatāra* of Śāntideva, 1960, where the mentioned statement belongs to verse 104, pp. 244–245.

119. Taishō, no. 666, 16: 457b28–457c3.

120. The *Saddharmalaṅkāvatārasūtra*, 1963, 2: 33.

121. The *Mahāyānasūtrālaṃkāra*, 1970, Ch. 9, v. 37, line *b* reads: *tad garbhā sarvadehinaḥ* (the embryo of that [Tathāgatahood] is all embodied beings). This statement is explained in the *Mahāyānasūtrālaṃkārabhāṣya*, Ch. 9, v. 37, in the following way: "Hence, all sentient beings are called the wombs of the *tathāgata*" (*ataḥ sarve sattvās tathāgatagarbhā ity ucyate*).

122. See the Tibetan translation of the *Mahāparinirvāṇasūtra* in the Peking ed., no. 788: 99*ab*-7.

123. See the *Hevajratantra*, 1976, Part 2, Ch. 4, v. 73, line *a*, which reads: "There is not a single sentient being that is not spiritually awakened due to perfectly awakening to its own nature."

124. The *Kālacakratantra*, Ch. 2, v. 91, lines *c-d*.

125. The *Kālacakratantra*, Ch. 5, v. 55, line *d*.

126. The *Ratnagotravibhāga*, Takasaki, 1966, Ch. 9, pp. 268, 277.

127. The *Śrīmālādevī*, 1974, Ch. 3, 106: *kṣaṇikaṃ bhagavan kuśalaṃ cittaṃ na kleśaiḥ saṃkliśyate / kṣaṇikam akuśalaṃ cittaṃ na saṃkliṣṭam eva tac cittaṃ kleśaiḥ/ na bhagavan kleśās tac cittaṃ spṛśanti.*

128. The *Sekoddeśa*, 1994, vs. 129–133.

129. The *Sekoddeśa*, vs. 122–123.

130. The *Vimalaprabhā* commentary on the *Kālacakratantra*, Ch. 5, v. 127.

131. Ibid.

132. The *Vimalaprabhā* commentary on the *Kālacakratantra*, Ch. 2, v. 91.

133. Ibid.

134. Cf. *Śikṣāsamuccaya*, 1961, p. 12: "Thus, when there is a spiritual ignorance, attachment, hatred, and delusion arise with regard to the sense-objects." A similar view is also held by the Sarvāstivāda school. E.g., the *Abhidharmakośa*, 1988, vol. 2, p. 402, reads: "All defilements accompany ignorance and are activated through ignorance." On the other hand, in the earliest Buddhist literature, one invariably encounters craving (*taṅhā*) and spiritual ignorance as the direct and primary causes of mental afflictions.

135. The *Kālacakratantra*, Ch. 2, v. 44.

136. The *Vimalaprabhā* commentary on the *Kālacakratantra*, Ch. 3, v. 2 reads: *rāgadveṣamohamānerṣyāmātsāryasamūhaḥ kaluṣam*. Cf. The Book of Analysis: Vibhaṅga, 1969, 232, 249: "Defilements are named this way because they make the body and mind to be afflicted and suffer"; the *Abhidharamkośa*, 1991, vol. 3, p. 113: "Mental afflictions (*kleśa*) are secondary mental afflictions (*upakleśa*) because they defile the mind."

137. The *Kālacakratantra*, 1986, Ch. 2, v. 23, and the *Vimalaprabhā*.

138. The *Kālacakratantra*, Ch. 5, v. 143, and the *Vimalaprabhā*.

139. The *Vimalaprabhā* commentary on the *Kālacakratantra*, Ch. 5, v. 65.

140. The *Kālacakratantra*, Ch. 2, v. 19, and the *Vimalaprabhā*.

141. The *Vimalaprabhā* commentary on the *Kālacakratantra*, Ch. 2, v. 19.

142. Ibid.

143. The *Vimalaprabhā* commentary on the *Kālacakratantra*, Ch. 5, v. 76; Ch. 1, p. 23.

144. The *Kālacakratantra*, Ch. 5, v. 68.

145. The *Kālacakratantra*, Ch. 5, v. 67.

146. According to the *Vimalaprabhā* on the *Kālacakratantra*, Ch, 5. v. 127, the obscurations of the body are the Skandha Māra; the obscurations of the mind are the Mṛtyu Māra; the obscurations of speech are the Kleśa Māra; and the prevalence of spiritual ignorance with regard to the world is the Devaputra Māra.

147. The *Vimalaprabhā* on the *Kālacakratantra*, Ch, 5. v. 127.

148. Ibid.: "Due to the cessation (*nirodha*) of the habitual propensity of the perishable [moment], there is a cessation of attachment, hatred, delusion, anger, and spiritual ignorance. Likewise, there is a sequential cessation of the twelve limbs [of dependent origination]. Due to the cessation of the twelve limbs, there is a cessation of the cycle of existence (*bhava-cakra*). Due to the cessation of the cycle of existence, there is Buddhahood, which is free of obscurations."

149. Ibid.

150. See Nāgārjuna's *Śūnyatāsaptatikārikā*, v. 37, in C. Lindtner, *Nagarjuniana*, 1982, p. 51.

151. The *Kālacakratantra*, Ch. 2, v. 82.

152. Ibid., Ch. 2, v. 83, and the *Vimalaprabhā*.

153. See ibid., Ch. 2, vs. 86–88, and the *Vimalaprabhā*.

154. The *Kālacakratantra*, Ch. 4, v. 219, line *d*: *tasmād eṣaḥ svakāyaḥ samasukho nilayo rakṣaṇīyaḥ parasya*.

155. The *Sekoddeśa*, 1994, v. 134.

156. The *Kālacakratantra*, Ch. 5, v. 70.

157. So far, I have been unable to identify the original source of this verse cited in the *Vimalaprabhā* commentary on the *Kālacakratantra*, Ch. 4, v. 124. It is possible that it is taken from the *Ādibuddhatantra*.

158. The *Vimalaprabhā* on the *Kālacakratantra*, 1976, Ch. 1, p. 4. Cf. the *Hevajratantra*, 1976, Part 2, Ch. 2, v. 50, which states that just as those who are burnt by fire treat the burn

with fire, so too those who are burnt by the fire of passion cure themselves by the fire of passion.

159. The *Sekoddeśa*, v. 135.

160. See the *Kālacakratantra*, Ch. 4, v. 110, and the *Vimalaprabhā*.

161. The *Sekoddeśa*, vs. 139–140.

162. The *Vimalaprabhā* commentary on the *Kālacakratantra*, 1986, Ch. 1, pp. 5–6.

163. The *Kālacakratantra*, Ch. 5, v. 71:

> The grape does not come from the *nimba* tree, nor ambrosia from poison, nor a lotus from the *udumbara* tree, nor the bliss of *nirvāṇa* from space, nor virtue from the power of non-virtue, nor *siddhis* from harming living beings, nor heaven from sacrificing animals, nor the supreme state of Śiva from restraining the sense-faculties, nor the omniscient language from the Vedas, nor the indestructible, immovable bliss from the mind that is not purified from the perishable [bliss].

164. The *Kālacakratantra*, Ch. 5, v. 199, line *c*.

165. The *Vimalaprabhā* commentary on the *Kālacakratantra*, Ch. 5, v. 127.

166. Cf. the *Hevajratantra*, Part 2, Ch. 2: 51, which states: "The world is bound by passion, and it is also released by passion."

167. The *Kālacakratantra*, Ch. 4, v. 224. Cf. the *Paramārthasevā*, cited by Bu ston [311], which reads:

> Fire and mercury are always enemies. Without fire there is no cohesiveness of mercury. Because it is non-cohesive, it does not transmute metals. Because metals are not transmuted, they do not become gold. Because they have not become gold, a substance is not improved. Due to the low quality of a substance, there is a lack of enjoyment in it. . . . "

168. According to the *Vimalaprabhā* commentary on the *Kālacakratantra*, Ch. 5, v. 127, there are five states of mercury: vapor (*dhūma*), *ciṭi-ciṭi* [sound], the jump of a frog, tremor, and motionlessness.

169. Ibid.

170. Ibid. Cf. the *Vajraśekharamahāguhyayogatantra*, Peking ed., no. 113, vol. 5, 4.3.7–8, which interprets the meaning of Vajrasattva in this way: "Gnosis of supreme spiritual awakening is called '*vajra*.' He who arises from the gnosis-*vajra* is called 'Vajrasattva.'" According to Naḍapāda's *Sekoddeśaṭīkā*, 1941, p. 73, the term *vajra* in the compound Vajrasattva refers to the indivisible (*abhedya*), empty form (*śūnya-bimba*), and the term *sattva* designates him "who is called the unity of the *rūpa-kāya*, speech, and mind in the desire-realm (*kāma-dhātu*), etc."

171. This verse from the fifth chapter of the *Ādibuddhatantra* is cited in the *Vimalaprabhā* commentary on the *Kālacakratantra*, Ch. 5, v. 127. Cf. the *Hevajratantra*, Part 1, Ch. 1, v. 4:

> *Vajra* is said to be indivisible (*abhedya*), and a being (*sattva*) is the unity (*ekatā*) of the three worlds. By means of this wisdom, it is known as Vajrasattva.

The *Yogaratnamālā*, commenting on this verse, identifies the *vajra* with emptiness, and it interprets a being (*sattva*) as a phenomenon consisting of the five psycho-physical aggregates.

172. The *Vimalaprabhā* commentary on the *Kālacakratantra*, 1986, Ch. 1, pp. 16–17. Cf. the *Yogaratnamālā* commentary on the *Hevajratantra*, 1976, Part 1, Ch. 1, v. 1, pp. 103–104, which interprets the word *evaṃ* in two ways: (1) as the union of the two sexual organs, the letter *e* designating the female sexual organ (*bhaga*), and the syllabe *vaṃ* denoting the male sexual organ (*vajra*); (2) and as the unity of two elements, two *mudrās*, and two *cakras*, the letter *e* being the earth-element, the *karma-mudrā*, and the *nirmāṇa-cakra*, and the syllable *vaṃ* being the water-element, the *dharma-mudrā*, and the *dharma-cakra*.

8. *The Transformative Body*

1. The *Vimalaprabhā* commentary on the *Kālacakratantra*, Ch. 4, v. 115.

2. The *Vimalaprabhā* commentary on the *Kālacakratantra*, Ch. 3, v. 1.

3. See the *Kālacakratantra*, Ch. 5, vs. 111–112, and the *Vimalaprabhā*.

4. The *Kālacakratantra*, Ch. 3, v. 5 and the *Vimalaprabhā*.

5. The *Vimalaprabhā* commentary on the *Kālacakratantra*, Ch. 3, v. 96, the *Kālacakratantra*, Ch. 3, vs. 99–100, and the *Vimalaprabhā*. According to the *Vimalaprabhā* commentary on the *Kālacakratantra*, Ch. 3, v. 97, in other related *tantras*, such as the *Guhyasamājatantra*, the first five initiations are designed to purify the five psycho-physical aggregates, respectively.

6. The *Vimalaprabhā* commentary on the *Kālacakratantra*, Ch. 3, v. 96.

7. The *Kālacakratantra*, Ch. 3, vs. 96–97, 99–100, and the *Vimalaprabhā*.

8. See the *Kālacakratantra*, Ch. 3, vs. 96–97, 99, and the *Vimalaprabhā*. Cf. the *Sekoddeśa*, vs. 10–14.

9. The *Kālacakratantra*, Ch. 3, vs. 13–14 mentions the following twenty-five vows: (1) the avoidance of killing (*hiṃsā*), lying (*asatya*), adultery (*para-strī*), stealing (*para-dhana*), and drinking liquor (*madya-pāna*); (2) the avoidance of gambling (*dyūta*), unwholesome food (*sāvadya-bhojya*), negative speech (*kuvacana-paṭhana*), and the religious teachings of the "demons" (Hindus), and *asuras* (Barbarians); (3) the avoidance of five types of killing: the killings of cows (*go*), children (*bāla*), women (*strī*), men (*nara*), and the Buddha, the teacher of thirteen men (*tri-daśa-nara-guru*), and the avoidance of harm (*droha*) to the five: friends (*mitra*), masters (*prabhu*), Buddhas (*tri-daśa-nara-guru*), the Buddhist community, and spiritual mentors (*viśvāsin*); (4) and avoidance of attachment to the objects of the five sense-faculties. According to the *Kālacakratantra*, Ch. 3, vs. 101–102, and the *Vimalaprabhā*, the fourteen root downfalls are: (1) causing mental grief to one's own spiritual mentor by engaging in the ten nonvirtues, (2) transgressing the spiritual mentor's injunctions, even behind the spiritual mentor's back, (3) anger toward one's own [*vajra*] brothers, regardless of their age or seniority, (4) abandoning loving kindness in four degrees: minimally, medially, strongly, and excessively, (5) releasing one's semen, (6) reviling the *siddhāntas*, or the system of perfections (*pāramitā-naya*), (7) giving a secret offering of sublime bliss to an immature person, that is, to a person established on the path of the Śrāvakas, (8) causing injury to the body by cutting it, etc., (9) aversion toward the "pure Dharma," that is, toward the Dharma of emptiness, (10) a false loving kindness, (11) a contrived ideation (*kalpanā*) with regard to the reality (*tattva*) of the Tathāgatas, which gives bliss and is devoid of name and the other attributes, (12) offending a pure being, such as a *yoginī*, (13) abandoning the received tantric pledges (*samaya*) during the tantric feast, and (14) aversion (*jugupsā*) toward women.

10. The *Kālacakratantra*, Ch. 3, v. 100, and the *Vimalaprabhā*.

11. Ibid.

12. The *Vimalaprabhā* commentary on the *Kālacakratantra*, 1994, Ch, 3, v. 100.

13. Bliss (*ānanda*), supreme bliss (*paramānanda*), special bliss (*viramānanda*), and innate bliss (*sahajānanda*).

14. The *Kālacakratantra*, Ch. 3, v. 105, and the *Vimalaprabhā*. Cf. the *Mañjuśrīnāmasaṃgīti*, v. 81:

> *trailokyaikakumārāṅgaḥ sthaviro vṛddhaḥ prajāpatiḥ*
> *dvātriṃśatlakṣaṇadharaḥ kāntas trailokyasundaraḥ.*

15. The *Sekoddeśa*, 1994, vs. 11–23.

16. The *Kālacakratantra*, Ch. 3, vs. 118–124, and the *Vimalaprabhā*.

17. The *Ādibuddhatantra*, quoted in the *Vimalaprabhā* commentary on the *Kālacakratantra*, Ch. 3, v. 120.

18. See the *Vimalaprabhā* commentary on the *Kālacakratantra*, Ch. 4, v. 100, Ch. 5, v. 13.
19. Ibid., Ch. 4, v. 110.
20. The *Kālacakratantra*, Ch. 4, v. 6, lines *a–b*:

śūnyaṃ bhāvād vihīnaṃ sakalajagad idaṃ vasturūpasvabhāvaṃ
tasmād buddho na bodhiḥ parahitakaruṇā cānimittapratijñā.

21. The *Kālacakratantra*, Ch. 4, v. 48.
22. The *Kālacakratantra*, Ch. 4, v. 8, and the *Vimalaprabhā*.
23. The mindfulness of the body, feelings, mind, and mental objects.
24. According to Bu ston [16], the eight corporeals are the four that consist of earth, water, fire, and wind, and the four that consist of form, smell, taste, and touch.
25. According to Bu ston [16], the eight qualities are great and small external forms, large and small, blue, yellow, red, and white.
26. According to Bu ston [16], the ten powers are: life and so on.
27. The *Ādibuddhatantra*, cited in the *Vimalaprabhā* commentary on the *Kālacakratantra*, Ch. 3, v. 9.
28. The *ālīḍha* posture is a standing posture in which the right leg is stretched forward and the left leg is retracted.
29. The *pratyālīḍha* posture is a standing posture in which the left leg is stretched forward and the right leg is retracted.
30. The *Vimalaprabhā* commentary on the *Kālacakrarantra*, Ch. 4, vs. 106, 14.
31. See the *Kālacakratantra*, Ch. 5, vs. 90–91, and the *Vimalaprabhā*.
32. See the *Vimalaprabhā* commentary on the *Kālacakratantra*, Ch. 4, v. 54.
33. See the *Vimalaprabhā* commentary on the *Kālacakratantra* , Ch. 4, v. 18.
34. Ibid., v. 20.
35. The *Kālacakratantra*, Ch. 4, v. 96, and the *Vimalaprabhā*.
36. The *Kālacakratantra*, Ch. 4, vs. 97–98, and the *Vimalaprabhā*.
37. The *Vimalaprabhā* commentary on the *Kālacakratantra*, Ch. 4, v. 51.
38. The *Ādibuddhatantra*, cited in the *Vimalaprabhā* commentary on the *Kālacakratantra*, Ch. 4, v. 49.
39. The *Kālacakratantra*, Ch. 4, v. 51.
40. See the *Kālacakratantra*, Ch. 4, vs. 98–99, and the *Vimalaprabhā*.
41. Ibid., vs. 101–106, and the *Vimalaprabhā*.
42. The *Vimalaprabhā* commentary on the *Kālacakratantra*, Ch. 5, v. 127.
43. It affirms that a so-called white meditation, which is characterized by peace, induces pacification and makes poison nontoxic; and a black meditation, which is characterized by wrath, induces killing and transports poison in the body, etc.
44. The *Vimalaprabhā* commentary on the *Kālacakratantra*, Ch. 5, v. 127.
45. Ibid.
46. The *Ādibuddhatantra*, cited in the *Vimalaprabhā* commentary on the *Kālacakratantra*, Ch. 4, v. 110.
47. The *Vimalaprabhā* commentary on the *Kālacakratantra*, Ch. 4, v. 110.
48. The *Kālacakratantra*, Ch. 4, v. 111, and the *Vimalaprabhā*.
49. The *Vimalaprabhā* commentary on the *Kālacakratantra*, Ch. 4, v. 111.
50. The *Vimalaprabhā* commentary on the *Kālacakratantra*, Ch. 5, v. 64.
51. The *Vimalaprabhā* commentary on the *Kālacakratantra*, Ch. 5, v. 127.
52. The *Vimalaprabhā* commentary on the *Kālacakratantra*, Ch. 4, v. 120.
53. Ibid.
54. The *Vimalaprabhā* commentary on the *Kālacakratantra*, 1986, Ch. 1, p. 21.

55. The *Ādibuddhatantra*, cited in the *Vimalaprabhā* commentary on the *Kālacakratantra*, Ch. 5, v. 127, states:

> After leaving the *karma-mudrā* and the conceptualized (*vikalpita*) *jñāna-mudrā*, one should meditate on the *mahā-mudrā* by means of the supreme, imperishable *yoga*.

56. The *Kālacakratantra*, Ch. 4, v. 120, and the *Vimalaprabhā*.

57. The *Vimalaprabhā* commentary on the *Kālacakratantra*, Ch. 5, v. 115, asserts that the Buddha taught in the *Samājatantra* that the ten signs appear during the nighttime *yoga*, and in the *Nāmasaṃgīti* that they arise during the daytime *yoga*.

58. See the *Kālacakratantra*, Ch. 4, v. 115, and the *Vimalaprabhā*.

59. The *Vimalaprabhā* commentary on the *Kālacakratantra*, Ch. 4, v. 117.

60. *Pūraka* designates closing of the right nostril and inhalation through the left nostril.

61. *Recaka* designates the closing of the left nostril and exhalation through the right nostril.

62. *Kumbhaka* is a breathing technique in which one holds the breath by closing the mouth and nostrils.

63. The *Vimalaprabhā* commentary on the *Kālacakratantra*, Ch. 4, v. 118.

64. The *Kālacakratantra*, Ch. 4, v. 116, and the *Vimalaprabhā*.

65. The *Vimalaprabhā* commentary on the *Kālacakratantra*, Ch. 4, v. 119.

66. The *Kālacakratantra*, Ch. 4, v. 117, and the *Vimalaprabhā*.

67. The *Vimalaprabhā* commentary on the *Kālacakratantra*, Ch. 4, v. 119.

68. See the *Kālacakratantra*, Ch. 4, v. 133, and the *Vimalaprabhā*.

69. The *Kālacakratantra*, Ch. 5, v. 119, and the *Vimalaprabhā*.

70. The *Kālacakratantra*, Ch. 5, v. 193:

> *eteṣāṃ muktihetoḥ sasutajinapatiḥ karmabhūmyāṃ praviśya*
> *garbhādhānaṃ hi kṛtvā paramakaruṇayā bodhim utpādayitvā*
> *mārakleśān nipātya kṣititalanilaye dharmacakraṃ pravṛttya*
> *kṛtvā nirmāṇamāyāṃ punar api bhagavān śuddhakāyaḥ sa eva.*

71. The *Śrīmālāsūtra*, Ch. 3: *tasmād bhagavaṃs tathāgatgarbho niśraya ādhāraḥ pratiṣṭhā saṃbaddhānām avinirbhāgānām amuktajñānām asaṃskṛtānāṃ dhramānām/ asaṃbaddhānām api bhagavan vinirbhāgadharmāṇāṃ muktajñānānāṃ saṃskṛtānāṃ dharmānāṃ niśraya ādhāraḥ pratiṣṭhā tathāgatagarbha iti/ tathāgatagarbhaś ced bhagavan na syān na syād duḥkhe' pi nirvin na nirvāṇecchā prārthanā praṇidhir veti vistaraḥ.*

72. The *Kālacakratantra*, Ch. 4, v. 120, and the *Vimalaprabhā*.

Appendix

1. The *Vimalaprabhā* commentary on the *Kālacakratantra*, Ch. 3, v. 168.

Bibliography

The Kālacakratantra Sanskrit Manuscripts

(*Ka* ms.) The *Kālacakratantraṭīkā* (*Vimalaprabhā*).
A microfilm copy of the manuscript is preserved in the Institute of Advanced Studies of World Religions: Buddhist Sanskrit Manuscripts (Strip No. MBB-1971-24–25).

(*Kha* ms.) The *Kālacakratantraṭīkā*.
A microfilm copy of the manuscript is preserved in the National Archives, Kathmandu by the Nepal-German Manuscript Preservation Project (Reel No. A 48/1; C. No. 5–240; V. No. 9).

(*Ga* ms.) The *Kālacakratantraṭīkā*.
A microfilm copy of the manuscript is preserved in the National Archives, Kathmandu by the Nepal-German Manuscript Preservation Project (Reel No. E 618/5; E. No. 13746).

(*Gha* ms.) The *Kālacakratantraṭīkā*.
A microfilm copy of the manuscript is preserved in the National Archives, Kathmandu by the Nepal-German Manuscript Preservation Project (Reel No. B. 31/16; C. No. 5–238; V. No. 68).

(*Ṅa* ms.) The *Kālacakratantraṭīkā*.
The manuscript is preserved in the National Archives, Kathmandu by the Nepal-German Manuscript Preservation Project (C. No. 5–241; V. No. 15).

(*Ca* ms.) The *Laghukālacakraṭīkā*.
The manuscript is preserved in the Library of the Asiatic Society, Calcutta (No. 10766).

(*Cha* ms.) The *Śrīmatkālacakratantrarāja*.
The manuscript is currently in the private possession of Mr. R. Gnoli, Rome, Italy. It was written down about seventy years ago on the request of Mr. G. Tucci.

(*Ja* ms.) *Sanskrit Manuscripts from Tibet* (Facsimile edition of the Kālacakra-tantra and of an unidentified palm-leaf manuscript, both from the Narthang monastery). 1971. Edited by L. Chandra. Śatapiṭaka Series, vol. 81, pp. 1–240. New Delhi: International Academy of Indian Culture.

Sanskrit, Tibetan, and Mongolian Sources

Abhidharmakoṣa & Bhāṣya of Ācārya Vasubandhu with Sphuṭārtha Commentary of Ācārya Yaśomitra, 2 parts. 1981. Edited by Dwarikadas Śāstri. Varanasi: Bauddha Bharati.

Abhisamayālaṃkāraprajñāpāramitopadeśaśāstra. Part 1. 1992. Edited by Th. Stcherbatsky and E. Obermiller. Bibliotheca Indo-Buddhica Series, vol. 99. Delhi: Sri Satguru Publications.

The Aṅguttara-Nikāya, vols. 1–5. 1958–1961. Edited by E. Hardy. Pāli Text Society. London: Luzac.

Aṣṭasāhasrikā Prajñāpāramitā. 1960. Edited by P. L. Vaidya. Buddhist Sanskrit Texts Series, no. 4. Darbhanga: Mithila Institute.

Āyuḥsādhana. (Tib. tr. *Tshe sgrub pa'i thabs*) Peking edition of *Tibetan Tripiṭaka*, edited by D. T. Suzuki, vol. 86, no. 4863.

Āyurvedasarvasvasārasaṃgraha. (Tib. tr. *Tshe'i rig byed mtha' dag gi snying po bsdus pa*) Peking edition of *Tibetan Tripiṭaka*, edited by D. T. Suzuki, vol. 148, no. 5879.

Āyussasutta. In the *Aṅguttara Nikāya*. 1885–1910. Edited by R. Morris, E. Hardy, and C. A. F. Rhys Davids. London: Pāli Text Society, vol. 3: 143.

Āyuṣmannandagarbhāvakrāntinirdeśanāmamahāyānasūtra. (Tib. tr.*'Phags pa tshe dang ldan pa dga' bo la mngal du 'jug pa bstan pa shes bya ba theg pa chen po'i mdo*) Peking edition of *Tibetan Tripiṭaka*, edited by D. T. Suzuki, vol. 23, no. 760.

Āyuṣparyantasūtra. (Tib. tr. *Tshe'i mtha'i mdo*) Peking edition of *Tibetan Tripiṭaka*, edited by D. T. Suzuki, vol. 39, no. 973.

Bodhipathapradīpa of Dīpaṃkara Śrījñāna. 1995. Edited and translated by Ramprasad Mishra. Delhi: Kant Publications.

Bu ston rin chen grub. 1965. *Dbang mdor bstan pa'i rnam bzhad: Dbang mdor bstan pa'i rnam bzhad bsdud pa'i snying po rab tu gsal ba* in *The Collected Works of Bu ston*, part 3 (Ga). Edited by Lokesh Chandra. New Delhi: International Academy of Indian Culture.

Bu ston Rin chen grub. 1965. *Dus 'khor chos 'byung: Rgyud sde'i zab don sgo 'byed rin chen gces pa'i lde mig ces bya ba* in *The Collected Works of Bu ston*, part 4 (Nga). Edited by Lokesh Chandra. New Delhi: International Academy of Indian Culture.

Buddhaghosa. 1942. *Atthasālinī*. Edited by P. V. Bapat and R. D. Vadekar. Poona: The Bhandarkar Oriental Research Institute.

Buddhaghosa. 1979. *The Path of Purification* (*Visuddhimagga*). Translated by Bhikkhu Ñāṇamoli. Kandy: Sri Lanka: Buddhist Publication Society.

The Caṇḍamahāroṣaṇa Tantra, Chapters 1–8: A Critical Edition and English Translation. 1974. Edited and translated by S. George Christopher. American Oriental Series, no. 56. New Haven: American Oriental Society.

The Caraka Saṃhitā by Agniveśa: Revised by Caraka and Dṛdhabala, with the Āyurveda-Dīpakā Commentary of Carakapāṇidatta. 1981. Edited by Jādavjī Trikamjī. New Delhi: Munshiram Manoharlal.

Chos kyi rnam grangs. 1986. Compiled by Mgon po dbang rgyal. Changdu: People's Publishing House.

Dharmadhātuvibhaṅgakārikā of Maitreyanātha: With a Commentary by Vasubandhu. 1990. Edited and translated by Acharya Tshultrim Phuntsok. Bibliotheca Indo-Tibetica, vol. 19. Saranath: Central Institute of Higher Tibetan Studies.

Dīgha Nikāya, vols. 1–3. 1890–1911. Edited by T. W. Rhys Davids and J. E. Carpenter. Pāli Text Society. London: Luzac.

Divyāvadāna: A Collection of Early Buddhist Legends. 1970. Edited by Edward B. Cowell and Robert A. Neil. Amsterdam: Philo Press Publishers.

Divyāvadānam. 1959. Edited by P. L. Vaidya. Buddhist Sanskrit Texts, n. 20. Darbhanga: The Mithila Institute of Post-Graduate Studies and Research in Sanskrit Learning.

Govindadḥasa. 1962. *Bhaiṣajya-ratnāvalī*. Edited by Narendranātha Mitra. Delhi: Motilal Banarsidass.

Guhyādyaṣṭasiddhisaṃgraha. 1988. Edited by Samdhong Rinpoche and Vrajavallabha Dvivedi.

Rare Buddhist Text Series, vol. 1. Sarnath, Varanasi: Central Institute of Higher Tibetan Studies.

Guhyasamāja Tantra or Tathāgataguhyaka. 1965. Edited by S. Bagchi. Buddhist Sanskrit Texts, no. 9. Darbhanga: Mithila Institute.

The Guhyasamāja Tantra. 1978. Edited by Yukei Matsunaga. Osaka: Toho Shuppan, Inc.

Guhyasamājatantrapradīpodyotanaṭīkāṣaṭkoṭivyākhyā. 1984. Edited by Chintharan Chakravarti. Tibetan Sanskrit Works Series, no. 25. Patna: Kashi Prasad Jayaswal Research Institute.

Hevajra Tantra: With the Commentary Yogaratnamālā. 1992. Edited and translated by G. W. Farrow and I. Menon. Delhi: Motilal Banarsidass.

Hevajra Tantra: A Critical Study, 2 parts. 1976. Edited and translated by D. L. Snellgrove. London Oriental Series, vol. 6. London: Oxford University Press.

Jñānavajra. *Āyurvṛddhisādhanadhvajāgranāma.* (Tib. tr. *Tshe 'phel ba'i sgrub thabs rgyal mtshan gyi rtse mo shes bya ba*) Peking edition of *Tibetan Tripiṭaka*, edited by D. T. Suzuki, vol. 79, no. 3868.

Kālacakragaṇitopadeśa Kālacakrānusārigaṇita. (Skt.) National Archives, Kathmandu, no. 152 VI, 22, Mf. B22/22.

Kālacakra-tantra and Other Texts, 2 vols. 1966. Edited by R. Vira and L. Chandra. Śatapiṭaka Series, vols. 69–70. New Delhi: International Academy of Indian Culture.

The Khuddaka-pāṭha, Together with Its Commentary Paramattha-jotikā, part 1. 1959. Edited by Helmer Smith. Pāli Text Society. London: Luzac.

Klong rdol bla ma. 1973. Edited by Lokesh Chandra. *Dus 'khor lo rgyus*: Klong rdol bla ma Nga dbang blo bzang: *Dang po'i saṅs rgyas dpal dus kyi 'khor lo rgyus dang ming gi rnam grangs* in *The Collected Works of Langdol Lama.* Edited by Lokesh Chandra. New Delhi: International Academy of Indian Culture.

Kokila. *Āyuḥparirakṣānāma.* (Tib. tr. *Tshe bsgrub pa'i gdams ngag*). Peking edition of *Tibetan Tripiṭaka*, edited by D. T. Suzuki, vol. 69, no. 3260.

Kun mkhyen dol po pa shes rab rgyal mtshan. 1992. *The 'dzam thang Edition of the Collected Works (gsung 'bum) of Kun-Mkhyen Dol-Po-Pa Shes-Rab-Rgyal-Mtshan*, vol. 6. Collected and presented by Professor Matthew Kapstein. The 'dzam thang Edition of the Collected Works (gsung 'bum) of Kun-Mkhyen Dol-Po-Pa Shes-Rab-Rgyal-Mtshan Series, vol. 8. Delhi: Konchog Lhadrepa House no. 31 New Tibetan Colony Manju-Ka-Tilla.

Madhyamakāvatāra par Candrakīrti. 1970. Edited by Louis de la Vallée Poussin. Bibliotheca Buddhica, vol. 9. Osnabrück: Biblio Verlag Reprint.

Mahāyānasūtrālaṃkāra. 1970. Edited by S. Bagchi. Buddhist Sanskrit Texts, no. 13. Darbhanga: The Mithila Institute.

The Majjhima-nikāya, vols. 2, 3. 1951. Edited by Lord Robert Charlmes. Pāli Text Society. London: Oxford University Press.

mKhas grub rje. 1983. *Dus 'khor ṭik chen*: Mkhad grub Dge legs dpal bzang: *Rgyud thams cad kyi rgyal po bcom ldan 'das dpal dus kyi 'khor lo mchog gi dang po'i sangs rgyas kyi trsa ba'i rgyud las phyung ba bsdud ba'i rgyud kyi 'grel chen rtsa ba'i rgyud kyi rjes su 'jug pa stong phrag bcu gnyis pa dri ma med pa'i 'od kyi rgya cher bshad pa de kho na nyid snang bar byed pa zhes bya ba* in *Yab sras gsung 'bum*, Mkhas grub (Kha). Dharamsala: Tibetan Cultural Printing Press.

Mongolian Kanjur, vol. 1. 1973. Edited by Lokesh Chandra. Śatapiṭaka Series Indo-Asian Literatures, vol. 101. Published by Dr. Mrs. Sharada Rani.

Nāgārjuna. *Madhyamakaśāstra of Nāgārjuna with the Commentary: Prasannapadā by Candrakīrti.* 1960. Edited by P. L. Vaidya. Buddhist Sanskrit Texts, no. 10. Darbhanga: The Mitthila Institute.

Nāropā. *Paramārthasaṃgrahanāmasekoddeśaṭīkā.* Edited by M. Carelli, in *Sekoddeśaṭīkā of Naḍapāda.* 1941. Gaekwad's Oriental Series, no. 90. Baroda.

Netti-Pakaraṇa. 1962. Edited by E. Hardy. London: Pali Text Society.

Niddesa I: Mahāniddesa, 2 vols. 1916–17. Edited by L. de la Valée Poussin and E. J. Thomas. Pāli Text Society. London: Oxford University Press.

Niṣpannayogāvalī of Mahāpaṇḍita Abhayākaragupta. 1972. Edited by Benyotosh Bhattacharya. Gaekwad's Oriental Series, no. 109. Baroda: Oriental Institute Reprint.

Padma dkar po. 1968. *'Brug pa'i chos 'byung* in *The Tibetan Chronicles of Padma dkar po*. Edited by Lokesh Chandra. Śata-piṭaka Series, vol. 75. New Delhi: International Academy of Indian Culture.

Padma dkar po. 1974. *Dpe med 'tsho'i lugs kyi rnal 'byor yan lag drug pa'i khrid rdo rje'I tshig 'byed*. In the Collected Works of Kun-mkhyen Padma dkar po, vols. 2, 17. Darjeeling: Kargyud Sungrab Nyamso Khang.

Praśāntamitra. *Māyājālatantrarājapañjikā* (*rgyud kyi rgyal po sgyu 'phrul dra ba'i dka' 'grel*). Peking edition of the *Tibetan Tripiṭaka*, no. 2714.

Puggalapaññati: Law as Designation of Human Types. 1969. Pāli Text Society Translation Series, no. 12. London: Luzac.

Rigs ldan Padma dkar po. 1965. *bsDus pa'i regyud kyi po dus kyi 'khor lo'i grel bshad rtsa ba'i rgyud kyi rjes su 'jug pa stong phrag bcu gnyis pa dri ma med pa'i 'od ces bya ba*. Edited by Bu ston Rin chen grub. *'Jig rten khams kyi le'u'i 'grel bshad dri ma med pa'i 'od mchan bcas*. Edited by Lokesh Chandra. *The Collected Works of Bu-ston*: part 1 (Ka). Śata-piṭaka Series, vol. 41. New Delhi: International Academy of Indian Culture.

Saddharmalaṅkāvatārasūtram. 1963. Edited by P. L. Vaidya. Buddhist Sanskrit Texts, no. 3. Darbhaṅga: The Mithila Institute.

Sādhanamālā. 1968. Edited by Benyotosh Bhattacharya. Gaekwad's Oriental Series, nos. 26, 41. Baroda: Oriental Institute Reprint.

Samādhirājasūtra. 1961. Edited by P. L. Vaidya. Buddhist Sanskrit Texts Series, no. 2. Darbhanga: Mithila Institute.

The Samyutta-nikāya of the Sutta-piṭaka, 5 vols. 1960. Edited by M. Feer Léon. Pāli Text Society. London: Luzac.

Śāntideva. *Śikṣāsamuccaya*. 1961. Edited by P. L. Vaidya. Buddhist Sanskrit Texts, no. 11. Darbhanga: The Mithila Institute.

Sekoddeśa: A Critical Edition of the Tibetan Translations. 1994. With an Appendix by Raniero Gnoli on the Sanskrit Text. Edited by Giacomella Orofino. Serie Orientale Roma, vol. 72. Roma: Instituto Italiano per il Medio ed Estremo Oriente.

Sbyor ba yan lag drug gi khrid skor bu-ston rin chen grub. Khrid Material for the Practice of Ṣaḍaṅgayoga of the Kālacakra. 1983. Prepared by Sherab Gyaltsen and Lama Dawa. Reproduction from a collection of rare manuscripts from the library of bla ma Senge of Yol mo. Gangtok, Sikhim: Palace Monastery.

Sbyor ba yang las drug gi khrid skor. Awadhūtipa bsod nams. 1983. Prepared by Sherab Gyaltsen and Lama Dawa. Reproduction from a collection of rare manuscripts from the library of bla ma Senge of Yol mo. Gangtok, Sikhim: Palace Monastery.

Sekoddeśaṭīkānāma. (Tib.) Peking ed. vol. 47, no. 2070.

Śrāvakabhūmi. 1973. Edited by Shukla Karunesha. Tibetan Sanskrit Works Series, vol. 14. Patna: K. P. Jayaswal Research Institute.

Śrīguhyasamājatantram. 1965. Edited by S. Baggchi. Buddhist Sanskrit Texts, no. 9. Darbhanga: The Mithila Institute.

Śrīkālacakratantragarbha. (Tib. and Mong.) 1966. In the *Kālacakra-tantra and Other Texts*, part 2. New Delhi: International Academy of Indian Culture.

Śrī Kālacakratantrarāja: Collated with the Tibetan Version. 1985. Edited by B. Bishwanath. Bibliotheca Indica: A Collection of Oriental Works. Calcutta: The Asiatic Society.

Śrīkālacakratantrottaratantrahṛdayam. (Tib. and Mong.) 1966. In the *Kālacakra-tantra and Other*

Texts, part 2. Śata-piṭaka Series, vol. 70. New Delhi: International Academy of Indian Culture.

Śrīlaghukālacakratantrarājasya Kalkinā Śrīpuṇḍarikeṇa Viracitā Ṭīkā Vimalaprabhā, vol. 3. 1994. Edited by Vrajavallabh Dwivedi and S. S. Bahulkar. Rare Buddhist Texts Series, vol. 13. Sarnath, Varanasi: Central Institute of Higher Tibetan Studies.

The Suśrutasaṃhitā of Suśruta with the Nibandhasaṃgraha Commentary of Śrī Ḍalhaṇācārya and the Nyāyancandrikā Pañjikā of Śrī Gayadāsācārya. 1980. Edited by Jādavjī Trikamjī and Nārāyaṇa Rāma Ācarya "Kāvyatīrtha." Jaikrishnadas Āyurveda Series, no. 34. Varanasi: Chaukhambha Orientalia.

The Sutta-Nipāta. 1985. Translated by H. Saddhatissa. London: Curzon Press.

Tantrarāja Tantra. 1981. Edited by Lakshmana Shastri. Delhi: Motilal Banarasidass.

Tāranātha. *dPal dus kyi 'khor lo'i chos bskor gyi byung khungs nyer mkho*. 1971. Edited by Ngawang Gelek Demo. *Tāranātha's Life of the Buddha and His Histories of the Kālacakra and Tārātantra*. Gadan Sungrab Minyam Gynphel Series, vol. 20. New Delhi: Ngawang Gelek Demo.

Therā and Therī-Gāthā: Stanzas Ascribed to Elders of the Buddhist Order of Recluses. 1966. Edited by Hermann Oldenberg and Richard Pischel. Pali Text Society. London.

The Tibetan Tripiṭaka: Peking Edition. 1955–1961. Edited by D. T. Suzuki. Tokyo-Kyoto: Tibetan Tripiṭaka Research Institute.

Vajracchedikā Prajñāpāramitāsūtra with the Commentary of Asaṅga. 1978. Critically edited and translated into Hindi by L. M. Joshi. Tibetan version of the Sūtra edited by Ven. Samdhong Rinpoche. Biliotheca Indo-Tibetica, vol. 3. Saranath, Varanasi: Central Institute of Higher Tibetan Studies.

Vajrahṛdayālaṃkāratantranāma (*dpal rdo rje snying po rgyan gyi rgyud*). Peking edition of the *Tibetan Tripiṭaka*, #86.

Vajramālābhidhānamahāyogatantrasarvatantrahṛdayarahasyavibhaṅga (*rnal 'byor chen po'i rgyud dpal rdo rje phreng ba ngon par brjod pa rgyud thams chid kyi snying po gsang ba rnam par phye ba*). Peking edition of the #82.

Vajraśekharamahāguhyayogatantra (*gsang ba rnal 'byor chen po'i rgyud, rdo rje rtse mo*). Peking edition of the *Tibetan Tripiṭaka*, #113.

"The *Vajrāvalī-nāma-maṇḍalopāyikā* of Abhayākaragupta." 1981. Edited by D. C. Bhattacharya. *Mélanges chinois et bouddhiques* 20: 70–95.

Vimalaprabhāṭīkā of Kalkin Śrīpuṇḍarīka on Śrīlaghukālacakra-tantrarāja by Mañjuśrīyaśas, vol. 2. 1994. Rare Buddhist Texts Series, vol. 12. Edited by V. Dwivedi and S. S. Bahulkar. Saranath, Varanasi: Rare Buddhist Texts Research Project, Central Institute of Higher Tibetan Studies.

Vimalaprabhāṭīkā of Kalki Śrī Puṇḍarīka on Śrī Laghukālacakra-tantrarāja, vol. 1. 1986. Edited by Upadhyāya, J. Bibliotheca Indo-Tibetica Series, no. 11. Saranath, Varanasi: Central Institute of Higher Tibetan Studies.

Visuddhamagga of Buddhaghosācariya. 1950. Edited by Henry Clark Warren and revised by Dharmananda Kosambi. Oriental Series, vol. 31. Cambridge, Mass.: Harvard University Press.

Sources in Other Languages

Abhidharmakośabhāṣyam. 1988–1990. 4 vols. Translated by Louis de la Vallée Poussin. English translation by Leo M. Pruden. Berkeley: Asian Humanities Press.

Abhinavagupta. 1988. *A Trident of Wisdom: Translation of Parātrīśikā Vivaraṇa*. Translated by Jaideva Singh. Albany: State University of New York Press.

Ainslie, Whitelaw. 1979. *Materia Indica*, vol. 1. London: Longman, Rees, Orme, Brown, and Green.

Akira, Hirakawa. 1990. *A History of Indian Buddhism from Śākyamuni to Early Mahāyāna*. Asian Studies at Hawaii, no. 36. Honolulu: University of Hawaii Press.

Ali, S. M. 1966. *The Geography of the Puranas*. New Delhi: People's Publishing House.

Alper, Harvey, P. ed. 1989. *Mantra*. New York: State University of New York Press.

Ames, William, L. 1993. "Bhāvavika's Prajñāpradīpa: A Translation of Chapter One: 'Examination of Causal Conditions' (*Pratyaya*)." Part 1. *Journal of Indian Philosophy* 21: 209–259. Netherlands: Kluwer Academic Publishers.

———. 1994. "Bhāvavika's Prajñāpradīpa: A Translation of Chapter One: 'Examination of Causal Conditions' (*Pratyaya*)." Part 2. *Journal of Indian Philosophy* 22: 93–135. Netherlands: Kluwer Academic Publishers.

Aśvaghoạ. 1950. *Vajrasūci of Aśvaghoṣa*. Edited and translated by Sujitkumar Mukhopadhyaya. Sino-Indian Studies, no. 2. Santiniketan: Sino-Indian Cultural Society.

Auboyer, Jeannine. 1961. *Daily Life in Ancient India from Approximately 200 BC to 700 AD*. English translation by Simon Watson Taylor. New York: Macmillan.

Banerji, S. C. 1978. *Tantra in Bengal: A Study in Its Origin, Development, and Influence*. Calcutta: Naya Prakash.

Beduhn, Jason, D. 1995. "The Metabolism of Salvation: The Manichean Body in Ascesis and Ritual." Doctoral dissertation. Bloomington: Indiana University.

Berzin, Alexander. 1997. *Taking the Kalachakra Initiation*. Ithaca, New York: Snow Lion Publications.

Beth, Simon, ed. 1985. *The Wheel of Time: The Kalachakra in Context*. Madison: Deer Park Books.

Bethlenfalvy, G. 1982. *A Hand-list of the Ulan Bator Manuscripts of the Kanjur Rgyal-rtse Them Spangs ma*. Budapest: Akadémiai Kiadó.

Bharati Agehananda. 1961. "Intentional Language in the Tantras." *Journal of the American Oriental Society* 81: 261–270.

———. 1970. *The Tantric Tradition*. London: Rider. Third Edition. First published 1965.

———. 1976. "Making Sense out of Tantrism and Tantrics." *Loka* 2: *A Journal from Naropa* 52–55.

Bhatacharya, Benyotosh. 1980. *An Introduction to Buddhist Esoterism*. Delhi: Motilal Banarsidass.

Bhattacharya, Brajamadhava. 1988. *The World of Tantra*. Delhi: Munshiram Manoharlal.

Bhattacharya, Haridas, ed. 1956. *The Cultural Heritage of India*, vol. 4: *The Religions*. Calcutta: The Ramakrishna Mission Institute of Culture.

Bhattacharya, Narendra, N. 1982. *History of the Tantric Religion* (*A Historical, Ritualistic, and Philosophical Study*). New Delhi: Manohar.

Birnbaum, Raoul. 1989. *The Healing Buddha*. Boston: Shambhala.

Bischoff, F. A. 1968. *Der Kanjur und Seine Kolophone*. 2 vols. Bloomington: The Selbstverlag Press.

Braarvig, Jens. 1994. "The Practice of the Bodhisattvas: Negative Dialectics and Provocative Arguments." Edition of the Tibetan text of the *Bodhisattva-caryānirdeśa* with a translation and introduction. *Acta Orientalia* 55: 113–160.

Broido, Michael, M. 1983. "*bshad thabs*: Some Tibetan Methods of Explaining the Tantras." In *Proceedings of the 1981 Csoma de Körös Symposium*. Edited by Ernst Steinkellner and H. Tauscher. Vienna: Wiener Studien zur Tibetologie und Buddhismuskunde.

———. 1988. "Killing, Lying, Stealing, and Adultery: A Problem of Interpretation in the Tantras." In the *Buddhist Hermeneutics*. Edited by Donald S. Lopez, Jr. Studies in East Asian Buddhism, no. 6. Honolulu: University of Hawaii Press.

Brooks, Douglas Renfrew. 1990. *The Secret of the Three Cities: An Introduction to Hindu Śākta Tantrism*. Chicago: University of Chicago Press.

A Buddhist Terminological Dictionary: The Mongolian Mahāvyutpatti. 1995. Edited by Alice

Sárközi in collaboration with János Szerb. Asiatische Forschungen. Monographienreihe zue Geschichte und Sprache der Völker Ost-und Zentralasiens, vol. 130. Wiesbaden: Harrassowitz.

Cabezón, Jose I. 1981. "The Concepts of Truth and Meaning in the Buddhist Scriptures." *Journal of International Association of Buddhist Studies*, 4, no. 1.

———. 1992. *A Dose of Emptiness: An Annotated Translation of the sTong thun chen mo of mKhas grub dGe legs dpal bzang*. SUNY Series in Buddhist Studies. New York: State University of New York Press.

———, ed. 1992. *Buddhism, Sexuality, and Gender*. Albany: State University of New York Press.

Caraka Saṃhitā. 1977. vol. 2. Translated by R. K. Sharma and B. Chowkhamba Dash. Sanskrit Studies, vol. 94. Varanasi: Chowkhamba Sanskrit Series Office.

Carelli, M. 1941. "Nāropā's Sekoddeśaṭīkā." *Proceedings and Transactions of the Tenth All-India Oriental Conference, Tirupati, March 1940*. Madras.

Chandra, Lokesh, ed. 1965. *The Collected Works of Bu-ston*. Śatapiṭaka Series, vol. 41. New Delhi: International Academy of Indian Culture.

———. 1984. "Vaipulya Sūtras and the Tantras." *Tibetan and Buddhist Studies* 2: 99–115. Edited by Louis Ligeti. Biblioteca Orientalis Hungarica, vol. 29/21. Budapest: Akadémiai Kiadó.

Chattopadhyaya, Alaka. 1996. *Atīśa and Tibet: Life and Works of Dīpaṃkara Śrījñāna in Relation to the History and Religion of Tibet*. Delhi: Motilal Banarsidass.

Chattopadhyaya, Brajadulal. 1998. *Representing the Other? Sanskrit Sources and the Muslims*. Delhi: Manohar.

Chimpa, L. 1990. A. Chattopadhyaya, tr. *Tāranātha's History of Buddhism in India*. Delhi: Motilal Banarsidass.

Chopra, R. N., et al. 1956. *Glossary of Indian Medicinal Plants*. New Delhi: Council of Scientific and Industrial Research.

Collins, S. 1990. *Selfless Persons: Imagery and Thought in Theravāda Buddhism*. Cambridge: Cambridge University Press.

Conze, E. 1966. "Buddhism and Gnosis," in *Le Origini dello Gnosticismo: Colloquio de Messina 13–18 Aprille 1966*: 665.

Cordier, P. 1909–1933. *Catalogue due Fonds Tibetain de la Bibliothèque nationale*. Paris: Imprimerie nationale.

Csoma de Körös. 1883. "A Note on the Origin of the Kāla-cakra and Ādi-Buddha Systems." *Journal of the Asiatic Society of Bengal* 2: 57–9. Reprinted in 1911 in the *Journal & Proceedings of the Asiatic Society of Bengal* 7: 21–3.

Dasgupta, Shashi Bhushan. 1969. *Obscure Religious Cults as Background of Bengali Literature*. Calcutta: Firma Mukhopadhyaya reprint.

———. 1974. *An Introduction to Tantric Buddhism*. Berkeley, London: Shambhala.

Dash, Bhagwan. 1994–1995. *Encyclopaedia of Tibetan Medicine: Being the Tibetan Text of Rgyud Bzhi and Sanskrit Restoration of Amṛta Hṛdaya Aṣṭāṅga Guhyopadeśa Tantra and Expository Translation in English*, vols.1–3. Delhi: Sri Satguru Publications, A Division of Indian Books Centre.

Dash, Bh., and L. Kashyap. 1994. *Iatro-Chemistry of Ayurveda: Rasa Sastra*. Todarananda Ayurveda Saukhyam Series, no. 9. New Delhi: Ashok Kumar Mittal.

Dash, Bhagwan. 1975. "Ayurveda in Tibet." *The Tibet Journal* 1 (July–September): 94–104.

———. 1975. *Embryology and Maternity in Ayurveda*. New Delhi: Delhi Diary.

Davidson, Ronald, M. 1981. "The Litany of Names of Mañjuśrī: The Text and Translation of the *Mañjuśrīnāmasaṃgīti*." In *Tantric and Taoist Studies in Honour of R. A. Stein*. Edited by Michel Strickman, vol. 1. Brussels: Institute Belge des Hautes Études Chinoises.

de Jong, J. W. 1960. "Review of D. L. Snellgrove, *The Hevajra Tantra. A Critical Study.*" *Indo-Iranian Journal* 4: 198–203.

———. 1984. "A New History of Tantric Literature in India." Acta Indologica 6: 91–113. (Précis in English of Matsunaga Yukei. 1980. *Mikkyo kyoten seiritsushi-ron*. Kyoto: Hozokan.)

Dey, A. C. 1980. *Indian Medicinal Plants Used in Ayurvedic Preparations*. Dehra Dun: Bishen Sings Mahendra Pal Singh.

Dhargyey, Geshe Ngawang. 1985. *A Commentary on the Kālacakra Tantra*. Translated by Gelong Jhampa Kelsang. Dharamsala: Library of Tibetan Works and Archives.

The Discourses of Gotama Buddha: Middle Collection. 1992. David W. Evans, tr. London: Janus.

Dowman, Keith. 1985. *Masters of Mahāmudrā: Songs and Histories of the Eighty-Four Buddhist Siddhas*. Albany: State University of New York Press.

Dyczkowski, Mark, s. G., tr. 1992. *The Aphorisms of Śiva: The Śiva Sūtra with Bhāskara's Commentary, the Vārttika*. Albany: State University of New York Press.

Eastman, Kenneth, W. 1981. "The Eighteen Tantras of the Tattvasaṃgraha/Māyājāla." *Transactions of the International Conference of Orientalists in Japan* 26: 95–6.

Edgerton, Franklin. 1972. *The Bhagavd Gitā*. Cambridge, Mass.: Harvard University Press.

Eimer, H. 1989. *Der Tantra-Catalog des Bu ston in Vergleich mit der Abteilung Tantra des tibetischen Kanjur: Studie, Textausgabe, Konkordanzen und Indices*. Indica et Tibetica, vol. 13. Bonn: Indica et Tibetica.

Eliade, Mircea. 1969. *Yoga: Immortality and Freedom*. Princeton: Princeton University Press.

Encyclopaedia of Buddhism, 2 vols. 1967. Edited by G. P. Malalasekera. Ceylon: Published by the Government of Ceylon.

Engle, A. 1982. "The Buddhist Theory of Self According to Ācārya Candrakīrti." Doctoral dissertation. Madison: University of Wisconsin.

Fenner, Edward Todd. 1979. "Rasayana Siddhi: Medicine and Alchemy in the Buddhist Tantras". Doctoral dissertation. Madison: University of Wisconsin.

Filliozat, Jean, ed. and tr. 1979. *Yogaśataka: Text médical attribué à Nāgārjuna*. Publications de l'institut Français d'Indologie, no. 62. Pondichéry: Institut Français d'Indologie.

Frauwallner, E. 1984. *History of Indian Philosophy*. Translated by V. M. Bedekar. Delhi: Motilal Banarsidass.

Fux, Herbert. 1969. "Śambhala und die Geschichte des Kālacakra—Einlamaistisches Thaṅka aus dem Osterreichischen Museum für Angewandte Kunst." *Alte und moderne Kunst* 107: 18–24.

Gen Lamrimpa. 1999. *Transcending Time: An Explanation of the Kālacakra Six-Session Guru Yoga*. Translated by B. Alan Wallace. Boston: Wisdom Publications.

Gnolli, R., and G. Orofino. *Nāropā. L'iniziazione, Traduzione e commento della Sekoddeśaṭīkā di Nāropā*. Milano: Adelphi. In press.

Gonda, Jan. 1963. "The Indian Mantra." *Oriens* 16: 244–97.

———. 1977. "Medieval Religious History in Sanskrit." In the *History of Indian Literature*. Wiesbaden: Otto Harrassowitz.

Griffiths, P. W. 1986. *On Being Mindless: Buddhist Meditation on the Mind-Body Problem*. La Salle, Ill.: Open Court.

Grönbold, Günter. 1969. *Ṣaḍ-aṅga-yoga: Raviśrījñāna's Guṇabharaṇīnāma ṣaḍaṅgayogaṭippaṇī mit Text, Übersetzung und literarhistorischem Kommentar*. München: Inaugural-Dissertation zur Erlangung des Doktorgrades der Philosophischen Fakultät der Ludwigs-Maxmilians Unversität zu Mänchen.

———. 1982. "Materialen zur Geshichte des Ṣaḍaṅga-yoga: III. Die Guru-Reihen im budistischen Ṣaḍaṅga-yoga." *Zentralasiatische Studien* 16: 337–347.

———. 1983. Der Sechsgliedrige Yoga des *Kālacakra-tantra*." *Asiatische Studien/Etudes Asiatiques* 37-2-1983.

———. 1991. "Das datum des Buddha nach tantrischen Texten." In *The Dating of the Historical Buddha*. I. Symposien zur Buddhismusforschung, vol. 4, part 1. Edited by H. Bechert. Göttingen. Vandenhoeck and Ruprecht.

———. 1996. *The Yoga of Six Limbs: An Introduction to the History of Ṣaḍaṅgayoga*. Santa Fe: Spirit of the Sun Publications.

Guenther, Herbert, V. 1976. *The Tantric View of Life*. Boulder, London: Shambhala.

———. 1973. *The Royal Song of Saraha: A Study in the History of Buddhist Thought*. Berkeley: Shambhala.

A Guide to the Bodhisattva Way of Life. By Śāntideva. 1997. Translated by Vesna A. Wallace and B. Alan Wallace. Ithaca, N.Y.: Snow Lion Publications.

Gupta, Parmanand. 1973. *Geography in Ancient Indian Inscriptions* (up to 650 A.D.) Delhi: D. K. Publishing House.

Gyatso, T., the Dalai Lama, and J. Hopkins. 1989. *Kalachakra Tantra: Rite and Initiation*. A Wisdom Advanced Book: Blue Series. London: Wisdom Publications.

Hahn, M. 1982. *Nāgārjuna's Ratnāvalī*, vol. 1. Bonn: Indica et Tibetica Verlag.

Harrison, Paul. 1990. *The "Samādhi" of Direct Encounter with the Buddhas of the Present*. Studia Philologica Buddhica Monograph Series, no. 5. Tokyo: International Institute for Buddhist Studies.

Harvey, Peter. 1993. "The Mind-Body Relationship in Pāli Buddhism: A Philosophical Investigation." *Asian Philosophy* 3/1: 29–41.

Hazra Kanai, Lal. 1983. *Buddhism in India as Described by the Chinese Pilgrims*, A.D. 399–689. New Delhi: Munshiram Manoharlal.

Hermann-Pfandt, Adelheid. 1992. *Ḍākinīs: Zur Stellung und Symbolik des Weiblichen im Tantrischen Buddhismus*. Indica et Tibetica, vol. 20. Bonn: Indica et Tibetica.

Hoffmann, H. 1951. "Literarhistorische Bemerkungen zur Sekoddeśaṭīkā des Nāḍapāda." *Festschrift Walthe Schubring*, 140–47. Hamburg: Cram de Gruyter & Co.

———. 1960. "Manicheism and Islam in the Buddhist Kālacakra System." *Proceedings of the IXth International Congress for the History of Religions, Tokyo and Kyoto 1958*. Tokyo.

———. 1964. "Das Kālackra, die letzte Phase des Buddhismus in Indien." *Saeculum* 15: 125–131.

———. 1969. "Kālacakra Studies: Manicheism, Christianity and Islam in the *Kālacakra Tantra*." *Central Asiatic Journal* 13: 52–63.

———. 1973. "Buddha's Preaching of the Kālacakra Tantra at the Stūpa of Dhānyakaṭaka." *German Scholars of India* 1: 136–140. Varanasi.

———. 1975. *Tibet: A Handbook*. Bloomington: Research Center for the Language Sciences, Indiana University.

Hookham, S. K. 1991. *The Buddha Within: Tathagatagarbha Doctrine According to the Shentong Interpretation of the Ratnagotravibhaga*. New York: State University of New York Press.

Hopkins, Jeffrey, tr. and ed. 1987. *Tantra in Tibet: The Great Exposition of Secret Mantra*, vol. 1. By Tsong-ka-pa. The Wisdom of Tibet Series. London, Sidney: Unwin Hyman.

Huntington, C. W., Jr., with Geshe Namgyal Wangchen. 1989. *The Emptiness of Emptiness: An Introduction to Early Indian Madhyamaka*. Honolulu: University of Hawaii Press.

Inada, K. K., ed. and tr. 1970. *Nāgārjuna: A Translation of his Mūla-madhyamaka-kārikā*. Tokyo: Hokuseido Press.

Indian Astronomy: A Source Book. 1985. Compiled by B. V. Subbarayappa and K. V. Sarma. Bombay: Nehru Centre.

Iyengar, Sampath. 1980. *Ancient Hindu Astronomy*. Madras: International Society for the Investigation of Ancient Civilization.

Jamgon Kongtrul Lodro Taye. 1995. *Myriad Worlds: Buddhist Cosmology in Abhidharma, Kāla-*

cakra and Dzog-chen. Translated and edited by the International Translation Committee of Kunkhyab Chöling, founded by the V. V. Kalu Rinpoché. Ithaca, N.Y.: Snow Lion Publications.

Johnston, E. H., ed. and tr. 1950. *The Ratnagotravibhāga-Māhāyanottara-tantraśāstra*. Patna: Bihar Research Society.

Jonas, Hans. 1963. *The Gnostic Religion: The Message of the Alien God and the Beginnings of Christianity*. Boston: Beacon.

Kane, Pandurang V. 1974. *The History of Dharmaśāstra: Ancient and Medieval Religious and Civil Law*. Vol. 1, part 1. Government Oriental Series Class B, no. 6. Poona: Bhandarkar Research Institute.

Kasulis, P. Th., R. T. Ames, and W. Dissanayake, eds. 1993. *Self as Body in Asian Theory and Practice*. Albany: State University of New York Press.

Kirfel, Willibald. 1920. *Kosmographie der Inder*. Bonn: K. Schroeder.

Klimkeit, Hans-Joachim. 1993. *Gnosis on the Silk Road: Gnostic Texts from Central Asia*. San Francisco: Harper San Francisco.

Kloetzli, Randolph, W. 1983. *Buddhist Cosmology*. Delhi, Varanasi, Patna: Motilal Banarsidass.

———. 1985. "Maps of Time—Mythologies of Descent: Scientific Instruments and the Purāṇic Cosmograph." *History of Religions* 25 2: 117–147.

Kulārṇava-tantra. 1965. Edited by Tārānātha Vidyāratna. Madras: Ganesh.

Kutumbiah, P. 1962. *Ancient Indian Medicine*. Madras: Orient Longman.

Kværne, Per. 1975. "On the Concept of Sahaja in Indian Buddhist Tantric Literature." *Temenos* 11: 88–135.

Lamotte, Etienne. 1974. "Passions and Impregnations of the Passions in Buddhism." In *Buddhist Studies in Honour of I. B. Horner*. Edited by L. Cousins, A. Kunst, and K. R. Norman. Dordrecht-Boston: D. Reidel.

———. 1980. *Indianisme et Bouddhisme; mélanges offert à Mgr. Etienne Lamotte*. Louvain: Université Catholique de Louvain.

———. 1980. *Le Traité de la grande vertu de sagesse de Nāgārjuna*. V. Louvain: Université Catholique de Louvain.

Lancester, L., ed. 1977. *Prajñāpāramitā and Related Systems*. Berkeley: University of California Press.

Lang, K. 1986. *Āryadeva's Catuḥśataka: On the Bodhisattva Cultivation of Merit and Knowledge* (AC). Indiske Studier, vol. 7. Copenhagen: Akademisk Forlag.

Larson, G. J. 1969. *Classical Sāṃkhya: An Interpretation of Its History and Meaning*. Delhi, Varanasi, Patna: Motilal Banarsidass.

Law, Bimala Churn. 1984. *Historical Geography of Ancient India*. New Delhi: Oriental Books Reprint Cooperation.

Lessing, F. D., and A. W. Wayman, trs. 1980, 2nd. ed. *Introduction to Buddhist Tantric Systems: Translated from Mkhas Grub Rje's Rgyud sde spyihi rnam par gzhag pa rgyas par brjod*. Delhi: Motilal Banarsidass.

Lindtner, Christian. 1982. *Nagarjuniana: Studies in the Writings and Philosophy of Nāgārjuna*. Indiske Studier, vol. 4. Copenhagen: Akademisk Forlag.

———. 1993. "The Central Philosophy of Ancient India." *Asian Philosophy* 3/2: 89–93.

Lingat, Robert. 1973. *The Classical Law of India*. Berekeley: University of California Press.

Lokesh, Chandra. 1971. *An Illustrated Tibeto-Mongolian Materia Medica of Ayurveda*. New Delhi: International Academy of Indian Culture.

———. 1971. *Exhibition of the History of Indian Medicine & Its Spread in Asia*. New Delhi: International Academy of Indian Culture.

Lopez, Donald S., Jr. 1990. *The Heart Sūtra Explained: Indian and Tibetan Commentaries*. Bibliotheca Indo-Buddhica, no. 76. Delhi: Sri Satguru Publications.

———. 1996. *Elaborations on Emptiness: Uses of the Heart Sūtra*. Princeton, New Jersey: Princeton University Press.

Mahidahassan, S. 1979. *Indian Alchemy or Rasayana: In the Light of Ascetism [and] Geriatrics*. New Delhi: Vikas.

Majmuidar, R. C. 1966. *The Struggle for Empire*. Bharatiya Vidya Bhavan's *History and Culture of the Indian People*, vol. 5. Bombay: Bharatiya Vidya Bhavan.

Makransky, John, J. 1997. *Buddhahood Embodied: Sources of Controversy in India and Tibet*. SUNY Series in Buddhist Studies. Albany, N.Y.: State University of New York Press.

Matsunaga, Yukei. 1964. "A Doubt to Authority of the Guhyasamāja-Ākhyāna-tantras." *Journal of Indian and Buddhist Studies* 12: 844–935.

———. 1965. "Indian Esoteric Buddhism as Studied in Japan." In *Studies of Esoteric Buddhism and Tantrism*, pp. 229–242. Edited by Gisho Nakano. Koyasan: Koyasan University.

McDermott, A. C. 1975. "Towards a Pragmatics of Mantra Recitation." *Journal of Indian Philosophy* 3: 283–98.

Mimaki, K. 1982. "Le Commentaire de Mi Pham sur le Jñānasārasamuccaya." In *Indological and Buddhist Studies: Volume in Honour of Professor J. W. de Jong on His Sixtieth Birthday*. Edited by L. A. Hercus et al. Canberra: Faculty of Asian Studies.

Mukhopadhyaya, G. N. 1923. *History of Indian Medicine*, vol. 3. Calcutta: University of Calcutta.

Mullin, Glenn H., tr. 1982. *Bridging the Sutras and Tantras: A Collection of Ten Minor Works by Gyalwa Gendun Drub the First Dalai Lama (1391–1474)*. Ithaca, N.Y.: Gabriel/Snow Lion.

———. 1991. *The Practice of Kalachakra*. Ithaca, N.Y.: Snow Lion Publications.

Murti, T. R. V. 1974. *The Central Philosophy of Buddhism*. London: George Allen and Unwin.

Muses, C. A., ed. 1982. *Esoteric Teachings of the Tibetan Tantra*. English translation by Chang Chen Chi. New York: Samuel Weiser.

Nagao, G. 1973. "On the Theory of Buddha-Body (Buddha-kāya)." *Eastern Buddhists* (new series) 6 (1): 25–53.

Nāgārjuna. 1994. *Dharmasaṃgraha*. Translated by Tashi Zangmo and Dechen Chime. Bibliotheca, vol. 27. New Delhi: Biblia Impex.

Nakamura, Hajime. 1987. *Indian Buddhism: A Survey With Bibliographical Notes*. Buddhist Traditions, vol. 1. Delhi: Motilal Banarsidass.

Namgyal, Takpo Tashi. 1986. *Mahāmudrā: The Quintessence of Mind and Meditation*. Translated and edited by P. Lhalungpa Lobsang. Boston: Shambhala.

Nattier, Jan. 1995. "A Prophecy of the Death of the Dharma." In *Buddhism in Practice*. Edited by Donald S. Lopez, Jr. Princeton Readings in Religions. Princeton, New Jersey: Princeton University Press.

Naudou, J. 1968. *Les Bouddhistes Kāśmiriens au Moyen Age*. Annales du Musée Guimet, vol. 68. Paris: Presses Universitaires de France.

Newman, John. 1985. "A Brief History of the Kalachakra." In *The Wheel of Time: The Kalachakra in Context*. Edited by Beth Simon. Madison: Deer Park Books.

———. 1987. "The Outer Wheel of Time: Vajrāyana Buddhist Cosmology in the Kālacakra Tantra." Doctoral dissertation. Madison: University of Wisconsin.

———. 1987. "The *Paramādibuddha* (The *Kālacakramūla-tantra*) and its Relation to the Early Kālacakra Literature." *Indo Iranian Journal* 30: 93–102.

———. 1988. "Buddhist Sanskrit in the Kālacakra Tantra." *The Journal of the International Association of Buddhist Studies* 11 (1): 123–140.

———. 1992. "Buddhist Siddhānta in the Kālacakra tantra." *Wiener Zeitschrift für die Kunde Südasiens* 36: pp. 227–234.

———. 1995. "Eschatology in the Wheel of Time Tantra." In *Buddhism in Practice*. Edited by Donald S. Lopez, Jr. Princeton Readings in Religions. Princeton, New Jersey: Princeton University Press.

Nihom, M. 1984. "Notes on the Origin of Some Quotations in the Sekoddeśaṭīkā of Naḍapāda." *Indo Iranian Journal* 27: 17–26.

Nishitani, Keiji. 1982. *Religion and Nothingness*. English Translation by Jan Van Bragt. Berkeley: University of California Press.

Obermiller, E., tr. 1986. *The History of Buddhism in India and Tibet by Bu-ston*. Bibliotheca Indo-Buddhica, no. 26. Delhi: Sri Satguru Publications.

———. 1987. *The Jewelry of the Scripture by Bu-ston*. Bibliotheca Indo-Buddhica, no. 42. Delhi: Sri Satguru Publications.

Orofino, Giacomella. 1994. "Divination with Mirrors: Observations on a Simile Found in the Kālacakra Literature." In *Tibetan Studies: Proceedings of the 6th Seminar of the International Association for Tibetan Studies*. Edited by Per Kvaerne, vol. 2. Oslo: Institute for Comparative Research in Human Culture.

Padoux, André. 1978. "Contributions à l'étude du *mantraśāstra*: I, La sélection des *mantra* (*mantroddhāra*)." *Bulletin de l'École française d'êxtreme-orient* 65: 65–85.

———. 1978. "Some Suggestions on Research into Mantra." *Indologica Taurinensia* 6: 235–39.

———. 1980. "Contributions à l'étude du *mantraśāstra*: II *nyāsa*: L'imposition rituelle des *mantra*." *Bulletin de l'École française d'êxtreme-orient* 67: 59–102.

Pagels, Elaine. 1979. *The Gnostic Gospels*. New York: Vintage Books.

Powers, John. 1995. *Wisdom of Buddha. The Saṁdhinirmocana Mahāyāna Sūtra: Essential Questions and Direct Answers for Realizing Englightenment*. Berkeley: Dharma Publishing.

Priyadaranjan, Ray. 1980. *Suśruta Saṃhitā: A Scientific Synopsis*. New Delhi: Indian National Science Academy.

Rāmānuja. 1959–1962. *Śrībhāṣya*. 2 vols. Edited and translated by R. D. Karmarkar. Poona: University of Poona.

Rastogi, Navjivan. 1979. *The Krama Tantricism of Kashmir, Historical and General Sources*, vol. 1. Delhi: Motilal Banarsidass.

Reigle, David. 1986. "The Lost Kālacakra Mūla Tantra on the Kings of Shambhala." *Kālacakra Research Publications*, 1. Talent: O. R. Eastern School.

Roerich, G. N. 1932. "Studies in the Kālacakra I." *Journal of the "Urusvati" Himalayan Research Institute of the Roerich Museum* 2: 11–23.

———, tr. 1988. *Blue Annals*. Delhi: Motilal Banarsidass.

Ruegg, David Seyfort. 1969. *La Théorie du Tathāgatagarbha et du Gotra: Etudes sur la Sotériologie et la Gnoséologie du Buddhisme*. Paris: Ecole Française d'Extreme Orient.

———. 1981. "Deux Problèmes d'éxègese et de pratique tantriques." *In Tantric and Taoist Studies in Honor of R. A. Stein*. Edited by Michael Strickmann. Mélanges Chinois et Bouddhiques, vol. 20: 212–26. Brussels: Institut Belge des Hautes Ètudes Chinoises.

———. 1981. *The Literature of the Madhyamaka School of Philosophy in India*. History of Indian Literature, vol. 7, fasc. 1. Wiesbaden: Otto Harrassowitz.

———. 1984. "Problems in the Transmission of Vajrayāna Buddhism in Western Himalaya About the Year 1000." *Acta Indologica* 6: 369–381.

———. 1989. "Allusiveness and Obliqueness in Buddhist Texts: *Saṃdhā, Saṃdhi, Saṃdhyā* and *Abhisaṃdhi*." In *Dialectes dans les litteratures indo-aryennes*. Edited by C. Caillat, pp. 295–328. Paris: College de France.

———. 1989. *Buddha-Nature, Mind and the Problem of Gradualism in a Comparative Perspective: On the Transmission and Reception of Buddhism in India and Tibet*. The Jordan Lectures in Comparative Religion, vol. 13. London: School of Oriental and African Studies.

Sadakata, Akira. 1997. *Buddhist Cosmolgy: Philosophy and Origins*. Tokyo: Kosei Publishing Company.

Sakai, Shinten. 1960. "Paramārthasevā." *Indogaku Bukkogaku Kenkyu*, vol. 8, no. 1.

Sāṃkhya: A Dualist Tradition in Indian Philosophy. 1987. Encyclopedia of Indian Philosophies, vol. 4. Edited by G. J. Larson and R. Sh. Bhattacharya. Delhi: Varanasi, Patna, Madras: Motilal Banarsidass.

Sasaki, G. H., ed. 1975. *A Study of Kleśa*. Tokyo: Shimizukobundo.

Schmidt, Michael, ed. and tr. 1978. "Das Yogaśataka: Ein Zeugnis altindischer Medizir [sic] in Sanskrit und Tibetisch." Doctoral dissertation. Friedrich-Wilhelms Univeristät.

Schopen, G. 1983. "The Generalization of Old Yogic Attainment in Medieval Mahāyāna Sūtra Literature: Some Notes on *jātismara*." *Journal of the International Association of Buddhist Studies* 6 (1): 109–47.

Schuh, Dieter. 1973. *Untersuchungen zur Geshichte der tibetischen Kalendarrechnung. Verzeichnis der orientalischen Handschriften in Deutschland*, Supplementband 16. Wiesbaden: Franz Steiner GMBH.

Sde srid sangs rgya mtsho. 1970. *Ayurveda in Tibet: A Survey of History and Literature of Lamaist Medicine*. (Tib.) Leh: Sonam W. Tashigang.

Shāstri, Hara, Prasad. 1897. "Notes on Palm-leaf MSS. in the Library of His Excellency the Mahārāja of Nepāl." *Journal of the Asiatic Society of Bengal* 66: 310–16.

Shaw, Miranda. 1994. *Passionate Enlightenment: Women in Tantric Buddhism*. Princeton: Princeton University Press.

Shiníci, Tsuda, ed. and tr. 1974. *The Saṃvarodaya-tantra: Selected Chapters*. Tokyo: The Hokuseido Press.

Shirō, Matsumoto. 1997. "The Doctrine of *Thatāgata-garbha Is Not Buddhist*." *In Pruning the Bodhi Tree: The Storm Over Critical Buddhism*. Edited by Jamie Hubbard and Paul L. Swanson. Honolulu: University of Hawaii Press.

Singh, Jaideva, tr. 1991. *The Yoga of Delight, Wonder, and Astonishment: A Translation of the Vijñāna-Bhairava*. Albany: State University of New York Press.

Skilling, Peter. 1980. "On the Five Aggregates of Attachment." *D'études Bouddhologiques* 11: 20–31.

Snellgrove, David. 1959. *The Hevajra Tantra: A Critical Study*. 2 vols. London: Oxford University Press.

———. 1959. "The Notion of Divine Kingship in Tantric Buddhism." In *The Sacral Kingship*. Contributions to the Central Theme of the VIIIth International Congress for the History of Religions (Rome, April 1955), pp. 204–18. Leiden: E. J. Brill.

———. 1987. *Indo-Tibetan Buddhism*, 2 vols. Boston: Shambhala.

Staal, Frits, J. 1993. *Concepts of Science in Europe and Asia*. Leiden: International Institute of Asian Studies.

Stalbein, William. 1980. "The Medical Soteriology of Karma in the Buddhist Tantric Tradition." In *Karma and Rebirth in Classical Indian Traditions*. Edited by Wendy Doniger O'Flaherty, pp. 193–216. Berkeley: University of California Press.

Stcherbatsky, F. Theodore. 1971. *Madhyānta-vibhaṅga: Discourse on Discrimination Between Middle and Extremes Ascribed to Bodhisattva Maitreya Commented by Vasubandhu and Sthiramati*. Soviet Indology Series, no. 5. Calcutta: Indian Studies—Past and Present.

———. 1989. *The Conception of Buddhist Nirvāṇa*. Delhi, Varanasi, Patna: Motilal Banarsidass.

Stearns, Cyrus. 1996. "The Buddha from Dol po and His Fourth Council of the Buddhist Doctrine." Doctoral disseration. Seattle: University of Washington.

———. 1996. "The Life and Tibetan Legacy of the Indian *Mahāpaṇḍita* Vibhūticandra." *Journal of the International Association of Buddhist Studies* 19/1: 127–171.

Steinkellner, Ernst. 1978. "Remarks on Tantric Hermeneutics." In *Proceedings of the Csoma de Körös Memorial Symposium*. Edited by Louis Ligeti. Bibliotheca Orientalis Hungarica, vol. 23. Budapest: Akadémiai Kaidó.

Takakusu, J., tr. 1970. *A Record of the Buddhist Religion as Practiced in India and the Malay Archipelago* (A.D. 671–695), *by I-Tsing.* Taipei: Ch'eng Wen.

Takasaki, Jikido. 1966. *A Study on the Ratnagotravibhāga* (*Uttaratantra*): *Being a Treatise on the Tathāgata Theory of Mahāyāna Buddhism.* Serie Orientale Roma, vol. 33. Roma: Instituto Italiano per il Medio ed Estremo Oriente.

Tāranātha's History of Buddhism in India. 1990. Translated by Lama Chimpa Alaka Chattopadhyaya. Delhi: Motilal Banarsidass.

Thapar, Romila. 1966. *A History of India*, vol. 1. London, New York: Penguin Books.

Thurman, Robert, tr. 1976. *The Holy Teaching of Vimalakīrti.* University Park: Pennsylvania State University Press.

———. 1993. "Vajra Hermeneutics." In *Buddhist Hermeneutics.* Edited by Donald S. Lopez, Jr. Delhi: Motilal Banarsidass.

Thus I Have Heard: The Long Discourses of the Buddha: Dīgha Nikāya. 1987. Translated by Maurice Walshe. London: Wisdom.

Tsong kha pa. 1976. *The Collected Works of Tsong Khapa or Khams gsum chos kyi rgyal po Tsong kha pa chen po'i gsung 'bum*, vol. 17. Delhi: Ngang dbang dge legs de mo.

———. 1977. *The Yoga of Tibet. The Great Exposition of Secret Mantra*, vols. 2–3. Translated and edited by Jeffrey Hopkins. The Wisdom of Tibet Series, vol. 4. London: George Allen and Unwin.

Tsuda, Shiníci. 1982. "'*Vajrayoṣidbhageṣu Vijahāra*': Historical Survey from the Beginnings to the Culmination of Tantric Buddhism." In *Indological and Buddhist Studies: Volume in Honor of Professor J. W. de Yong on his Sixtieth Birthday.* Edited by L. A. Hercus et al., pp. 595–616. Canberra: Faculty of Asian Studies.

Tucci, G. 1958. *Minor Buddhist Texts*, Part 2. Rome: IsMeo.

Umāsvāti. 1994. *That Which Is: Tattvārtha Sūtra.* Translated by Nathmal Tatia. The Sacred Literature Series. San Francisco: Harper Collins.

Urban, Hugh B. 1999 "The Exreme Orient: The Construction of 'Tantrism' as a Category in the Orientalist Imagination." *Religion* 29/2: 123–146.

Valée Poussin, Louis de la. S.v. 1922. "Tantrism (Buddhist)." In *Encyclopedia of Religion and Ethics.* Edited by James Hastings, vol. 12: pp. 193–97. New York: Charles Scribner's Sons.

Van Lysebeth, André. 1988. *Tantra, le culte de la Féminité.* Paris: Flammarion.

Wallace, Vesna A. 1995. "The Buddhist Tantric Medicine in the *Kālacakratantra.*" *The Pacific World: Journal of the Institute of Buddhist Studies*, New Series, nos. 10–11: 155–174.

Wallace, Vesna A., and B. Alan Wallace, trans. 1995. *A Guide to the Bodhisattva Way of Life* (*Bodhicaryāvatāra*) *by Śāntideva.* Ithaca, N.Y.: Snow Lion.

Warder, A. K. 1991. *Indian Buddhism.* Delhi: Motilal Banarsidass.

Warren, Henry C. 1982. *Buddhism in Translation.* New York: Atheneum.

Wayman, Alex. 1973. *The Buddhist Tantras: Light on Indo-Tibetan Esotericism.* New York: Samuel Weiser.

———. 1976. "The Significance of Mantras, from the Veda down to Buddhist Tantric Practice." *Indologica Taurinensia* 3: 483–97.

———. 1977. *Yoga of the Guhyasamājatantra.* Delhi: Motilal Banarsidass.

———. 1985. *Chanting the Names of Mañjuśrī.* Boston: Shambhala.

Werner, K., ed. 1989. *The Yogi and the Mystic: Studies in Indian and Comparative Mysticism.* London: Curzon Press.

White, David G. 1996. *The Alchemical Body: Siddha Traditions in Medieval India.* Chicago: University of Chicago Press.

Williams, P. 1989. *Mahāyāna Buddhism: The Doctrinal Foundations.* London, New York: Routledge.

Williams, Michael A. 1996. *Rethinking "Gnosticism": An Argument for Dismantling a Dubious Category*. Princeton: Princeton University Press.

Wujastyk, Dominik. 1998. *The Roots of Āyurveda: Selections from Sanskrit Medical Writings*. Penguin Classics. Delhi: Penguin Books India.

Zysk, Kenneth G. 1991. *Asceticism and Healing in Ancient India: Medicine in the Buddhist Monastery*. New York: Oxford University Press.

———. 1993. "The Science of Respiration and the Doctrine of the Bodily Winds in Ancient India." *Journal of the American Oriental Society* 13/2: 198–213.

Index

Buddhist schools, four. *See also individual school names*
four non-Buddhist groups and, 33–34
KCT view of, as conversionary means, 32–33
Bu ston, 35–36

Cakras
four, 22, 158
six, 77–82
Carvāka, critique of materialism of, in KCT, 15
Caste. *See* Social classes
Clan (*kalka*), 115
Class. *See* Social classes
Compassion
as result of Vajrayāna, in *Vimalaprabhā*, 11
temporal aspects of sixteen types of, 94
Consciousness, in Yogācāra and KCT, 16
Consorts
impartiality of tantric practitioner regarding, 125
offering of, to spiritual mentor, 123–124
Cosmography, variations between, in KCT, *Abhidharmakośa*, and Jaina tradition, 87–88. *See also* Hindu tradition; Jaina tradition; *under Kālacakratantra;*
Cosmos. *See also* Universe
as body of Jina, 64–65
configuration and measurement of, in KCT and *Abhidharmakośa*, 66–68, 70–71
conventional nature of size and configuration of, 66–67
dissolution of, 59
and individual, 56–57, 57–64, 66
as manifestation of gnosis, 154
origination of, 58–59
two types of, 57
as universal sacrifice, 216
Cyclic existence
and cause and effect, 98
manifestation of wheel of time as, 95
material nature of, 58
mental causes of, 173

Day-and-night, 92, 93
Death, 23, 24
Deities
generation of, in KCT practice, 191–198
of *Kālacakra-maṇḍala*, 209–211
Deity-*yoga*, of stage of generation, 190–200
Dependent origination
cessation of, and transformation of cosmic and bodily *cakras*, 77, 80
classification of twelve links of, into cause and effect, 98
and four *vajras*, 157
and origination of all phenomena, 14
and origination of human psycho-physiology, 22
and pilgrimage sites and signs of zodiac, 77
sequential arising of twelve links of, 98–99
thirty-six links of, 99–100
three categories of, in KCT, Mahāyāna Buddhism, and Abhidharma, 98
and time, in body of individual, 100
and twelve zodiacs, 97–100
Dharma-dhātu, 151
as Mahāyāna precedent for gnosis of KCT, 153
Dhātu, three understandings of, in KCT, 153
Disciple. *See* Tantric trainee
Divine pride, 190
Dogmatism, warnings against, in KCT, 32
Doṃba class, in *gaṇa-cakra* and *kālacakra-maṇḍala*, 126–129
Dreaming state, and self-awareness, 151–152
Drops, four
capacities of, 158
and generation of links of dependent origination, 158
purification of, 189

Earth-*maṇḍala*, configuration of, in KCT and *Abhidharmakośa*, 71
Education
Buddhist monastic system of, 43–44
theological and scientific, in India, 43
Elements
and arising of ten karmic winds, 58
and body of individual, 22–23
and conception, 59–60
in environment and body, 60–61
humoral disorders and, 53